PROPERTY LAW REFORM, SUSTAINABILITY AND THE COMMONS

Property Law Reform, Sustainability and the Commons

Vincent SAGAERT
Dorothy GRUYAERT
Marie-Laure DEGROOTE
Kato DE SCHEPPER
Vincent JANSSEN
Flore VAVOURAKIS
(eds.)

LARCIER INTERSENTIA
Cambridge – Antwerp – Chicago

Intersentia
Lefebvre Sarrut Belgium SA
Rue Haute, 139/6
1000 Bruxelles
Belgium
contact@larcier-intersentia.com

Distribution for the UK and
Rest of the World (incl. Eastern Europe)
Ingram Publisher Services UK
1 Deltic Avenue, Rooksley
Milton Keynes MK13 8LD
United Kingdom
Tel: +44 1752 202 301 | Fax: +44 1752 202 331
Email: orders@nbninternational.com

Distribution for France and other countries
Interforum Editis
92 avenue de France
75013 Paris
France

Distribution for the USA and Canada
Independent Publishers Group
Order Department
814 North Franklin Street
Chicago, IL 60610
USA
Tel: +1 800 888 4741 (toll free) | Fax: +1 312 337 5985
Email: orders@ipgbook.com

Cover design by Danny Juchtmans / www.dsigngraphics.be

ISBN 978-1-83970-451-2
D/2024/7849/107

British Library Cataloguing in Publication Data. A catalogue record for this book is available from the British Library.

PREFACE

The current book is the commercial edition of the scientific conference organized at the University of Leuven on Property Law Reform, Sustainability and the Commons.

The beginning of the 21st century marks a turnabout in the relations between human beings and the world of goods. Ideas about the abundance of natural resources, and thus of exclusivity of rights to use the product of these resources, are shifting towards an awareness that the resources are limited and that there is an urgent need for responsible use of these.

Property law is shifting along with these societal developments. Property law determines our relationship with goods. The idea of absolute exclusivity, which was predominant at the beginning of the 19th century, is regressing at the beginning of the 21st century. The idea of abundance for those goods which are not subject to exclusive property rights has also been abandoned. The tragedy of the anti-commons leads to an unsustainable relationship with the world of goods. The lack of conceptual limitations on using natural resources can also negatively impact the long-term viability of the world.

The question arises whether new property law legislation incorporates these changed views on property relations. Several law reforms have enacted new property laws over the last decades. The specific occasion for this conference was the reform of the Belgian Civil Code, which entered into force on 1 September 2021. However, there have also been other new property law enactments, such as the Chinese Civil Code (2020), but also the Argentinian Civil Code (2015), the Civil Code of Hungary (2013), the Romanian Civil Code (2009) etc. The question arises whether these (and other law reforms) demonstrate further developments concerning the earlier generation of law reforms of the second half of the 20th century, such as the Dutch Civil Code (1992) and the Quebec Civil Code.

The editors of this book are very grateful to all authors who have contributed to this book. The contributions offer a multi-layered and often innovative insight into the issues of sustainability and the commons, particularly in response to recodifications. We also thank Vicky van Kelst for the precious assistance in organizing the conference.

Vincent Sagaert also acknowledges the Eisenhower Fellowships for awarding him a Global Fellowship, which has contributed to the ideas expressed in this book. All the opinions expressed in this book remain of course personal to the author.

Leuven, 10 June 2024
Dorothy Gruyaert and Vincent Sagaert

CONTENTS

PART I

PROPERTY LAW REFORM IN CONTEXT

REFORMING OWNERSHIP: FROM PRIVATE, THROUGH COMMUNAL, TO PUBLIC PROPERTY

Magdalena HABDAS
Professor, University of Silesia in Katowice

I. INTRODUCTION

Ownership is one of the most important social, economic and legal notions. It may be argued that ownership precedes the state, because it allows to designate the territory over which a given state exercises its power and introduces binding laws, providing its citizens with security. External or internal attempts to disrupt the allocation and access to ownership result in conflicts and loss of safety for the citizens.[1] Throughout the ages, ownership has served both communal, as well as individual interests, although it may be argued that private ownership has ultimately been assessed as having a productive advantage over public one.[2] Nevertheless, the importance of the existence of non-exclusive property to the proper functioning of the society and economy was noticed already by the Romans. It should be noted that Roman law did not have a developed concept of ownership as a right, therefore having an object and the object itself were not differentiated.[3] However with regard to things, Romans created a continuum of property types by distinguishing: *res divini iuris*, *res commones*, *res publicae*, *res universitatis*, *res nullius* and *res privatae*.[4]

The Romans appreciated synergies that were created by the existence of various property types and did not treat non-exclusive property as being antagonistic to private property, because private property benefits from the

---

1 S. BYRD, J. HRUSCHKA, "The Natural Law Duty to Recognize Private Property Ownership: Kant's Theory of Property in His Doctrine of Right" (2006) 56 *University of Toronto Law Journal* 217, 218

2 R.A. EPSTEIN, *Supreme Neglect. How to Revive Constitutional Protection for Private Property*, Oxford University Press, Oxford 2008, 19.

3 G.L. GRETTON, "Ownership and its Objects" (2007) 71 *Rabels Zeitshriftung* 802, 806.

4 E. WESTON-BROWN, "A Common Morality: Toward a Framework for Designing Fiscal Instruments to Respond to Global Climate Change" (2010) 15 *Widener Law Review* 391, 401-403.

existence of nonexclusive property, and the latter is only worth creating and maintaining, if private property exists and is protected.[5] Importantly, the Romans regarded public property, particularly with regard to immovables, as belonging to the society as a whole in the sense that the public, and not an identified individual, benefitted from their use. Public things remained essential for societies long after the Romans were gone and their *usus publicus* usually subjected them to some sort of supervision of public bodies, if not put them neatly within ownership of public bodies.[6] The Romans, through the concept of *res publica*, also introduced the distinction between public law and private law. The *res publica*, property held in common that is not possessed or exercised personally or exclusively, belongs to the society which promotes justice and the sharing of common interests.[7] This in turn paved the way for civil law jurisdictions to distinguish between public and private ownership, which after World War II and the emergence of socialist states was perceived as a distinction between opposing and competing types of ownership. Nevertheless, the original premise between this distinction was the type of use and interest that the object of ownership, and the right itself were designed to satisfy, with public property implying a use by the public or in the public interest and public ownership resembling guardianship rather than private holding.[8]

The displacement of communist regimes of Eastern Europe in the late 1980s may suggest that these types of ownership need no longer be contrasted, as private ownership is generally viewed as a constitutional and political value which ensures freedom, efficiency and personal autonomy, while public ownership is an embarrassing remnant of less developed, often authoritarian states.[9] Meanwhile, the need to maintain a continuum of property types, like public, common, and private ownership, prevails as it allows to move from a mentality focused on mere productivity to one based on morality and sensitivity towards environmental and social concerns.[10] Privatization of numerous lands and resources is not always beneficial, also because it may lead to inefficiencies caused by the over-fragmentation of rights, resulting in suppressing innovation, or preventing the pooling of resources for a more efficient reorganization. In addition, private ownership may not work well in cases of providing goods and

---

5 C.M. Rose, "Romans, Roads, and Romantic Creators: Traditions of Public Property in the Information Age" (2003) 66 *Law and Contemporary Problems* 89, 91, 99-100.

6 M. Habdas, "Who needs a park or a city square? The notion of public real estate as res publicae" (2011) 4 *Journal of South African Law* 626, 633.

7 E. Zoller, "Public Law as the Law of the Res Publica" (2008) 32 *Suffolk Transnational Law Review* 93, 94-95.

8 A. Gambaro, "Public and Private Land Property: The Current Meaning of a Traditional Distinction" in B. Pozzo (ed.), *Property and Environment. Old and New Remedies to Protect Natural Resources in the European Context*, Stämpfli Publishers Ltd., Berne 2007, pp. 66-67.

9 A. Lehavi, "Mixing Property" (2008) 38 *Setton Hall Law Review* 137, 144.

10 Weston-Brown (2010), 407.

services for which profit is not the main objective, for example, education, social services, healthcare or environmental protection.[11]

In the context of the above, the role of public ownership in a post-communist country is particularly controversial, bearing in mind its previous predominance in an authoritarian system, based on a centrally steered economy. The challenge of adequately incorporating public ownership into a new socio-economic system had to be addressed in Poland, where in 1990 a change from a socialist state to a democracy based on market economy was effected. At that time, the main objective of the legislator was to prevent the state from controlling the ownership of means of production and from emphasizing the role of social ownership.[12] The object of this paper is to determine whether property law reforms implemented in post-communist Poland have removed public ownership from the discourse, or whether, based on Roman concepts, the legislator embraced the need to provide a continuum of property types, particularly in the light of sustainable development. Polish law will be examined beginning with the interwar period of the XXth century, through the communist state, and post the 1990 market reforms. As will be shown, ownership displays a variety of forms, all necessary in a democratic system based on a market economy.

II. OWNERSHIP IN THE INTERWAR PERIOD OF THE TWENTIETH CENTURY

Poland disappeared from the maps of Europe for a period of over a 100 years due to the partitions of Poland. The First Partition of the Polish-Lithuanian Commonwealth took place in 1772 and consisted of Russia, Austria and Prussia annexing parts of Polish territory. The Second Partition, by Russia and Prussia, occurred in 1793 and resulted in depriving Poland of most of its territory. The final, Third Partition by Russia, Austria and Prussia was carried out in 1795 (following the failed Kościuszko Uprising) and brought about the complete disintegration of the country, which disappeared from the map of Europe until 1918.[13] During the time of partitions, previously Polish territories were governed by laws of the occupying forces, which meant that Poland was exposed to three, main legal orders, namely the Austrian, Prussian (German) and Russian ones. However, in Spisz and Orava, small regions located in southern parts of previously Polish territories, Hungarian law was in force. In addition,

---

11 Lehavi (2008), 145-148.

12 A. Stelmachowski, "Modele własności i ich uwarunkowania społeczno-ustrojowe", in T. Dybowski (ed.), *System Prawa Prywatnego. Prawo rzeczowe. Tom 3*, C.H. Beck – PAN, Warszawa 2007, pp. 123-125.

13 See R. Bubczyk, *A History of Poland in an Outline*, Wydawnictwo UMCS, Lublin 2011, pp. 81 – 116; cf. N. Davies, *Heart of Europe. A Short History of Poland*, Oxford University Press, Oxford 2001.

French law, most notably the Napoleonic Code, was introduced in the Duchy of Warsaw, created by Napoleon in 1807. After Napoleon's abdication in 1814 and based on decisions taken at the Congress of Vienna, the Duchy was transformed in 1815 into the Kingdom of Poland (Congress Poland), essentially a puppet state of the Russian Empire. Nevertheless, the French Civil Code retained its usefulness, as it was adopted in 1825, with a couple of revisions regarding mainly personal and matrimonial law, as the new Civil Code of the Kingdom of Poland.[14]

This legal mosaic, prevalent on Polish territories for more than a century, influenced the discourse on ownership after Poland's reconstitution in 1918. Regaining independence made it imperative to unify the law and to adequately reflect and regulate the new political and economic situation, also taking into account past experiences with solutions operating in foreign legal systems. Although the work on property law was not completed before the outbreak of the Second World War, important decisions as to how ownership was to be viewed were made in the Constitution of the Second Polish Republic from 17th March 1921.[15] In its Article 99, the constitutional legislator declared that Poland acknowledges all types of ownership, namely: (1) personal – belonging to individual citizens; (2) collective – belonging to citizens' associations, institutions, local governments, and (3) state – belonging to the state itself, thus showing an understanding of a continuum of property types, starting with private ownership, moving through communal ownership, and ending with state/public ownership.

In the said provision, the legislator further stipulated that acknowledging all types of ownership is one of the most important pillars of the new social and political system and that the protection of their property is guaranteed to all citizens, institutions and communities. It was also explained that in specified situations, an act of parliament may allow the extinguishment or a restriction of personal or communal property only due to higher interests and for compensation. Additionally, only an act of parliament may designate, for the benefit of the public, certain types of property as exclusive state property, including the possibility to limit in the public interest, citizens and their organizations in their unabridged use of land, water, minerals and other treasures of nature. Finally, in the considered provision, it was stipulated that land is one of the most important factors of the existence of the Polish nation and the state. The laws will define the State's right to compulsory purchase of land and to regulate land trade, taking into account the principle that the agricultural

[14] W. Dajczak, "Historical Development of Private Law in Poland" in W. Dajczak, A.J. Szwarc, P. Wiliński (eds), *Handbook of Polish Law*, ParkPrawo, Bielsko-Biała 2011, pp. 43-44.

[15] *Journal of Statutes* 1921, no. 44, item 267.

system of the Republic of Poland is to be based on agricultural farms capable of proper production and constituting personal property.

The above constitutional provision evidences that in interwar Poland, ownership was viewed as a right which could fulfil various needs, starting with private ones, and ending with public ones. The latter context was conducive to distinguishing public things, i.e. objects owned by the state and other public bodies for the purpose of facilitating the performance of their duties. Based on categories developed in German law, public things included: the financial property of the state (money and other property that generates income, e.g. securities, income from state enterprises, forests), administrative property (objects directly utilized to perform public duties, e.g. public schools, public hospitals, public libraries, public offices, soldier barracks), and property for public use (goods to be used by the general public). The latter category comprised things public by nature (air, light, the sea) or by purpose (public roads, bridges, city parks and squares) which were owned either by the state or by a public entity (e.g. a church). It was emphasized, that financial property comprised typical objects of ownership and was completely governed by private law regulations, whereas the other two categories were governed by public law, with private law applicable exceptionally to unresolved matters.[16] A similar approach was to identify things available for use by the general public (*usus publicus*) as public goods. Consequently, an object could be public if: a) it was owned by a public entity (all things regardless of whether private or public law provisions applied), or b) was open to public use – *usus publicus* (regardless of whether the owner was a private person or a public entity), or c) was both owned by a public entity and subject to public use. The management and dispositions of public things were governed by public law and their protection rested with police authorities, regardless of the person obliged to maintain the object. Disputes concerning these things belonged to the jurisdiction of administrative court jurisdiction, however the notion of ownership and civil liability for injuries remained private law matters.[17] The views on types of ownership and the category of *res publicae* were also a reflection of the Roman tradition that divided law into private and public, nevertheless the notion of ownership, even when it was qualified by administrative law regulating public things, remained within the realm of private law.

---

16 S. Kasznica *Polskie prawo administracyjne. Pojęcia i instytucje zasadnicze,* Księgarnia Akademicka, Poznań 1946, pp. 143-145.

17 T. Bigo *Prawo administracyjne. Część ogólna. Stenogram wykładów Uniwersyteckich,* J. Rodkowski, Lwów 1932, pp. 201-206, 213-214; also see P. Radzimiński, "Pojęcie rzeczy publicznych w polskiej nauce prawa administracyjnego" in E. Knosala, A. Matan, G. Łaszczyca (eds), *Prawo administracyjne w okresie transformacji ustrojowej* Zakamycze, Kraków 1999, pp. 81-88.

III. OWNERSHIP AND THE COMMUNIST STATE

Although the outbreak of the Second World War halted the work of Polish legal scholars on the unification of Polish law, the intensive work performed in the interwar period in the area of property law resulted in a quick enactment of the decree on the Law of Real Rights 1946 (hereinafter: "LRR")[18] after the war had ended. Ideas concerning ownership and other property rights were based on a mixture of French and German solutions, which were in force on Polish territories during the partitions. The decree regulated the notions of things, ownership, usufruct, easements, mortgage, pledge, real burdens and possession. Ownership was addressed in Article 28 LRR, where it was concisely stated that the owner may, within limits specified by law, use the object to the exclusion of other persons and dispose of the object. This stipulation emphasized the owner's right to exclude as well as potential limits of owner's right that may follow from restrictions in statutory provisions.

As the implementation of communism in Poland progressed in the late 1940s and early 1950s, the definition of ownership was becoming increasingly obsolete, as it failed to explicitly reflect new ideals of a socialist state. The nationalization of industry and trade, efforts to eliminate individual farm ownership, administrative control of leases of private apartments in cities and basing the economy on centrally planned objectives were characteristic of the new political system that needed to be adequately supported by the legal system.[19] At that time it was noted in legal scholarship that the LRR definition of ownership is lacking elements which differentiate ownership on the basis of its object and the entity that holds the right and thus treats ownership in a unilateral and abstract manner, typical of capitalist legal systems.[20] The lack of more detailed determinants of the content and function of ownership that could serve as a starting point for differentiating various types of ownership was viewed as contrary to the needs of the emerging socialist system, as well as to the new constitutional regulation.[21] This became more obvious after the enactment the Constitution of the People's Republic of Poland of 22 July 1952 (hereinafter "CRP 1952").[22]

Pursuant to Article 8 CRP 1952, national property in the form of mineral deposits, waters, state forests, mines, roads, railway, water and air transport, means of communication, banks, state industrial plants, state agricultural farms and state machinery centers, state trading enterprises, municipal enterprises and facilities was made subject to special care and the protection of the state and all

18 Journal of Statutes 1946, no. 57, item 319.

19 Dajczak (2011), 45-46.

20 J. Wasilkowski, *Prawo własności w PRL. Zarys wykładu*, PWN, Warszawa 1969, pp. 101-102.

21 S. Breyer, *Mienie. Przepisy ogólne dotyczące własności. Treść i wykonywanie własności*, Zrzeszenie Prawników Polskich, Katowice 1966, p. 36

22 Journal of Statutes 1952, no. 33, item 232.

citizens. In Article 11 CRP 1952 it was stipulated that the Polish People's Republic supports the development of various forms of the cooperative movement in cities and villages and provides it with comprehensive assistance in fulfilling its tasks, with special care and protection provided to cooperative property, which constitutes social property. According to Article 12 CRP 1952 the state recognized and protected, on the basis of applicable laws, individual ownership and the right of inheritance of land, buildings and other means of production belonging to farmers, craftsmen and cottage workers. Finally, in Article 13 it was stipulated that the state guarantees full protection and the right of inheritance of citizens' personal property. In addition, in Article 77 CRP 1952 it was stated that every citizen was obliged to protect social property and strengthen it as a steadfast basis for the development of the state, a source of wealth and strength of the country. Persons who committed sabotage, subversion, damage or other attacks on social ownership were to be punished to the fullest extent of the law.

The above constitutional provisions created an intricate differentiation between various types of property (ownership). The first, and ideologically, most important type of ownership was social property, which formed the basis of the socialist state. Social property was divided into two types of ownership, namely:
- socialist, national ownership; and
- the ownership of cooperatives and other social organizations, such as political parties and workers' unions, sometimes called group (communal) ownership.

Socialist, national ownership belonged indivisibly to the State, according to the principle of the unity of state ownership, expressed in Article 128 of the Polish Civil Code 1964 (hereinafter: "PCC 1964"). This principle enabled the State to control the means of production and to implement the centrally planned economy, by distributing resources among state enterprises. In violation of typical, private law rules on legal personality and patrimony, state enterprises, which were legal persons, were not recognized as owners of public property, but were treated merely as managers of property which belonged to the state. They could hold other rights to national property, including property rights, but not ownership of such property.[23]

Social property, despite the differences between national ownership and group ownership, enjoyed special protection. Apart from the mentioned Article 77 CRP 1952, the new Polish Civil Code, enacted on 23 April 1964 and in force since 1 January 1965, stipulated in Article 127 that it was the duty of every citizen to protect social property from impending damage (§ 1). A citizen who, protecting social property, had suffered damage to a person or property, would be compensated. If, as a result of the protection of social property, this

---

23 Stelmachowski (2007), 80–82, 92–114; Z.K. Nowakowski, *Prawo rzeczowe. Zarys wykładu*, PWN, Warszawa 1980, p. 22-61.

citizen lost his life, the persons towards whom the deceased had a statutory maintenance obligation, and other relatives to whom the deceased voluntarily and permanently provided means of subsistence, could request an appropriate pension (§ 2). In the event that the protection of social property was the professional or official duty of the injured party, the compensation payable was to be determined based on separate provisions (§ 3).

The second type of property covered the individual ownership of means of production and belonged to physical persons and well as legal persons which were not organizations of the social economy. Within this type of property, individual ownership of working farmers was distinguished from individual, capitalistic ownership of, for example,. businesses, land, plant and machinery. The latter was not protected at the level of the constitution, but rather, according to Article 12 CRP 1952, its protection followed from acts of parliament. However since social property was favored, legislation was aimed at limiting the scope of individual property, especially by the nationalization of numerous private enterprises and some land during the 1940s. This meant that such ownership did not enjoy constitutional guarantees and could be easily restricted by statutory legislation.[24] Finally, the third type of property was personal property, which could only belong to physical persons and consisted of consumable goods fulfilling the personal needs of that person and his/her family, such as cars, home appliances, but also residential houses and apartments.[25] This type of property enjoyed, according to Article 13 CRP 1952 constitutional protection.

The above constitutional principles were mirrored in the PCC 1964. Pursuant to Article 126 social property was either socialist national (state) property or cooperative property or the property of other social organizations of the working people, with national (state) property vested in the State Treasury or other State legal entities (Art. 128 PCC 1964). According to Article 129, when interpreting and applying the provisions of PCC, it was to be taken into account that social ownership, as the basis of the system of the Polish People's Republic, remains under special protection of the law. In Article 130 PCC 1964 it was stated that land, buildings and other means of production which are not the exclusive object of social ownership may, on the basis of and within the limits of laws, be owned by natural persons (individual property). Finally, Article 131 PCC 1964 declared that the State guarantees ownership and complete protection of individual farms, which are a permanent and equal element of the socio-economic system of the Polish People's Republic. Personal property was defined in Article 132 and 133 PCC 1964. The former stipulated that personal property is the ownership of things intended to meet the personal material and cultural needs of the owner and his relatives. Such property also included the ownership of small means of

---

24 S. Wójcik, "Prawo rzeczowe" in S. Grzybowski (ed.), *Prawo Cywilne,* PWN, Warszawa 1979, p. 100.

25 Stelmachowski (2007), 105-113.

production that are used to produce items intended to meet the personal needs of the owner and his relatives. In the latter provision it was further explained that personal property may include in particular: a single-family house or a residential unit, together with the farm buildings necessary for their use, items belonging to household appliances, household items and motor vehicles. In agricultural production cooperatives, personal property also included, within the limits specified in statutes, buildings and farm equipment, livestock, poultry, tools and other things intended for running a farm on a farm plot.

The socialist state relied heavily on administrative law and particularly in the field of property law attempts were made to discredit and abandon the Roman distinction between private and public law. It was argued that since the economy is predominantly based on state owned means of production, private law implications and the nature of rights have lost their importance and are not an indispensable element in administrative law considerations.[26] Since the socialist system was characterized by the unity between personal/private and social interests, it was assumed that the division of law into private and public had lost its utility.[27] In particular, attempts were made to view state ownership not as a private law institution, but rather as a separate instrument of public law.[28] Despite this, it must be noted that property law, even when it concerned social property, never ceased to be be within the scope of private law. Moreover, private ownership of farmland as well as of small business was never extinguished and the strong civil law tradition ensured that the PCC 1964, apart from adding some concepts necessarily connected with the socialist state, retained its Roman law roots and important features of civil law regulations of the major European codifications of the nineteenth century.[29]

Nevertheless, the definition of ownership in PCC 1964 was changed in comparison with the one introduced in the LRR 1946. According to the new regulation of Article 140 PCC 1964 within the limits specified by statutory law, and the principles of social coexistence, the owner may use an object to the exclusion of other persons in accordance with the socio-economic purpose of his right, in particular he may collect fruits and other income from the object. Within the same limits, he may make dispositions of the object. When compared with Article 28 LRR 1946, the definition of ownership gained new indicators as to its limits. The boundaries of ownership set out in Article 140 refer not only

---

26 J. Starościak, *System Prawa Administracyjnego. Tom 1,* Ossolineum, Wrocław-Warszawa-Kraków-Gdańsk 1977, p. 491.

27 For more see K. Opałek, *Problemy metodologiczne nauki prawa*, PWN, Warszawa 1962, p. 180 *et seq.*; J. Nowacki, *Prawo publiczne – prawo prywatne*, Wydawnictwo Uniwersytetu Śląskiego, Katowice 1992, p. 39 *et seq.*

28 K. Sójka-Zielińska, "Państwo, a własność u progu powszechnej industrializacji" (1984) 36 *Czasopismo Prawno-Historyczne* 57, 69.

29 M. Raff, "One Summer in Gdańsk: Poland's Leadership in Transition from the Socialist Legal Model" (2010) 3 *Humanities Research* 69, 74-80.

to limitations contained in the law, but also to ones derived from the principles of social coexistence and the socio-economic purpose of ownership. As pointed out by W. Rozwadowski, such an approach to defining ownership differed from the Roman tradition and the tradition of Western European countries, where ownership is defined as the power to do everything except for what is forbidden by the law. The author emphasized that in the new definition, the owner is not entitled to do everything as long as it does not violate the law, but may only do what the law, principles of social coexistence, and socio-economic purpose of the right allow him to. He thus concludes that the Polish PCC definition of ownership is modelled on the substance of Russian and the subsequent Soviet provisions.[30]

IV. OWNERSHIP IN A DEMOCRATIC STATE BASED ON MARKET ECONOMY

After the fall of communism in 1989/1990 and the introduction of a market economy, the legislator needed to revisit the notion of ownership both at the constitutional and private law level. The previous distinction into various types of ownership, which were heavily connected with the ideology and economy of the social state had lost their utility in a democratic state based on a market economy. The CRP 1952 was comprehensively amended in December 1989 to reflect the new political and economic reality, which included removing provisions relating to national and social ownership. Instead, the changed Article 7 CRP 1952 stipulated that the Republic of Poland protects property (ownership) and the right to inherit and guarantees the full protection of personal property. Interestingly, the amended 1952 Constitution still retained the notion of personal property, however this was assessed as of no practical significance and in terms of an oversight or a mistake, rather than as a conscious attempt to maintain this distinctive type of property.[31]

Following the amendment of the Constitution, the first important amendment of the PCC 1964 was enacted as early as 31 January 1989[32] and came into force the following day. It invalidated the principle of the unity of state ownership by stipulating that national property may be held by the State or by other types of state legal persons. The next amendment of the PCC

---

[30] W. Rozwadowski, "Własność w polskim prawie cywilnym. Przemiany strukturalne – potrzeba nowelizacji" (2002) VII *Studia z Dziejów Państwa i Prawa Polskiego* 275, 276–278.

[31] T. Dybowski, "Własność w przepisach konstytucyjnych wedle stanu obowiązywania w 1996 roku" in J. Trzciński, A. Jankiewicz, *Konstytucja i gwarancje jej przestrzegania. Księga Pamiątkowa ku czci Prof. Janiny Zakrzewskiej*, Trybunał Konstytucyjny – Wydawnictwa, Warszawa 1996, p. 306, J. Ignatowicz, *Prawo rzeczowe*, PWN, Warszawa 1994, p. 40; Stelmachowski (2007), p. 124.

[32] Journal of Statutes 1989, no. 3, item 11.

1964 was much more comprehensive and was introduced by the act of 28 July 1990.[33] Its objective was to remove any references made to socialist ideology as well as institutions which were incompatible with the market economy. In the law of property rights law significant changes concerned ownership. It was no longer divided into various types, so Article 126-133 PCC 1964 were deleted. At the onset of political and economic changes it was clear that continuing to institutionally differentiate between social, individual, and personal property was unacceptable, because all forms of ownership were to be awarded equal protection.[34]

Classifying ownership according to the premise that the lowest and politically discredited type of ownership was private property while social property embodied the most valuable type of ownership was completely useless for a market economy. This, however, did not denote that public ownership was no longer a category that could and should be acknowledged.[35] It was obvious that private property had been selected as the basis of a free market economy, but that was not a reason to neglect noticing that there are differences between ownership, depending on the object of the right and the entity holding the right. Even directly after the transformation it was necessary to designate private, communal (self-governments), and state ownership. The last two categories required special regulations, because of the entities holding the right and the public interest and tasks inextricably connected with these types of public entities. The differentiation between public and private property was noted to be one of the most basic divisions of ownership. It did not suggest that the former was an institution of public law, while the latter remained within private law. On the contrary, ownership is always an institution of private law, however its public character may be evident from the object of ownership, its predominant use, as well as the entity holding the right. The type of entity continues to be an important consideration, particularly since performing various public tasks is typically the duty of public authorities.[36] It should be emphasized that the most serious drawback of the socialist legal system was not the differentiation of ownership types, but employing these only in terms of a political ideology, completely separated from social and economic reality.[37]

A new constitution of the Republic of Poland was enacted on 2nd April 1997 (CRP 1997)[38] and it addresses ownership in the following provisions:

---

33 Journal of Statutes 1990, no. 55, item 321.

34 Ignatowicz (1994), 54.

35 W. Seiffert, "Przemiany własnościowe we wschodnich Niemczech i Europie Wschodniej" in *Postępy prywatyzacji w krajach Europy Centralnej i Wschodniej. II Międzynarodowe Sympozjum Prywatyzacyjne*, Katowice-Kielce 1994, p. 112.

36 A. Stelmachowski, *Zarys teorii prawa cywilnego*, PWN, Warszawa 1998, p. 187.

37 M. Bednarek, *Przemiany własności w Polsce. Podstawowe koncepcje i konstrukcje normatywne*, Wydawnictwo Naukowe Scholar, Warszawa 1994, p. 96.

38 Journal of Statutes 1997, no. 78, item 321, as amended.

- Article 20 ("*A social market economy, based on the freedom of economic activity, private ownership and solidarity, dialogue and cooperation between social partners, shall be the basis of the economic system of the Republic of Poland*");
- Article 21 Section 1 ("*The Republic of Poland shall protect ownership and the right of succession*");
- Article 64 Sections 1–3 ("*Everyone shall have the right to ownership, other property rights and the right of succession. Everyone, on an equal basis, shall receive legal protection regarding ownership, other property rights, and the right of succession. The right of ownership may only be limited by means of a statute and only to the extent that it does not violate the substance of such right*");
- Article 165 Section 1 ("*Units of local government shall possess legal personality. They shall have rights of ownership and other property rights*").

The above list must be supplemented by Article 218 which stipulates that the organization of the State Treasury and the manner of management of the assets of the State Treasury shall be specified by statute. In this provision, the legislator does not mention ownership *expressis verbis*; however, assets are deemed to include the right of ownership.

The CRP 1997 does not contain any provisions that explicitly differentiate among different types of ownership or introduce different levels of protection. Conversely, according to Article 64 section 2 of the Constitution, equal protection has been awarded to the right of ownership, regardless of who the holder of the right is. The Polish Constitutional Tribunal has also confirmed that CRP 1997 does not contain a stratification of ownership based on the type of the owner, nor does it provide for specific protection of state property. In particular, Article 20 CRP 1997 does not introduce special constitutional protection of communal (self-government) property. In conclusion, the Polish Constitutional Tribunal emphasized that under the CRP 1997 there is a uniform understanding of the concept of ownership and the principle of equal protection of property regardless of the entity holding the right.[39]

Despite no explicit enumeration of property types in the CRP 1997, it would be unjustified to conclude that the legislator does not notice varieties of ownership. In Article 20 CRP 1997 private ownership is mentioned and thus allows to conclude that apart from private ownership, other types of ownership exist. In Articles 165 and 218 a reference to the ownership of local governments and of the State Treasury, respectively, is made. Since Article 20 is located in the first chapter of the CRP 1997, which concerns the principles of Poland's socio-economic system, it is clear that the express reference to private ownership is substantiated by the need to accentuate that Polish economy is to be based on

39 Constitutional Tribunal judgment of 21 March 2000, K 14/99, Z.U. 2000/2/61.

private means of production and not on public ones, characteristic of a socialist state and a centrally planned economy. This does not eliminate the existence of public ownership, but it does exclude the possibility of building an economy based predominantly on public, as opposed to private, ownership of means of production.[40]

For the above reasons, it is viable to state that despite the lack of an express division of ownership into various types, the CRP 1997 does not contradict the existence of various categories of ownership.[41] The mentioned judgment of the Polish Constitutional Tribunal emphasizes that ownership is to be understood uniformly, in the sense that it is the most basic form of property appropriation as regulated by private law and thus always deserves equal protection. A uniform understanding of ownership as a right does not, however, indicate that various forms of ownership, which satisfy diverse needs, do not exist, with public, communal and private ownership serving as basic examples of the varying functions, objects and holders of the right.[42] In particular, it must be noted that public ownership should not be treated as a 'lesser' type of ownership, because its essence is to satisfy various, important public needs. It can thus not be treated as 'no one's' property[43], but as property which enables public bodies to perform their statutory tasks of public interest.

V. APPRECIATING VARIOUS PROPERTY TYPES

The whiplash of socialist ideology, in which ownership was institutionally divided into different types and connected with varying levels of protection probably influenced the legislator's decision to only explicitly mention private property. Although this decision is understandable, it cannot be viewed as aimed at denying that ownership is a complex phenomenon. In particular, ownership of physical persons is easily qualified as private property, but ownership of legal persons is not as straightforward to qualify. This is because legal persons have a plethora of different legal forms and can pursue divergent objectives.[44] For this reason alone it is obvious that private ownership, despite being the foundation of the current socio-economic system, is not the only type of ownership present in the economy and the line between private and public is not always well-

---

40 Constitutional Tribunal judgment of 7 May 2001 (K 19/00), OTK 2001/4/82.

41 B. Banaszak, *Prawo konstytucyjne*, C.H. Beck, Warszawa 2010, p. 251.

42 R. Antonów, "Społeczne funkcje własności" in E. Kozerska, P. Sadowski, A. Szymański (eds), *Problemy własności w ujęciu historyczno-prawnym*, Uniwersytet Opolski, Opole 2008, p. 90.

43 C. Kosikowski, "Zasada ochrony własności" in W. Sokolewicz (ed.) *Zasady podstawowe polskiej konstytucji*, Wydawnictwo Sejmowe, Warszawa 1998, pp. 234-235.

44 S. Wójcik, "Problem pojęcia 'własność prywatna' w III Rzeczypospolitej" (1991) 7-8 *Rejent* 7, 17.

defined.[45] It is viable to state that there is a stratification, or, according to the terminology presented by W. Pańko[46], a decomposition, of ownership based on criteria relating to the object of ownership (e.g. agricultural property, property in natural resources, urbanized real estate) or the entity holding the right (e.g. state property, local government property, private property, etc.). As a result, the typical entitlements of an owner may and will vary, because ownership comes in many different forms and serves various purposes. Consequently, it would be incorrect to hold that after the fall of communism, Poland does not allow the existence of property forms other than private.[47] Such a contention would blatantly disregard legal and economic realities of modern societies and be counterproductive in creating conditions for social welfare.

Apart from explicitly naming private ownership, the CRP 1997 contains no further provisions which signal a special role or a legal regime for arguably valuable goods. There is thus no special constitutional protection of historical objects, natural resources or economically important immovables. There is also no obligation for the legislator to regulate the principles of utilizing or making dispositions regarding such objects.[48] It may be argued that although differentiation between ownership based on the type of owner is not necessarily beneficial, it would be useful to indicate the need of properly regulating ownership that relates to objects which perform special functions and are important to the public interest or state economy.[49] One reason for advocating the above is the need to protect the national legacy in the field of culture, art or science and maintain, as far as possible, public access to such goods. The other reason is the need to protect the natural environment and implement a sustainable management of land, water, forests and other natural resources, which would benefit from special, constitutional protection. This seems the more justified, because private ownership interests may often come in conflict with more general, public ones.[50]

Such solutions may be found in constitutions of other European states. For example, in Article 132 of the Spanish Constitution it is stated that the legal system governing public domain and community property shall be regulated by law, on the principle that they shall be inalienable and imprescriptible and not subject to attachment or encumbrance (s. 1). Furthermore, the property of the State public domain shall be that established by law and shall, in any case,

---

45 Stelmachowski (1998), 189.

46 W. Pańko, *O prawie własności i jego współczesnych funkcjach*, Wydawnictwo Uniwersytetu Śląskiego, Katowice 1984, pp. 97 *et seq.*

47 E. Gniewek, Prawo rzeczowe, C.H. Beck, Warszawa 2022, p. 48-59, 71.

48 Banaszak (2010), 250.

49 A. Łabno-Jabłońska, „Nowa konstytucyjna regulacja prawa własności w Polsce" in A. Agopsowicz, T. Kurowska, M. Pazdan (eds), *Zagadnienia prawa cywilnego, samorządowego i rolnego: pamięci Profesora Waleriana Pańki*, Wydawnictwo Uniwersytetu Śląskiego, Katowice 1993, p. 39.

50 Kosikowski (1998), 235.

include coastal area, beaches, territorial waters and natural resources of the economic zone and the continental shelf (s. 2). The State and National Heritage, as well as their administration, protection and preservation, shall be regulated by law (s. 3). This provision is primarily an expression of the political choice to build a system based on private ownership of land and public ownership of natural resources.[51] Although the Spanish constitution, similarly to CRP 1997, adopted a uniform concept of property rights, unlike Polish solutions, the obligation and principles of creating a separate regulation for public property, covering the public domain and municipal property, have been clearly indicated. Article 42 of the Italian constitution stipulated in Section 1 that property may be public or private and that economic goods may belong to the State, to public bodies, or to private persons. In Section 2 of the said provision, the legislator provides that private ownership is recognized and guaranteed by laws which determine the manner by which it may be acquired and enjoyed, and its limits, in order to ensure its social function and to make it open to all. In addition, in Article 44, the lawmaker stipulates that for the purpose of securing a rational use of the land and of establishing equitable social relations, the law shall impose obligations on, and limitations to, private ownership of land, shall determine limits to its extent, depending on the regions and the various agricultural areas, shall encourage and impose land reclamation, the transformation of large estates, and the reorganization of productive units; it shall assist small and medium sized farms (s. 1). It is further stated that the law shall make provisions in favor of mountainous areas (s. 2). Consequently, the Italian constitution emphasizes the social function of ownership, the two main types of property, namely public and private, as well as the protection of valuable types of land.[52]

When compared with these examples of constitutional provisions on ownership, the Polish regulatory framework seems to be extremely concise and could benefit from a more robust regulation of at least the main principles that should apply to particularly valuable objects of ownership, such as natural resources, environmentally precious land or historical goods. It would also be beneficial to state the premises that should govern statutory regulation of state and self-government property, due to its public function.[53] The fact that the Polish constitution does not regulate public property or ownership of objects with a public interest purpose means that the constitutional regulation may not

---

51 E. Merino-Blanco, *Spanish Law and Legal System*, Thomson- Sweet & Maxwell, London 2006, p. 258.

52 For more see G. Alpa, V. Zeno-Zencovich, *Italian Private Law*, Routledge-Cavendish, London 2007, pp. 121 *et seq.*

53 R. Illinicz, "Własność państwowa i jej ochrona w świetle Konstytucji RP" in C. Kosikowski, *Zasady ustroju społecznego i gospodarczego w procesie stosowania Konstytucji*, Wydawnictwo Sejmowe, Warszawa 2005, p. 61.

provide sufficient guarantees of protecting this particular type of ownership.[54] Meanwhile, there is no doubt that even after the political change that took place in Poland after 1989, the need and legal justification for distinguishing public property in addition to private property have not disappeared, especially since it is difficult to deny that the content and functions of property will be different, depending on the subject of this property, its object and the function that this object is to perform.

It should also be noted that property has an organizing function, which ensures apart from the safeguard of the social balance and peace, an equally important economic function. Ownership motivates one to take care of the property and its productivity. In addition, it provides the owner with independence and allows him to accumulate wealth, which protects against waste and affects the safety of future generations.[55] The interdependence between private and public property should not be underestimated. The lack of appropriate experience with private property prevents the proper development of the culture of being an owner, which in turn leads to a lack of understanding and respect for property other than private. Therefore, acknowledging public property that is used to achieve other purposes than private ones remains an important element of the market economy. However unlike in the previous era, public property should enhance and not exclude the prevalence of private property, particularly in the area of means of production.

VI. OWNERSHIP IN PRIVATE LAW

Although the 1989 amendment of CRP 1952 and the new CRP 1997 introduced significant changes in the concept of ownership, the definition of Article 140 PCC 1964 has remained unchanged. As noted in section IV above, Article 140 PCC 1964 provides that an owner may, within the limits specified by statutory law and the principles of social coexistence, use an object to the exclusion of other persons in accordance with the socio-economic purpose/designation of his/her right. In particular (s)he may collect fruits and other income from the object as well as dispose thereof, all within the mentioned limits. The boundaries of ownership present in Article 140 PCC 1964 are a source of controversy, because apart from mentioning limits following from statutory provisions and the principles of social co-existence, another imposed limitation is the socio-economic designation of the right.

The dispute seems to concern only the decision to leave the boundary of the socio-economic purpose of ownership, since principles of social coexistence

---

54 Kosikowski (1998), pp. 238-239; J. Szachułowicz, *Własność publiczna*, Wydawnictwo Prawnicze, Warszawa 2002, p. 10.

55 Kosikowski (1998), p. 228.

are associated with the social function embedded in ownership.[56] It has been suggested that the socio-economic designation contained in Article 140 PCC 1964 should be deleted as it was strictly connected with the socialist approach to ownership and was introduced only to strengthen the formal division into different types and forms of ownership. Consequently, the mentioned designation would have completely lost its meaning in a democratic state with a free market economy.[57] The definition was formulated in 1964, in a completely different political and economic system, with the purpose of legitimizing the State's intervention and control over private property and therefore it should now be perceived as obsolete.[58]

In this context it is necessary to realize that although the socio-economic designation was indeed introduced during socialism in order to achieve a particular objective, it is a general clause that changes its content according to changes in the legal and economic system. It would be a mistake to think that the substance of this general clause has remained unchanged, because the very objective of having a general clause is to allow it to adapt to the changing circumstances. The limits of ownership are not predetermined once and for all, but change according to the changes in society, economy, the law, and the purpose of the object in question, thus evidencing the resilience of property law. Ownership is a flexible right and its limits identified by the legislator, particularly the limit of socio-economic purpose, allow to view a given right of ownership in the light of its object, holder, and possible interests of the society.[59] It would also seem that this solution additionally allows to include a social context within the notion of ownership which is particularly important considering the fact that, unlike in the German constitutional provisions (*see* Article 14 of the German *Grundgesetz*), where the social function is built into the concept of ownership, the CRP 1997 does not contain a similar provision. Furthermore, it allows to acknowledge that depending on the object of ownership and the subject holding the right, property may perform different functions and afford owners different entitlements.

Ownership is the strongest and fullest right that a person may hold with respect to an object. This right must be consistently understood in the whole legal system regardless of which sector of the economy one is considering.

---

56 W. Pańko, *Własność gruntowa w planowej gospodarce przestrzennej. Studium prawne*, Wydawnictwo Uniwersytetu Śląskiego, Katowice 1978, pp. 36–37.

57 Z. Radwański, M. Zieliński, "Uwagi de lege ferenda o klauzulach generalnych w prawie prywatnym" (2001) 2 *Przegląd Legislacyjny* 11, 29; M. Safjan, "Klauzule generalne w prawie cywilnym (przyczynek do dyskusji)" (1990) 11 *Państwo i Prawo* 48, 57–58; T. Zieliński, "Klauzule generalne w demokratycznym państwie praw*nym*" (1992) XXIII *Studia Iuridica* 195, 206.

58 B. Ziemianin, K.A. Dadańska, *Prawo rzeczowe*, Wolters Kluwer, Warszawa 2008, pp. 43–44.

59 T. Dybowski, "Zasady współżycia społecznego i społeczno-gospodarcze przeznaczenie prawa, a prawo własności" (1967) 6 Nowe Prawo 721, 731–733.

This is imperative since all socialist divisions of types and forms of ownership were abolished in 1990. Therefore, a person or an entity either is or is not an owner.[60] This applies not only to private persons, but also to public entities. Their ownership is always a right defined in Article 140 PCC 1964, however, its shape will vary depending on the socio-economic purpose of the right. This purpose will not only depend on the holder of the right, but also on the object and its features. If ownership is shaped by the socio-economic purpose of the right, then it must be possible to distinguish various types of ownership based on Article 140 PCC 1964. It is undeniable that private ownership has a different socio-economic purpose than public ownership, so the PCC 1964 definition does afford a sensible basis for distinguishing private and public ownership. It does not, however, allow one to conclude that public ownership is not genuine ownership, but a different right or a separate institution.[61] The Polish Constitutional Tribunal has also confirmed that the socio-economic designation of the right of ownership is a general clause that does not violate the constitutionally protected economic system based on social market economy (Art. 20 CRP 1997).[62]

It should be emphasized that the legislator himself often clarifies his idea of the socio-economic purpose of property rights by introducing specific regulations, for example, regarding various types of real estate and the rules for their use by specific entities. In particular, the management and disposition of objects, especially immovables, held by the State or local governments are often subject to additional regulations, because they are abstract entities and require the legislator's intervention in order to reflect the desired principles and aims of public property management. As a result, the boundaries of ownership defined by statutes and the socio-economic purpose of the right intersect[63], which should not be equated with the fact that these boundaries always coincide.

The boundaries that follow from express statutory provisions are not sufficient to determine the entire content of ownership, because the legislator in specific provisions will not be able to comprehensively regulate all aspects of the ownership of divergent objects in the hands of various categories of entities. The clause with regard to the socio-economic purpose of property rights is needed precisely in these cases where it is not necessary or possible to introduce detailed regulations (usually they are selective, not comprehensive). In the latter cases, it is useful to refer to more general, flexible assumptions, subject to an assessment taking into account both the object of ownership, its use and the entity holding

[60] W.J. Katner, "Mienie komunalne jako podstawa działalności gospodarczej samorządu terytorialnego" (1993) 57 *Acta Universitatis Lodziensis Folia Iuridica* 65, 73–74.

[61] A. Agopszowicz, "Mienie komunalne", in A. Agopszowicz, Z. Gilowska, M. Taniewska-Peszko (eds), *Prawo samorządu terytorialnego w zarysie*, C.H. Beck, Warszawa 2001, p. 94.

[62] Constitutional Tribunal Judgment of 17 Oct. 2000, SK 5/99, OTK 2000/7/254.

[63] Gniewek (2022), 75.

the right.[64] It is worth noting that due to the rapid development of technology and changes in social needs, there are often areas that are either not regulated at all or of which the regulation is incomplete. The significant diversity and complexity of contemporary relations and situations, as well as rapid and often profound changes in social and economic relations, and therefore also changes in concepts and valuations, have as a consequence that the legislator must refer to general clauses. Expressing a constant and strict criterion in special and explicit regulations may in many cases prove to be difficult and even pointless.

VII. CONCLUSIONS

Ownership is a social, economic and legal concept of the utmost importance for the functioning of any given state and its society. Regulations regarding ownership both shape and reflect the political character of a State and provide information as to the freedoms that its citizens enjoy. Private ownership has long been noted for its importance in harbouring respect for property, providing motivation for innovation, as well as for the development of the society and economy. The example of Poland, which after World War II became a communist state, is an important lesson in showing, how basing the economy on a faulty mix of mainly public ownership is not conducive to creating and maintaining a civil society. The transition to a market economy in the 1990s resulted in granting private ownership its rightful place in the economy, however, as noted by academia, ownership is a pluriform right. Despite the fact that ownership must be a right understood uniformly in the whole legal system, i.e. both in public and private law, its content will vary depending on the object of the right, its use and the subject holding the right.

The Polish constitutional regulation of ownership is concise in the sense that apart from expressly naming private ownership, it does not contain more detailed provisions on public ownership or public things and the principles that should bind the legislator when further regulating them. Nevertheless, the PCC 1964 definition of ownership has retained two indicators, namely the principles of social-coexistence and the socio-economic purpose of ownership, which allow to view ownership through its social function and special objectives that may follow from the object of ownership, its use, and the entity holding the right. This allows to more precisely describe any given ownership right, also by classifying it as private, common, or public. Unfortunately, upon the introduction of the market economy, the general rule expressed in Article 141 PCC 1964 has been deleted. Meanwhile, the directive contained therein that whoever is entrusted

64 Cf. M. Habdas, *Publiczna własność nieruchomości*, Lexis Nexis, Warszawa 2012, pp. 186 et seq.; Dybowski (1967), 733; R. Mikosz, "*Ograniczenia własności (na przykładzie prawa górniczego)*, (1982) 5 *Problemy Prawne Górnictwa* 9, 56-57.

with the management of public property is obliged to manage it in a manner which allows for the best performance of objectives in connection with which the management has been entrusted to that person, retains its value even today.

Public and common ownership must necessarily supplement an economic system based on private ownership, because of synergies between these types of ownership. Although liberty is an ingredient of private property, the latter also has a public element necessarily connected with being a member of a given society. In particular, certain types of immovables may be affected with a public interest, in the sense that their purpose and use can potential affect the general public.[65] Private property should thus be considered in the context of a whole legal system, remembering that it is also possible to create a system of collective property and a system of common property. Importantly, none of these systems exist separately, but always complement one another. Certain objects and immovables important for the society because of their historic, environmental or functional value are better managed through non-private property systems. Consequently, when considering ownership, the emphasis should not be placed on ascertaining whether there is a need for non-private property, but how to achieve the right balance between private and public ownership.[66] This exercise, although already performed in Poland at the end of the XXth century, is increasingly important in the context of sustainable development and preserving the civil society, resistant to authoritarian regimes.

---

65 P. Kens, "Liberty and the Public Ingredient of Private Property" (1995) 55 The Review of Politics 106-107.

66 J. Waldron, *The Right to Private Property*, Claredon Press, Oxford 1990, pp. 38-42; 44-46.

GLOBALIZATION THROUGH THE RECODIFICATION OF PROPERTY LAW?

Amnon LEHAVI
Atara Kaufman Professor of Law, Harry Radzyner Law School
Academic Director, G City Real Estate Institute, Reichman University

The globalization of markets, technology, and interpersonal networks poses a growing challenge for national legal systems. Property law is traditionally considered a "domestic" field of law, not only because of its structural features (such as the in rem or numerus clausus principles), but also because it promotes distinct cultural, economic, political, and social values. The decision if property law ***should*** *be globalized also requires a choice among potential globalization strategies (****how*** *to do so). This article examines four globalization strategies: (1) soft law; (2) conflict of laws; (3) approximation; and (4) supranationalism. It does so by comparing two different types of assets, land and digital assets, which have both been dramatically affected by current processes of globalization, albeit in diverging ways. This article argues that different strategies of globalization – and, correspondingly, distinct forms of recodification or other changes to property law doctrines – should be adopted for distinct types of assets, including, for that matter, land and digital assets.*

I. INTRODUCTION: PROPERTY LAW AND GLOBALIZATION STRATEGIES

We live in a time witnessing an increasing movement of capital, goods, services and persons across national borders. Disruptive technologies and other scientific, technological and economic innovations play a key role in this process and entail an enormous potential for pushing forward societies, corporations and individuals in pursuing their goals on a global scale.[1] At the same time, such processes also encounter multiple challenges, from safety or health risks such as in the case of the global spread of COVID-19, to current political, social and economic forms of backlash against globalization. These latter forces allegedly

1 E. AUTIO et al., "Digitalization and Globalization in a Turbulent World: Centrifugal and Centripetal Forces" (2021) 11 *Global Strategy Journal* 3.

seek to restore national priorities, independence and a sense of local pride – but in so doing, they may advance populism, isolationism and xenophobia – while targeting supranationalism and globalization as their foes.[2]

From a legal perspective, the success of globalization depends to a large extent on the ability to mitigate the gaps between the largely borderless nature of markets, interpersonal networks and digital technology, and the domestic characteristics of legal systems. Legal disparity among national systems, which exists across different branches of law, results from a variety of reasons that go beyond historic trajectories or different methodologies. Such divergences are due also, to a large extent, to country-specific social, economic, cultural and political considerations.[3] These latter considerations are also dynamic in nature, in the sense that changes to such societal elements or values may occur over time, and these changes might accordingly reshape (albeit at a diverging pace) the relevant national legal systems.[4] In other cases, legal divergences may result from "legal competition," by which jurisdictions compete with each other in order to attract economic and other activities that may prove worthwhile for the host jurisdiction, such as in the case of offering tax incentives for luring investment or providing lenient rules for corporate governance.[5] In contrast to legal differences driven by country-specific histories or values, measures of legal competition actually seek to harness opportunities that global markets or global settings offer, i.e. improving a certain jurisdiction's standing in a cross-border competition over mobile assets and entities. In some cases, however, these legal disparities may cause sophisticated actors to exploit gaps and loopholes in ways that may adversely affect the competing jurisdictions themselves. This may motivate jurisdictions to collaborate to prevent excessive cases of "legal arbitrage," without otherwise undermining legal differences embedded in more profound values and policies.[6]

While these challenges exist across all fields of law, the task of adapting property law to an era of globalization faces unique complexities. This is due in large part to the structural components of property law – most prominently the *in rem* or third-party applicability feature of property, by which property law is based on establishing a single set of rights, duties, priorities and powers with regard to assets. Such delineation of property interests also governs legal

---

2 *See*, e.g., EDITORIAL, "Europe is Threatened by Right-Wing Alliances" *Le Monde* (English), 20 June 2023.

3 D. Caruso, "Private Law and State-Making in the Age of Globalization" (2006), 39 *N.Y.U. J. Int. L & Pol.* 1.

4 G. Roland, "Understanding Institutional Change: Fast-Moving and Slow-Moving Institutions" (2004) *Stud. Comp. Int. Dev.* 109, 109-111, 116-18 (portraying the different pace at which politics, law, and culture change over time).

5 A. Lehavi, "From Global Databases to Global Norms? The Case of Cultural Property Law" (2023) 44 *U. Penn. J. Int. L.* 359, 368 (hereinafter: "Lehavi, Cultural Property Law").

6 *Ibid.*, pp. 368-371 (explaining why jurisdictions collaborate with each other against some types of legal arbitrage).

relations among distant parties that have no privity of contract, or another preset legal basis for governing conflicting claims. The third-party applicability feature of property law, and the subsequent need to inform third parties of the existence of such legal interests, has traditionally led national legal systems to embrace some sort of a *numerus clausus* (closed list) principle in property law.[7] This has typically meant that new types of legal interests that would also bind third parties should be designed top-down by the legislative, executive, or judicial branches, and these cannot be created by private parties through contract. Obviously, if all legal systems were to embrace the same, or very similar, procedural and substantive rules for property law, then the switch from national to cross-border governance of property would not have been too burdensome in practice. This is not the case. National legal systems continue to exhibit significant differences from one another in the design and operation of property law.[8] Such divergences thus challenge a smooth transition to globalism.

At the same time, the very need to design property law in a centralized manner, namely through lawmaking institutions such as legislatures, administrative agencies, and courts, allegedly requires a particularly dramatic move towards top-down interstate ordering. This is so because property law cannot allegedly rely on cross-border private ordering to ease the friction between global markets, interpersonal networks, and technology, and the *in rem* ordering of rights to assets. In other words, a cross-border ranking of property norms with an *in rem* effect seems to require, to varying degrees, effective cross-border institutions on a legislative, administrative and adjudicative level. Thus, somewhat paradoxically, property law is at the same time the most "domestic" in nature, but it may allegedly require the most dramatic transition towards formally enforceable cross-border governance.

But is this really the case? Does property law mandate the use of a single method in order to decrease the gap between property law and the cross-border nature of markets, interpersonal networks and technology? This article argues that this assumption does not hold, and that just as processes of globalization do not follow a single route, the appropriate legal strategy for addressing various cross-border scenarios need not take a single form. In other words, the decision if property law **should** be globalized also requires a choice among potential globalization strategies (**how** to do so) – with such a choice involving an array of both normative and practical considerations.

---

7 *See, e.g.*, T.W. Merrill and H.E. Smith, "Optimal Standardization in the Law of Property: The Numerus Clausus Principle" (2000), 110 *Yale Law Journal* 1; B. Akkermans, *The Principle of Numerus Clausus in European Property Law*, Intersentia, Antwerp 2008.

8 Y.C. Chang, *Property Law: Comparative, Empirical, and Economic Analyses*, Cambridge, Cambridge University Press, 2023.

In previous work[9], I referred to four legal strategies that should be considered in the context of the globalization of property law (although other strategies may also be available or developed).

First, the "**soft law strategy**," which refers to nonbinding principles or institutions that aim to serve as potential legislative or administrative templates, guides to best practices, tools of interpretation, and so forth, in order to promote the prospects of cross-border coordination.[10] Although such principles or institutions are not directly binding on states, and accordingly, are not formally enforceable by domestic and supranational institutions – unlike "hard law" instruments – soft law or private ordering mechanisms can practically influence the ways in which both states and private actors design arrangements that pertain to property law doctrines across borders.[11]

It is important to note, however, that various types of soft law instruments may have distinctive features that affect the degree of their "softness." This is so both in terms of the level of flexibility embedded in the norms themselves – namely, whether such norms are designed as clear "rules" or as open-ended "standards" that leave room for discretion and interpretation – and also in terms of the actual power dynamics that may influence national governments, professional organizations, or private actors in deciding whether to adopt such soft law instruments. Thus, for example, soft law rules may become "harder" if the adoption of certain model laws may serve as a "take-it-or-leave-it" condition for financial aid granted by international agencies such as the World Bank or the International Monetary Fund,[12] or when the adoption of certain "rules of ethics" practically guides also the formal conduct of members of organizations across borders, such as in the case of museums or cultural institutions that comprise the International Council of Museums (ICOM).[13]

Second, the "**conflict of laws strategy**," which seeks to advance new or improved private international law rules that deal with jurisdiction, choice of law, and enforcement of foreign proceedings in cases of disputes that involve parties or assets across borders. One example, in the context of property law, concerns the European Union's Regulation No. 650/2012 on jurisdiction, applicable law,

---

9 *See* A. Lehavi, *Property Law in a Globalizing Law*, Cambridge, Cambridge University Press, 2019, pp. 35-37 and 53-89.

10 For the general distinction between "hard law" and "soft law" in the international setting, see, e.g., G. Shaffer and M.A. Pollack, "Hard and Soft Law" in J.L. Dunoff and M.A. Pollack (eds), *Interdisciplinary Perspectives on International Law and International Relations: The State of the Art*, Cambridge, Cambridge University Press, 2013, pp. 197-222.

11 For a suggested definition and analytical analysis of soft law, see, e.g., L. Sossin, and C. Van Wiltenburg, *The Puzzle of Soft Law* (2021), 58 *Osgoode Hall Law Journal* 623, 628-631.

12 A. Lehavi and A. N. Licht, "BIT and Pieces of Property" (2011) 36 *Yale Journal of International Law* 115, 124-125.

13 International Council of Museums (ICOM), *Code of Ethics for Museums* (2017), https://icom.museum/wp-content/uploads/2018/07/ICOM-code-En-web.pdf. ICOM brings together museums in 138 countries and territories.

and enforcement of decisions in matters of succession[14], intended to ensure that a **given succession** is *"treated coherently, by one single court applying one single law,"*[15] although it in no way alters the substantive national rules on succession. Similarly, the EU adopted regulations for implementing "enhanced cooperation" in the area of jurisdiction, applicable law, and enforcement of decisions in property matters concerning both married couples (Council Regulation (EU) 2016/1103)[16] and registered partners (Council Regulation (EU) 2016/1104).[17] Agreed to by 18 Member States, such an "enhanced cooperation" framework follows a conflict of laws strategy in property matters upon the dissolution of spousal relations with a cross-border dimension, seeking to increase legal certainty about rules on jurisdiction, applicable law, and enforcement in an area of law otherwise marked by considerable substantive national differences.[18]

Third, the "**approximation strategy**," which resorts to binding cross-border instruments that require states to approximate their respective property law doctrines. This may be done through treaties or conventions that introduce "minimum standards of protection" in a certain field of law, while leaving to states, and their courts, the power of lawmaking and enforcement of such norms. A prominent example is the Agreement on the Trade-Related Aspects of Intellectual Property Rights (TRIPS).[19] While the TRIPS Agreement requires all signatory states to introduce certain minimum standards for the various intellectual property rights, and it vests some authority for inter-state dispute resolution with a panel of the World Trade Organization (WTO)[20], it still leaves the operation and enforcement of intellectual property rights mostly to domestic law.

---

14 Regulation (EU) No. 650/2012 of the European Parliament and of the Council of 4 July 2012 on Jurisdiction, Applicable Law, Recognition and Enforcement of Decisions and Acceptance and Enforcement of Authentic Instruments in Matters of Succession and on the Creation of a European Certificate of Succession, *Official Journal* (L 201/107), 4 July 2012.

15 European Commission, "Succession and Wills", https://commission.europa.eu/strategy-and-policy/policies/justice-and-fundamental-rights/civil-justice/family-law/successions-and-wills_en#eurulesoninternationalsuccession (last accessed on 12 March 2024).

16 Council Regulation (EU) 2016/1103 of 24 June 2016 Implementing Enhanced Cooperation in the Area of Jurisdiction, Applicable Law and the Recognition and Enforcement of Decisions in Matters of Matrimonial Property Regimes, *Official Journal* (L 183/1), 8 July 2016.

17 Council Regulation (EU) 2016/1104 of 24 June 2016 Implementing Enhanced Cooperation in the Area of Jurisdiction, Applicable Law and the Recognition and Enforcement of Decisions in Matters of the Property Consequences of Registered Partnerships, *Official Journal* (L 183/30), 8 July 2016.

18 See CEELI INSTITUTE, *Application of EU Instruments in Civil Justice* (2021), pp. 5-24, http://ceeliinstitute.org/wp-content/uploads/2022/01/Application_EU_Instr_2021_CIVIL_EN_01.pdf.

19 Agreement on Trade-Related Aspects of Intellectual Property Rights, April 15, 1994 (Marrakesh Agreement Establishing the World Trade Organization, Annex 1C, 1869 UNTS 299).

20 H.B. Pauwelyn, A.T. Guzman and J.A. Hillman, *International Trade Law*, 3d ed., Wolters Kluwer, New York 2016, pp. 128-138.

Fourth, the "**supranationalism strategy**," which establishes supranational norms of property law, with corresponding institutions that have binding lawmaking and enforcement powers. Such supranational norms enjoy a superior legal status over national norms in case of conflict, even if the application of such supranational provisions may be tempered or limited by adopting principles that defer to domestic rules in some cases. Prominent examples are the property clauses included in binding human rights treaties, such as Article 1 of the First Protocol of the European Convention on Human Rights.[21] In reviewing the conformity of local lawmaking to the binding provisions of this supranational property clause, the European Court of Human Rights has gradually developed a set of supranational criteria for interpreting and applying this clause. The Court has thus established "fair balance," "proportionality" and other principles as supranational standards, while subjecting them to some level of deference to states by introducing a "margin of appreciation."[22]

The choice among the various globalization strategies (or the potential combination of which) entails both functional and normative considerations. Alongside questions such as when the globalization of legal norms may be practically essential for a certain global market to function, considering, inter alia, the actual scope of the market's cross-border activity, it is also necessary to consider key normative issues. Is the specific global market truly efficient and fair? Does it ignore the legitimate interests of certain actors – be they private or public – in favor of other, more powerful stakeholders? Are there essential local or national values or goals that are being unduly sidelined in the process? As this article shows, the potential answers to both these functional and normative considerations – and their prospective implications for the choice among the different globalization strategies – may vary according to the particular type of assets at stake. The following sections study these questions, first, in the context of land, and then, in the case of digital assets.

II. LAND

A. GLOBAL LAND MARKET? ON CROSS-BORDER MEGA DEALS

Land law has been traditionally considered the most "domestic" branch of property law. This is so not only due to the immovability of land, but also because of land's natural scarcity, its centrality for human life (considering both

---

21 Protocol 1, Art. 1 of the European Convention for the Protection of Human Rights and Fundamental Freedoms, 4 November 1950, 213 UNTS 221.

22 See Y. Arai-Takahashi, *The Margin of Appreciation Doctrine and the Principle of Proportionality in the Jurisprudence of the ECHR*, Intersentia, Antwerp 2002.

"use value" and "market value"), and its social and political meaning within communities and nation-states.[23] Accordingly, cultural, social, economic, or political changes that took place within a certain society at a certain time in history have also prompted the redesign of land law to reflect these changes. Thus, in the great civil codes of European countries, enacted after the French revolution and expressing a rejection of feudal models of land governance, property law focused on ownership as the "*right of one particular subject, who for an unlimited duration of time can exercise sole and full power over a physical object and who can exclude anyone else.*"[24] More recently, newly independent states, economies in transition and countries that underwent major political changes have revised their land laws.[25]

At the same time, foreign ownership, or control of land by individuals or corporations is far from being a new phenomenon. Going well beyond non-transactional forms of foreign control of land due to colonialism, military occupation and similar geopolitical phenomena – individuals, business corporations, religious institutions, and other entities have owned, possessed, or otherwise controlled land in territories outside of their countries of origin, holding title that was formally registered or otherwise legally validated by the host country's institutions. This reality has also led over time to the need to resolve legal disputes involving parties from different jurisdictions, with the *lex rei sitae* rule serving traditionally as the default for both jurisdiction and applicable law.[26]

The dominance of this baseline version of the conflict of laws strategy has, however, come under pressure once foreign land ownership became a target of contentious policies undertaken by different countries, such as newly independent states in the post-colonial era, including expropriation of land and other assets from foreign owners for little or no compensation[27], imposition of regulatory requirements with a discriminative or otherwise unequal effect on non-domestic stakeholders[28], or even the imposition of limits or bans on foreign land ownership.[29]

---

23 See C.M. Rose, "Property as the Keystone Right?" (1996) 71 *Notre Dame Law Review* 329.

24 S. Van Erp, *All Good Things Come to an End, but Access Remains*, Wolf Legal Publishers, Oisterwijk 2021, p. 19.

25 See A. Lehavi, "The Global Law of the Land" (2010) 81 *University of Colorado Law Review* 425, 430-438.

26 S. Van Erp, "Lex Rei Sitae: The Territorial Side of Classical Property Law," in C. GODT (ed.), *Regulatory Property Rights: The Transforming Notion of Property in Transnational Business Regulation*, Brill Nijhoff, Leiden/Boston 2016, pp. 61-81.

27 During the 1950s, a number of newly independent countries embarked on a series of massive expropriations of properties and enterprises controlled by foreign investors. Lehavi and Licht, *supra* note 12, p. 118-128.

28 *Ibid.*

29 A 1980 academic study has shown, however, that such limits were also imposed by Western countries, including Australia, Canada, France, the Netherlands, New Zealand, Scandinavian

This phenomenon, which had originally troubled investors from Western countries that operated in developing economics – but is currently of potential concern to foreign investors across the globe – has led to the gradual development of bilateral investment treaties (BITs) and other cross-border legal mechanisms aimed at better protecting foreign investors, including land owners, against government excess.[30] In essence, BITs implement three measures that deviate from a simple application of the *lex rei sitae* rule in relevant cases. First, a BIT typically involves a set of commitments by host countries to extend certain standards of treatment for foreign investment – ones that do not necessarily exist in the host country's domestic laws; second, it grants a direct right of action for individual investors against host countries in case of an alleged breach of such commitments; and third, resolution of disputes is typically governed by international arbitration, most often through the International Centre for Settlement of Investment Disputes (ICSID).[31]

This means, in principle, that a foreign land owner, who contests a certain government measure that is allegedly in conflict with a commitment that had been undertaken by the host government under the relevant BIT, may rely on this supranational norm embedded in the bilateral investment treaty, and can also resort to a supranational dispute-resolution institution. While the actual number of formal investor-state dispute resolution (ISDS) proceedings concerning land has been relatively small as compared to disputes concerning other types of foreign investments[32], and although BITs do not apply to land law disputes that involve private parties (meaning that the *lex rei sitae* rule continues to govern such cases), it is noteworthy that supranationalism may be employed as a strategy for land, beyond the general context of property clauses in human rights conventions.

Moreover, an analysis of arbitration proceedings held under ICSID and other institutions points to significant success by claimants.[33] This is so because arbitration tribunals often interpret and implement BIT commitments such as "fair and equitable treatment," "full protection and security" or "indirect expropriation" as granting foreign investors, including land owners, greater legal

---

states, West Germany, and the United States. J. Weisman, "Restrictions on the Acquisition of Land by Aliens" (1980) 28 *Am. J. Comp. L.* 39, 41-42.

30 Lehavi and Licht, *supra* note 12, pp. 118-128.

31 INTERNATIONAL CENTRE FOR SETTLEMENT OF INVESTMENT DISPUTES, "The ICSID Caseload – Statistics" (2023), https://icslbid.worldbank.org/sites/default/files/Caseload%20Statistics%20Charts/The_ICSID_Caseload_Statistics.1_Edition_ENG.pdf (providing statistics about all investment cases brought before ICSID between 1972 and 2022).

32 *See* UNITED NATIONS CONFERENCE ON TRADE AND DEVELOPMENT (UNCTAD), IIA Issue Notes, "Review of 2021 Investor-State Arbitration Decisions: Insights for IIA Reform" (Issue 1, July 2023) (reviewing 31 ISDS decisions rendered in 2021, and pointing to the dominance of energy-related cases, as compared with other types of assets).

33 The ICSID Caseload Statistics, *supra* note 31, pp. 13-14 (showing that 48 percent of cases decided by arbitral tribunals upheld the claims in part or in full).

protection than that provided by the host jurisdiction. Although arbitration awards do not follow a *stare decisis* principle and are not otherwise coordinated in the same way that court decisions are, one can nevertheless identify the emergence of a supranational body of case law that challenges, at least to a certain degree, the longstanding reign of local land law and regulation.[34]

In fact, over the past few years, countries and international bodies, such as the United Nations Conference on Trade and Development (UNCTAD), have pointed to the potential ill-effects of arbitration awards moving the pendulum probably too much in favor of powerful investors at the expense of countries' ability to design public policy and need to respond to changing conditions. This has led to a gradual reform in crafting new-generation BITs, aimed at creating a better balance between protecting the legitimate interests of investors and recognizing host countries' "right to regulate".[35]

In the context of foreign investment in land, any contemporary analysis of the proper balance between the interests of foreign stakeholders and host countries, and of the potential implications for adopting a globalization strategy that is both normatively worthy and functionally effective, must consider a dramatic development that has been taking place around the world, especially since the 2007-2008 food crisis.[36] This crisis has led to an unprecedented wave of large-scale land acquisitions in developing countries rich in arable lands, mostly in Africa, Latin America, and parts of Asia. The purchasing parties mostly come from capital-rich countries in the West, Gulf States, and emerging economies with large or fast-growing populations – and consequently, with increasing needs for food and sources of energy – such as China, India, and South Korea.[37]

While such large-scale land acquisitions originating from Western countries are usually done by private corporations, in the case of capital-rich emerging economies, such acquisitions are often directed and orchestrated by the respective governments, such as via state-owned enterprises. This points to the emergence of a public policy in these investor countries: Instead of relying on markets for imports, land acquired by investor countries in destination countries serves as a source of "quasi-domestic" production of food crops, biofuels, timber, etc. This phenomenon, also dubbed as "land grab" or the "rush for land,"[38] is often embedded in an even broader policy of gaining control

---

34 *Ibid.* (offering a detailed analysis of the ways in which different arbitration awards address key investment issues).

35 UNCTAD, *World Investment Report 2023: Investing in Sustainable Energy for All*, New York, 2023, pp. 71-79.

36 *See, generally*, LEHAVI, *supra* note 9, pp. 91-98.

37 S. NARULA, "The Global Land Rush: Markets, Rights, and the Politics of Food" (2013), 49 *Stanford J. Int. L* 101.

38 *See, e.g.*, O. DE SCHUTTER, "The Green Rush: The Global Race for Farmland and the Rights of Land Users" (2011) 52 *Harvard Int. L. J.* 503; *J.* WIGGINTON, "Large-Scale Land Investment in Africa: An Issue of Self-Help and Self-Determination" (2013) 20 *U.C. Davis J. Int. L. & Pol.* 105.

over other resources in the target countries, while harnessing such control also for expanding the political influence of investor countries over destination countries. China's operations in Africa are probably the most notable example, with a clear positive correlation between its geopolitical strategy and the scope of investment in land, infrastructure, and minerals.[39]

Statistics are often hard to compile because many of these deals are kept secret by both investors and host countries. Critics attribute this to the fact that many of the host countries are plagued by weak governance, poor records of formally recognizing rural or tribal land tenure, and lack of accountability and access to information, often resulting in alleged cases of corruption.[40] Land Matrix, an independent global land monitoring initiative[41], presents data, as of 2023, about over 2,100 large-scale land acquisitions concluded so far for a total of over 64 million hectares worldwide, out of which about 570 deals done in African countries for over 12 million hectares.[42] Providing details not only about individual transactions, but also aggregate information about the global web of transaction deals, investor profiles, and country profiles[43], the Land Matrix database points clearly to the imbalance between investors (and their home countries) and host countries with this power imbalance adversely impacting the interests of local residents and communities.[44] Accordingly, the concept of a "global land market" may prove controversial, at least from a normative perspective, with potential consequences for considering globalization strategies. The scope of foreign ownership and other forms of access, use and control of land across national borders has thus changed considerably, not only as a matter of quantity, but also as one of quality.

Under the conventional paradigm, transaction-based foreign land ownership involved mostly individuals purchasing a property as a pied-à-terre or household investment, real-estate developers, corporations acquiring land to set up a manufacturing plant or infrastructure project, religious institutions getting a foothold to expand their mission abroad, and so forth. The host country was considered as otherwise holding the general powers over land law and policy, with the *lex rei sitae* rule referring to the home jurisdiction's courts and applicable law. In the current era of large-scale land acquisitions, in which

---

39 *See* THE ECONOMIST, "China in Africa: Unequal Partnership – Special Reports" (28 May 2022).

40 S. Borras, Jr. and J. Franco, "Global Land Grabbing and Trajectories of Agrarian Change: A Preliminary Analysis" (2012), 12 *Journal of Agrarian Change* 34.

41 LAND MATRIX, "The Land Matrix Initiative", https://landmatrix.org/about/the-land-matrix-initiative/ (last accessed on 12 March 2024).

42 *Ibid.*, "Data", then "Map", https://landmatrix.org/map/ (last accessed on 12 March 2024).

43 *Ibid.*, "Data", then "Charts", https://landmatrix.org/charts/country-profiles/ (last accessed on 12 March 2024).

44 *See, e.g.*, S. Smis, D. Cambou and G. Ngende, "The Question of Land Grab in Africa and the Indigenous Peoples' Right to Traditional Lands, Territories and Resources" (2013) 35 *Loyola of Los Angeles Int'l & Comp. L. Rev.* 493.

investors (whether private corporations or state-owned enterprises) may also leverage the potential application of BITs and resort to international arbitration, host countries – especially those located in the developing world – may often find themselves incapable of exercising their right to regulate or otherwise address societal, economic, or political changes. Moreover, in countries that are otherwise typified by lack of transparency and accountability to their own residents and local communities, the latter may find themselves in a particularly vulnerable position as a matter of both political power and legal protection. Such concerns may be further exacerbated by the fragmentation of norms and institutions, which I now move to address.

B. THE LEGAL FRAGMENTATION OF NORMS AND INSTITUTIONS

To illustrate the complex and multi-layered features of land law in the age of a "global land market" – ones that may implicate, *inter alia*, customary norms, domestic law, international investment commitments, and human rights treaties, consider a petition filed by the Sawhoyamaxa Indigenous Community of the Enxet People to the Inter-American Commission on Human Rights, alleging that the government of Paraguay violated the American Convention on Human Rights.[45]

The tribe argued that the government had failed to complete its own initiative to recover part of the ancestral lands of the tribe of over 14,000 hectares in the Chaco region. This was so although Paraguayan constitutional law recognizes the right of indigenous peoples to preserve their way of life in their habitat and to protect the claimed lands. As a result, community members had to live in inhumane conditions, resulting in a number of deaths due to lack of food and medical care. The tribe argued that the government's omission of not restoring possession of the land to it amounted to a violation of Article 21(1) of the American Convention on Human Rights, by which "[E]*veryone has a right to the use and enjoyment of his property.*"[46] The government contended, on its part, that although it was committed to resolving the matter, the lands in question had been formally purchased by a German investor, who used the land for beef production. Consequently, the executive branch's efforts to expropriate the land had been met with staunch resistance by the legislature in view of the provisions of the 1993 BIT between Germany and Paraguay.[47]

45 *Sawhoyamaxa Indigenous Community v. Paraguay*, 2006 Inter-Am. Ct. H.R. (ser. C.), No. 146, 29 March 2006. This section is based, in part, on Lehavi, *supra* note 9, Chapter 3.

46 Organization of American States, American Convention on Human Rights, 22 November 1969, O.A.S.T.S. No. 36, 1144 U.N.T.S. 143, Art. 21(1).

47 *Sawhoyamaxa* case, *supra* note 45, para. 115.

In March 2006, ruling in favor of the tribe, the Inter-American Court reasoned that the enforcement of bilateral investment treaties may not allow a state to infringe its obligations under the American Convention of Human Rights. As for the problem of conflicting rights to the land, the Court reasoned that although it is "*not a domestic judicial authority with jurisdiction to decide disputes among private parties,*" it is nevertheless competent to "*analyze whether the State ensured the human rights of the members of the Sawhoyamaxa Community.*" According to the Inter-American Court, the government's recognition of the tribe's rights to traditional lands remains "*meaningless in practice if the lands have not been physically* [...] *surrendered because the adequate domestic measures necessary to secure effective use and enjoyment of said right* [...] *are lacking.*"[48]

The court therefore ordered Paraguay to adopt measures to return the land to the Sawhoyamaxa Community. In June 2014, after many delays, and two other rulings by the Inter-American Court in favor of indigenous tribes in Paraguay, President Horacio Cartes signed into law a bill that orders the expropriation of the land from the German owner and its return to the tribe.[49]

The *Sawhoyamaxa* case vividly illustrates the challenges of a fragmented system of supranational, national, and sub-national norms and institutions, and the consequent implications for trying to devise a proper globalization strategy that weighs both normative and functional considerations. Thus, this specific case implicates: (1) an international human rights convention (American Convention) and a respective international tribunal; (2) a supranational investment treaty (Germany-Paraguay BIT) with its distinctive potential arbitration forum; (3) general provisions in Paraguay's constitution and national legislation about the recognition of traditional tribal rights and commitment to land restitution; (4) the land law of Paraguay with its land titling system and the property rights that emanate from it; and (5) customary norms, institutions and practices of sub-society groups – all of which are tied up in this case to the same piece of land.

What is even more intriguing in this case is the lack of a clear-cut hierarchy among the different sets of norms applying in the matter. In fact, one could argue for a circular pattern that is driving the structure of legal norms, while constantly tilting the balance of legal interests back and forth among the different parties. To start with, national land law would regularly trump any nonconforming forms of subnational traditional land tenure (thus supporting the position of the investor, formally registered as the owner). However, national constitutional law provisions, committed to land restitution, might supersede

48 *Ibid.*, paras 136-43.

49 G. Constantine, "Paraguay: Indigenous Community Records Rare Land Rights Victory", *Eye on Latin America*, 20 June 2014, https://eyeonlatinamerica.wordpress.com/2014/06/20/paraguay-indigenous-land-rights-victory/.

national land law, especially if constitutional rights are viewed as implicating also "horizontal" relations among persons and not only "vertical" ones (i.e., state v. persons). Then, the BIT, including commitments by the state against certain acts of expropriation, denial of "fair and equitable treatment," etc., may make the case in favor of the foreign investor, who would argue that these commitments should serve as a *lex specialis* in protecting the investment. Then, the American Convention on Human Rights is viewed by the court as prevailing, in case of conflict, over other commitments that the state has undertaken in a bilateral investment agreement – thus moving the pendulum again towards the side of the indigenous tribe in its conflict with the German land owner (even though the latter was not a formal party to the proceeding before the Inter-American Court and Germany is obviously not a signatory to the American Convention). Moving one step further, the very recognition of the tribe's right to property under Article 21(1) of the American Convention by the Inter-American Court is based on the customary land tenure – the same subnational norm superseded by Paraguay's national land law – thus coming a full circle (some would say, a vicious circle).

The difficulty incurred here is not only one of normative fragmentation, but also one of institutional incompleteness. Recall the Inter-American Court's statement, by which it is "*not a domestic judicial authority with jurisdiction to decide disputes among private parties.*"[50] But when a court or tribunal decides on the superiority of some property rights or interests over others, it cannot simply disregard the broader implications of its decision. Therefore, even though the court is allegedly concerned only with the public law aspect; that is to say, constitutional or human rights aspect with respect to indigenous tribes, it in fact also implicates the private law aspect of the dispute and the entire array of *in rem* rights, duties, priorities, and powers.

Obviously, when a dispute concerning both public law and private law facets of land rights is argued before a national court in a pure domestic matter, the court cannot look selectively only at some of the legal norms that have a bearing on the case. Moreover, if a certain national constitution is understood as having also a "horizontal" dimension – as is the case in countries such as South Africa and to a lesser extent in jurisdictions like Germany[51] – the court would have to account for the entire set of legal norms that grant *in rem* priority to some parties over others. This is a responsibility that cannot be entirely avoided also in the supranational setting.

The Inter-American Court may have been absolutely sincere in its account that it is not a domestic court with power to decide a private dispute, but this is exactly the gap that is currently making property jurisprudence even more

---

50 *Sawhoyamaxa* case, *supra* note 45, para. 136.

51 See, generally, G.A. Alexander, *The Global Debate over Constitutional Property: Lessons for American Takings Jurisprudence*, University of Chicago Press, Chicago 2006.

burdensome than it should be in a world of incomplete globalization. For a system of property to make any sense, even in the current state of normative fragmentation, courts and tribunals asked to decide in effect on *in rem* aspects of rights to land cannot simply overlook the existence of other legal norms that might govern the entire set of rights, powers, and priorities in regard to the asset. A state of events in which each judicial forum could simply disregard relevant norms as it chooses is not a viable globalization strategy for land law.

C. LAND AND GLOBALIZATION: IMPLICATIONS FOR NATIONAL LAW

In light of the above characteristics of the alleged "global land market" and the current set system of norms and institutions in operation, what is the most proper way to move forward with a globalization strategy for land law – one that would have both normative and functional merits?

My key argument is that both intra-market and extra-market considerations advise against validating the concept of a "global land market" as justifying a universal adoption of cross-border approximation or supranationalism of substantive norms and decision-making institutions. While many land transactions that involve foreign stakeholders are done in well-functioning markets, ones that grant access to both domestic and international actors and that follow certain market practices that are shared by land markets in different territories, other factors point to a genuine heterogeneity and place-specific features that justify keeping the focus on domestic law – while seeking potential improvements that would benefit both foreign and domestic stakeholders.

In this respect, the critical mass of large-scale land acquisition points to a growing imbalance in favor of foreign investors (whether private corporations or state-owned enterprises), with residents and local communities in host countries often finding themselves in a vulnerable position when their interests are being sidelined by weak, corrupt, or nontransparent host governments.

Accordingly, while BITs and similar mechanisms were originally devised with the idea of correcting one type of imbalance – that which existed between vulnerable foreign investors and powerful host governments, by adding a layer of supranational norms and dispute-resolution institutions – the very same strategy may create, even if inadvertently, a different type of imbalance. This is so in regard to both host governments, who may be in dire need of capital investments but may then find themselves unable to exercise their right to regulate and respond to genuine changes, and to local residents and communities who may be unaware of such supranational norms and institutions, or otherwise unable to take measures to address their potential implications. Unlike property clauses in human right treaties, such as Article 1 of Protocol 1 of the European Convention of Human Rights, or Article 21 of the Inter-American Convention of Human Rights, which may protect both domestic and foreign right holders against certain types of government excess, other supranational instruments such as BITs can actually increase existing imbalances. This may further undermine a simplistic view of a "global land market" as justifying moving away from local land law and regulation in favor of supranational norms that may be a misfit for land.

Accordingly, the conflict of laws strategy should continue to adhere to the general dominance of the *lex rei sitae* rule, governing both the jurisdiction that has power to adjudicate a conflict pertaining to *in rem* ordering of rights, duties, priorities and powers, and the substantive law that would apply to the matter. The *lex rei sitae* continues to be dominant not only because of historical path-dependence, but also because it has cultural, social, economic, and political merit in considering the key role of land continues to play for individuals, communities, and nation-states.

At the same time, national legal systems should be clearer and more transparent – both to their own residents as well as to foreign citizens – about the web of legal interests, including potential conflicts/ambiguities, between domestic law and cross-border legal instruments that create rights or duties concerning land. Such clarity and transparency should also ensure better access to information, via registries and other available sources, with a particular focus on free digital access that would available not only to sophisticated actors, but also to local residents and communities. In this respect, certain soft law mechanisms could be developed by international agencies about how to make such information more accessible. This should be done without undermining the key role that local law and regulation and the *lex rei sitae* rule should play – while scrutinized local norms to ensure efficiency and fairness toward all types of stakeholders, be they local or foreign.

III. DIGITAL ASSETS

A. THE CURRENT GAP BETWEEN THE MARKET TRENDS AND LEGAL CONCEPTS

The term "digital assets" covers a broad plethora of digital or virtual resources. While earlier literature referred to items such as e-mail and social media accounts, electronic media in digital form such as music, videos, and books, or reward points earned by persons participating in a retail program[52], the current focus on digital assets is on items such as cryptocurrencies or non-fungible tokens (NFTs).[53] The global market for the latter types of digital assets is rapidly

[52] N.M. Banta, "Property Interests in Digital Assets: The Rise of Digital Feudalism" (2017), 38 *Cardozo L. Rev.* 1099.

[53] STATISTA, "Digital Assets Report 2023" (14 July 2023), p. 3 (cryptocurrencies are a "*digital currencies that use an online ledger with strong cryptography to secure online transactions*"; an

growing, such that the revenue forecast for cryptocurrencies is estimated to grow from USD 32 billion to 65 billion between 2021 and 2027, and that for NFTs from USD 0.8 billion to 3.2 billion during the same period.[54] NFTs have been particularly dominant in media coverage and professional circles as the object of a brand new global market – with prices reflecting the general "hype" around it, such as in the case of the 2021 record-breaking sale of a JPG file created by artist Mike Winkelman (known as Beeple) in an online auction held by Christie's for USD 69.3 million.[55] Yet, as I argue below, while the market for NFTs rapidly grows, it remains a legally obscure concept – both on the national and global levels – and the same dissonance holds also for other types of digital assets.

This problem, attesting to what I term the "infancy of property law" in the context of digital assets, is also manifested in the case of the related (but not identical) concept of data. Thus, while legal systems are addressing, to a growing degree, including by case law, the question whether data can be considered as "property" – such piecemeal attempts are far from developing a new and consistent body of law.[56] Thus, as Sjef van Erp notes, the theoretical and conceptual analysis of data is hindered by "the blind focus on the unitary concept of ownership."[57] What is needed, as both a conceptual tool and a normative guide, is a focus on the idea of "data management" for determining "in an orderly, efficient and effective way who has access, control, is entitled to portability, the possibility of erasure and who has the power to share, pool and transfer the data."[58]

To illustrate the current gap between market dynamics and legal concepts (resulting to a large degree from the infancy of property law in the matter) in the context of NFTs as a prominent example of digital assets, consider the following observations in the current literature on NFTs.

In their article in *Business Horizons*[59], Raeesah Chohan and Jeannette Paschen argue that an NFT "can be thought of as a certificate of ownership. It is a digital asset that records the ownership of intangible, digital objects (e.g. videos, images, tweets), or of tangible items (e.g. real-world artwork, event tickets) using blockchain technology."[60] In so doing, the two co-authors seem to convey the market's popular view of what is being sold and bought in the case of an NFT.

In contrast, Juliet Moringiello and Christopher Odinet study the legal features of NFTs, as compared with other instances of tokenization developed in

---

NFT is "a *unique identifier that represents ownership of real-world or digital assets, such as art, music, collectibles, in-game items, and even real estate*").

54 *Ibid.*, p. 6.

55 S. Reyburn, "JPG File Sells for $69 Million, as 'NFT Mania' Gathers Pace", *New York Times*, 11 March 2021.

56 *See* Lehavi, *supra* note 9, pp. 200-205.

57 Van Erp, *supra* note 26, p. 49.

58 *Ibid.*, p. 38.

59 R. Chohan and J. Paschen, "NFT marketing: How Marketers can Use Nonfungible Tokens in their Campaigns" (2023) 66 *Business Review* 43.

60 *Ibid.*, p. 44.

law (such as negotiable instruments, securities, deeds of real estate, and bills of lading), and for that purpose, they also survey a dataset of terms of service from the most prominent NFT platforms.[61] They conclude that "NFTs do not actually embody property rights in a reference asset," and that [t]*hey are not **tethering** – they do not embody property rights in a reference thing.*"[62] Simply put: As the legal situation currently stands, a property right in a digital token does not attest to a property right in an underlying asset.

This gap has obvious implications that go beyond national legal systems. It bears considerably also on the cross-border aspect of the market for digital assets and on the implicit assumption that often drives market actors by which the use of blockchain technology facilitates globalization,[63] especially given the nature of blockchain as "*a distributed ledger technology that autonomously records peer-to-peer transactions across decentralized computers without a central authority.*"[64] The infancy of property law on digital assets is thus manifested on both local and national scales.

B. UNIDROIT PRINCIPLES ON DIGITAL ASSETS AND PRIVATE LAW

It is against the background of this major gap between market trends and legal concepts that one should consider the "Digital Assets and Private Law" project undertaken by the International Institute for the Unification of Private Law (UNIDROIT).[65] The genesis of the project goes back to 2015, when UNIDROIT received a proposal from the Ministry of Justice in Hungary suggesting the development of model laws in the domain of "business informatics," followed by a proposal from the Industry and Trade Ministry of the Czech Republic to include also topics that relate to the distributed ledger technology (such as blockchain) and inheritance of digital properties.[66]

---

61 J.M. Moringiello & C.K. Odinet, "The Property Law of Tokens" (2022) 74 *Florida L. Rev.* 607.

62 *Ibid.*, p. 641 (emphasis in the original).

63 *See*, e.g., O. Joel, "How Blockchain Can Improve Globalization" (3 January 2020), https://cointelegraph.com/news/how-blockchain-can-improve-globalization.

64 STATISTA, *supra* note 53, p. 3.

65 UNIDROIT is an intergovernmental organization that promotes hard law and soft law instruments. It was set up in 1926 by the League of Nations and re-established in 1940 on the basis of a multilateral agreement, the UNIDROIT Statute. UNIDROIT, "About UNIDROIT," www.unidroit.org/about-unidroit/ (last accessed on 12 March 2024).

66 See UNIDROIT, "Digital Assets and Private Law – Study LXXXII – Digital Assets and Private Law Project". www.unidroit.org/work-in-progress/digital-assets-and-private-law/#1690494083914-ffdfbf1a-0cf5 (last accessed on 12 March 2024) (hereinafter: "UNIDROIT, Digital Assets and Private Law").

The impetus for the project approved by UNIDROIT in September 2020, with a more refined scope of "digital assets and private law," was thus the request coming from member states who asked UNIDROIT to develop a model law that would aid them in constructing a legal framework for dealing with the emerging phenomenon of digital assets. This attests to the self-recognition by these states about the "infancy" of their national property law in the context of digital assets.[67]

Following meetings of the Digital Assets and Private Law Working Group, and a process of public consultation that included the distribution of the draft principles in January 2023, the UNIDROIT Governing Council adopted in May 2023 the UNIDROIT Principles of Digital Assets and Private Law with the purpose of promoting them in different jurisdictions to facilitate their implementation.[68] As stated in the website that introduces the UNIDROIT Principles:

> "Broadly, the Project aimed to provide legislative guidance and to develop principles relating to the legal nature, transfer and use of digital assets. This would include a legal taxonomy of digital assets and an analysis focusing on proprietary interests while considering specific issues arising in various contexts [...] The approach to be followed was neutral, seeking to accommodate diverse types of assets and technologies, along with various legal cultures. The principles identified embody best practices and international standards and enable jurisdictions to take a common approach to legal issues arising from the transfer and use of digital assets."[69]

While this section cannot discuss in detail all themes covered by the UNIDROIT Principles, two issues seem particularly relevant for the question of adopting a globalization strategy to address the proprietary aspects of digital assets considering both functional and normative issues.

First, the UNIDROIT Principles identify themselves as a soft law instrument, such that while they do offer guidance and a suggested set of clear rules, "[t]*he Principles do not prescribe a specific approach to implementation by States, but rather leave to the jurisdiction in question to decide how to implement them and incorporate them into its national law.*"[70] However, while this statement may be read as granting states substantial leeway not only in deciding whether to adopt the UNIDRPOIT Principles but also in revising them to fit a particular national

67 *Ibid.*

68 UNIDROIT, "Draft UNIDROIT Principles On Digital Assets And Private Law" (2023) (Annex to the UNIDROIT Governing Council Document on the Principles of Digital Assets and Private Law (C.D. (102) 6) (May 2023), www.unidroit.org/wp-content/uploads/2023/04/C.D.-102-6-Principles-on-Digital-Assets-and-Private-Law.pdf (hereinafter: "UNIDROIT Principles").

69 UNIDROIT, "Digital Assets and Private Law," *supra* note 66.

70 UNIDROIT Principles, *supra* note 68, p. 6 ("IV. Overview of the Principles," para. 20).

setting, this instrument emphasizes the important of consistency and similarity of norms across legal systems:

> "It is recommended that States adopt legislation consistent with these Principles. This will have several benefits. It will increase the predictability of transactions involving these assets that occur in those States. In addition, as these transactions frequently involve persons in different States, the greater the consistency among States, the greater the predictability in cross-border transactions. The increased predictability should reduce the costs of these transactions, both in direct transaction costs and pricing."[71]

Therefore, the "softness" of this instrument is practically hardened by the functional observation made in the UNIDROIT Principles that in order for the largely global market for digital assets to work well, the substantive and procedural rules adopted by states should be as similar as possible (even if not identical) because disparity would significantly increase market costs. Such an approach comes close to the strategy of approximation in the case of hard law instruments, such as conventions. Therefore, rather than serving simply as a general conceptual guide to the new world of digital assets, which could be freely tailored and redesigned by each national jurisdiction, the UNIDROIT Principles promote a functional justification for the actual harmonization of legal norms across borders.

Second, while the UNIDROIT Principles identify themselves as "jurisdiction neutral", they do make certain conceptual and normative choices that are better aligned with certain jurisdictions, thus requiring other jurisdictions to make a comparatively bigger transition in adopting these principles into their legal systems. This is particularly the case with the suggested "innocent acquisition" doctrine for digital assets, as articulated in Principle 8.[72] According to this principle, "[a]*n innocent acquirer takes a digital asset free of conflicting proprietary rights ('proprietary claims'),*"[73] and "[n]*o rights based on a proprietary claim relating to a digital asset can be successfully asserted against an innocent acquirer of that digital asset.*"[74] Principle 8 establishes also other provisions, including the conditions required for an acquirer to qualify as "innocent."[75]

Opting for a detailed "innocent acquirer" doctrine is far from being "jurisdiction neutral" in the sense that it adopts a normative approach that is closer to the way in which some legal jurisdictions address proprietary conflicts resulting from problems in the chain of title or possession in the case of other types of assets – immovable and movable ones. Roughly speaking, at least some

71 *Ibid.*, p. 11 ("Introduction – I. Reasons for the Principles," para. 0.4).
72 *Ibid.*, pp. 43-35 ("Principle 8: Innocent Acquisition").
73 *Ibid.*, p. 43 (Principle 8(2)).
74 *Ibid.* (Principle 8(3)).
75 *Ibid.* (Principle 8(1)).

common law jurisdictions (such as in the United States) tend to adopt a more stringent application of the principle of *nemo dat quod non habet* ("he who does not have cannot give") that favors the original owner over subsequent buyers/possessors, while civil law systems are generally more prone to protect "good-faith purchasers" under such circumstances, at least after a certain period of time.[76]

However, at closer inspection, the legal diversity that exists today among legal systems in regard to the "good-faith purchaser" (or the "innocent acquirer") doctrine is even more spread out than a simple common law/civil law divide. As Yun-chien Chang shows in a comparative study on the good-faith purchase doctrine from 246 jurisdictions around the world, there are at least 21 variants of this doctrine that exist – from a nearly strict application of the *nemo dat* rule to a broad and immediate protection of good-faith acquisition, and with many interim doctrines located along this spectrum.[77] Thus, even among the 12 countries that can be depicted as following a universal *nemo dat* rule ("Type A" group), nine countries allow good-faith possessors to acquire ownership of the goods, after a certain period of time, through the doctrine of "acquisitive prescription."[78]

What this enormous diversity means is that in order to comply with the suggested rules of the UNIDROIT Principles for digital assets, basically *all* legal systems will have to make some sort of an adjustment or exception to their current legal doctrine concerning the application of the *nemo dat* or "good-faith purchaser" doctrines in the general context of movable and immovable goods. The UNIDROIT Principles make a specific set of normative choices in regard to this doctrine in the case of digital assets, and because of the functional consideration of advocating consistency among legal systems to facilitate the global market – this requires a cross-border legal reform.

C. DIGITAL ASSETS AND GLOBALIZATION: TOWARD HARMONIZED CODIFICATION?

In contrast to land, both intra-market and extra-market considerations point to the need for a considerable degree of consistency of legal norms across national legal systems in the case of digital assets. While the legal strategy employed by UNIDROIT is one of a soft law instrument (rather than a hard law one in the

---

76 *See* D. Klerman and A. Shortland, "The Transformation of the Art Market: Law, Norms, and Institutions" (2022), 23 *Theoretical Inquiries in Law* 219, 222-223.

77 Y.C. Chang, *Property Law: Comparative, Empirical, And Economic Analyses*, Cambridge University Press, Cambridge 2023, pp. 259-268.

78 *Ibid.*, p. 262. The doctrine of "acquisitive prescription," termed "adverse possession" in common law countries, exists in some version in 175 of 202 jurisdictions surveyed in Chang's study of this doctrine. *Ibid.*, pp. 125-137.

form of a convention), the underlying goal of the UNIDROIT Principles is to promote approximation of legal norms by way of self-implementation by states.

The prospects of such a process, by which countries would adopt these soft law principles by codifying them, entirely or almost verbatim, in their respective national laws, may be enhanced by yet another distinguishing factor between the legal ordering of land and that of digital assets. While in the case of land, any effort to enable at least some degree of globalization requires the mitigation of certain disparities among otherwise well-established doctrines in national property laws (ones embedded in historical, social, political and cultural nation-specific attributes), the motive for globalization in the case of digital assets is largely driven by the infancy of property law in the context of digital assets. While not entirely working with a clean slate – at least in the sense that embracing certain normative or conceptual principles such as in the case of the "innocent acquirer" would require certain national legal systems to carve out an exception to general doctrines that apply to other types of assets – such a process might prove more feasible both professionally and practically. As noted above, the initiative for UNIDROIT's Digital Assets and Private Law project came largely from member states – who sought guidance in the design of an unchartered territory within property law, and in so doing, approached an intergovernmental organization dedicated in its title and essence to the unification of private law, even if it is done through soft law instruments.

Finally, there is another factor that may prove significant in enabling soft law instruments, such as the UNIDROIT Principles, to lead to a change as a matter of both law and practice. This has to do with the way in which such instruments correspond with cotemporary industry practices of prominent market actors, and especially whether these two sets of norms and practices can reinforce one another in leading to a new common dominator across markets and legal systems.

Thus, as I have shown elsewhere in the context of cultural property, a key factor in the ability to change the behavior of both public and private actors in regard to protecting the rightful owners of cultural artifacts against their cross-border theft, loot, or illegal export has to do with the simultaneous and mutually-reinforcing changes in legal instruments and market practices.[79] In particular, the norm that requires traders and buyers of cultural property to engage in "due diligence" about the provenance of cultural items and other factors pertaining to the legitimacy of the global market trade in arts and antiquities, has been emerging over the past few decades in both soft law and hard law instruments[80], as well as in market-based initiatives and rules of ethics adhered to by cultural

---

79 Lehavi, "Cultural Property Law," *supra* note 5, pp. 377-394.

80 The key legal instrument in the matter is the 1995 UNIDROIT Convention on Stolen or Illegally Exported Cultural Objects, Jun. 24, 1995, 2421 U.N.T.S. 457, which sets out the requirement for "due diligence" in Art. 4.

institutions, such as museums that are members of ICOM.[81] Such a mutually-reinforcing development of a new set of norms may lead national jurisdictions, which are not necessarily part of a binding cross-border instrument in the matter, to gradually move towards such a new cross-border paradigm, including by the adoption of soft law mechanisms.

These interrelations between soft law instruments and industry practices may prove particularly meaningful in the case of the global market for digital assets and the emerging set of norms that apply to them. Thus, the success of a soft law instrument such as the UNIDROIT Principles in being embraced and implemented by states will depend to a large extent on the correlation between these principles and the substantive and procedural practices adopted by key market actors.

IV. CONCLUSION

This article offers a new framework for addressing the globalization of property law. It does so by inspecting both functional and normative considerations on whether the governance of a certain type of asset should remain within the province of national jurisdictions or move towards some type of cross-border governance, and – if so – which globalization strategy would be most normatively appropriate and practically feasible. Offering a comparative study of the current inter-market and extra-market features of land vis-à-vis digital assets, this article calls for a different set of conclusions for each type of asset. In the case of land, in view of the current imbalances and flaws that typify foreign investment and large-scale land acquisitions, the focus should remain on local law and governance and the *lex rei sitae* rule, while providing parties across borders better access to information. Digital assets call for another type of strategy. While a soft law approach is more feasible, it should and can aspire for harmonization to facilitate a genuine global market.

---

81 See text accompanying *supra* note 13.

OWNERSHIP, THE (ANTI-) COMMONS AND RECODIFICATION: A CONTINUOUS PENDULUM

Vincent SAGAERT
Full Professor of Private Law, University of Leuven
*Eisenhower Fellow 2023**

I. INTRODUCTION

1. **General** – Students do not frequently think of property law in terms of an instrument for enhancing policy and value perspectives, at least not in most civil law countries. They rather see property law as a legal-technical domain in which abstract reasoning and conceptual dogmatism prevail over a balancing of policy interests. However, and this is a common feature for all articles in this book, essential in property regulation is the balancing of interests: between the private individual and the State, private rights *versus* public interest, economic benefits *versus* social and environmental protection, individual freedom *versus* collective regulation, etc. This balancing exercise is even sharper in an era of property law reform, for instance in the framework of a recodification. There is always a property policy underlying a recodification of property law and this property policy has a direct and major impact on daily life.

In this view, property law must be resilient in times of drastic societal changes without disrupting the society as a whole. From a legal perspective, it questions the scope, ambitions, and approach to be taken when a recodification process is being undertaken, especially if one takes into account that recodifications often only occur in or after an era of drastic (geo-)political changes. During the recodification, those who are responsible for the process should coordinate its foundational impact and policy reasons. As we will develop, this is especially true in the recodification of property law, more so than in the recodification of other areas of private law.

* Several insights expressed in this article are the result of the Eisenhower Fellowship the author received in 2023. All opinions expressed in this article are personal and cannot bind any organization.

2. Scheme and purpose of the contribution – The purpose of this contribution is not to write a comprehensive analysis on how property law reform works. On the contrary, this contribution aims to demonstrate that such "abstract" comprehensive analysis is impossible. In spite of the ambitions of some, each recodification is context-related. There will never be a final recodification. Even if one can discuss the method, the scope, the democratic process, etc. of each and every (re)codification, it is always dependent upon, and in a dialectic relationship with, economic, social, political and security circumstances. A recodification process is intertwined with the context within which it operates. The focus on sustainability and refining absoluteness can be totally different in ten years' time. History shows that the starting points for a recodification are always contingent – and in recent times even volatile. This does not mean that we should not take them into account, or that we should not take today's challenges seriously. On the contrary, it is an additional argument for addressing these challenges as they arise, in the understanding of the relativity of eternity.

In the titles and paragraphs below, we will try to reconcile this "contextual" nature of private law recodification with the foundational nature of the process of recodification. These contextual and foundational features are especially prominent in the recodification of property law. In the last paragraphs of this contribution, we will apply our findings to the reform of Belgian property law, which resulted in the establishment of a new Belgian Civil Code.

II. THE "CONSTITUTIONAL NATURE" OF (PROPERTY LAW IN) THE CIVIL CODE

3. The Civil Code as actual Constitution – A Civil Code is, at least in civil law countries, the constitution of private law. This idea was already reflected in the Babylonian Code of Hammurabi, traditionally considered as one of the oldest legal codifications (1750-1755 BC). This Code developed, on the same level as provisions on slavery and criminal law, rules on for example tort, family law and specific contracts (lease, sale).

In general terms, private law, and its codification, provides for the foundational rules for the continuity and harmony of a society. It must ensure, across changes in the political regime, a stable pattern of social relations between citizens.[1] This also is a constitutional dimension of private law. Although the idea of the constitutionalisation of private law does not express any existing *legal* hierarchy between civil law rules and constitutional rules[2], it breathes the

1 H. Collins, *The European Civil Code: the Way forward*, Cambridge University Press, Cambridge 2008, p. 103.

2 For an analysis in French law: J. Carbonnier, "Le Code civil", in P. Nora (dir.), *Les lieux de mémoire*, II, Gallimard, Paris 1986, 3; R. Cabrillac, "Le Code civil est-il la véritable constitution de la France?", *Revue juridique Themis* 2005, 249-259.

foundational nature of the Civil Code in codified legal systems. In a non-legal sense, private law tends to have quasi-constitutional effects.

A recodification of private law thus equals, as regards its legal impact, a constitutional reform within the field of private law. It is a rare moment of reflection in history. It disrupts the framework which is meant to ensure continuity and must therefore be handled very carefully. One of the most authoritative 20th century French scholars, Jean CARBONNIER, expresses the importance of recodification by characterizing it as a turning point in history: He argues that a codification of law is a moment to close the past and to open the future.[3]

4. **Recodification of property law** – What is true for private law in general, is even more valid for property law in particular. Property law determines the manner in which human beings deal with goods, both artificial goods and natural resources, and animals. It seals the interactions between humans and nature, but also largely shapes the (patrimonial) interactions between humans among themselves. In this regard, property law is predeterminant for both the fulfillment of economic (patrimonial) outcomes and for the safeguard of non-economic interests (environment, animal welfare, public health, etc.). The architecture of property law constitutes therefore, not surprisingly, the foundations for the structure of private law.[4] By way of consequence, it determines the foundations of social life. To quote Harvard Law Professor J.W. SINGER: "*property law is not just a mechanism of coordination; it is a quasi-constitutional framework for social life. Property is not merely the law of things. Property is the law of democracy.*"[5] This goes back to the early consciousness about the way in which property law shapes social relations. MAITLAND already wrote in the beginning of the 20th century: "*The whole government system – financially, military, judiciary – is part of the law of private property.*" In this regard, property law would even absorb public law to a large extent. The human flourishing theory, promulgated by Professor G.S. ALEXANDER, even goes one step further: Property law does not only determine relations between human beings, but also determines the internal state of mind of a private individual.[6] All this makes the recodification of property law, wherever it takes place, into a hazardous exercise, which should be well contemplated and deliberated. This highly fundamental nature of property law also emerges to make its reform more difficult and, both on an academic and political level, more sensitive than for instance the reform of contract law.

---

3 J. CARBONNIER, "Le Code civil", 308-325.

4 H.E. SMITH, "Property as the Law of Things", (2012) *Harvard LR*, 1691: "*Property is a platform for the rest of private law.*"

5 J.W. SINGER, "Property as the Law of Democracy", (2014) *Duke LJ*, 1287-1335.

6 G.S. ALEXANDER, *Property and Human Flourishing*, Oxford University Press, Oxford 2018, 392 p.

5. French attempts to recodify property law as illustration – We can illustrate this challenging and complex process of recodifying property law along a fairly recent example. In the early 21st century, both the French academia (through the Association Henri Capitant) and the French legislator expressed the ambition to reform the Napoleonic Civil Code, at the commemoration of its bicentenary. In doing so, they aimed to avoid that the 200th anniversary of the French Civil Code would initiate its funeral. While most core fields of private law (succession, fiducia, security rights, obligations, and tort) were successfully and fundamentally revised during this wave of legislative reform, property law has, until now, remained unamended. As a result, property law (second book of the Civil Code of 1804) remains without any doubt the most archaic and, according to some, anachronistic chapter of the old Civil Code.

It is not that there were no attempts to reform property law. The French Association Henri Capitant, which has served as a special kind of *ad hoc* "*law commission*" for numerous successful law reforms, launched a first proposal in 2008, and reviewed that proposal in function of the criticism in 2009. Even if the drafts(wo)men emphasized the pragmatic nature of the proposed texts, the very first provision of the draft already reflected a huge policy decision which challenged the foundational principles of the code: "*All provisions of this book are of public order, except if provided otherwise.*" Some legal scholars indicated this umbrella provision as nothing less than a new world of things.[7] This provision, which caused criticism in French scholarship, was removed for the second, revised version of the Draft in 2009.

Finally, both drafts continued to encounter a lot of criticism on an academic level[8] and the Association Capitant failed to obtain sufficient political and academic support for the project. The sensitivity on the fundamental principles of both projects was apparently insurmountably high. The property law reform faced many sacred principles which, at first glance, seemed to be academic, but proved to have an intrusive societal impact. It reflects and illustrates the sensitivity and foundational nature of the exercise. The result is that the outdated and obsolete rules, focusing on a rural society and shaped in function of the past (feudalism) instead of the future, nowadays still apply in France.

---

7 C. Atias, "L'enracinement du droit des biens dans la nouvelle ère du droit civil français", (2009) *Recueil Dalloz*, 1165 *et seq.*

8 W. Dross and B. Mallet-Bricout, "L'avant-projet de réforme du droit des biens", (2009) *Recueil Dalloz*, 508 et seq.; F. Zenati, "La proposition de refonte du livre II du code civil", (2009) *Rev. Trim. Dr. Civ.*, 211 *et seq.* (the latter author qualifies this draft as "non-sense", both from a substantive and methodological point of view).

III. PROPERTY LAW AS POLICY INSTRUMENT FOR THE ANTI-COMMONS IN THE EARLY NINETEENTH-CENTURY RECODIFICATIONS?

6. Constitutional nature of new ownership concept – The end of the 18th and beginning of the 19th century marks, on both sides of the Atlantic Ocean, an era of fundamental societal changes. With regard to the European continent, the French codification of 1804 is often considered to be the mother of modern codifications. The French codification of 1804 dealt the death blow to the Feudal land system. The Civil Code of Napoleon was nothing less than the cornerstone in the construction of the new French Nation.[9]

It is clear that, in the aftermath of – and as a reaction against – the French Revolution, ownership was one of major devices to revolve social structures. Ownership was clearly considered in 1789 as an instrument which, in its modern conceptualization, would help to build a society rid of feudal structures and hierarchical "bindings". Ownership was the noose to hang feudalism on. The French Civil Code was the legal framework within which ownership as "a space of freedom" had to replace ownership as "a source of obligation". The background for this "civil" concept of ownership in 1804 is the Declaration of Human Rights and Citizens of 1789[10], in which Article 1 states that "[p]*eople are born and live in freedom and have equal rights*" and is complemented by the second sentence of Article 2 providing that *"these rights are liberty, ownership, security and resistance against oppression."*[11] Ownership was thus mentioned among the most fundamental rights of the revolution and thus acquired constitutional status. The last provision of the Declaration gave specific content to the general protection. A free translation sounds as follows: "*Nobody can be deprived (expropriated) from its ownership, as inviolable and sacred right, except for reasons of public interest, on the basis of a legal ground and subject to the condition that a just and prior compensation is provided*" (Art. 17).[12]

---

9 Cf. W. Dross and B. Mallet-Bricout, "L'avant-projet de réforme du droit des biens", 514-515.

10 The Declaration was approved by the "*Assemblée nationale*", who had reformed itself to "*Assemblée constituante*", on 20-26 August 1789 in Versailles.

11 The full and original text of the first two articles is as follows:
"*Art. 1. Les hommes naissent et demeurent libres et égaux en droits. Les distinctions sociales ne peuvent être fondées que sur l'utilité commune.*
Art. 2. Le but de toute association politique est la conservation des droits naturels et imprescriptibles de l'Homme. Ces droits sont la liberté, la propriété, la sûreté, et la résistance à l'oppression."

12 The original French text being as follows: "*La propriété étant un droit inviolable et sacré, nul ne peut en être privé, si ce n'est lorsque la nécessité publique, légalement constatée, l'exige évidemment, et sous la condition d'une juste et préalable indemnité.*" In the same logic, the Constitution of 1791 guarantees "*l'inviolabilité des propriété ou la juste et préalable indemnité de celles dont la nécessité publique, légalement constatée, exigerait le sacrifice.*" In order to illustrate the importance of ownership in the revolutionary era, the Decree of 18 March

While the latter provision has been a historical ancestor to the modern constitutional provisions with regard to ownership, the general concepts of Article 1 and 2 compelled the legislators to develop a modern civil concept of ownership. These features have to be deduced from the definition in Article 544 of the French Civil Code, which provides that "*ownership is the right to enjoy and dispose of things in the most comprehensive manner, provided they are not used in a way prohibited by statutes or regulations.*" The new concept automatically applied not only in France, but also in Belgium and the Netherlands, which were back then French provinces.[13] The definitions in later 19th century Civil Codes on the European continent take, in spite of some technical differences, the same approach.

7. **Anti-commons concept of ownership** – The concept of ownership in Article 544 is often said to aim to distinguish ownership from other, limited, property rights. It would establish a hierarchy of property rights, emphasizing the prevalence of ownership over limited property rights. Ownership is, according to this provision, the ultimate property right from which all other property rights are derived.[14]

In fact, exclusion was one of the driving forces for the codification of private law in the early 19th century. The words "in the most comprehensive manner" (in French: "*de la manière la plus absolue*") seal the exclusive nature of the right, creating on the one hand the possibility for the rightsholder to exercise his powers in an unlimited manner[15] and on the other hand giving all remedies to the rightsholder to oppose against unlawful interferences by third parties or the State. Applied to land, a landowner would have an unlimited right to exercise and develop his real estate according to his own needs with the exclusion of any interference by third parties. The definition of ownership of Article 544 Civil Code would, in a widely spread opinion, be the expression of the victory of individualism and private autonomy at the beginning of the 19th century.[16] This absolute and exclusive ownership was, in

1793 introduced the death penalty for anyone proposing an agricultural Statute or any other document violating territorial, commercial and industrial properties (Décret du 18 mars 1793, punissant quiconque proposerait une loi agraire).

13 Both countries were subject to the French regime in 1804.

14 Comp. L. Duguit, *Manuel de droit constitutionnel*, E. De Boccard, Paris 1923, 294: "*Il voulait affirmer qu'il existe pour celui qui est ou sera propriétaire un droit qui est exclusif du droit que pourraient revendiquer les autres* [...]." A.J. Van der Walt, *Property in the margins*, 34. The prevailing nature of ownership also emerged from the so-called neo-personalist scholarship of S. Ginossar, *Droit réel, propriété et créance. Elaboration d'un système rationnel des droits patrimoniaux*, LGDJ, Paris 1960, 224 p.

15 Although the beginning of the 19th century still marked quite some public property burdens. They gradually disappeared in the course of the 19th century.

16 H. De Page, *De l'interprétation des lois*, Librairie des sciences juridiques, Brussels 1925, II, 176; A. Le Paige, "Avenir de la propriété", (1946) *Journal des tribunaux*, 545: "*Le propriétaire de 1804 a réellement le droit d'user de la chose suivant son bon plaisir.*"; M. Planiol, *Traité élémentaire de droit civil*, LGDJ, Paris 1928, I, nr. 2329; G. Ripert, *De l'exercice du droit de propriété dans ses rapports avec les propriétés voisines*, Rousseau, Paris 1902, 15: "*Ce système,*

other words, a free space for individual freedom and personal fulfilment, in which the "dominus" was exempt from any interference by third parties (contrary to the Feudal system).[17] In the words of MATTEI, *"the Napoleonic Code was the synthesis and sanction of this selfserving ideological construction of the bourgeoisie."*[18] It thus aims to create a legal cornerstone preventing a return to feudalism.

The ownership concept must also, and mainly, be read from a historical perspective: It does mainly aim to demarcate the modern ownership concept from the feudal ownership concept. It aims to eradicate the division of ownership between *dominium utile* and *dominium directum* and make one, uniform non-fragmented ownership concept instead.[19] In that regard, the words "*in the most comprehensive manner*" are oriented towards exclusivity rather than towards absoluteness of ownership. The gravity of ownership makes that all limited property rights would come to an end and finally reintegrate within that ownership concept. In the words of VAN DER WALT: "*it marks the victory of modern civil law over feudal law.*"[20] The scholarship of (mainly the second half of) the 19th century has translated this exclusivity into absoluteness and has given a political translation to the concept.

8. Ownership as a hinge for a new world (or a block to the old one?) – Given the historical burden underlying this provision, it must not surprise us that this anti-commons description of ownership belonged to the realm of the new private law. It is not surprising neither that the new ownership concept is considered to be the anchor point, not only for the whole system of private law, but also for the new societal structure which was proposed to set up. This also emerges from the preliminary reports during which the draft for a new Civil Code was debated. PORTALIS, one of the four main draftsmen, declared: "*The entire body of the Civil Code is devoted to defining everything to do with the exercise of the right to property, the fundamental right on which all social institutions are based, and which, for every individual, is as precious as life itself, since it provides the means to preserve it.*"[21]

---

c'est celui du libre conflit d'intérêts, de l'individualisme absolu, c'est la disparition presque complète de l'élément social dans la propriété."

17 U. MATTEI, *Basic principles of property law. A comparative legal and economic introduction*, Greenwood Press, London 2000, 122: "*The French legislator lent to posterity a formidable rhetoric celebrating the relationship between property and freedom in general and the freedom of land law against the feudal structure of the Ancien Régime in particular.*"

18 U. MATTEI and A. QUARTA, "Property Law", in U. MATTEI and A. QUARTA (ed.), *Ecology, Technology and the Commons*, Elgar Publishing, Cheltenham 2018, 23.

19 A.M. PATAULT, "La propriété non exclusive au XIXième siècle: histoire de la dissociation juridique de l'immeuble", (1983) *Rev.hist.dr.*, 217-237.

20 A.J. VAN DER WALT, *Property in the margins*, Hart Publishing, London 2009, 29.

21 The original text was as follows: "*Le corps entier du Code civil est consacré à définir tout ce qui peut tenir à l'exercice du droit de propriété, droit fondamental sur lequel toutes les institutions sociales reposent et qui, pour chaque individu est aussi précieux que la vie même, puisqu'il assure le moyen de la conserver.*" P.A. FENET, *Recueil complet des travaux préparatoires du Code civil*, Videcocq, Paris, IX, 132.

Other commentators and draftsmen also qualified ownership as the hinge for the entire system of private law and, even further, for the society they were building.[22]

It demonstrates the ambivalent nature of the ownership concept in 1804. While it was intended to be the building stone for a new society, it was rather shaped as a blocking stone towards the past than as a gate on the future. The concept of ownership was instrumentalized as a *re*-action rather than as a *pro*-action. Closing the past seemed to be more important than opening the future.

9. Not exclusive to civil law – This concept of ownership was, however, not only pre-dominant on the continent, pursuant to the French Revolution, but also – and more surprisingly – in the common law. We refer to the famous expression of BLACKSTONE, which in a historical perspective preceded the French Revolution. He described ownership as the "*sole and despotic dominion which one man has over the external things of the world, in total exclusion of the right of any other individual in the universe.*"[23] This idea of ownership, denominated as an egocentric dominion[24], was and is the prevailing view in the common law, although it contradicts the feudal property concepts.

10. Historical development in the 19th century – As we have said, the core feature of the post-revolutionary concept of ownership was *exclusivity* and, thus, *exclusion*. This exclusivity, initially, did not necessarily imply absoluteness of the powers conferred upon the owner. The *absolute* nature of the powers of an owner was only dogmatically conceptualized in the later developments of the (second half of the) 19th century. This theoretical concept has been used and strengthened in the political process which has taken place in different legal systems from around 1850 onwards. In these decades, the restrictions of case law with regard to the prohibition of abuse of rights and neighborhood relations, disappeared.[25] Under this liberal approach, ownership is a simple concept: It

22 Also J. GRENIER: "Tous les titres du code civil ne sont que des développements des règles relatives à l'exercice du droit de propriété" (FENET, XI, 158). Also J.-J. CAMBACÉRÈS: "*La législation civil règle les rapports individuels et assigne à chacun ses droits quant à la propriété: le code civil doit donc considérer: 1° les personnes, relativement* [...] *aux caractères qui leur donnent l'exercice du droit de propriété sur quelques biens; 2° les choses pour déterminer si elles sont susceptibles ou non d'une propriété privée et comment le droit de propriété s'établit sur elles par d'autres causes que par l'effet des qualités personnelles; 3° les obligations que les hommes contractent entre eux relativement au droit de propriété.*" See also: H. DE PAGE, *Traité élémentaire de droit civil belge*, Bruylant, Brussels 1957, V, nr. 894: "*On peut dire que le droit privé presque entier est exposé dans le Code du seul point de vue de la propriété.*"

23 W. BLACKSTONE, *Commentaries on the Laws of England 2*, Clarendon Press, Oxford 1766.

24 R. MURRAY, "Environmental obligations and the Western liberal property concept", (1998) *Melbourne University Law Review*, 662 *et seq.*

25 For instance Court of Appeal Paris 8 July 1858, (1859) *Sirey*, II, 180: "*Que l'exercice de ce droit est absolu et voisin, comme du plus ou moins d'intérêt qu'il présente pour celui qui en use; qu'il n'appartient pas aux magistrats lorsque ce principe est invoqué par l'une des parties, d'en paralyser ou d'en atténuer l'application par de simples considérations d'équité.*"

is the individual's right to unrestricted control, disposition, and use of objects. The number of public restrictions on ownership decreased. The absoluteness of ownership arose, based on a political inspiration, i.e. a liberal interpretation of ownership as the expression of individual freedom.[26]

This liberal approach was supported by philosophical and economic viewpoints.[27] Liberal philosophy considered the free space provided by the owner's freedom as the best guarantee for self-development.[28] In Hegelian terms: ownership was "*die aüssere Sphäre unserer Freiheit.*"[29] Economists, on their side, have argued in favor of the individual's autonomy to act as this would be the best incentive to pursue economic efficiency.[30] That does not mean that, according to some of its proponents, a redistribution of resources was excluded, but such redistribution could only take place on the basis of government's welfare policy which is external to ownership regulation. Ideal instruments to realize this redistribution of wealth could, according to this view, be found in tax law or social security law.

IV. THE END OF HISTORY FOR PRIVATE LAW? FROM ETERNITY TO IMPLOSION

11. Perceived sustainability of the civil code – In the eyes of Napoleon, the pillars of the early 19th century were sustainable by nature and were intended

26 R.A. Epstein, *Takings: Private Property and the Power of Eminent Domain*, Harvard University Press, Cambridge 1985, 60: "*Each person can do with his own land what he pleases as long as he does not physically invade the land of another.*" This is commonly also the interpretation of the theory of Locke on the appropriation of land. However, others describe how this interpretation of Locke's theory has only come in during the first half of the 20th century (G.S. Alexander and E.M. Penalver, *An Introduction to Property Theory*, Cambridge, 2012, 54-56 and the references given there).

27 The argumentation is based on: *cf.* J.W. Singer, *Entitlement. The Paradoxes of Property*, 4.

28 J. Waldron, *Right to private property*, Oxford, Oxford University Press, 1990, 60. This idea that property is the most ideal manner to achieve self-realization was already implied in the argumentation of Aristotle in Ancient Greece: "*When everyone has his own separate sphere of interest, there will not be the same ground for quarrels; and the amount of interest will increase, because each man will feel that he is applying himself to what is his own*" (*The Politics of Aristotle*, Book II, 5, §§ 5 *et seq.*). However, he further clarifies that he sees private ownership as a means to promote friendship and to facilitate generosity and moderation. He also excluded, in his ideal model of city, public property from private ownership. Public property, for the common good, could not be appropriated (G.S. Alexander and E.M. Penalver, *An Introduction to Property Theory*, CUP, Cambridge 2012, 83-84). In other words: Aristotle did not think of property in terms of individual sovereignty to be exercised in isolation towards third parties. The individual right was only a prerequisite to build up a political society ("polis").

29 G.W.F. Hegel, *Grundlinien der Philosophie des Rechts oder Naturrecht und Staatswissenschaft im Grundriss*, Frankfurt-am-Main, 1821, § 41.

30 R. Posner, *Economic Analysis of the Law*, Little Brown, Boston 1986, 32: "*If every valuable (meaning scarce as well as desired resource were owned by someone (universality), ownership connoted the unqualified power to exclude everybody else from using the resource (exclusivity) as well as to use it oneself, and ownership rights were freely transferable or as lawyers say alienable (transferable), value would be maximized.*"

to last for ever. A famous citation, expressed during his asylum in Sint-Helena, is that "*My real glory is not to have won forty battlefields, Waterloo will delete the memory to all the victories. What will last forever, is my Civil Code.*"[31] The pillars of the Civil Code, and more specifically the pillars of ownership, were thought to be characteristic to all post-feudal eras. To re-phrase it in well-known philosophical terms: property law had come, in the view of Napoleon, to the end of its history.[32] The utilitarian, neo-liberal approach of ownership reflected and strengthened the final societal structures, as they saw daylight after the French Revolution. The ambition for survival through this Code of Napoleon has remained intact, for private law, for two centuries. The French Civil Code has proved to be stable and has resisted, to political turbulence and constitutional changes, especially in the French homeland. In French law, property law is – after more than two centuries – still intact.

Developments in the first decades of the 19th century seemed to confirm the idea of Napoleon that his Code could have ambitions for perpetuity. The end of the Napoleonic Empire did not dim the star of his Code civil. Belgium maintained the Napoleonic Code even after its independence and the Netherlands formally adopted a new Civil Code, but largely along the same lines and rules as the Napoleonic Civil Code. As we have illustrated, the liberal approach towards ownership was even politically strengthened in the second half of the 19th century. The exclusivity developed after the death of Napoleon from a reaction against the past (feudalism), to a (liberal) policy instrument of the present (cf *supra*, n° 8). It re-enforced the position of the early 19th-century codes.

12. A social dimension for ownership – However, the conscience gradually emerged that the 1804 Code was just building a context-specific and policy-oriented legislation. The traditional ownership concept resulted in the tragedy of the anti-commons, meaning that the power to exclude leads towards a non-efficient and inequitable use of the limited natural resources. This also proved to be true for the ownership concept, where under-use of natural resources was a direct and natural threat due to an excessive emphasis on anti-commons.

The awareness has grown that the bundle of rights constituting ownership must be developed in line with the social impact the exercise of the right can have on third parties and society as a whole.[33] Without endangering the full powers of an owner, which belongs to the essence of capitalism and the current socio-economic order, the social function of ownership has won, through the centuries, weight, limiting the free space of the owner. In other words:

---

31 The original French text is "*Ma vraie gloire n'est pas d'avoir gagné quarante batailles; Waterloo effacera le souvenir de tant de victoires; ce que rien n'effacera, ce qui vivra éternellement, c'est mon Code civil.*"

32 F. Fukuyama, *The End of History and the Last Man*, The Free Press, New York 1992, 418 p.

33 To quote the famous words used by Joseph SAX: "Ownership does not exist in isolation". (J. SAX, "Takings, Property and Public Rights", (1971) *Yale LJ*, (149) 152.

Ownership can inherently impose obligations upon the owner. The Blackstonian approach to ownership (cf. *supra*, n° 9) has been refined through a development affecting the expressions of ownership, which has, over the past few decades, been denominated as the relational dimension of ownership.[34] Ownership is, in this more recent conceptualization, not a despotic dominium in which the owner can be isolated from society and has absolute remedies against anyone trying to interfere with it. It is, in property law, not merely about the relation between the holder of the right and the thing which is the object of the right. The awareness that the exercise of property rights (including ownership) can have an impact on other individuals, and sometimes on the fundamental rights of other individuals, has been growing. The highest property right – ownership – does not escape to the idea that the rightholder is not in an isolated relation with the object of the right, but also with third parties. The exercise of ownership can only respect another's ownership if it is done in respect of the ownership of somebody else. The respect for somebody else's interests, is a prerequisite for the existence of individual ownership in a society. In the words of Frank Michelman: "*No trust, no property*".[35] That was also the approach gaining influence on the European continent, even in France.[36]

In many countries, the number of land burdens, imposed in the public interest, increased again in the course of the 20th century.[37] One realized that the exercise of ownership was not a matter of a (wo)man alone.[38] Exercise of

34 Y. Emerich has prominently argued in favor of such approach (Y. Emerich, *Droit commun des biens: perspective transsystémique*, Éditions Yvon Blais, Cowansville 2017, 518 p.). See also: W. Lucy and C. Mitchell, "Replacing Private Property: The Case for Stewardship" (1996) *Cambridge Law Journal*, 568 ("*Locutions about property in 'things' must be interpreted as including implicit reference to other persons since 'things' are plainly unable to exercise rights or be bound by duties. Hereinafter, the concept of property is regarded as a generic term for sets of rules that define the relationships between persons and some resources.*"). in French law: F.-G. Trebulle, "Droit communautaire de l'environnement: vers une consécration de l'analyse fonctionnelle de la propriété?", (2006) *Rev. Dr. Imm.*, 436 ("*A la conception traditionnelle de la propriété privée, même renouvelée par la prise en compte de sa fonction sociale, il faut substituer une conception intégrant les divers rattachements en tenant compte de la multiplicité des fonctions assumées.*"); G. Lardaux (ed.), *Les propriétés*, LGDJ, Paris 2022, 284 p.

35 In the modern property theory: F. Michelman, *Ethics, Economics, and the Law of Property*, New York, Nomos 1982, 31. Comp. C.M. Rose, "Property as Keystone Right", (1996) *Notre Dame L.R.*, 363 ("*A property regime thus depends on a great deal of cooperation, trustworthiness, and self-restraint among the people who enjoy it*".); J.W. Singer, *Entitlement. The Paradoxes of Property*, 18 ("*There is no core of property we can define that leaves owners free to ignore entirely the interests of others. Owners have obligations, they have always had obligations. We can argue about what those obligations should be, but no one can seriously argue that they should not exist.*")

36 In French law: L. Duguit, *Les transformations du droit privé*, 1912, 148 *et seq.*; M. Planiol, *Traité élémentaire de droit civil*, 1925, I no. 2333; J. Boivin-Champeaux, *Restrictions apportées à la propriété dans un intérêt esthétique*, Paris, Ph. D. Thesis, 1913.

37 For French law: J.L. Halperin, *Histoire du droit des biens*, Economica, Paris 2008, 309.

38 To quote the famous words used by Joseph Sax: "*Ownership does not exist in isolation*". (J. Sax, (1971) *Yale L.J.*, 152.

one's ownership can affect others. Public law restrictions have been increasing and have become more intrusive in the course of the 20th century, in view of the increasing attention for town planning, urban development, soil pollution, preservation of historic buildings, etc. Environmental law burdens became more prominent for a landowner. This development is the co-called "communization" or "social dimension" of ownership. These restrictions can have both a private law origin and a public law origin. This development induces a "*reflux on the absolutist nature of ownership*"[39], which has been acknowledged across the borders of national legal systems in French[40], Belgian[41], Dutch[42] and German[43] law.

13. Underlying paradigm for social ownership – Paradoxically, the philosophical foundations for this concept are often found in the writings of John Locke. Although he is a 17th century philosopher, he is often considered to be one of the founding fathers of modern property theory. He already acknowledged the corrective function of property rights in the chapter "Of Property": "*As much as any one can make use of to any advantage of life before it spoils; so much he may by his labour fix a property in. Whatever is beyond this, is more than his share, and belongs to others. Nothing was made by God for Man to spoil or destroy.*"[44]

At first sight, this relational approach of property rights is more natural to common law than to civil law. In common law, property law is, given the dependent nature of property, considered as a stick of powers and duties, governing the relation between individuals.[45] Common law property rights

39 F.G. Trebulle, "Environnement et droit des biens", in Association Henri Capitant (ed.), *Le droit et l'environnement*, Paris, Dalloz, 2010, 86.

40 P. Catala, "La transformation du patrimoine dans le droit civil moderne", *Rev. trim. dr. civ.* 1966, (185) 199, no. 18; L. Duguit, "La propriété fonction sociale", in *Les transformations générales depuis le code Napoléon*, Paris, 1920; L. Trobatas, *La fonction sociale de la propriété privée. Le point de vue technique. Le régime administratif de la propriété civile*, Paris, 1930.

41 J. Hansenne, *Les biens. Précis*, Liège, Presse universitaire, 1996, I, p. 582, no. 630; R. Derine, *De grenzen van het eigendomsrecht in de negentiende eeuw*, Anvers, De Sikkel, 1955, 306; V. Sagaert, "Nieuwe perspectieven op het eigendomsrecht na tweehonderd jaar Burgerlijk Wetboek", in B. Tilleman and P. Lecocq (ed..), *Droit des biens*, La Charte, Bruges 2005, 43-85.

42 J.H. Gilissen, *Eigendomsrecht en eigendomsplichten*, Bergmans, Tilburg, 1946, 281 p.

43 L. Lau, *Die Sozialpflichtigkeit des Eigentums*. Würzburg, 1997.

44 J. Locke, "Of Property" in *Second Treatise of Government*, London, 1690, section 31. This idea was grounded in the connection he makes between property and labour, which serves as justification for private property. Compare: H.S. Marguerat, "Locke's Correlative Property Limits/Responsibilities to His Property Rights", in *Private Property Rights and the Environment. Palgrave Studies in Environmental Policy and Regulation,* Cham, Palgrave Macmillan, 2019.

45 The reference to the bundle (or stick) of rights is of course inspired by W.N. Hohfeld, "Fundamental Legal Conceptions as Applied in Judicial Reasoning", (1917) *Yale Law Yournal*, 710 *et seq.* Also: U. Mattei and A. Quarta, "Property Law", p. 14.

are relational by nature. It is not familiar with the "ownership in land" but is based on "estates". Of course, it is important to note that a fee simple is, for all practical purposes, a functional equivalent of "ownership" in the civil law, but the connotation of dependence always remains. This conceptual difference with a civil law ownership still translates a relational conception of the stick of powers of the rightholder.

14. Implosion of Napoleon's France at the bicentenary – This countermovement resulted, for private law as a whole, in the implosion of the influence of French private law on in Europe. While French law was the model law throughout the 19th century, its position indirectly degraded in the 20th century.[46] The inspirational force of the French Civil Code for more modern codifications gradually diminished.[47] The Italian recodification in 1948 took distance from the French-inspired rules in the Italian civil law.[48] The German BGB became the new star in heaven. From the beginning of the 20th century, French private law got rapidly caught up by German codification, which proved to be more influential to later Civil Codes, both in Western Europe and Eastern Europe. Meanwhile, the influence of French law and French legal scholarship on European harmonization projects such as the Draft Common Frame of Reference, which at one stage had the ambition to become a European Civil Code, was minor. While French law was a model, the track to follow by other legal systems, in the early decades of the 19th century, it became – in exaggerated terms – the Cinderella of European private law in the course of the 20 and 21st century.

15. Reform of core fields of private law – In France, the celebration of the bicentenary of the Civil Code in 2004 finally was the occasion to become aware of the necessity to reform, in order to avoid that the anniversary would result in its "*requiem*".[49] The French had become aware that the influence of their Civil Code in European private law was in decline.[50] Therefore, French politics and academics (with a major role for the Association Capitant) initiated efforts in

---

46 D. Tallon, "Grandeur et décadence du Code civil français", in *Mélanges Marcel Fontaine*, Larcier, Brussels 2003, 281 *et seq.*

47 This analysis is also made by French scholars: C. Blanc-Jouvan, "L'influence de Code civil sur les modifications récentes", in *Le Code civil 1804-2004. Livre du bicentenaire*, Dalloz, Paris 2004, 477 *et seq.*

48 Royal Decree n° 262 of 16 March 1942.

49 G. Cornu, "Un code civil n'est pas un instrument communautaire", (2002) *Recueil Dalloz*, 351.

50 Also: F. Barrière, "Le Code civil français aujourd'hui: influences", in J.P. Dunand and B. Winiger, *Le Code civil français dans le droit européen*, Bruylant, Brussels 2005, p. 106, no. 28; C. Blanc-Jouvan, " L'influence de Code civil sur les modifications récentes ", in *Le Code civil 1804-2004. Livre du bicentenaire*, Dalloz, Paris 2004, 477 *et seq.*

order to modernize the Civil Code on several "key domains".[51] This resulted shortly afterwards in several fundamental reforms, such as succession law[52], the law on property security rights[53], the introduction of a French fiducia[54] and more recently the law of obligations.[55]

Especially for property law, such a reform proved to be a hazardous exercise and finally failed (cf. *supra*, n° 5). We will illustrate the delicacy of the reform of property law through the reform of property law in Belgium (cf. *infra*, n° 4 *et seq.*).

V. SUSTAINABILITY IN THE MODERN PROPERTY LAW REASONING

16. Introduction – An important dimension for a recodification *anno* 2024 is the principle of sustainability. The concept of ownership as absolute dominion resulted, for many decades, in the total absence of a "dialectic" relation between property law and environmental law. Environmental law was, conceptually, the born enemy of property law: while the latter aims to safeguard individual freedom, environmental law aims to limit individual freedom in the perspective of sustainability and collectiveness. Property law is grounded in the anti-commons, and solely focused on profit-maximization, while environmental law is based on the idea of the commons.[56] The social, economic and political

---

51 D. Tallon, "La rénovation du titre III, livre III du Code civil: une approche comparative", (2004) *Revue des contrats*, 1190. Also: "*Il n'est pas déraisonnable de participer simultanément à la rédaction de ce qui pourrait devenir un jour un code européen des obligations et à la réécriture de la partie du Code civil français.*" (J. Ghestin, "Le Code civil en France aujourd'hui" in D. Heirbaut et G. Martyn (ed.), *Bicentenaire du Code civil en Belgique*, Anvers, Kluwer, 2004, 321). "*Loin d'exclure les recodifications nationales, la perspective d'une codification européenne leur donne une certaine urgence. Il doit y avoir synergie entre les deux entreprises, et non blocage de l'une par l'autre.*" (M. Grimaldi, "Les grandes lignes de l'évolution du Code civil en France depuis 1804", (2004) *Journal des Tribunaux*, 449).

52 Loi n° 2006-728 du 23 juin 2006 portant réforme des successions et des libéralités, Journal Officiel 24 June 2006.

53 Ordonnance of 23 March 2006 introducing a Book IV in the French Civil Code.

54 Act of 19 February 2007 introducing a fiducie in Art. 2043 et seq. of the French Civil Code: cf. V. Sagaert, "The Trust Book in the DCFR: A civil lawyer's Perspective, in S. Van Erp, B. Akkermans and A. Salomons (ed.), *The Future of European Property Law*, Sellier, Munich 2012, 31-46.

55 Ordonnance of 10 February 2016, as modified in the Loi n° 2018-287 of 20 April 2018. For a Belgian reception: S. Stijns and S. Jansen (ed.), *The French Contract Law Reform. A source of Insipiration?*, Intersentia, Antwerp 2016, 230 p.

56 Compare B. Akkermans, "Sustainable Property Law", (2018) *European Property Law Journal*, 1-3. For an analysis of the antinomy between anti-commons and commons, which historically developed in law and economics theory: H. Gordon, "The economic Theory of a Common-Property Resource: the Fishery", (1968) *Journal of Political Economy*, 32 *et seq.*; F.A. Friedman, "The Economics of the Common Pool: Property Rights in Exhaustible Resources", (1971) *UCLA Law Review*, 855-873; M.A. Heller, "The Boundaries of Private Property", (1999) *Yale L.J.*, 1197 e.v. Also J. Buchanan en Y.J. Yoon, "Symmetric tragedies:

foundations underlying the early 19th century property law, all contradicted environmental awareness. Using the words of the famous Paris professor Jean CARBONNIER, the inclusion of environmental law in property law would encompass the Creation of the world itself.[57]

Times have drastically changed since the beginning of the 19th century. The relationship between law and sustainability has become the object of fundamental research by a full generation of property law scholars, such as Bram AKKERMANS[58], Dorothy GRUYAERT[59], Bjorn HOOPS[60], Jill ROBBIE[61], and many other scholars. This book is a reflection of this scholarly movement.

With regard to property law reform, sustainability has two dimensions: (1) the sustainability of the statutory text itself and (2) the sustainability of the content of the rules inserted into the texts.

17. Sustainability of the Civil Code – On the one hand, it should be the ambition and desire of the legislator, in reforming property law, to create a sustainable instrument. Codifications in the past, not in the least the civil Code of 1804, demonstrate that, in spite of the perspective to create a perpetual legislative instrument (cf. *supra*, n° 11), the sustainability of a codification becomes vulnerable to the extent that the Code contains enumerations grounded in a contemporary societal context. Generally speaking, a Code should not be a static instrument, but should be able to be dynamic and adaptable to changing realities. It is therefore preferable to limit the number of applications and enumerations which are grounded in a temporary context, but which can not survive technical, digital and environmental developments. Open standards, which can persist through technological and economic developments, must prevail. Property law regulation should therefore not start from applications and enumerations, but from general principles. To give a concrete example: the movable or immovable nature of solar panels is currently the object of debate,

Commons and Anticommons Property", (2002) *Journal of Law and Economics*, 453-473. In French law: A. CHAIGNEAU (réd.), *Fonction de la propriété et commun. Regards comparatistes*, Société de législation comparée, Paris 2017, 197 p.

57 It would risk to "*embrasser la Création toute entière.*" (J. CARBONNIER, *Les biens*, PUF, Paris 2000, no. 46).

58 B. AKKERMANS, "Sustainable property law?", (2018) *EPLJ*, 1-3; *Ibid.*, "Sustainable obligations in property law", in S. DEMEYERE and V. SAGAERT (ed.), (ed.), *Contract and Property with an environmental Perspective*, Intersentia, Antwerp 2020, 29-46; B. AKKERMANS, *Sustainable Property Law. Reckoning, Resilience and Reform*, Eleven Publishing, The Hague, 2022, 22 p.; *Ibid.*, "Sustainable Ownership – new obligations towards achieving a sustainable society", (2021) *EPLJ*, 277-303.

59 D. GRUYAERT, "Privaat en publiek goederenrecht en duurzaamheid", (2021) *TBH*, 495-550.

60 B. HOOPS, "Property Meeting the Challenge of the Commons" in U. MATTEI, A. QUARTA, F. VALUARNERA and R.J. FISHER (eds.), *Property Meeting the Challenge of the Commons*, 2023, 223-250.

61 J. ROBBIE, "Moving Beyond Boundaries in the Pursuit of Sustainable Property Law", in B. AKKERMANS and G. VAN DIJCK (eds), *Sustainability and Private Law*, Eleven International Publishing, the Hague 2019, 59-78.

with major financial impact, in most national legal systems. Does that however mean that property law legislation should introduce a rule on that specific application? I would not take it for granted that solar panels will look the same in 2050. Probably solar panels will have become an inherent part of the roof tiles, and a specific rule with regard to solar panels would risk to make any new legislation rapidly obsolete. Thus, for the sake of sustainability, a property law reform should avoid to include enumerations and applications.

18. Sustainability of the substantive rules – More important for the sake of this chapter is the second dimension of sustainability. Property law is the law which determines in the most direct manner the powers humans can exercise over things. Things can be both natural or artificial, but in the end, they are created by "mother earth". In the long run, property law determines, by way of consequence, also our use of natural resources, and the responsibility and long-term perspective which we should comply with in this perspective. The latter is the subject matter of radical societal change in the early 21st century. This awareness that property law directly impacts the sustainability issues in society underlies the development of property law from the early 19th century codifications up to the beginning of the 21st century. As Jill Robbie states: "*As property law rules are those which most directly regulate use of these resources, these rules cannot be untouched by the transformation of our laws, policies and lives that will be required in order to contend with this task.*"[62]

19. The relation between property law and environmental law – This sustainability dimension of property law results in several innovative perspectives, which could largely differ from the perspective a 19th or even 20th century legislator would have had. Property law has, in the past, often been regarded as an isolated field of law. However, especially with regard to land law, the way in which a legislator regulates property law (reform) should be in line with the regulations in what is traditionally perceived as other fields of law.

First of all, there is the need for a dialectic dimension between property law and environmental law or – more generally – between private real estate law and public real estate law, the latter including zoning law, soil pollution regulation, waste law, eminent domain, etc. Environmental law constitutes a regulatory framework for the exercise of property rights (building, zoning, soil pollution, etc.). It is not surprising therefore that environmental law was in the civil law, conceptually, the born enemy of property law: While the latter aims to safeguard individual freedom, environmental law aims to limit individual freedom in the perspective of sustainability and collectiveness. However, a more dialectic

62 J. Robbie, "Moving Beyond Boundaries in the Pursuit of Sustainable Property Law", in B. Akkermans and G. Van Dijck (eds), *Sustainability and Private Law*, Eleven International Publishing, the Hague 2019, 78.

relationship between both fields of law is probably the way forward and is already the case in American legal education and scholarship, where property law and environmental law are often included in the same classes and publications.[63]

Apart from environmental law, property rights have another traditional counterpart in housing rights. Housing law aims to optimize the use of the available portfolio in the view of demographic developments. Housing issues could raise questions for the legislator as to whether the legislation should give a remedy in case of non-used properties. Can the rule that ownership cannot extinguish due to non-use be upheld in a society where there is a shortage of houses? Should the legislator give a counterweight to the risk of oligarchic real estate possession? These are policy choices which a legislator could, and perhaps should, be aware of. These questions relate to social sustainability of the rules.

While property rights are traditionally grounded in the concept of exclusivity, environmental law and housing law are by nature targeted at inclusion. Embedding the starting principles of the several fields of law, and articulating these in property law, is essential. This will automatically result in a mitigation, or at least a refinement, of the principle of exclusivity. This does not mean that all property should be shared or be in common, but rather that property should be made more inclusive, taking into account the societal impact of the exercise of property rights.

20. Relational approach in the constitutional dimension of property law – As we have said, the manner to which one looks to the ownership concept, has quasi-constitutional impact (cf. *supra*, n° 6). It is therefore no surprise that national constitutional legislators have protected ownership rights on a constitutional level, but have related this protection also to environmental protection. The best-known example is probably Article 14 of the German Constitution, on which we will come back later (cf. *infra*, n° 23). We have also found inspiring examples of this in Eastern-European constitutional texts explicitly referring to environmental protection as one element of limitation to property rights. For instance, the Romanian Constitution provides in Article 41, (6) that "*the right to property obliges to comply with the obligations relating to environmental protection and safeguard of good neighborship, as well as of other obligations burdening ownership, in accordance with the law or custom.*" We also refer to Article 11 (3) of the Czech Charter for Fundamental Rights and Freedoms[64], which provides that "[*o*]*wnership entails obligations. It may not be misused to the detriment of the rights of others or in conflict with legally protected public interests. It may not*

---

[63] For a more in depth analysis: V. Sagaert, "Property Law, Contract Law and Environmental Law: shaking hands between (historical) enemies?" in S. Demeyere en V. Sagaert (ed.), *Contract and Property with an Environmental Perspective*, Intersentia, Antwerpen 2020, 1-29.

[64] Resolution of the Presidium of the Czech National Council of 16 December 1992 on the declaration of the Charter of Fundamental Rights and Freedoms as a part of the constitutional order of the Czech Republic.

be exercised so as to harm human health, nature, or the environment beyond the limits laid down by law." Finally, and may be most surprisingly, we can refer to the Russian Constitution: "*Possession, utilization and disposal of land and other natural resources shall be exercised by the owners freely, if it is not detrimental to the environment and does not violate the rights and lawful interests of other people.*"[65] Not all modern constitutional texts explicitly refer to the environmental obligations of the owner but the examples illustrate the development which we describe. The constitutional embedment of the environmental protection in the protection of ownership gives a legal stability and sustainability to this dimension of the property right. In traditional constitutional systems, environmental law mostly depends upon contingent political factors and developments.

This development is also echoed in the case law of the European Court of Human Rights, especially with regard to Article 1 of the First Additional Protocol to the European Convention on Human Rights. We refer to the judgment in *Hamer v. Belgium*, which we cite – given its importance – literally[66]:

> "78. The Court notes that this case concerns rules applicable to town and country planning and environmental protection, areas in which the States enjoy a wide margin of appreciation.
> 79. It reiterates that while none of the Articles of the Convention is specifically designed to provide general protection of the environment as such (see Kyrtatos v. Greece, no. 41666/98, § 52, ECHR 2003-VI), in today's society the protection of the environment is an increasingly important consideration (see Fredin v. Sweden (no. 1), 18 February 1991, § 48, Series A no. 192). The environment is a cause whose defence arouses the constant and sustained interest of the public, and consequently the public authorities. Financial imperatives and even certain fundamental rights, such as ownership, should not be afforded priority over environmental protection considerations, in particular when the State has legislated in this regard. The public authorities therefore assume a responsibility which should in practice result in their intervention at the appropriate time in order to ensure that the statutory provisions enacted with the purpose of protecting the environment are not entirely ineffective."

Especially relevant in the *Hamer*-judgment is the consideration that "*financial imperatives and even certain fundamental rights, such as ownership, should not be afforded priority over environmental protection considerations, in particular when the State has legislated in this regard.*" This judgment raises two equally valid legal considerations.

The Court seems to imply, on the one hand, that it does not see a hierarchy between environmental protection and the safeguard of ownership. The right

---

65 Art. 36 (2) of the Constitution of the Russian Federation.

66 ECHR, 27 November 2007, *Hamer* v. *Belgium*, www.echr.coe.int. These considerations have been confirmed in the later case law of the Court: ECHR, 15 December 2015, www.echr.coe.int, cons. 100-101; ECHR, 10 March 2009, www.echr.coe.int, cons. 33.

to property has no priority in relation to environmental protection. Through this case law, the European Court of Human Rights obliges Member States to integrate environmental law within their property law concepts and structure. On the other hand, the Court does not go as far as to recognize inherent environmental obligations which go beyond the regulatory and statutory provisions. In doing so, the Court adheres to the default rule of liberty and burdens imposed upon ownership as exceptions to the normal situation.

VI. DOGMATIC REVOLUTION: INTERNALIZATION OF THE PROPERTY REGULATION

21. **Traditional dual approach to ownership** – The classic liberal approach of ownership is a dual approach: freedom is the rule, regulation is the exception. The definition of ownership reflects this structure: an owner is free to use his good, except for what is prohibited by the law. Property and regulation are, in this view, understood to be opposites.[67] The property question is always raised in terms of: "*how many regulations should/can/will ownership be subject to?*". Freedom is thought of as general principle, the regulation as exception to this principle. According to this conceptual view, the restrictions are imposed externally to ownership, do not belong to the nature of ownership and can even be seen as a threat to ownership. VON JHERING illustrated this approach in the beginning of the 20th century by warning for the limits on the burdens which can be imposed upon private ownership, presenting these regulatory measures as sources threatening private ownership: "*There comes a time when the individual can cry out: 'Enough pressure, I'm tired of being a slave to society. There must be a boundary between it and me that it cannot cross, a land over which I alone will be my master, and which is forbidden to it.*'"[68] In the second half of the 20th century numerous scholars in different legal systems recognized that the external burdens had become a real threat on the principled approach of private ownership.[69]

22. **Alternative "relational" concept of ownership** – An alternative approach to ownership has been developed under the American legal realism theory in the 20th century. In the beginning of the 20th century, the analysis was made that the liberal approach did not take into account social reality, which had to confront unequal bargaining powers, labor and consumer protection rules, social exclusion, etc. This theory argues that the liberal ownership model can

---

67 J.W. SINGER, *Entitlement. The Paradoxes of Property*, 3.

68 Free translation from R. VON JHERING, *L'évolution du droit*, Marescq, Paris 1901, 353.

69 See e.g. A. MEIER-HAYOZ, "Vom Wesen des Eigentums" in *Revolution der Technik. Evolutionen des Rechts, Festgabe K. Oftinger*, Zürich, 1969, 99.

only properly function in a state where all people have equal standing. In such a scenario, the government's role could diminish to a large extent, and delegate ownership issues to the free competition between owners. This analysis resulted in the development of the "legal realism" theory. In this approach, ownership regulation is not opposite to the sovereignty dimension of ownership, but is part of it. As SINGER[70] summarizes: *"Private property and regulation are not mortal enemies. In fact, private property cannot exist without regulation."*[71]

This line of reasoning would bring the ownership notion much closer to the American concept of ownership. The latter is often defined in terms of a bundle of rights which can be disaggregated into distinct entitlements owned by different persons.[72] Such "Hohfdeldian" approach[73], leads to a much more functional or relative, less "sacrified" concept of ownership compared to traditional civil law ownership. In this approach, there is no hierarchy between property rights with ownership as ultimate *"sanctissimum"*. It offers the advantage of being able to allocate each stick of the bundle to the person who would deal with it in the most efficient manner. In this sense, it is a utilitarian, legal-economic approach of ownership.[74]

23. Cross-border influence – The relational concept of ownership is often wrongfully thought to be an Anglo-American approach of ownership. This view can also be found in continental-European legal systems.

70 We do not mean to have said that SINGER was an adept of legal realism. He wanted to balance the classic ownership model with the legal realism theory: "*We need an alternative to both the ownership and bundle-of-rights models. My goals is to unite what is best in both these approaches by directing our attention to the ways that property law responds to and is shaped by social relations.*" (J.W. SINGER, *Entitlement. The Paradoxes of Property*, 8).

71 J.W. SINGER, *Entitlement. The Paradoxes of Property*, 8. Also: L. UNDERKUFFLER, "On Property: an Essay", *Yale L.J.* 1990, (127) 129: "[P]*roperty, in the historical view, did not represent the autonomous sphere of the individual to be asserted against the collective; rather, it embodied and reflected the inherent tension between the individual and the collective. This tension – now seen as something external to the concept of property – was in fact internal to it.*"

72 This theory has been developed by G. CALABRESI and A.D. MELAMED, "Property Rules, Liability Rules and Inalienability: One View of the Cathedral", (1972) *Harv. L.R.*, 1089-1128. J.W. SINGER, *Entitlement. The Paradoxes of Property*, 6. Comp.; G.S. ALEXANDER and E.M. PENALVER, *An Introduction to Property Theory*, 2. For a critical analysis: J. PENNER, *The Idea of Property in Law*, 1: "*On the 'bundle of rights' picture, 'property' is not really a useful concept of any kind. It doesn't help judges understand what they're doing when they decide cases, because it doesn't effectively characterize any particular sort of legal relation.*" Comp. with the exclusion approach of T.W. MERRILL and H.E. SMITH, "What happened to Property in Law and Economics", (2001) *Yale LJ*, 360 *et seq.*

73 W.N. HOHFELD, "Some fundamental legal concepts as applied in judicial reasoning", (1913) *Yale LR*, 16-59. See also, with application, on property law: J.W. SINGER, "Legal realism now", (1988) *California LR*, 467-544.

74 Also: G.S. ALEXANDER and E.M. PENALVER, *An Introduction to Property Theory*, 30.

A remarkable example is Article 14 (2) of the German Constitution: "*Ownership obliges. Its exercise will also contribute to the whole society.*"[75] The "active form" used by the German constitutional legislator implies that the obligations derive from the ownership itself, and thus are inherent to ownership. We can also refer to other constitutional texts such as, setting aside the communist texts in the Eastern European context, the Italian Constitution[76], the Spanish Constitution[77] and, in a later stage, the French Constitutional Act with regard to the Environmental Charter.[78] All these texts integrate the limitations of ownership within the ownership itself, thus restricting the bundle of powers awarded to the owner without affecting the core of the ownership.[79]

Albeit absent in French statutes, the idea of an inherent obligation in ownership can also be found in French legal writings. For instance, DUGUIT argued already in the first quarter of the 20th century that ownership would have a social function which naturally implies the existence of limitations. An owner has, according to this influential French scholar the social obligation to invest his property in such manner that it contributes to social welfare and cohesion.[80] The same idea can be found in the writings of PLANIOL: "*Ownership is largely justified by the services it renders to humanity.*"[81] Other scholars have characterized ownership as a "mixed right" partly attributing powers to an individual, but partly also ensuring that the goods benefited the full community.[82] The mixed nature of owernship reflect the inherent double-

75 The original text is as follows: "*Eigentum verpflichtet. Sein Gebrauch soll zugleich dem Wohle der Allgemeinheit dienen.*"

76 Art. 42 (2) of the Italian Constitution: "*Private ownership shall be recognized and guaranteed by laws which shall determine the manner by which it may be acquired and enjoyed, and its limits, in order to ensure its social function and to make it open to all.*"

77 Art. 33 (2) of the Spanish Constitution: "*The social function of* [property rights and inheritance rights] *shall determine the limits of their content in accordance with the law.*"

78 Loi Constitutionnelle no. 2005-205 of 1 March 2005 relative à la Charte de l'environnement (JORF n°0051 du 2 mars 2005. Art. 1 of the Constitutional Act provides that "each individual has the right to live in a balanced environment which respects health." ("*Chacun a le droit de vivre dans un environnement équilibré et respectueux de la santé.*").

79 The acknowledgment of a theoretical foundation of such obligations as an inherent part of ownership seems more natural in the common law concept of ownership than in the civil law concept of ownership. In the common law, one could consider it is an obligation of a life tenants in relation to the holder of the residuary interest in the land. The relational dimension of ownership is inherent to the common law notion of fee simple. In the civil law, the conceptual framework is not as evident, as land ownership is a stand alone.

80 See e.g. L. DUGUIT, *Manuel de droit constitutionnel*, 295: "*La conception de la propriété, que s'étaient formées les auteurs de la Déclaration et ceux du Code civil, ne répond certainement plus à l'état actuel du droit.* [...] *Aujourd'hui, la propriété cesse d'être le droit subjectif de l'individu et tend à devenir la fonction sociale des détenteurs de capitaux mobiliers et immobiliers. La propriété implique pour tout détenteur d'une richesse l'obligation de l'employer à accroître la richesse sociale et par là l'interdépendance sociale.*"

81 M. PLANIOL, *Traité élémentaire de droit civil*, I, 768, no. 2323.

82 A. ROUAST, "Les droits discrétionnaires et les droits contrôlés", (1944) *Rev. trim. dr. civ.*, (1) no. 11. This view was subject to criticism: E. GAILLARD, *Le pouvoir en droit privé*, LGDJ, Paris (1985), 32-33.

sided rights and social obligations of ownership. An internalization of property burdens also results in a "*responsabilization*" of an individual owner. Internal limitations of his ownership are a prerequisite to a proper exercise of his powers. To the extent that the obligations are not opposed to his individual interest, but an inherent part of his individual interest, it is an *a priori* condition for his bundle of powers, and not an *a posteriori* deprivation of pre-existing powers.

VII. THE NEW BELGIAN CIVIL CODE: OWNERSHIP IS RESILIENT WITH THE COMMONS

A. GENERAL BACKGROUND

24. New Belgian Civil Code – As we have said, Belgian statutory rules on civil law dated back from 1804. As Belgium was at that moment a French province, the Napoleonic Civil Code automatically entered into force in 1804 on the Belgian territory and Belgium did – surprisingly in a comparative perspective – not enact a new Civil Code at the moment of its independence in 1830. Contrary to the French mother system[83] – which reformed succession law, property security law, estate law (including a fiducia) and (in a later stage) the law of obligations – Belgium did not grasp the opportunity of the 200th anniversary of the Civil Code to reform most fundamental dimensions of civil law. Family law and family patrimonial law have had to develop along the case law of the European Court for Human Rights and the Belgian Constitutional Court. However, the classical trilogy – contract, property and tort – remained largely unamended.[84] European Directives impacting one of these fields of law have been implemented by the Belgian legislator outside the Civil Code in a separate statute or exceptionally – but without affecting the common rules – in the Civil Code (such as the Consumer Sales Directive).

It must, therefore, not be a surprise, that Belgian law had become obsolete, archaic and grounded in a largely rural society. With some sense for provocation, Belgian law had, in these three crucial fields of private law, become a type of common law, in which statute only played a secondary role and case law has become a major field of law. This raised numerous questions, both on a private law level and from a democratic perspective.

---

83 See for an overview, in comparative perspective, of the French reforms: V. Sagaert (ed.), *La réforme du droit privé français. Un aperçu franco-belge*, Larcier, Brussels 2008, 182 p.

84 We make abstraction of the few specific fields in which the legislator inserted amendments in the Civil Code, for instance with regard to condominium law (1994, 2010, 2018), penalty clauses (1998), consumer sales contracts (under European influence), etc.

25. **Reform process** – The Belgian Minister of Justice Koen Geens[85] therefore initiated in 2016 an ambitious reform project for several quintessential chapters of Belgian civil law. The project was framed in the policy paper, authored by the Minister of Justice and entitled "*Jump towards the law of tomorrow: recodification of the foundational statutes*", and approved by the Belgian government on 20 July 2017.[86] This policy paper provides for the foundations of the reform of the basic statutes, not only in civil law but also in commercial law, criminal law and company law.[87]

With regard to civil law, five expert committees – on (1) the law of evidence, (2) property law, (3) general law of obligations, (4) tort law and (5) loan agreements – were established in order to develop draft statutes, which did not start from, or operate within, the framework of the existing texts of the Napoleonic Civil Code, but which started from scratch. The expert committees had a large margin of liberty in their operations and choices, but there was a general coordination between the operations of the different expert groups.[88] For instance, with regard to property law, several meetings with the contract law group have been organized in order to align both substance and form.

With regard to property law, the Minister of Justice has appointed the professors Pascale Lecocq[89] and Vincent Sagaert[90] as experts in 2016. They developed the first draft, which was submitted to public consultation in order to enhance the support base and to receive input on the technical and policy dimension of the draft (December 2017 – February 2018). It was the first time in Belgian history that this procedure, inspired by the European legislator, was used for Belgian civil law. The drafters received more than 200 pages with observations, criticism and suggestions. The final Act introduces 188 statutory provisions and an Explanatory Memorandum of 450 pages, numbered from Article 3.1 to Article 3.188, which can be found online on the website of the Belgian Parliament[91] in French and Dutch. We refer for a more elaborate analysis of the statute in English to other publications.[92]

---

85 He is also emeritus Professor Company Law at the University of Leuven.

86 The paper which is the foundation for the several reform projects provides for the underlying rationale of the reform and is online at www.koengeens.be/policy/hercodificatie .

87 For a comprehensive analysis of the reform of the Belgian Civil Code: cf. D. Heirbaut, "Blitzkrieg Codification: The 2020 Belgian Civil Code", in In: M. Graziadei and L. Zhang (eds.), *The Making of the Civil Codes. Ius Gentium: Comparative Perspectives on Law and Justice*, Singapore, Springer 2023, 127-148.

88 Two academics – one from the Flemish-speaking side and one from the French-speaking side – preside and coordinate the several working groups: Eric Dirix (University of Leuven), who has been replaced after his death by Vincent Sagaert, and Patrick Wéry (Université de Louvain-la-Neuve).

89 Full Professor at the University of Liège.

90 Full Professor at University of Leuven.

91 The explanatory memorandum and all other acts which were produces during the parliamentary preparation of the Act can be found in French and in Dutch on www.dekamer.be/kvvcr/showpage.cfm?section=/flwb&language=fr&cfm=/site/wwwcfm/flwb/flwbn.cfm?lang=N&legislat=55&dossierID=0173.

92 We refer to the special issue of the *European Property Law Journal* 2021, 1-176.

B. SUSTAINABILITY AND THE COMMONS IN THE NEW BELGIAN CIVIL CODE: SOME ILLUSTRATIONS

26. Accounting for sustainability in property law – As we have illustrated, drafting a Civil Code in the early 21st century requires more attention for the sustainability approach of property law. The law of things should be concerned about the sustainability of things. Property law is the law which in the most direct manner deals with the powers we can exercise on things.[93]

The reflections of more sensibility for the commons are popping up in the new Belgian property law, not as groundbreaking principles shaking the system, but as concrete examples of the central role property law has to play in a responsible behavior towards things. We give, in the following paragraphs, some illustration of this attention, without any ambition to give an exclusive overview.[94]

27. Moderation of the anti-commons – Article 3.50 CC provides that "[t]*he right of ownership directly grants to the owner the right to use, enjoy and dispose of the object of his right. The owner has full powers, subject to the restrictions imposed by laws, regulations or the rights of third parties*." Article 3.50 does not repeat the exclusive nature or the absolute nature of ownership, as it was the case under its predecessor. This already emerges from the extent of the object of land ownership. Article 3.63 CC limits the vertical extent of land ownership. The right of ownership on the land extends only to an altitude above or depth below the surface of land that may be useful to the owner in the exercise of his powers. Consequently, he cannot object against the use by a third party at an altitude or depth on which the current owner, in view of the use and condition of the land, could not reasonably exercise his powers of use.

Another important concretization within the framework of this contribution is the moderation of the anti-commons in those cases in which exclusion is only used in a harmful manner or, at least, triggers disproportionate harm in relation to the advantage it has. The Belgian Civil Code mitigates the excessive results of an exclusivity approach to property under the umbrella of a "*de minimis*" approach. For instance, the right to roam is an expression of the withdrawal of the anti-commons in property law. Belgian law, pursuant to the Scandinavian

93 As J. Robbie states: "*As property law rules are those which most directly regulate use of these resources, these rules cannot be untouched by the transformation of our laws, policies and lives that will be required in order to contend with this task.*" (J. Robbie, "Moving Beyond Boundaries in the Pursuit of Sustainable Property Law" in B. Akkermans and G. Van Dijck (eds), *Sustainability and Private Law*, Eleven International Publishing, The Hague, 2019, 77-78; cf. B. Akkermans, "Sustainable Property Law?", (2018) *EPLJ*, 1-3.

94 We could also refer to Articles 3.133-3.134 CC, which imposes limits to the possibility to grub-up trees, even if the latter are unlawful, and to Art. 3.65 CC, which limits the possibility of the owner of ground which is adjacent to a river to use the water of the river. The former articles are dealt with by Dorothy Gruyaert in this book.

countries where it has its historical foundations but also Dutch and German law, has introduced a right to roam onto non-fenced and non-used plots of land under the condition that it does not cause any damage and that there is no sign that the right to roam is excluded on that land.[95] Another illustration of the same idea is that the owner of a plot of land must tolerate that his neighbour has access to that immovable, after he has given prior notice, if this is necessary to carry out construction or repair work or to repair or maintain the non-common fence, unless the owner has legitimate grounds for refusing such access.[96] Again, the exclusivity of ownership is mitigated in favor of a more balanced approach between neighbours.

28. **Sustainability in the micro-environment** – A prominent example of such balance, which refines the exclusivity within proportionate borders, is the field of neighborhood nuisance. The neighborhood is the micro-environment. Thus, care for the neighborhood is a preliminary step towards care for the environment. Nuisance law, in our view, is not complementary to environmental law, but is an integral part of it.[97] Belgian law has developed, and anchored for the first time in the legislation in the new Civil Code, an elaborate set of rules, which is grounded in the basic idea of the balance the rights of all owners. If, the owner in question has, according to the circumstances at stake, disrupted the balance between the adjacent property rights in a manner that he caused a harm exceeding the normal harm due to neighborship, he can be held liable. This could even result in a limitation of the use of the ownership. The objective balancing between neighboring properties is the standard for liability.[98]

Traditionally, issues between neighbours are, from a legal perspective, solved along the lines of abuse of rights. However, this traditional approach lacks refinement, as it only takes into account the interests of both neighbours, and difficultly copes with surrounding circumstances.[99] Therefore, the Belgian legislator has developed a large statutory framework for nuisance law. We have in earlier publications worked around the idea that nuisance law is an engine for the care for environment.[100] Setting the standard for nuisance should be independent from the question whether the neighbor has committed a wrongful act, as it mainly affects the equilibrium existing between neighboring parcels. It should, in this view, find its place in property law and not in tort law. This is what

95 Art. 3.67, par. 3 of the Belgian Civil Code.
96 Art. 3.67, § 2, par. 1 of the Belgian Civil Code.
97 B. Ponti, *Nuisance Law and Environmental Protection*, Lawtext Publishing Limited, 2013, 204 p.
98 Art. 3.101 CC.
99 We refer to the article of Dorothy Gruyaert in this book for the question whether public interest can be considered in applying the abuse of rights doctrine.
100 V. Sagaert, "Property Law, Contract Law and Environmental Law: shaking hands between (historical) enemies?" in S. Demeyere and V. Sagaert (ed.), *Contract and Property with an Environmental Perspective*, Antwerpen, Intersentia 2020, 18-20.

the Belgian legislator has done in Article 3.101 of the Belgian Civil Code. The first paragraph of this provision determines as follows: "*Neighbors each have a right to use and to enjoy their immovable property. In the exercise of their use and enjoyment, they shall respect the created balance by not imposing any nuisance on the neighbor that exceeds the normal inconveniences of the neighborhood and is attributable to them. In order to assess the excessive nature of the nuisance, all the circumstances of the case shall be taken into account, such as the time, the frequency and the intensity of the nuisance, the pre-occupation or the public use of the immovable property from which the nuisance originates.*"

The Belgian legislator has further strengthened this idea of balancing property interests by allowing a preventive nuisance action if there is a serious and specific risk for health, safety or pollution. In other words: one does not have to wait until the pollution or health problems have occurred, but one can ask to a judge to prevent these infringements. Sustainability is the common ground for allowing such an action, as it is better to prevent nuisance in the micro-environment than to grant for a remedy. Care for the environment begins at your own door, in taking care of your neighborhood, both with your neighbors and in relation to the green areas in the neighborhood. This can result in a (mutual) limitation of the use ("regulation") of ownership and in another layer for the social dimension of private ownership. Given demographic and geographic developments, people are living in increasingly dense conditions and closer to each other. It is for these reasons obvious that neighborhood and nuisance law have an increasingly important role in property law reform and a more intrusive function in property law discourse.

29. Optimization of ground use – Another example of a more sustainable approach in recodifying property law in the Belgian Civil Code is the growing attention for the third dimension of ownership. The legislator, not only in private law but also in public law, traditionally approaches land in two dimensions, in terms of land surface. He did hardly contemplate the use of the land above or below the surface. However, land ownership should not be thought of in terms of flat land, but rather in terms of property volumes on, above and underneath the land. Such a three-dimensional approach serves both ecological and economic benefits. The possibility to create multiple uses of his land, by stacking property volumes above and underneath each other reinforces the optimized use of the mother earth and helps to safeguard the spare green areas in Belgium on the flatland. If a landowner can constitute different volumes with different uses and destinations of his land, then he can not only optimize the value of the land, but also safeguard other lands from being built. If one has more possibilities to build above and underneath each other, there is less need to use the free space on other parcels. The new Belgian civil code deliberately expands the possibility to create "ownership of volumes" under the legal form of perpetual (irrevocable) building rights on volumes. In doing so, the legislator undermines a basic foundation of property law, which is called the "accession". A perpetual building right excludes, without time limit and without termination possibility, the accession and thus also infringes the exclusive nature and pre-eminence of ownership.

30. Common resources – Sustainability is not only dependent upon the manner in which we use our private resources, but also upon the way in which we deal with public resources. We have become gradually more aware of the scarcity of fresh air, clean water etc. A codification must thus limit the way in which we exhaust these. A long-term perspective must prevail over short-termism. Article 3.43 of the Belgian Civil Code reflects this awareness: "*Common objects cannot be appropriated in their entirety. They do not belong to anyone and are used in the public interest, including the interest of future generations. Their use is common to all and is governed by special laws.*" Air, water, minerals, must be used with a long term perspective ahead, they cannot be exhausted for the current generation. This is a clear example of the transgenerational approach in the new Belgian property law, creating responsibilities in favor of future generations. Even if it is uncertain whether this provision can award a specific remedy in specific litigation, it remains an important legal instrument of awareness.

VIII. CONCLUSION

32. **Final reflections** – The relationship between ownership, sustainability and the commons presents a difficult interaction, as is often the case if three subject matters are in a relationship. There is some dialectic interaction between these three dimensions, even on a purely legal basis. History demonstrates that ownership, and the way it is used, is an important engine, not only in a dogmatic perspective, but also as tool for societal challenges. History also shows that the pendulum has shifted on pivotal moments in history. The role of ownership in the recodifications in the early 19th century clearly demonstrates that ownership is a central device and engine for the building of a society. Contemporary societal challenges are different than the ones in the early 19th century. The enemy is not ancient feudalism, but a future tragedy of the commons. This perspective should be pre-eminent in 21st century recodifications. Inserting sustainability issues in property law can have a major impact on the traditional divisions and paradigms of private law.

As the historical opposition between property law and environmental law is re-defined, the need for integration of environmental law within property law increases, and the re-connection between private law and public law will be enhanced. Environmental law as integrative component of property law, as it is since long the case in US legal thinking, will not only have societal impact, but also requires a re-setting of dogmatic paradigms. The traditional *summa divisio* between public and private law will have to be readjusted.

PROPERTY LAW REFORM AND THE REGISTRATION OF PROPERTY TRANSFER IN LAND

A New Approach to the Indefeasibility of the Immovable Properties' Transactions

Nasrin Tabatabai HESARI
*Associate Professor of Private Law, Faculty of Law and Political Science, University of Tehran**

Soroush SAFIZADE
*PhD Student in Private Law, University of Tehran Farabi College***

I. INTRODUCTION

1. Although "revolution" may seem like an exaggeration, the implementation of land registration in immovable property' transactions brought about a significant shift, even in such manner that it can be labeled as a "revolution".[1] which is the reason why the term is being used. There was a notable transformation in the field of property transactions, as compared to the traditional conveyancing model, without an adequate model of publicity.

Actually, the traditional model involved the creation or transfer of property rights being completed through a contract. The presence of land registration in the conveyancing system added another step in the transfer formalities.

2. According to Alain Pottage, this change resulted in a new grammar in the land conveyancing system[2], which, despite its importance in creating contractual security and security of tenure, also created new challenges in the legal system.

---

* nasrintaba@ut.ac.ir.
** safizade.soroush@ut.ac.ir.
1 A. POTTAGE. 'The originality of registration' (1995). 15 *Oxford Journal of Legal Studies*, 377.
2 *Ibid.*

One of the most important challenges is to determine what happens where a transactional deed has been registered and subsequently determined to be defective? To clarify this question, let us consider the following case example:

Imagine person A sells a plot of land to person B. The transactional deed is registered adequately into the land register. Based on this registration, B subsequently transfers ownership over the land to C, and this transaction is also registered. Later, it is discovered that the contract between A and B is either void or voidable due to an error in transferor's consent, such as if their consent were induced by unfair means or there was no consent from the transferor. What is the legal effect of this voidness/voidability for the contractual relation and property transfer between B and C? Can A regain possession of the land from C? Answering these questions presents in a lot of legal systems an ambiguity between opposing principles.

On the one hand, the principle of *Nemo plus iuris ad alium transferre potest quam ipse habet*, states that one cannot sell what one does not own, and it has been discovered that B did not own the land in question.

On the other hand, C purchased the plot of land, because the Land Registry indicated B as the owner which we can attribute to the registration error due to transactional error.

3. This situation results in the illegal transfer of ownership over the land, causing a competing ownership between the original owner (A) and third-party purchaser (C). Therefore, the chain of title has a legal ambiguity, and land registration systems must address the question of who is protected by the legal system. It is a policy choice between A, who owns the land under ordinary property law, and C, who seeks to acquire the ownership right. Furthermore, it raises the question of what method should be used to protect them.

In addition, another question arises regarding how the Belgian and Iranian land registration systems handle this issue. Is there any difference between the previous Belgian and Iranian property laws and the new laws in this area? Have recently approved property law reforms, such as the new Belgian Property Law Code and the Article 62 of the Law on Permanent orders of the Development Programs of Iran, made any changes to this approach?

4. A legal answer to the challenges in each legal system is directly related to the country's registration system. Therefore, first of all, it is necessary to determine the type of registration system and the situation of registration in the real estate transaction, according to the country's system. From there one, we can address the legal system of the two countries under study and examine their solutions to legally deal with these challenges.

II. MONOJURAL V. BIJURAL

5. To solve the first challenge in conflicts between the owner and the buyer, land registration systems can be divided in two categories on the basis of the approach they follow.

6. The first is known as "Monojural or Negative systems" which solves the challenge based on the general rules of property law. Essentially, a person acquires ownership only if two conditions are met: The transferor owns the land, and the transfer was done correctly. Registration of a conveyance itself is declarative, so it cannot be constitutive for the creation of a property right over the land. Therefore, registration of a defective conveyance confers, in the purest form of this category, no rights at all to the transferee. Since *Nemo plus* ... is the fundamental rule, you cannot sell what you do not own.

In these systems, the key moment for indefeasibility is put at the beginning of the chain of titles. The title is not immune from competing claims, and transaction occurring after this point (good root of title) can be resolved under general property law. So, in our case example, the priority should be given to the original owner (A).[3]

Since subsequent title in these systems can be voided easily, these legal systems are based on what is known as a "Defeasible System".

7. The second type of land registration system, known as "Bijural or Positive System" (also called Torrens) was created with the intention of strengthening the validity of information contained in the Land Registry by setting aside general rules of property law, such as the *Nemo plus*-rule.[4]

This approach was first seen in "title by registration system" or "Torrens System", in which the purchaser acquires ownership by registration rather than transactional conveyance. The purchaser does not need the digging of the chain of title as they can rely on the information provided in the land register, which is guided by mirror and curtain principles.[5] So, the point of indefeasibility is located at the end of the chain of title providing a title that is immune from competing claims.

It means, in its purest form, that all registered titles are indefeasible, and any transactional errors occurring before the point of indefeasibility become registration errors that can only be resolved under land registration law. The registration creates a good root of title, giving priority to the registered acquirer.

---

3 M. Vuckovic, "Formalism in legal transactions in roman and in modern law example of real property" (2017). 2 *Ius Romanum*, 561.

4 P. O'Connor, 'Deferred and immediate indefeasibility: Bijural ambiguity in registered land title systems' (2009). *13 Edinburgh Law Review*, 194.

5 N. Tabatabai Hesari. *Basics and the effects of the land registry system*, Enteshar Co 2014, pp.47-57

The system of "Immediate Indefeasibility", is most adequately described by Barwick CJ in the *Breskvar v Wall* in the High Court of Australia:

> "The Torrens system of registered title of which the Act is a form is not a system of registration of title but a system of title by registration. That which the certificate of title describes is not the title which the registered proprietor formerly had, or which but for registration would have had. The title it certifies is not historical or derivative. It is the title which registration itself has vested in the proprietor. Consequently, a registration which results from a void instrument is effective according to the terms of the registration."[6]

8. The negative systems in the 19th century, faced fundamental problems in the field of land transfers worldwide. The main reason was that the property law rules could not ensure the security of transferees.[7] Someone may have purchased a piece of land, but in a negative system, if it is later discovered that the seller was not the real owner due to a transactional error in the chain of title, the actual owner could claim the land according to the general rules of property law. It is a severe infringement of the security of tenure.

The buyer would, in case of only having a contractual claim against their seller. Even if the seller had been the genuine owner, it is still possible that a third party may own an interest in the land unbeknownst to the buyer before concluding the contract leading to a need for the chain of titles to be reviewed with each new sale or mortgage, causing uncertainty, complexity and costs for buyers.[8]

9. Negative systems also face important backsides from a law and economics perspective. Obeyance to the general rules of property law, and especially the *Nemo plus-* rule, resulted in the decline in the market and economy in the countries that follow a negative system. The "Deferred Indefeasibility" doctrine was, in a historical perspective, developed to address this issue.[9] According to experts, the latter doctrine requires examining provisions related to the priority of the registered owner in addition to, and as a correction of, the general rules of property law.[10]

In the judgment *Clements v Ellis*, Dixon, in a note, cited numerous provisions that recognize the scope for general rules of property law to operate, these provisions include allowing the registrar to correct or amend certificates of title

6 P. O'Connor, "Deferred and immediate indefeasibility: Bijural ambiguity in registered land title systems", (202) 203.

7 B. C. Crown, (2010). "Whither torrens title in Singapore?" (2010), 22 *Singapore Academy of Law Journal* .10, 11.

8 *Ibid.*

9 N. Tabatabai Hesari. *Basics and the effects of the land registry system*, pp. 47-57

10 R. Edwards and J. O'Reilly, "The duel between immediate and deferred indefeasibility". (1999) 1 *Singapore Journal of Legal Studies*, 83.

issued in error. Finally, he concluded that the priority rule cannot be understood as more than a general statement to be read subject to other provisions:

> "The justification for destroying an existing legal estate or interest, which has already been duly established upon the register, is [...] found only in the necessity of protecting those who subsequently deal in good faith and for value in a manner which, upon its face, the register appears to authorize and who then obtain registration."[11]

10. Based on the deferred Indefeasibility doctrine, there is another way to provide security in the land transactions without the need to change the entire system. All that is needed is to move the point of indefeasibility from the beginning and end point of the chain of titles and place it somewhere else in the transactional chain. This means that transactional errors occurring before this point become registration errors, and can only be solved under registration law, giving priority to the transferee. However, transactional errors occurring after this point, can only be solved under property law, giving priority to the real owner.[12]

Therefore, land registration only has an indefeasibility effect on transactions after the invalid transfers. For instance, if a property is transferred based on a void contract and the title of transferee is registered in the land registry, it is possible to file a lawsuit to annul the transaction and amend the land registry book before it is subsequently transferred to the third party. However, as soon as it is transferred to the third party and the third party's title is registered, it would, in such intermediary system, not be possible anymore to file a lawsuit to cancel the transaction and get the land back from buyers' possession.[13]

III. BELGIAN PROPERTY LAW REFORM AND THE BIJURAL AMBIGUITY ISSUE

11. As it is known, Belgian law has been subject to a property law reform by the Act of the 4 February 2020, which entered into force on 1 September 2021.[14] To answer the question of how the Belgian legal system solves the described ambiguity, it is first useful to consider whether there are any differences between the former provisions and the new property law with regard to the land registration.

---

11 *Ibid.*, 84.

12 Scottish Law Commission, *Discussion Paper on Land Registration: Void and Voidable Titles*, The Stationery Office 2004, 24-25.

13 *Ibid.*, 70-71.

14 We refer to the contribution of Vincent Sagaert in this book and the references there.

It is worth mentioning that both in the former and the new provisions, consent from parties is, as a matter of principle, a necessary but also sufficient condition to create and transfer property rights in land. The role of land registration is rather limited in this respect: It only affects the opposability of title in relation to a third-party with competing property rights which is in good faith. The registration in the land register is not constitutive for internal effects, but only activates the efficiency of the transfer in relation to certain, protected third parties. Therefore, both provisions have one crucial thing in common: maintaining a Negative or Declarative System in land transfer conveyance. However, a comparative view of the previous and new legal provisions reveals that the negative system in the old and the new law tend to differ in nature, mainly with regard to the correction of errors. A development can be seen from a pure negative system in the previous law to a mixed system (between monojural and bijural) in the new law.

Upon comparison of these two laws and analysis of the evolution of bijural systems in comparative law, as mentioned in the first section of this article, it emerges that the new law has a more protective perspective towards transferees in good faith as compared to the previous law.

The previous provisions of Belgian land law allowed parties to challenge the validity of property transactions in land even after the registration of the latter, thus permitting to amend data which were integrated in the land register, within the applicable prescription period (in accordance with the provisions of Article 2265[15], for ten or twenty years). This meant that third parties could not fully rely on the information on land registry to determine the legal status of the land in question.[16]

Therefore, Belgium existed for many decades as a defeasible or pure negative system, and if a registered transactional error was discovered, the true owner (A) was entitled to reclaim their land under the previous Belgian Property Law regardless of whether the third party (C) acted in good faith or bad faith.

12. During the reform of the Civil Code in 2020, it seems that lawmakers have taken into consideration the rights of third parties (transferees) to access accurate information. The new law has provided the protection of registered good faith third parties, rather than the original owner. In Article 3.17 of the new Belgian Civil Code[17], the legislator has recognized and has acknowledged

---

15 "*Celui qui acquiert de bonne foi et par juste titre un immeuble, en prescrit la propriété par dix ans, si le véritable propriétaire habite dans le ressort de la cour d'appel dans l'étendue de laquelle l'immeuble est situé; et par vingt ans, s'il est domicilié hors du dit ressort.*"

16 Scottish Law Commision, *Discussion Paper on Land Registration: Void and Voidable Titles*, p. 211-212.

17 Art. 3.17. "*Effets de l'extinction des droits réels La renonciation, la révocation, la résolution pour inexécution, la résiliation de commun accord, la confusion et la déchéance ne portent pas atteinte aux droits des tiers qui sont acquis, de bonne foi, sur le droit réel anéanti.*
La renonciation à un droit réel vaut seulement pour l'avenir. Si le droit réel est né par un acte juridique à titre onéreux, la renonciation ne porte pas atteinte aux obligations personnelles, présentes et futures, due en contrepartie de la constitution de ce droit."

"the principle of protecting third parties in good faith" in cases where there is an issue with the chain of title. This is a novel approach, as it puts the indefeasibility point prior to the last transaction if the purchaser is deemed in good faith. As the presence of the third party in good faith is a condition for protection, the implementation of this Article means that the Belgian land registration system is now subject to a deferred indefeasible system.

13. This marks a shift from the defeasible system (pure negative) to the indefeasible one (mixed system) by the Belgian legislature. Two questions that can be raised under the new regime: Who is the third party; and what is the good faith?

14. The third party is a flexible concept that will have a different meaning depending on the subject under discussion.[18] For example, in the law of property, any person other than the owner is referred to as the third party. In the contract law system, simply, the notion of the third party is consistent with its etymology – the third party is the third person, i.e. the one other than the two (or more) contracting parties.[19]

This flexibility extends even more in the Law of Registration. For example, when discussing the right of access to registered information, the term of "third party" refers to the beneficial persons who must be informed about the legal status of the property and the transactions associated with it. Nevertheless, this concept of third party is not the same as that used in the registration of land transfers. In the registration of land transfers, land law scholars argue that the registration of acts relating to the creation, modification or extinction of property rights would increase the security and protection the property rights of people who conclude contracts and obtain rights based on the information contained in the land books.

15. These persons constitute the concept of the third party in the principle of "protection of third parties in good faith" which refers to a person who, relying on a registered invalid proprietary contract, enters into an agreement and acquires property rights.[20]

According to some experts, "third party in the special sense of registration"[21], can be defined as someone who has acquired rights in good faith on a terminated property right. This concept is identical to the one stated in Article 3.17 of the Belgian Civil Code.

18 L. Toma, "Tiers et biens en Roumainz", in Association Henri Capitant (ed), *Les tiers* (Brussels: Bruylant 2015), 446.

19 W. Dross, "Tiers et biens en France", in Association Henri Capitant (ed), *Les tiers*, 377-378.

20 L. Toma, "Tiers et biens en Roumain", 442-443.

21 G. Boutin, "Rapport General", in Association Henri Capitant (ed), *Les tiers*, Bruylant 2015, p. 300.

16. However, being a third party is not sufficient in order to be protected under the land registration system. Evidence of the affirmation that this third party was in good faith is another condition to be eligible for support. In the traditional civil codes, good faith is considered a two-dimensional concept with both positive and negative aspects.[22] The negative side refers to ignorance and lack of awareness[23] while the positive side refers to one's efforts to obtain information, but failing to do so.[24]

However, in land transfer registration, good faith has specific requirements.

It is said that the third party must meet certain conditions to be considered in good faith. In this case, the third party is in good faith that their property right is based on a registered transfer with the person whose right is registered in the land book, and at the time of registration, no action or notice was recorded regarding the register or transaction errors, and the person had no knowledge (or should not have had knowledge) about the inaccuracy.[25]

Lamontagne and Duchaine argue that the occurrence of good faith depends on fulfilling three conditions. First, the third party does not (and should not) know the truth of the matter. Second, based on the information in the land register, the third party has entered into a transaction. Third, the third party has registered its acquisition in the land book.[26]

Which concept does the Belgian legislator use? Article 3.17, paragraph 1 of the new Belgian Civil Code provides as follows: "*The abandonment, revocation, dissolution due to non-performance, termination in mutual agreement, concurrence and deprivation do not affect the rights of third parties that have been acquired in good faith on the terminated property right.*" The concept of good faith is outlined in Article 3.17 of the new provisions, which introduces two important terms: "acquired rights" and "on the terminated property right." The term "acquired rights of the third party" specifically pertains to land title registration in the land registry. While using the term " third party in good faith" in Article 3.17 of the new Belgian Civil Code, it appears that the Belgian legislator was referring to the traditional concept of good faith found in the civil code, rather than to the good faith principle within a land transfer registration system. This is in line with the definition of good faith outlined in Section 5.117[27] of the new obligations book of Civil Code, which specifies the

---

22 M.H. Abbaszadeh, (2010), *Reliance to appearance in contracts*, ph.D thesis in Private Law, University of Tehran 2010, 70.

23 R. Marcellino Dala, *Aquisição tabular: efeito atributivo no artigo 5º do código do Registo Predial*, Master thesis, University of Lisbon 2019, 60.

24 *Ibid.*, p. 61.

25 L. Toma, "Tiers et biens en Roumain", 446.

26 G. Gidrol-Mistral, "Publicite des droits et prescription acquisitive: Des liaisons dangereuses" (2016) 46 *Revue Generale de Droit*, 318.

27 Art. 5.117. Bonne foi: Au sens de la présente sous-section, le débiteur de la restitution cesse d'être de bonne foi:
1° dès qu'il a connaissance effective de la cause de nullité du contrat;
2° dans les autres cas, dès qu'il est en demeure.

good faith disappears if one has knowledge or should have known about certain information.

Under Article 3.30 of the New Property Law Code, the registration of land is mandatory in order to establish opposability against the *bona fide* third party. Additionally, the phrase "on the terminated property right" implies that the third party has relied on information obtained from the land registry. As a result, these two conditions signify that the concept of good faith within the land registration system has been acknowledged through the new Property Law Book.

IV. IRANIAN LAND REGISTRATION SYSTEM: DEFEASIBLE SYSTEM OR BELIEF IN INDEFEASIBILITY

17. Iranian land law scholars analyze the Iranian land registration system by dividing it into two periods based on the title indefeasibility index and the validity land registry's information within the land registry system, namely before and after 1972.[28] Nevertheless, legislative developments from 2015 onwards have resulted in the emergence of a third period in the Iranian land registration system concerning the title indefeasibility index. Therefore, the following paragraphs will examine the model of the Iranian land registration system within these three periods.

A. 1931-1972: THE PERIOD OF IMMEDIATE INDEFEASIBILITY

18. Legal scholars have referred to this time period as the "Golden Age" and the empire era of the rule of Article 22 of the "Law of Registration of Documents and Real Estates."[29] In this Article, the legislator provided as follows:

> "As soon as an immovable property is registered in the land registry according to the law, the government will recognize only the person in whose name the immovable property is registered or the person to whom the immovable property has been transferred and this transfer is also registered in the land registry."

According to this provision, not only in any proceedings but also prior to taking any action, the land registry book should be regarded as a primary criterion for

28 M. Asgharzade Bonaab, *Practical Registration Law*, Vol. I, Majd 2021, p. 121-124.

29 M.J. Jafari Langroudi, *Law of Registration*, Ganje Danesh 2013, p. 131.

the determination of the question who holds the ownership right.[30] Moreover in a strict interpretation, no court did not possess any authority to invalidate the content of the land registry book and the title certificate.[31] Perhaps, due to this reason, some foreign scholars still believe that Iranian land registration system adheres to the immediate indefeasibility model, which encompasses any errors, mistakes or deficiencies in the title transfer process.[32]

B. 1972-2015: THE DEFEASIBILITY ERA

During this period, known as the phase of Article 's vulnerability according to some scholarly writings, it became evident that the number of registration errors is far exceeded the threshold that would compel the legislator to uphold the unconditional validity .[33] Therefore, an amendment was made to Article 25 of the Law of Registration of Documents and Real Estates on January 8, 1973. The third paragraph of the revised provision states that any contradiction between the land registry books and the authentic act or the final court decisions will lead to the modification of the land registry books. This reform served as the legal ground for the reduction of the weight of the land registration with regard to the validity of the title of property transfer, particularly due to the inclusive interpretation of the term "authentic act" mentioned in the third paragraph. It encompassed not only the notarial documents, but also the Article 1287 of the Iranian Civil Code, which includes "*all documents that has been received by public legal officers who have the authority to draw up such acts at the place where the act was written and with the requisite formalities.*"

19. Even if the real estate office contradicts the defense and distribution of the declaration, the supervisory board is obliged to issue a ruling for the office 's amendment. This circumstance led to amendments in the land register whenever a contradiction with the authentic act occurred.[34] During this period, Iran's judicial process readily rendered decisions to invalidate title certificates based on ordinary documents and unregistered transactions. Hence, this era can be referred to as the period of the defeasibility rule in Iran.

---

30 D. Bahrami. *Descriptive and Analytical Foundations of Property and Documents Registration Law.* Mizan 2022, pp. 177-178.

31 D. Bahrami, *Real Property Registration Law in Iran.* Mizan 2015, p. 599.

32 L. Griggs, *The Doctrinal Coherence of the Torrens System of Land Registration in Australia: Evolution or Revolution?*, Doctoral Thesis, Bond University 2017, p. 8.

33 Asgharzade Bonaab, *Practical Registration Law*, p. 123.

34 J. Jafari Langroudi, *Law of Registration*, p. 138.

C. 2015 UNTIL TODAY: THE PERIOD OF DEFERRED INDEFEASIBILITY

20. Issuance of the advisory opinion No. 2664/102/95 dated October 25, 2016 of the Guardian Council of the Constitution, declaring the invalidity of the private deeds based on Article 22 of the Law of Registration of Documents and Real Estates as contrary to *Sharia*, along with the approval of Article 62 of the Law on Permanent orders of the Development Programs, which allows the prioritization of private deeds approved by the court over the authentic act, led some analysts to the conclusion that the defeasibility of title certificate and the modification of land registry books have been officially recognized as the intended policy of legislator.[35] In Article 62, the legislator provided as follows:

> "All transactions related to registered immovable property such as sale, settlement, lease, mortgage, as well as the promise or commitment to carry out such transactions must be officially registered in the notary offices. Private deeds of immovable property transactions cannot be enforceable against third parties and cannot legally contradict an authentic deed except in cases where they are approved by the court as having Shariah validity."

Contrary to the aforementioned conclusions, case law during this period indicates that the restoration of the authority of Article 22 in a balanced manner has been regarded as the primary policy. It neither possesses a fictitious authority nor is interpreted based on the policy of defeasibility. In light of this, the case law made efforts to interpret the provisions such as Article 22 and Article 62 with the aim of transitioning towards a deferred indefeasibility system.

According to the majority position in case law and legal scholarship, most judges believe that the opposability and validity of private documents against third parties is established only when the third party does not act in good faith.[36] Therefore, registered information has priority over unregistered information and is considered accurate and legally non-infringing.[37] This is grounded in the underlying rationale the person whose name is recorded in the land registry book is recognized as the rightful owner by Article 22, whereas unregistered transactions are not recognized under Articles 46 and 48 of Law of Registration of Documents and Real Estates.[38] However, if the registered

---

35 A. Mirzanezhad, J. (2016). "Delay on Articles 22, 46, 47 and 48 of the Deeds and Land Registration act under the pretext of the new opinion of the Guardian Council" (2016), 5 *Raay Journal*, 46-49.

36 A. Khodabakhshi, *Law of lawsuits*, Vol. 7, Enteshar Co (2019), pp. 36-51.

37 N. Tabatabai Hesari, H. Azari, and M. Saber. "Ensuring 'stability of the real estate legal situation' in the Iranian land recording system" (2017) 3 *International Comparative Jurisprudence*, 192.

38 N. Tabatabai Hesari, H. Azari, and M. Saber . "The Effect of Iranian Land Administration System in Transactions Real Properties' Security: In the Light of Public Confidence Theory".

owner obtained their title without good faith, private documents can be used to challenge the registered ownership.

V. CONCLUSION

21. Bijural ambiguity refers to the conflict between the general property law rules and the law of registration. This conflict arises due to the historical development of land registration systems, which assume that transactional errors result in competing ownership between the original owner and the third-party purchaser.

In this process, ensuring the validity of the registered titles is a key objective of land registration systems. These systems have as major function to play a crucial role in securing transaction costs. The prevailance of the buyer's rights over the rights of the original owner is a result of the departure from traditional property law principles – particularly the "*Nemo plus iuris ad alium transferre potest quam ipse habet* rule, in favor of positive land registration systems. Such exception on a most fundamental principle is mostly grounded in the need for legal security in real estate transactions. However, it is important to note that this approach is not universally accepted, particularly in land registration systems known as negative, monojural or defeasible system. In the latter systems, the traditional rules of property law still prevail, emphasizing the protection of the real owner in any circumstance.

22. The comparative investigations conducted in this article reveal that the Belgian land registration system tradionally adopted a different approach prior to the approval of the new provisions in the property law book of the Civil Code. Although both the previous and new laws have maintained a monojural or negative system, there has been a shift from a defeasible system to a deferred indefeasible system in which the protection of the third party in good faith is taken into account.

In the new Civil Code, the legislator has restricted the protection only to the third parties acting in good faith. It means that individuals who are not directly involved in an invalid transfer, but have unknowingly relied on the information provided by the land registry and subsequently registered their transfer in the land registry's book, are eligible for protection.

Although the Iranian land registration system initially adopted the principle of immediate indefeasibility, relying on Article 22 of the Law of Registration of Documents and Real Estates, it underwent adjustment over time. In this process, despite the advisory opinion No. 2664/102/95 dated October 25, 2016,

---

(2017) 5 *International Journal of Academic Research in Economics and Management Sciences*, 150.

issued by the Guardian Council of the Constitution, and Article 62 of the Law on Permanent orders of the Development Programs, which introduced elements of title defeasibility, there was a significant shift towards this direction starting from 1972 with the amendment of Article 25 of the Law of Registration of Documents and Real Estates. However, due to the jurisprudence and interpretation provided, implementation of defeasibility approach has been prevented, leading the Iranian land registration system towards a deferred type of indefeasible system.

PART II

PROPERTY LAW AND SUSTAINABILITY

IN SEARCH FOR SUSTAINABLE PROPERTY RELATIONS

Bram AKKERMANS*
Professor of Property Law, Maastricht University Faculty of Law
Fellow, Maastricht European Private Law Institute (M-EPLI).

I. INTRODUCTION

As we move into the twenties of the new millennium there is ample evidence that we are in a climate crisis.[1] Although this is not the first crisis of this century, it is certainly more prevailing.[2] In terms of eco-sustainability, the world is dealing with an increase in global temperatures and a loss of biodiversity. As most of the land surface of the planet is governed by private property rights, the way in which this land is managed, has a great effect on eco-sustainability.[3]

In the past centuries, a system has arisen in which exclusivity and extraction are the leading principles, and that is based on economic growth by accrual of wealth.[4] This property law, which VAN ERP has called the classical system of property law, plays an instrumental part in the structure

* I am greatly indebted to Víðir Smári PETERSEN for helpful and insightful comments on an earlier version of this paper. Any mistakes – of course – remain my own.

1 See IPCC Special Report on climate change, desertification, land degradation, sustainable land management, food security, and greenhouse gas fluxes in terrestrial ecosystems, available at www.ipcc.ch/srccl/, as well as the Sixth Assessment Report by the IPCC, especially by the Third Working Group; most recently AR6 Climate Change 2022: Mitigation of Climate Change, available at www.ipcc.ch/report/sixth-assessment-report-working-group-3/.

2 See J. LOVETT, "Tragedy or Triumph in Post-Katrina New Orleans?: Reflections on Possession, Dispossession, Demographic Change and Affordable Housing" (2013) *Fordham Urb. L. J. City Square* 40, 22, available at http://urbanlawjournal.com/3-tragedy-or-triumph-in-post-katrina-new-orleans-by-john-a-lovett/, reprinted in (2015) *Journal of Affordable Housing and Community Development* 23, 289; E. VAN DER SIJDE, "What can (South African) property lawyers learn from resilience thinking? An exploratory note on the aftermath of the Covid-19 pandemic" in Z.-Z. Boggenpoel *et al.* (Eds.), *Property and Pandemics: Property Responses to Covid-19*, Juta, Cape Town 2021, p. 352 *et seq.*

3 See D. GRINLINTON and P. TAYLOR (Eds.), *Property Rights and Sustainability. The Evolution of Property Rights to Meet Ecological Challenges*, Leiden / Boston, Martinus Nijhoff Publishers 2011, p. 414.

4 See B. AKKERMANS, "Duurzaam Goederenrecht. Naar een herijking van ons goederenrechtelijk stelsel?" (2018) *Tijdschrift voor Privaatrecht (TPR)*, p. 1437 *et seq.*

of our society.[5] The classical model fits into an imaginary of a world in which economic growth and welfare maximization are the key organizing principles.[6] The set of rules of property law, also referred to as "the property *nomos*", is organized around this larger idea or imaginary of what society should look like.[7] The risk of changing the rules without addressing the notion of *nomos* and imaginary is incoherency. Incoherency in property law creates issues of legal certainty. Property law deals with durable relationships that sometimes span across multiple generations. Especially property relations relating to land use are often created for a very long duration of time. These property rights are part of a complex system of rules that rely on coherency of the system.[8] Incoherency or changes within the system – for example, through additions of new previously unknown property rights – lead to uncertainty and increased efforts for all users.[9]

In terms of the rules of property law themselves, there are three levels at which private law property can be approached. First, there is the level of property theory that provides the foundations on the basis of which the system of property law functions. Second, there is the organizational level of the system, in which general principles govern the rules of property law. Third, there are the technical rules of property law that apply to property relations between two private parties.[10] This contribution will explore the necessary transition from a classical property *nomos* towards a property *nomos* for sustainable relations. In doing so the contribution explores some of the fundamental elements a sustainable property law must contain and where these come from.

---

5 S. Van Erp, "From 'classical' modern European property law" in *Essays in Honour of Konstantinos D. Kerameus/Festschrift für Konstantinos D. Kerameus*, Vol. I, Ant. A Sakkoulas – Bruylant, Athens- Brussels 2009, p. 1517 *et seq*.

6 On key organizing principles see J. Robbie, "Moving Beyond Boundaries in the Pursuit of Sustainable Property Law" in B. Akkermans and G. van Dijck (Eds.), *Private law and sustainability*, Eleven International Publishing, The Hague 2020, p. 59; B. Akkermans, *Sustainable Property Law. Reckoning, Resilience, and Reform*, Eleven International Publishers, The Hague 2022, p. 17.

7 See L. Fox O'Mahony and M. Roark, *Squatting and the State. Resilient property in an age of crisis*, Cambridge University Press, Cambridge 2022, p. 26-27.

8 On systematic considerations in private law property law see B. Akkermans, *The principle of numerus clausus in European property law*, Intersentia, Antwerp 2008, p. 387 *et seq*.

9 See T. Merrill and H. Smith, "Optimal Standardization in the Law of Property: The Numerus Clausus Principle" (2000) *Yale Law Journal* 110, 1 *et seq*.

10 On the three levels of analysis, see Akkermans (n. 5); S. van Erp, *European and National Property Law: Osmosis or Growing Antagonism? Walter van Gerven Lectures* (6), Europa Law Publishing, Groningen 2006, 25 p.; Akkermans, "Sustainable Property Law" in B. Akkermans (Ed.), *Edward Elgar Research Agenda on Property Law*, Edward Elgar, Northampton 2024, p. 161 *et seq*.

II. SUSTAINABLE PROPERTY LAW?

Sustainability means taking care of our own needs without compromising the ability of future generations to meet their needs.[11] Although there are more definitions of sustainability and sustainable development, all approaches take a multi-dimensional and multi-generational view.[12] That generally means that any approach of sustainability is at odds with the classical system of property law that is focused on the present and future of the current property rightsholder.[13]

In recent years, more attention has been given to the underlying values of the system of property law. Especially Gregory ALEXANDER has been highly instrumental in bringing attention to the question of the purpose of property law.[14] Alexander exposed how our post World War II systems of property law have become dominated by a utilitarian economic growth mindset.[15] The classical system of property law has become closely connected to these underlying values.[16] Traditionally this classical system of property law is studied with a historical doctrinal research method, either in national law only or in a comparative setting.[17] Since the rise of law and economics in the 1970s, an economic analysis of law was added to this.[18] Economic analysis offers deep insights into the translation of underlying values of efficiency, economic growth and welfare maximization into the technical rules of property law.[19] Against this – rather descriptive – analysis of the law of property, a new approach to scholarship arose under the name of "progressive property law".[20] Progressive property scholarship offers a more normative approach in which not only the

---

11 See WORLD COMMISSION ON ECONOMIC DEVELOPMENT (WCED), *Our Common Future*, Oxford University Press, Oxford 1987, para 27.

12 See J. BLEWITT, *Understanding Sustainable Development (3rd edition)*, Routledge, London 2018, p. 426.

13 That is not to say that inter-generational aspects are absent from classical property law, such as in case of estate planning, but an inter-generational perspective is rare. There are also critical views such as those of LIFSHITZ, GILBOA and KAPLAN who argue that the right of ownership cannot offer sufficient means to protect the interests of future generations. See J. LIFSHITZ, M. GILBOA and Y. KAPLAN, "The Future of Property", (2023)*Cardozo Law Review* 44:4, p. 1443 *et seq.*

14 See G. ALEXANDER, *Property and Human Flourishing*, Oxford University Press, Oxford 2018, p. 366.

15 G. ALEXANDER and E. PEÑALVER, *Introduction to Property Theory*, Cambridge University Press, Cambridge 2012, p. 11 *et seq.*

16 See S. VAN ERP (n. 6), p. 1517 *et seq.*

17 See S. VAN ERP, "Civil and Common Property Law: Caveat Comparator – The Value of Legal Historical-Comparative Analysis" (2003) *European Review of Private Law* 3, 394 *et seq.*

18 See R. COASE, "The Problem of Social Cost" (1960) *J. Law & Economics* 3, 7; R. POSNER, *Economic Analysis of Law*, Little Brown, Boston 1973, 415 p.; ALEXANDER and PEÑALVER (n.16), p. 11 *et seq.*, H. SMITH, "Property as the Law of Things" (2012) 125 *Harvard Law Review*, 7, 1691 *et seq.*

19 On technical rules see S. VAN ERP (n. 11), p. 13 *et seq.*

20 G. ALEXANDER, E. PEÑALVER, J. SINGER and L. UNDERKUFFLER, "A Statement of Progressive Property" (2009) *Cornell LR* 94, 743.

current state of affairs, but also a reimagination of what property law should be, is included. In this respect progressive property law is very much a response to the more descriptive traditional and law and economics approaches. In the past decade, property scholars have begun slowly attempting to move beyond the progressive property approach. An example of such a new approach is "Resilient Property Theory" as advocated by Lorna Fox O'Mahony and Marc Roark.[21] Resilient property theory looks at the law in action and looks at the set of property and other rules that cause problems.[22] Another approach is to use the sociological concept of "social imaginary" to conceptualist the development of the legal system that would be desirable.[23]

The question of sustainable property can therefore be approached from various angles. In terms of a doctrinal approach, there are more ad hoc approaches, such as dealing with the rules of accession in case of placing solar panels, or the reorganization of governance structures of apartment owners so that they can create an energy community. In terms of progressive property law and resilient property theory, there is a more abstract discussion on what the system of property law should be capable of in terms of sustainability. What is "sustainable property law" therefore depends on the aim as well as the method chosen. Depending on the level or scale at which the field is approached, a more or less coherent *nomos* can be observed.[24] Progressive property law and resilient property theory contribute to a call for coherence in the approach to be taken.

III. CHOICES FOR DIRECTIONS TO TAKE

As the previous discussion shows, creating sustainable property law is a complex matter. Depending on the perspective that is taken, sustainable property law may concern very practical solutions to small scale problems, as well as a large discussion of the underlying values of the system of property law as whole.

There are other legal systems in the world that are also confronted with large challenges, comparable to the size of the challenge of eco-sustainability. Perhaps the best-known example of such a system is the law of South Africa. Since the mid-1990s, South Africa has been in transition towards a democratic society based on strong values of equality and the rule of law. Leading this development is a transformative constitution that not only provides a strong catalogue of social fundamental rights, but which, through a constitutional court, gives direction to transformation of South African society. This unique experience

21 See Fox O'Mahony and Roark (n. 8).

22 See Fox O'Mahony and Roark (n. 8), p. 201 *et seq.*, p. 337 *et seq.*

23 See B. Akkermans (n. 7), p. 15 *et seq.*

24 On scale see: M. Roark and L. Fox O'Mahony, "Scaling Property Law" in B. Akkermans (Ed.), *Edward Elgar Research Agenda for Property Law*, Edward Elgar, Northampton 2024, p. 93 *et seq.*

teaches valuable lessons for other systems that are confronted with problems of a similar transformative nature.

The development of sustainable property law offers a comparable transformative objective, but of course lacks a constitutional document of an equally transformative nature. Still, lessons from South African law can provide valuable insights into the thought patterns and fundamental principles that underly such transformative process.[25] Transformation is not revolution; it means a gradual development and not an abruptly introduced completely new legal system. Property rights are durable legal relations. Fundamentally changing the concept of ownership by influence of the state is considered expropriation and, in the absence of very specific justifiable reasons, an abuse of the power of eminent domain.[26] Therefore, working with the existing "lawscape" is a given.[27] This generally provides two options. First of all, the current rules can be used. These can be applied, but can – if necessary – be reinterpreted to fit into the transformative direction in which the legal system is taken. Interpretation of rules can go a long way, but at some point, the results may become *contra legem*.[28] In those cases, a second approach may be needed which would require new rules to be introduced.

In a seminal piece on property and constitution André van der Walt develops a nuanced approach, which takes the form of an algorithm, on the basis of which the transition in South African law can be given shape.[29] The most important foundation of Van der Walt's approach is the idea that law forms a single system, in which there is a hierarchy between sources. It is the constitution that is the highest source of law that gives direction for the developments. However, practical rules are to be developed and used at the lowest possible level, following the general principle of subsidiarity. When current rules, either through their application or through reinterpretation, cannot be used, the creation of new rules comes into play. Such new rules will either deal with situations previously unregulated or will replace rules that cannot be interpreted without an interpretation *contra legem*. Examples of new rules, for instance offered by legislation that regulates the number of days or locations in which homeowners can enable home sharing through platforms such as Airbnb.[30]

25 On thought patterns and fundamental principles in property law see Van Erp (n. 11), p. 13 *et seq.*

26 On expropriation see B. Hoops, *The Legitimate Justification of Expropriation*, Juta, Cape Town 2017.

27 On the term "lawscape", see N. Graham, Lawscape: *Property, Environment, Law*, Routledge, New York 2011.

28 See A. van der Walt, *Property and Constitution*, Pretoria University Law Press, Pretoria: 2012.

29 Van der Walt (n. 29), p.19 *et seq.*

30 See www.amsterdam.nl/veelgevraagd/vergunning-en-registratienummer-voor-vakantieverhuur-f477f.

Reinterpretation of rules for example includes governments using their existing regulatory power to limit the amount of rent that owners can ask from tenants.[31]

IV. NEW DIRECTIONS USING EXISTING DOCTRINE

A. OBLIGATIONS OF SUSTAINABILITY?

A lot has been written in the context of sustainability about completely new directions and rules that could be taken. Examples of these are offered by, for example, regulation in the energy transition. This contribution will focus on the re-use of existing doctrine to investigate if these can provide solutions to one of the most pressing problems in sustainable property law.

There is a debate in sustainable property law that concerns a shift from the rights of a landowner towards the obligations that a landowner may have. Such obligations can have a public law nature, but there is also a debate on the search for sources in private law on which such obligations can be constructed. Of course, private law obligations already exist in property law, such as the duty to tolerate or not to do something in case of a right of servitude. Sometimes, but much more rare, private law obligations can also be positive in nature, such as the duty to maintain the exercise of a right of servitude, the duty to maintain the object in case of existence of a right of usufruct, or the duty to ensure that the holder of a right of *emphyteusis* (long lease) has access to the land. Following the abolition of feudal tenure during the French Revolution, especially civil law systems are very wary for personal positive obligations. A negative obligation can run with the land and burden the land; a positive obligation almost always burdens a person in their capacity as a right holder.

In the context of sustainability, a focus on obligations rather than rights is much more natural. Sustainability does not only offer a set of behavioral standards, but also entails the inherent obligation to take into account current and future use. After all, future generations must also be able to meet their needs. Such obligations may be mostly negative in nature, referring to the obligation not to do something, such as an overly extractive use of a piece of land. However, there is also a possibility that obligations have a positive nature, requiring the owner of a piece of land to actively do something, such as the obligation to use the land in a regenerative manner.[32] Especially in the context of the application of human flourishing theory as a foundational idea to property,

[31] See wet van 9 april 2021 tot wijziging van Boek 7 van het Burgerlijk Wetboek en de Uitvoeringswet huurprijzen woonruimte (Wet maximering huurprijsverhogingen geliberaliseerde huurovereenkomsten) (Law maximising increase in rent in lease contracts on the free rental market) (BWBR0045063).

[32] See B. Akkermans and K. van Melle, "Regeneratieve eigendom – naar een hernieuwde benadering", in B. Akkermans, B. Hoops, E. van der Sijde and B. Verheye (Eds,),

such as dealt with above, the acceptance of positive obligations becomes much more normalized.[33] In human flourishing theory the fulfillment of the social thesis in which a holder of a property right does not only benefit themself, but also takes responsibility for the flourishing of fellow community members, leads to the acceptance of moral obligations of caretaking. Such obligations can easily be more positive in nature, such as an obligation to invest in sustainable measures such as solar panels and heat pump systems, or an obligation to leave the edges of the field upon harvest for others, or to hire other members of the community to work for you in order to share wealth and income.[34] However, to transform these moral obligations into legal obligations is much more difficult.[35] Of course there are some legal devices to impose duties on others in private law, such as through trust law or by way of a legacy in a testament, but most of the current property law rules are created in a *nomos* that focuses on rights and not obligations. Only obligations directly connected to the enjoyment of a property right are accepted.[36] Situations where obligations may need to arise, but where there is no direct connection to the enjoyment of a property right in the traditional sense, cause issues in classical property law. These obligations cannot arise for want of a source. Nevertheless, there may be compelling reasons why obligations should arise, especially in the context of sustainability. Situations already discussed include a landowner compelled to invest in sustainable energy measures, or an owner compelled to share their wealth with others. In these situations, the current rules of property law do not provide a solution and the next step is to investigate whether existing rules and doctrine can be interpreted in such a manner that they can provide a basis for these obligations and therefore significantly contribute towards a sustainable property law.

Of course, there is a route through public law which is always open. However, the true strength of a private property law solution lies in the fact that not the state enforces change, but we change the way in which private parties relate to each other, without direct state interference. Traditionally, there is one private law doctrine that influences property rights: the doctrine of abuse of rights. As an answer to the very liberal notions of ownership in 19th century France, the doctrine of abuse of rights was created to limit the powers of an owner in private law itself.[37] An owner has a lot of powers over the object on which they

---

Privaatrecht 2050. De weg naar Ecologische Duurzaamheid, Die Keure, Brugge 2020, p. 193 *et seq.*

33 See, on this, B. Akkermans, "Sustainable Obligations in (Dutch) property law", in S. Demeyere and V. Sagaert (Eds.), Property and Contract from an Environmental Perspective, Intersentia, Antwerp 2020, p. 29 *et seq.*

34 See, Akkermans and Van Melle (n. 33), p. 203 *et seq.*

35 Such transformation is also not always desirable as it may directly contradict the underlying values of the legal system.

36 See Alexander (n.15), p. 39 *et seq.*

37 See E. van Dongen, "Rechtsmisbruik in het Belgische en Nederlandse recht: over individuele vrijheid, maatschappelijke zorgvuldigheid en asociale rechtsuitoefening", (2022) *Tijdschrift voor Privaatrecht*, p. 1049 *et seq.*

hold a right of ownership, but if the sole purpose of use is to cause a nuisance to another, especially a neighbor, such a use of power is not permissible.[38]

The doctrine of abuse of rights is actually wider than just for property rights. VAN DONGEN, citing PINO, has recently offered a comparative approach to further clarify this doctrine.[39] An abuse of rights arises when (1) a person is the holder of a right, (2) that right can be exercised in different ways, (3) there is a circumstance in which the exercise of the right is lawful, but the current exercise is objectionable, and (4) the exercise of the right creates an imbalance between the advantage for the right holder and the sacrifice of the "other(s)". When these criteria are met, the owner is precluded from using their right of ownership in the current manner. In other words, the abuse of rights doctrine offers a negative interference of the right of ownership.[40] That makes sense when the context in which the doctrine was developed is taken into account. In the 19th century there were authors who argued that the powers of the owner were almost unlimited and that their right of ownership was a true absolute right. This included for example the power of an owner even to destroy their object, such as the ability to set fire to a painting.[41]

In the 21st century, it is perhaps time to further develop this doctrine. When we reimagine our society as a society that must live within its planetary boundaries, and where post-growth economics and human flourishing theory underly the *nomos* of property rules needed to give effect to this, this places current rules and doctrine in a different perspective. The aim of property law is then no longer just to enrich the owner by extracting as much use and value from the object, but instead requires a responsible stewardship.[42] It could be argued that such an approach also sets a standard of behavior that right holders must comply with. Not adhering to that standard may cause friction and when, under the fourth criterium for abuse of right, an extractive or exclusive use leads to a considerable imbalance between the right holder and the "other", perhaps such a use can be interpreted as an abuse of right. The owner may be prevented from exercising their right in such a manner.

---

38 For a comparative overview see B. AKKERMANS and W. SWADLING, "Property Rights on Land and Movable Objects", in S. VAN ERP and B. AKKERMANS (Eds.), *Texts, Cases and Materials on Property Law, Ius Commune Casebooks for the Common Law of Europe*, Hart Publishing, Oxford 2012, p. 211 *et seq.*

39 VAN DONGEN (n. 37), p. 1054, G. PINO, *Ragion practica* (2005), p. 165.

40 Possibly such an abuse also creates obligations in tort law for compensation, but as this concerns the law of obligations, this falls outside the scope of this contribution.

41 See C. DEMOLOMBE, *Traité de la distinction des biens; de la propriéte; de l'usufruit de l'usage et de l'habitation; Tome Premier*, 4th edition, Auguste Durand/L Hachette et Cie, Paris 1870, p. 464-465, AKKERMANS and SWADLING (n. 38), p. 222-223.

42 See E. LEES, "Property in the Anthropocene", (2019) 43 *William & Mary Environmental Law and Policy Review* 2, p. 541 *et seq.*

B. CONSTRUING POSITIVE OBLIGATIONS WITH EXISTING DOCTRINE

Perhaps it is also possible to go beyond this extension of the negative interference with ownership. In recent years in some legal systems, most notably in the Netherlands, the law of tort has been used to experiment with some positive obligations. In the famous climate case of *Urgenda v. State of the Netherlands*, a group of citizens attempted to hold the Dutch state accountable for climate obligations it took on.[43] The reasoning is that instead of financial compensation, a court of law holds the tortfeasor to the obligation they infringed. Although tort law is not designed for this, there are examples of similar issues, such as with the English tort of conversion that is used to protect title to personal property in English law.[44]

Possibly therefore the doctrine of abuse of rights is also open as a legal basis for the construction of a positive obligation of a landowner *propter rem*, *i.e.* an obligation that follows directly from the private law property right of ownership itself. Whether or not such an obligation can arise requires a reimagination and revaluation of the concept of landownership. Landownership is a crucial part of our social imaginary of a planet in which its occupants live within planetary boundaries. Foundational values of that imaginary are offered by planetary flourishing theory. That means that there must be a widely accepted social thesis in which everyone wants to belong to and be part of a society that supports a certain kind of political, social and moral culture, that maintains a decent background material structure, and that recognizes that we need to keep within the planetary boundaries so that not only we but also the planet can flourish.[45] It is with this *nomos* that property law comes into play. Our property *nomos* is a crucial part of achieving this new social imaginary as it is the set of rules and regulations that deal with governance of land use. As a society we allocate private parties the ability to hold a primary property right, usually the right of ownership.[46] That right is part of a larger system that includes both public and private law. Traditionally, it has been private law that has a facilitating function, enabling the owner to do with the land what they want. Public law, on the contrary, offers limitations on the powers of the owner. This has led to a classical *nomos* in which the state is seen as a limiting power that must restrict limitations

---

43 Court The Hague, 24 June 2015 (ECLI:NL:RBDHA:2015:7196), Court of Appeal The Hague, 9 October 2018 (ECLI:NL:GHDHA:2018:2610) and Dutch Supreme Court 20 December 2019 (ECLI:NL:HR:2019:2007).

44 See M. Hinteregger, "The Protection of Property Rights", in S. van Erp and B. Akkermans (Eds.), *Texts, Cases and Materials on Property Law, Ius Commune Casebooks for the Common Law of Europe*, Hart Publishing, Oxford 2012, p. 161 *et seq.*

45 See Akkermans (n. 11), p. 16 *et seq.*

46 On primary property rights see Van Erp (n. 6), p. 1517 *et seq.*

as much as possible and protect the private law enjoyment of property.[47] In the context of a new social imaginary, a new *nomos* arises in which private and public law take new perspective. From this perspective, an already ongoing reinterpretation of constitutional provisions such as Article 1 First Protocol to the European Convention on Human Rights (ECHR) to include positive state obligations makes a lot of sense. Additionally, other international agreements such as the Paris Climate Agreement, in as far as they provide binding targets, provide positive obligations for states.

Another very interesting example is offered by the Green Deal of the European Union.[48] The EU Green Deal is a policy leading to a package of fundamental legislation.[49] One of the most notable examples of binding legislation is the European Climate Law.[50] These initiatives are part of the "Fit for 55 Strategy" designed to put the EU on a climate target of a reduction of greenhouse gas emissions in the EU by at least 55% in 2030. The EU Climate Law requires Member States to submit National Energy and Climate Plans (NECPs) that will be reviewed in the EU legal framework. The Green Deal and, especially, the European Climate Law make a lot of sense in the context of a reimagined imaginary of flourishing within planetary boundaries. Article 192 of the Treaty on the Functioning of the European Union (TFEU) provides a legal basis to adopt EU legislation to fulfill the objectives listed in Article 191 TFEU. Article 191 TFEU mentions, *inter alia*, preserving, protecting and improving the quality of the environment, protecting human health, and promoting measures at international level to deal with regional or worldwide environmental problems, and in particular combating climate change, as clear objectives. It could be argued that in the same way as Articles 34, 45, 56 and 63 TFEU and implementing binding EU legislation form the European Economic Constitution, Articles 191, 192 TFEU and implementing binding EU legislation make for a European Green Constitution.[51] In a social imaginary of planetary flourishing the *nomos* of

47 See V. Smari Petersen and B. Akkermans, "Eminent Domain, Regulatory Takings and the Right to Property", in C. Bevan (Ed.), *Handbook of Property, Law and Theory*, Edward Elgar, Northampton 2024, forthcoming.

48 See https://commission.europa.eu/strategy-and-policy/priorities-2019-2024/european-green-deal_en.

49 Communication from the Commission to the European Parliament, The European Council, The Council, The European Economic and Social Committee and the Committee of the Regions, The European Green Deal COM/2019/640 final.

50 Regulation 2021/1119 of the European Parliament and of the Council of 30 June 2021 establishing the framework for achieving climate neutrality and amending Regulation No 401/2009, OJ L243, 9.7.2021, p. 1-17.

51 On the EU Economic Constitution and property law see B. Akkermans, "European Union Constitutional Property Law: searching for foundations for the allocation of regulatory competences", in B. Akkermans, J. Hage, N. Kornet and J. Smits (eds.), *Who does what? On the allocation of competences in European private law*, Intersentia, Antwerp 2015, p. 165 *et seq*.

property rules is therefore guided by rules from the EU Green Constitution that affect all national legislation. After all, the EU is supranational law and generally applies directly to vertical legal relations. Occasionally even, EU law has horizontal direct effects.[52] The rules of European Union law together with rules of national law form a single system of law that govern a single market.[53] National state obligations under measures of EU constitutional law of course primarily affect vertical relations between the state and the EU level, as well as possibly between the state and private parties. However, horizontal effects in which private parties are directly affected by the EU constitutional rules are rare. One example is perhaps the EU Energy Performance Certificates Directive, that – although it must be implemented into national law – does directly affect private landowners.[54]

This approach can be reimagined as well. There is a very small body of scholarship that suggests that in order to give effect to a state obligation, that state must offer a well-functioning system of private law.[55] In a *nomos* that is giving effect to a planetary flourishing imaginary, this would be a perfect example of collaboration between public law and private law norms and values. In order to give effect to the positive obligation of a state to meet the climate objectives from the EU Green Constitution, the system of private law, the system of property law in particular, must comply with these constitutional objectives and make a significant contribution. Such an approach requires a strong methodology on the basis of which this normative assignment can be translated into the rules that govern and facilitate everyday life. The aforementioned approach of Van der Walt comes to life here.[56] The adapted algorithm for the EU context offers a clear way forwards by stating *inter alia:*

> "h. The legislature must make legislation that gives effect to sustainability and the UN SDGs;
> i. The executive creates policy to guarantee and promote sustainability and the UN SDGs;
> j. The judiciary has as its tasks to interpret existing legislation and existing legal relations in such a way that they are aligned with sustainability and the UN SDGs;
> k. Legislation and legal relations that do not comply with these concrete SDGs and the policy made by the executive, cannot continue to exist;

52 See, e.g., P. Craig and G. de Búrca, *EU Law: Text, Cases and Materials*, 7th edition, Oxford University Press, Oxford 2020, p. 314 *et seq.*

53 Akkermans (n. 51), p. 182 *et seq.*

54 Directive 2010/31/EC of the European Parliament and the of the Council of 19 May 2010 on the energy performance of buildings.

55 See, e.g., German Constitutional Court 15 July 1981, 58 BVerfGE 300 (1981) (Groundwater Case),

56 See Van der Walt (n. 29), p. 23-24.

> l. It is the task for [...] legal academics to find out how legislation can be made, changed and interpreted in the context of sustainability and the SDGs."[57]

The doctrine of abuse of rights can be brought into this new imaginary, *nomos*, and constitutional perspective. When exercising a right of ownership, the owner can be held to refrain from doing something as they would be abusing their right of ownership. Possibly, the owner can also be compelled to do something as not acting may also constitute an abuse of right. Several examples of where this may arise come into mind.

First, in agricultural food production, especially in densely populated countries such as the Netherlands and Belgium, livestock and crop growing often happen side by side. Animal diseases, such as bird flu or fourth and mouth disease, may break out and bacteria enter the soil and ground water. That same water can be used by farmers to irrigate their crops causing food poisoning to humans when they consume these products.[58] A farmer using his right of ownership in such a manner fulfills the Pino / Van Dongen set of criteria. The use of ownership is lawful and can be exercised in many different manners. The current exercise is objectionable and creates an imbalance between the profit of the farmer and the public health interest. Besides a negative obligation to prevent contamination, the farmer could also be under a more sustainable obligation to use their land in a different manner and choose between livestock and crops, or to take additional measures to actively contribute to public health.[59]

A second example also comes from rural land. In some countries, such as Iceland, a lot of former wetlands have been transformed into farmland in the past century. The result of this public policy has been a major loss of biodiversity and a significant contrition to greenhouse gas emissions leading to climate change.[60] The government is running a program to restore wetlands, but not achieving its objectives in a timely manner. Perhaps here too, there are situations in which the owner can be compelled to restore (parts of) their land to a wetland status because otherwise they would be abusing their right of ownership.

---

57 B. Akkermans, "Sustainable Property Law. Towards a Revaluation of System of Property Law", in B. Akkermans and G. van Dijck (Eds.), *Private law and sustainability*, Eleven International Publishers, The Hague 2020, p. 54-55.

58 See, for examples on this, J. Benedict, *Poisoned. The True Story of the Deadly E.Coli Outbreak that Changed the Way Americans Eat*, February Books, New York 2013, which also formed the basis for the Netflix Documentary Poisoned: The Dirty Truth about Your Food, www.netflix.com/tudum/articles/poisoned-the-dirty-truth-about-your-food-release-date-news.

59 Another route could also be to conceptualise an obligation to offset the operations of the farmer if they choose livestock farming.

60 V. Smari Petersen, "Climate Change and the Social Function of Property – A Human Flourishing Reading of Article 1 of Protocol No 1 to the European Convention on Human Rights", in B. Hoops *et al* (Eds), *Takings for Climate Justice – Rethinking Expropriation Law*, Eleven Publishing, The Hague 2024, forthcoming. J. Madgwick, CEO, Wetlands International, on the World Economic Forum's website here (last visited 15 January 2024): www.weforum.org/agenda/2022/03/wetlands-climate-change/.

Finally, in urban settings as well positive obligations may arise out of the abuse of rights doctrine. Apartment owners are increasingly confronted with pressure to invest in reusable energy sources. The law on apartments is structured in a very complex manner attempting to mimic a situation of private ownership of apartments as if an apartment were a piece of land as much as possible. However, the proximity and technical connection creates complex legal relationships between apartment owners. Investing in reusable energy as apartment owners usually only applies to shared areas and not to apartment owners individually.[61] When apartment owners have the financial means, they could perhaps be obliged to invest in clean and reusable energy by forming an energy community in which they generate electricity not only for common areas, but also for all the apartment owners together. Not doing that, in the light of a planetary flourishing imaginary, could be reinterpreted as an abuse of right. Obligations towards the other apartment owners, or an association of apartment owners, depending on the legal system, may arise to positively contribute to achieve this aim. Such obligations would then not come directly from a higher source but arise *propter rem* to give effect to positive state obligations under the EU Green Constitution.

V. A REIMAGINED SUSTAINABLE PROPERTY LAW

As the world more and more comes to terms with the reality of climate change and the need to act to mitigate negative effects, a wide landscape of initiatives has arisen.[62] The collection of rules and regulations applying to the law of property, the *nomos* – sometimes also referred to as the "lawscape" – is very wide and very diverse.[63] Moreover, it is a manifestation of the classical model of property law. The starting point is private autonomy that requires justification for limitations imposed on this. It has led to a system in which extraction for private benefit is the norm rather than regeneration.

Thinking about sustainability, especially with an intergenerational perspective, brings friction with this classical approach to the surface. Private initiatives sometimes lead to wonderful results that become examples for other people and organizations in other countries. Many cooperative initiatives, for example for housing or farming, fulfill this objective. However, sustainability is also abused by some to continue mostly on the former ways, such as fossil fuel companies providing green energy. Therefore, other terminology is increasingly

---

61 See B. Hoops and B. Akkermans, "Goederenrecht en duurzaamheid", (2023) *Weekblad voor Privaatrecht, Notariaat en Registratie (WPNR) 7407*, p. 335-336.

62 See J. Merz *et al*, "World's scientist warning: the behavioural crisis driving ecological overshoot", (2023) *106 Science Progress 3*, https://doi.org/10.1177/00368504231201372.

63 See Graham (n. 28).

sought, such as "resilience" rather than "sustainability" to provide a much narrower definition of the shared objective. Resilience in a transformative sense means thinking about how systems and therefore the property *nomos* can be adapted to the challenges ahead.[64] The concept of social imaginary offers an even more abstract transformative direction in which resilient property law is to be taken.

In order to do this in a systemic manner with clear and transparent methodology, common agreement on the problem must be reached. The problem of eco-sustainability is clearly a wicked problem.[65] The problem cannot be solved with simple measures and requires fundamental change to legal systems as well as human behavior across borders on a global scale. At the same time each legal system also is faced with its own variation of the problem as solutions must be implemented in a particular system of law. Common thought patterns in the approach can be identified and a methodology of a reimagined social imaginary and a property *nomos* in which transformative constitutional principles provide direction for development, offers the systemic approach that is needed. At the same time, this method leaves room for differences and deviation in technical rules at the national level depending on the specifics of a legal system.

Depending on the level of scale that is dealt with, states and private actors can act together or by themselves to implement creative new solutions that offer a positive contribution towards the objective of an eco-sustainable planet. This sheds new light on positive state obligations, but also on private initiatives. One of these private initiatives is a reimagined use of the commons. The commons are a type of collective property in which several stakeholders each hold a property interest in the same object.[66] Commons are an old form of collaborative holding of property that predate the rise of national states and national codifications of private law. Commons have been analyzed extensively in the past, most notably from an economic perspective.[67] In recent years, commons have also received renewed attention from scholars such as Ugo Mattei and Alexandra Quarta.[68] Mattei and Quarta give a transformative interpretation to what commons are and what they can do. Mattei and Quarta write that "*commons institutions limit the excesses of all power concentration through direct decision-*

64 Van der Sijde (n. 3), B. Akkermans (n. 7).

65 On wicked problem theory see H. Rittel and M. Webber, "Dilemmas in a General Theory of Planning", (1973) *4 Policy Sciences 155.*

66 See F. Capra and U. Mattei, *The Ecology of Law. Toward a Legal System in Tune with Nature and Community*, Berrett-Koehler Publishers, Oakland 2015, p. 164-167.

67 See, *inter alia*, S. Munzer, "The Commons and the Anticommons in the Law and theory of Property", in M. Golding and W. Edmundson, *The Blackwell Guide to the Philosophy of Law and Legal Theory*, p. 148 *et seq.*, Wiley, London 2005, A. Stojanovic, "Commons in the Past and the Future of Law and Economics", (2019) *19 Global Jurist 3*, p. 21 *et seq.*

68 U. Mattei and A. Quarta, *The Turning Point of Private Law*, Edward Elgar, Northampton 2018, p. 48-50.

making by communities who take care of the commons [...]."[69] A commons in this perspective becomes a tool of democratization of property governance allowing for management of public goods such as natural resources or services.[70]

This more inclusive and transformative approach to commons fits very well within the reimagined *nomos* of sustainable property law developed in this contribution. Even more, instead of very contradictory to the traditional notion of exclusive and extractive ownership, it becomes an almost natural solution for joined governance of important resources. Moreover, it is a solution in which public law and private law collectively enable private parties to arrange for their own affairs. Interesting examples of such approaches to commons are offered by energy communities, but also by cooperative farming solutions. Such new initiatives lead to a different way of landholding where not only those with formal property right, but also other community members are directly and actively involved and support each other's flourishing through, for example, solidarity payment schemes in cooperative farming, enabling community members of less financial wealth to participate fully.

VI. CONCLUSION

Sustainable property law facilitates a transformative world in which no longer the individual landowner is at the organizational centre, but in which communities together connect and share resources in a regenerative manner. This approach does not mean that no private ownership exists anymore. To the contrary, it is private ownership that enables sharing in the first place and not everything, such as the privacy of the home, needs to be shared. However, in case of affluence, there may be an obligation to share in this approach.

A new social imaginary in which planetary boundaries provide not only the outer limit of how humankind treats the planet, but also give transformative direction on how the planet should be dealt with within these limits, provides input for a methodology to transform classical into sustainable property law. As the problem of climate change and loss of biodiversity becomes more and more pressing, legal systems must respond at every scale possible. This does not only concern the rise of positive state obligations, but also a reconfiguration of property law to incorporate regenerative ownership and positive obligations *propter rem*. Such a reconfiguration of property law can come from new policy and legislation but can also be achieved by reinterpretation and reinvention of existing private law doctrine. One such solution is the doctrine of abuse of rights. By providing it with a new purpose, obligations – both negative and positive – *propter rem* can be construed. Similarly private law initiatives such

69 Mattei and Quarta (n. 67), p. 52.
70 Mattei and Quarta (n. 67), p. 53.

as a reinvented commons facilitate private parties to create governance schemes that allow for an inclusive sharing or entitlement and decision making. Energy communities and cooperative housing and farming initiatives become examples of pioneering.

The development of sustainable property law can therefore be achieved by using a coordinated and methodological approach instead of keeping making *ad hoc* initiatives. A coordinated effort ensures that the system of property law is maintained and that, even though more flexibility is created through recognition of personal obligations depending on the context in which property rights are held, legal certainty also remains ensured. Systems of property law require as much foreseeability as possible, as property relations remain to have effect against third parties. In doing so a new version of property law arises allowing us to keep those aspects that fit the redevelopment algorithm. New possibilities are added to the system allowing for private sustainability initiatives, but following the redevelopment algorithm these will fit in the system instead of upsetting it.

NEIGHBOURHOOD AS MICRO-ENVIRONMENT IN THE RECODIFICATION OF PROPERTY LAW

Zsa-Zsa BOGGENPOEL
Professor in Private Law, Stellenbosch University

I. INTRODUCTION

Societies are becoming increasingly diverse, and people are living in closer proximity to each other.[1] It is inevitable that conflicts will arise amongst neighbouring owners, especially in urban areas where properties tend to be situated in closer proximity to one another.[2] At the same time, resources are becoming progressively more limited. The pursuit of a property (law) system that is also sensitive to the quest for climate and social justice should also become front and centre – even as one considers competing interests of individuals as neighbours on privately-owned land. So, how does one begin to conceptualise neighbour law provisions in a new Civil Code that account for these challenges? This was of course the monumental task that Vincent SAGEART and several other colleagues endeavoured during the (recent) Belgian Law Reform process, a process that has brought about several thought-provoking provisions in the new Belgian Civil Code, some of which will be addressed in this chapter.

The recent reforms that took place in the context of Belgian law are particularly interesting if one considers various changes that are taking place (or have taken place) in some other jurisdictions as well, including a number of interesting changes in South African law. South Africa has undergone substantial law reform in the last three decades, prompting considerable amendments to the conceptual understanding of ownership and the use of common and often limited resources – also in the context of neighbour law.[3] Interesting problems arise in the context of the extent to which neighbour law impacts on other areas

---

1 H. MOSTERT, "Nuisance", in D. VISSER & E. REID (eds.), *Private law and human rights: Bringing rights home in Scotland and South African*, 2013, pp. 256-293, 258 available at, https://papers.ssrn.com/sol3/papers.cfm?abstract_id=2275964 258 (accessed 30 August 2023).

2 A.J. VAN DER WALT, *The law of neighbours*, Juta, Cape Town 2010, p. 240.

3 A.J. VAN DER WALT, *The law of neighbours*, Juta, Cape Town 2010, pp. 45-49.

of the law in South Africa, like constitutional law, which includes environmental law. This chapter will foreground some of the developments in South Africa against the suggested changes in the new Belgian Civil Code.

The chapter will begin by providing a brief, and admittingly superficial, background to the reform or transformation of the South African (property) law landscape. This is done so that one can begin to have a conversation about how neighbour law is the micro-environment against which many reforms within a particular jurisdiction exist. Thereafter, the chapter will address the provisions of the new Belgian Civil Code in the context of nuisance law. In the final part of the chapter, some concluding remarks are provided regarding the idea of neighbourhood as a micro-environment for the recodification of property law.

II. AN OVERARCHING ACCOUNT OF THE SOUTH AFRICAN LAW REFORM LANDSCAPE

In 1997, South Africa adopted its first democratic Constitution as the supreme law of the land. From a societal perspective, the impact of the Constitution cannot be overemphasized. Its role has always been to bridge the gap caused by years of colonial and apartheid oppression. The Preamble of the South African Constitution states unequivocally that we, the people of South Africa recognise the injustices of our past and strive towards a society based on democratic values, social justice and fundamental human rights.[4] KLARE writes that "[a] *particularly appealing feature of the South African Constitution is its self-consciousness that it is an instrument committed to social transformation and reconstruction*".[5] In the final South African Constitution, we therefore see "*a grand constitutional text replete with broad phrases and redolent with magnificent hopes to overcome past injustice and move toward*[s] *a democratic and caring society*".[6] Besides its clear societal impact, the South African Constitution has also very pertinently sought to be the litmus test against which all other laws should be viewed.

From the perspective of the impact of the Constitution on the pre-existing sources of law, it is also important to note that no source of law – including the common law regulating neighbour law – is shielded from constitutional authority. In fact, the words of CHASKALSON in *Pharmaceutical Manufacturers Association of South Africa and Another: In re Ex parte President of the Republic*

4 The Preamble of the South African Constitution.

5 K.E. KLARE, "Legal culture and transformative constitutionalism" (1998) 14 *SAJHR*, 146–188, 155.

6 K.E. KLARE, "Legal culture and transformative constitutionalism" (1998) 14 *SAJHR*, 146–188, 149.

of South Africa and Others serves as a lodestar for the particular approach that should be adopted in this regard. CHASKALSON stated that[7]:

> "I cannot accept this contention which treats the common law as a body of law separate and distinct from the Constitution. There are not two systems of law, each dealing with the same subject matter, each having similar requirements, each operating in its own field with its own highest court. There is only one system of law. It is shaped by the Constitution which is the supreme law, and all law, including the common law, derives its force from the Constitution and is subject to constitutional control."[8]

Upon reflection, three decades since the enactment of the Constitution, South Africans are still trying to deal with what these reforms mean for law and society. This then, is the macro-context within which (in the words of KLARE) the project of constitutional enactment, interpretation and implementation in individual cases, like neighbour law cases, in the South African law should be viewed.[9] The extent to which the reforms and transformation as envisaged by the Constitution – as briefly highlighted above – is to influence existing rules of the common law in South Africa, is an ongoing project. This was shown fairly recently in a South African neighbour law case, namely *Ellaurie v Madrasah Taleemuddeen Islamic Institute*[10], where one sees how the court has to grapple with the question of whether constitutional rights and values could be incorporated into the long-standing reasonableness test in nuisance law. It is imperative to find a way of ensuring that societal changes necessitated by these overarching reforms are incorporated into a particular property law system that has existed for a long time. After all, neighbour law is in fact a micro-environment in property law reform – and reforms that often take place in favour of broader goals, like climate justice or social justice, have to be incorporated into long-standing legal constructs like ownership that exist within a property law paradigm.

Against this background, two thought-provoking statements become relevant as this chapter focusses on neighbour law as a micro-environment in property law reform.[11] One statement is that property law is shifting along with societal developments. The idea of absolute exclusivity, which was pre-

---

7 2000 (2) SA 674 (CC).

8 *Pharmaceutical Manufacturers Association of South Africa and Another: In re Ex parte President of the Republic of South Africa and Others* 2000 (2) SA 674 (CC) para 44.

9 K.E. KLARE, "Legal culture and transformative constitutionalism" (1998) 14 *SAJHR*, 146–188 150.

10 2021 (2) SA 163 (KZD). See also *Madrasah Taleemuddeen Islamic Institute v Chandra Giri Ellaurie and Another* [2022] ZASCA 160 (24 November 2022).

11 On 17-18 March 2023, the *Property Law Reform, Sustainability and the Commons* conference was held at the University of Leuven in Belgium. The statements discussed here were provided by conference organizers for delegates to consider and engage with in their respective papers. It forms the backbone for the analysis in this chapter.

dominant in the beginning of the 19th century, is regressing in the beginning of the 21st century. The second statement concerns the question about whether new property law legislation incorporates these changed views of property relations. These are important statements as one begins to investigate whether we are seeing the necessary shifts in the way in which neighbour law cases are being adjudicated. More specifically, it remains important to ask: To what extent are these statements true if one considers some of the developments that have taken place in the context of neighbour law, in different jurisdictions.[12] The Belgian Civil Code provisions on nuisance law provide an interesting anchor to engage in such a discussion. The following section consequently sets out those provisions, before the chapter returns to South African law to mirror how South African law deals with some of the aspects highlighted.

III. NUISANCE LAW PROVISIONS IN THE BELGIAN CIVIL CODE: SOME INTERESTING COMPARISONS

A. INTRODUCTION

Nuisance law is dealt with in Article 3.101 of the New Belgian Civil Code:

> "§ 1. Neighbors each have a right to use and to enjoy their immovable property. In the exercise of their use and enjoyment, they shall respect the created equilibrium by not imposing any nuisance on the neighbor that exceeds the normal disturbances of the neighborhood and is attributable to them. In order to assess the excessive nature of the nuisance, all the circumstances of the case shall be taken into account, such as the time, the frequency and the intensity of the nuisance, the pre-occupation or the public use of the immovable property from which the nuisance originates.
> § 2. The person who violates the established balance shall be obliged to restore it. The court shall decide which of the following measures are appropriate to restore the equilibrium:
> 1. a financial compensation that compensates for the excessive nuisance;
> 2. compensation for the costs related to the compensatory measures on the obstructed immovable property in order to reduce the nuisance to a normal level;
> 3. to the extent that this in itself does not create a new imbalance and does not preclude the normal use and enjoyment of the immovable property, an injunction to cease the act that disturbs the balance or to take measures on the immovable property which causes the nuisance to reduce it to a normal level."

12 The focus here will be on nuisance law, although it is interesting to observe a number of other provisions in the new Belgian Civil Code in the context of neighbour law. For instance, see the provisions on encroachments (Art. 3.62) and common fences (Art. 3.103-3.113).

In short, we therefore see a starting point in terms of what neighbours can expect and should do in the context of their conduct on neighbouring land. We also see some indication of particular factors that would be taken into account to determine whether the nuisance is actionable, and then of course an indication of the remedies that may be considered in instances where a neighbour's conduct purportedly amounts to nuisance. It may be worthwhile to pause here for a moment and focus on this starting point in nuisance law before proceeding in the next part of the chapter to the interesting provision (Art. 3.102) in the Civil Code aimed at preventing nuisances that impact negatively on the environment.

B. PREVENTING NUISANCES: SOME COMPARATIVE PROVISIONS

The starting point of the new Belgian Civil Code, that owners are ordinarily entitled to ward off interferences that result in "nuisance" is not new, or particularly ground-breaking. As SAGEART, DEGROOTE and VAN DER VOORDE mention in their respective contributions about the new Belgian Civil Code, the point of departure of the nuisance provisions is not novel in as much as it is a confirmation of well-established principles of Belgian law, namely that in the exercise of the ownership of property such an owner ordinarily may not cause nuisance to neighboring land – at least not the type of nuisance that exceeds the normal inconveniences of a neighbourhood.[13] One could even go as far as saying that from a comparative perspective, there seems to be the same types of starting points as far as the general limitation on the use of ownership exists preventing conduct that may impact negatively on neighboring properties.

Interestingly, Article 976 of the Civil Code of Quebec provides that "[n]*eighbours shall suffer the normal annoyances that are not beyond the limit of tolerance they owe each other, according to the nature or location of their land or local usage.*" This is essentially the same starting point as the Belgian provision outlined above, and some indication is also given of what will be taken into account in determining whether the equilibrium was disrupted. Furthermore, in section 8 of the Civil Code of Philippines, there are quite interesting and extensive provisions regarding private and public nuisance, and the purported consequences thereof. There is also Article 682, which provides an easement against nuisances, providing that "[e]*very building or piece of land is subject to the*

13 See M. DEGROOTE, "Neighbor relations in the new Belgian property law" 2021 (10) *EPLJ*, 66-80; V. SAGEART, "The background and general principles of the new Belgian property law" 2021 (10) *EPLJ*, 3-25; J. VAN DER VOORDE "'Accidental' environmental property law in Belgium, France and Germany" in J. ROBBIE (ed.), *Property Law Perspectives VII*, 2021, pp. 155-175.

easement which prohibits the proprietor or possessor from committing nuisance through noise, jarring, offensive odor, smoke, heat, dust, water, glare and other causes." Furthermore, Article 683 stipulates that "[s]*ubject to zoning, health, police and other laws and regulations, factories and shops may be maintained provided the least possible annoyance is caused to the neighborhood.*" The same starting points are therefore evident. Similarly, in the Civil Code of Hungary, in Chapter 6 under the general rules, Section 5:23, there is a general limitation on the use of things. This provision states that "[w]*hile using the thing, the owner shall refrain from any conduct unnecessarily disturbing others, in particular the neighbours, or which would jeopardise the exercise of their rights.*" This seems like a similar point of departure to the other jurisdictions. This starting point and the question about whether the equilibrium has been disrupted has also played out in interesting ways in South Africa. Of course, the devil is in the detail in terms of how courts (in the respective jurisdictions) will go about determining whether the equilibrium between neighbours has been disrupted purportedly causing more harm to a neighbor than should be expected.

C. SOUTH AFRICA: AN INTERESTING COMPARATOR

In terms of the South African common law, the notion of "neighbours" concerns neighbouring owners and their mutual and reciprocal rights and obligations to use their land in a reasonable manner, so as not to infringe upon a neighbouring owner's entitlements of use and enjoyment flowing from his or her ownership of the land.[14] In this regard, the starting point seems to be the same as in Belgian law – but also appears to be similar to the other jurisdictions – as briefly alluded to above. It is in this context that it becomes interesting to view the common law conception of ownership, generally accepted in South Africa, in light of the often-quoted case of *Gien v Gien*[15], where AJ Spoelstra held that:

> "The right of ownership is the most comprehensive real right that a person can have in respect of a thing. The point of departure is that a person can, in respect of immovable property, do with and on his property, as he pleases. This apparently unfettered freedom is, however, a half-truth. The absolute power of an owner is limited by the restrictions imposed thereupon by the law."[16]

---

14 J.R.L. Milton, "The law of neighbours in South Africa" 1969 *Acta Juridica*, 123-269, 152-156; D. Van Der Merwe, *Oorlas in die Suid-Afrikaanse reg*, 1982, pp. 437-441.

15 1979 (2) SA 1113 (T).

16 *Gien v Gien* 1979 (2) SA 1113 (T) at 1120C-E. In *Van der Merwe v Taylor* 2008 (1) SA 1 (CC) para 26 the Constitutional Court described the concept of ownership as "*potentially confers upon the owner the most complete or comprehensive right in or control over a thing*". The Court held further that: "*The most comprehensive control over the property does not imply unfettered freedom to do with the thing as one pleases. However comprehensive, and although protected against arbitrary deprivation under section 25(1), ownership like any other right, is*

Accordingly, this description of ownership as the most complete right does not suggest that ownership is absolute or that no limitations may be placed on it.[17] Rather, it is accepted that ownership has always been subject to limitations.[18] Accordingly, where the landowner's exercise of his or her *ius utendi* interferes or disturbs the neighbouring landowner's similar use right, the law limits both their rights by imposing reciprocal obligations on them.[19] Each landowner is obliged not to impose a heavier burden on neighbouring owners that they are obliged to accept.

Nevertheless, the notion of ownership as assigning absolute power over property, especially insofar as it relates to the ability to exclude others from using and enjoying the resource, was a widely accepted interpretation of the concept[20], which suited the purposes of the South African government well during the time of apartheid – during the pre-constitutional era.[21] In the South African context, ownership entitlements and the ability to exercise ownership, were specifically also affected by the race-based approach to land during the apartheid era.[22] Despite the abolition of apartheid statutes, which formalised discriminatory, race-based land use and ownership, the legacy of dispossession remains prevalent under a democratic post-apartheid

---

not absolute." See further G. Muller, R. Brits, J.M. Pienaar and Z. Boggenpoel (eds.), *Silberberg and Schoeman's The law of property*, LexisNexis, Pretoria 6 ed 2019, pp. 125-134; C.G. Van Der Merwe and A. Pope, "Property", in F.D. Bois (ed.), *Wille's principles of the South African law*, 9 ed 2007, pp. 405-665, 410; A.J. van der Walt, *The law of neighbours*, Juta, Cape Town 2010, p. 275.

17 C.G. Van Der Merwe, *Sakereg*, 2 ed 1989, pp. 176-178; G. Muller, R. Brits, J.M. Pienaar and Z. Boggenpoel (eds.), *Silberberg and Schoeman's The law of property*, LexisNexis, Pretoria 6 ed 2019, pp. 125-134.

18 A.J. van der Walt and G.J. Pienaar, *Introduction to the Law of Property*, Juta, Cape Town, 7 ed 2016, p. 93; C.G. Van Der Merwe, *Sakereg*, 2 ed 1989, pp. 176-178; H. Scott, "Absolute ownership and legal pluralism in Roman law: Two arguments" (2011) *Acta Juridica*, 23-34, 23; P. BIRKS, "The Roman law concept of dominium and the idea of absolute ownership" (1985) *Acta Juridica*, 1-37, 1; D. Visser, "The absoluteness of ownership: The South African common law in perspective" (1985) *Acta Juridica*, 39-52, 39.

19 *Gien v Gien* 1979 (2) SA 1113 (T), 1121B.

20 H. Mostert, "Land as a 'national asset' under the Constitution: The system change envisaged by the 2011 Green Paper on Land Policy and what this means for property law under the Constitution" (2014) 17 *PELJ*, 760-797 at 773.

21 *Daniels v Scribante* 2017 (4) SA 341 (CC) paras 14-21, 90. See also the following cases that illustrate the use of neighbour law as a means of preventing the establishment of new (mostly black) residential areas in the vicinity of established (mostly white) neighbourhoods: *East London Western Districts Farmers' Association v Minister of Education and Development* 1989 (2) SA 63 (A); *Diepsloot Residents' and Landowners' Association v Administrator Transvaal* 1993 (3) SA 49 (T); *Diepsloot Residents' and Landowners' Association v Administrator Transvaal* 1994 (3) SA 336 (A); *Minister of Public Works v Kyalami Ridge Environmental Association* 2001 (3) SA 1151 (CC); *Joubert v Van Rensburg* 2001 (1) SA 753 (W).

22 J.M. Pienaar, "'Unlawful occupier' in perspective: History, legislation and case law" in H. Mostert, and M.J. De Waal (eds.), *Essays in Honour of CG van der Merwe*, 2011, pp. 309-329, 311-314.

society.[23] As a result, in the constitutional dispensation, private ownership continues to exist, but must coincide with modern day practice, be aligned with future needs of the South African society, and endorse constitutional and transformational demands.[24] So, what we see is an existing body of law – nuisance law founded on the ideals mentioned above – within the ambit of constitutional and transformation demands and reforms. This makes for an exciting playground when one begins to interrogate neighbour law as a micro-environment for property law reforms.

Under a constitutional framework that requires the promotion and protection of human rights and is founded on fundamental values such as human dignity, equality and freedom, there is a need to develop a society based on "*good neighbourliness and shared concern.*"[25] Accordingly, Van der Walt refers to "neighbours" as "*people living more or less closely together as members of communities, citizens of the new constitutional democracy without necessarily actually residing on or using adjoining parcels of land*".[26] It is in this context that the principle of reasonableness governing nuisance law aims to harmonise and balance out respective rights, interests and obligations and solve disputes.

While there are many descriptions of "nuisance"[27], it seems that the common conception is that a nuisance is an action (or omission) that disturbs or interferes with the "*use and enjoyment of neighbouring property in a way that exceeds what could reasonably be expected of a neighbour to tolerate.*"[28] In this regard, the law of nuisance encapsulates "*mutual and reciprocal rights and obligations of reasonable use and tolerance that neighbouring owners and occupiers owe one another.*"[29] This idea of reciprocity, which we also see in other jurisdictions including Belgium, entails that neighbours must use their land reasonably but are also obliged to tolerate and accept reasonable inferences or "annoyances" emanating from normal and lawful use of land by their neighbours and the community. In sum, this foundational principle of reasonableness in the law of nuisance should require neighbouring owners and occupiers[30] to refrain

---

23 A.J. van der Walt, *The law of neighbours*, Juta, Cape Town 2010, p. 381.

24 G. Muller, R. Brits, J.M. Pienaar and Z. Boggenpoel (eds.), *Silberberg and Schoeman's The law of property*, LexisNexis, Pretoria 6 ed 2019, p. 93; *First National Bank of SA Ltd t/a Wesbank v Commissioner for the South African Revenue Services; First National Bank of SA Limited t/a Wesbank v Minister of Finance* 2002 (4) SA 768 (CC) paras 49-50; *Offit Enterprises v Coega Development Corporation (Pty) Ltd* 2011 (1) SA 293 (CC) para 46.

25 *Port Elizabeth Municipality v Various Occupiers* 2005 (1) SA 217 (CC) para 37.

26 A.J. van der Walt, *The law of neighbours*, Juta, Cape Town 2010, p. 49.

27 D. Van Der Merwe, "Neighbour law" in R. Zimmerman and D. Visser (eds.), *Southern Cross: Civil law and common law in South Africa*, 1996, pp. 759-784 at 759; G. Muller, R. Brits, J.M. Pienaar and Z. Boggenpoel (eds.), *Silberberg and Schoeman's The law of property*, LexisNexis, Pretoria 6 ed 2019, p.125.

28 A.J. van der Walt, *The law of neighbours*, Juta, Cape Town 2010, p. 239.

29 G. Muller (ed) *General principles of the South African property law* (2019) 85; J.R.L. Milton, "The law of neighbours in South Africa" (1969) *Acta Juridica*, 123-269 at 137.

30 A.J. van der Walt, *The law of neighbours*, Juta, Cape Town 2010, p. 241.

from using their property in a way that causes unnecessary or unreasonable discomfort or harm to a neighbour or the community.[31]

Whether a particular infringement emanating from neighbouring properties, in the form of smoke[32], unpleasant smells[33], fumes, disease[34], vibrations or noise[35] is unreasonable, is entirely a contextual question.[36] South African courts have adopted the objective reasonableness standard to determine whether the interference amounts to unreasonable use of the property.[37] In particular, the question is whether a reasonable or "*normal man of sound and liberal tastes and habits*", rather than a "*perverse or finicking or over-scrupulous person*", would have tolerated the interference.[38] To determine whether a neighbour's use is objectively reasonable, a range of contextual factors may be taken into account, including[39]: the locality (zoning) and use of the property in the neighbourhood in which the alleged nuisance takes place (milieu)[40]; the gravity, extent and duration of the interference[41]; the personality or sensitivity and motive of the

---

31 D. Van Der Merwe, "Neighbour Law" in R. Zimmermann and D. Visser (eds.), *Southern Cross –Civil Law and Common Law in South* Africa, 1996, p. 759; G. Muller, R. Brits, J.M. Pienaar and Z. Boggenpoel (eds.), *Silberberg and Schoeman's The law of property*, LexisNexis, Pretoria 6 ed 2019, pp. 125-126; A.J. van der Walt, *The law of neighbours*, Juta, Cape Town 2010, p. 237.

32 C.G. Van Der Merwe, *Sakereg*, 2 ed 1989, p. 188; J. Church and J. Church, "Nuisance" in W.A. Joubert, J.A. Faris and L.T.C. Harms (eds.), *The law of South Africa*, vol 19 2 ed 2006, pp. 115-145, para 188.

33 C.G. Van Der Merwe, *Sakereg*, 2 ed 1989, p. 188; J. Church and J. Church, "Nuisance" in W.A. Joubert, J.A. Faris and L.T.C. Harms (eds.), *The law of South Africa*, vol 19 2 ed 2006, pp. 115-145 para 186.

34 *PGB Boerdery Beleggings (Edms) Bpk and Another v Somerville 62 (Edms) Bpk and Another* 2008 (2) SA 428 (SCA).

35 C.G. Van Der Merwe, *Sakereg*, 2 ed 1989, p. 187-188; J. Church and J. Church, "Nuisance" in W.A. Joubert, J.A. Faris and L.T.C. Harms (eds.), *The law of South Africa*, vol 19 2 ed 2006, pp 115-145, para 187; *Blacker v Carter* 1905 19 EDC 223; *Graham v Dittman & Son* 1917 TPD 288; *Van de Berg v OVS Landbou Ingenieurs (Edms) Bpk* 1956 (4) SA 391 (O); *Die Vereniging van Advokate (TPA) v Moskeeplein (Edms) Bpk* 1982 (3) SA 159 (T); *Mosekeeplein (Edms) Bpk v Die Vereniging van Advokate* (TPA) 1983 (3) SA 896 (T); *De Charnoy v Day Star Hatchery (Pty) Ltd* 1967 (4) SA 188 (D); *Ferreira v Grant* 1941 WLD 186; *Leith v Port Elizabeth Museum Trustees* 1934 EDL 211; *Gien v Gien* 1979 (2) SA 1113 (T); *Nelson Mandela Metropolitan Municipality v Greyvenouw CC* 2004 (2) SA 81 (SE); *Laskey v Showzone* CC 2007 2 SA 48 (C); *Prinsloo v Shaw* 1938 AD 570.

36 A.J. van der Walt, *The law of neighbours*, Juta, Cape Town 2010, p. 272.

37 *Holland v Scott* 1882 EDC 307; *Prinsloo v Shaw* 1938 AD 57; *Die Vereniging van Advokate (TPA) v Moskeeplein (Edms) Bpk* 1982 (2) All SA 164 (T) at 167. See also *Vogel v Crewe* 2004 (1) All SA 587 (T).

38 *Prinsloo v Shaw* 1938 AD 570 at 590. See further A.J. van der Walt, *The law of neighbours*, Juta, Cape Town 2010, pp. 275-276.

39 G. Muller, R. Brits, J.M. Pienaar and Z. Boggenpoel (eds.), *Silberberg and Schoeman's The law of property*, LexisNexis, Pretoria 6 ed 2019, p. 126.

40 *Malherbe v Ceres Municipality* 1951 (4) SA 510 (A); *Laskey v Showzone CC* and Others 2007 (2) SA 48 (C).

41 See *Allaclas Investments (Pty) Ltd and Another v Milernton Golf Club* 2008 (3) SA 134 (SCA); *Laskey v Showzone* 2007 (2) SA 48 (C).

person affected[42]; the utility (benefit) impact for neighbouring owners and occupiers and the community at large; the social and economic conditions and customs that prevail in the community; the practicality of preventing the alleged nuisance; and/or whether there are less restrictive means or measures available to minimise the neighbour's discomfort or harm.[43] These are ordinarily understood as the general principles relating to reasonableness, at least in the context of nuisance law in South Africa. These notions of reasonableness and normal use are essentially commonplace and accepted quite easily in South African law as the standard to determine whether certain conduct amounts to nuisance. However, these notions may need to be more fully fleshed out and reconsidered in the new constitutional dispensation.[44]

In the recent case of *Ellaurie v Madrasah Taleemuddeen Islamic Institute* this point is illustrated. In this case, there are two neighbouring properties owned by the applicant and the respondent respectively. The applicant averred that:

> "The Call to Prayer [emanating from the respondent's property] is a foreign sound, which invades his private space. He alleged that it deprives him of the enjoyment of his property and interrupts his peace and quiet. It further disrupts his sleep, listening to music and meditation. ... [T]he Call to Prayer which came from the respondent's property also – according to the applicant – gave the suburb in which the parties lived a distinctly Muslim atmosphere. The applicant went on to claim that it attracts those of the Islamic faith and keeps non-Muslims away. The Muslim community in the area had apparently increased by 30 percent in the past 15 years and turned it into a Muslim enclave."[45]

Despite the High Court highlighting that the applicant is "*unashamedly opposed to the Islamic faith*" and that the applicant regards Islam as "*a false religion that discriminates against non-Muslims as non-believers*", the court nevertheless awarded an interdict on the basis that the religious practices, the Call to Prayer, infringed upon the applicant's use and enjoyment of his property rights. The High Court judgment has very little engagement with the sound and established reasonableness principle in neighbour law. The court simply granted

---

42 See *Holland v Scott* 1882 EDC 307 at 322; *Prinsloo v Shaw* 1938 AD 570 at 590.

43 *Regal v African Superslate (Pty) Ltd* 1963 (1) SA 102 (A); *Gien v Gien* 1979 (2) SA 1113 (T); *Laskey v Showzone* 2007 (2) SA 48 (C). It is of course interesting, and I thank K. De Schepper for reminding me of this, that under Belgian law, some of these factors cannot be taken into account for the question whether there is excessive nuisance. For instance, the personal sensitivity of the affected person and whether there are less restrictive means to minimise the effect for the neighbour are factors that are only considered when determining a sanction for nuisance, rather than the determination of whether a nuisance has occurred or whether it was excessive.

44 T. Kotze and Z. Boggenpoel, "Living together as neighbours: Rethinking the reasonableness standard in nuisance law under the Constitution" (2021) 24 *PELJ*, 1-32.

45 *Ellaurie v Madrasah Taleemuddeen Islamic Institute* (3848/2019) [2020] ZAKZDHC 32 (21 August 2020) paras 6-7.

an interdict in favour of an owner and essentially failed to consider the various factors applicable, including the opposing rights and interests of the property owners and the community as a whole, in establishing whether the actions of the respondent truly amounted to an actionable nuisance. The court neglected to consider the locality or character of the neighbourhood, the social utility of the Call to Prayer for the broader community (especially during a time of a pandemic where people arguably find comfort in their religious practices) and whether there are less restrictive means of mitigating the noise caused by the Call to Prayer. It also failed to determine whether the applicant is not simply an over-scrupulous or oversensitive neighbour.

Interestingly, this case went on appeal to the Supreme Court of Appeal (SCA), where the SCA mentioned that although owners *do* have the right to undisturbed use and enjoyment of property, such a right is not unlimited.[46] The court went on to mention that "[a] *limited interference with property rights and enjoyment thereof by owners of other properties in the same neighbourhood is expected and acceptable in law.*" The reasonableness test is therefore, according to the court, the standard to determine whether the nuisance is actionable. Furthermore, the SCA in *Ellaurie* emphasised the factors to determine the reasonableness threshold, showing quite pertinently that sensitivity of a particular person to the purported harm should be taken into account. In this regard, the court concluded that "*the interference or harm occasioned to the plaintiff was not unreasonable, because he suffered from a condition that caused him to be extraordinarily sensitive to the noise nuisance on which his claim was founded.*" The court therefore viewed Mr. Ellaurie as an especially and extraordinarily sensitive complainant. Moreover, Mr. Ellaurie also failed to show the nature and level of noise and how long it lasted. Reasonableness could therefore not be determined because Mr. Ellaurie was a particularly sensitive person. On this basis, the SCA held that Mr. Ellaurie's application for an interdict failed. It is also worth mentioning that the court took freedom of religion – a constitutional right in South Africa – into account in finding in favour of the Madrasah. The court found that "*the submission was well made on behalf of the Madrasah that the reasonableness assessment in this case had to take into account and balance the countervailing constitutional rights.*"[47]

What remains to be researched in South African law is whether the common-law reasonableness test of nuisance law can sufficiently take constitutional rights into account? It remains crucial to consider the interplay between reforms as envisaged under the Supreme Constitution, and the micro-environment of neighbour law, which is essentially grounded in the common law. This is because very often courts must adjudicate private disputes between

46 *Madrasah Taleemuddeen Islamic Institute v Chandra Giri Ellaurie and Another* [2022] ZASCA 160 (24 November 2022) para 7.

47 *Madrasah Taleemuddeen Islamic Institute v Chandra Giri Ellaurie and Another* [2022] ZASCA 160 (24 November 2022) para 18.

neighbours where human rights (or other constitutional rights) are potentially at stake. Normatively, the law of nuisance should be influenced by human rights mechanisms to transform neighbour law more broadly. In this sense, intuitively, one would expect some indication that the institution of ownership is impacted by a changed application of neighbour law in the constitutional dispensation. Interestingly in this regard, SCOTT did a survey of South African nuisance and encroachment law cases up to 2005 and concluded that at least in the context of nuisance law cases, she did not detect a general tendency to deviate from the existing approach to ownership – being absolute ownership as a point of departure.[48] VAN DER WALT criticises SCOTT's conclusion.[49] He points out that the cases that Scott used to come to her conclusion required "*nothing more than small incremental adaptations that improve*[d], *clarif*[ied] *or expand*[ed] *on well-settled doctrinal explanation*[s] *of the reasonableness standard*".[50] Therefore, the examples that Scott used in her analysis took place according to VAN DER WALT "*within the sphere of equal privilege and power amongst neighbouring landowners*."[51] In SCOTT's defence, she does mention: "A*n issue, which I find interesting, but which falls outside the scope of this article, refers to the limitation of ownership by specific individual human rights protected in the Constitution of the Republic of South Africa 1996*."[52] It may be in these instances, where even Scott may have to concede that nuisance law has resulted in a changed theoretical understanding of ownership.

The interplay between the constitutional, human rights paradigm and law of nuisance may raise expectations around different lifestyles, where property and other constitutional rights and interests of diverse and changing neighbourhoods may be difficult to balance out and reconcile. Property rights may conflict with other fundamental human rights such as, the right to equality (Section 9), privacy (Section 14), personal security and development (Section 12), the right to exercise a profession (Section 22), environment (Section 24), housing (Section 26), health (Section 27) and religious/cultural freedom (Sections 15 and 28). These constitutionally protected rights could (and arguably should) influence the understanding of the reasonableness standard in nuisance law. This does not mean that the exercise of human rights will in all instances amount to reasonable use of the property. In this respect, courts are tasked with the responsibility of ensuring that all considerations and factors must be weighed up to establish whether the use of the property amounts to an actionable nuisance. This issue came up the judgment of *Ellaurie v Madrasah Taleemuddeen Islamic*

48 S. SCOTT, "Recent developments in case law regarding neighbour law and its influence on the concept of ownership" (2005) 16 *Stell LR*, 351-377.

49 A.J. VAN DER WALT, *The law of neighbours*, Juta, Cape Town 2010, pp. 43-48.

50 A.J. VAN DER WALT, *Property in the margins*, Hart, Oregan, 2009, p. 25, footnote 56.

51 A.J. VAN DER WALT, *Property in the margins*, Hart, Oregan, 2009, p. 25, footnote 56.

52 See S. SCOTT, "Recent developments in case law regarding neighbour law and its influence on the concept of ownership" (2005) 16 *Stell LR*, 351-377 at 352.

Institute as mentioned above. This raises very important questions about the role of nuisance law in regulating not only the conduct on neighbouring parcels of land as such, but also as a mechanism to prevent broader social harms, like harm to the environment. This observation is interesting in light of the provision that has been added to the Belgian Civil Code, namely Article 3.102.

D. ARTICLE 3.102 OF THE NEW BELGIAN CIVIL CODE

This provision regarding the use of nuisance claims to protect the broader environment or public interest-related claims based on nuisance, like public health, safety and welfare, which is of course limited to serious and manifest risks to safety, health and pollution[53], is really encouraging and thought-provoking. DEGROOTE explains that this addition to the new Civil Code, provides an additional private law mechanism to ensure an element of sustainability – in some modest form.[54] In her analysis of the importance of this provision, she emphasises that it recognises that property law is not just about regulating private relationships as regards nuisances and its impact on private individual's ownership, and finding appropriate remedies for such nuisances; it is also about recognising the social obligations that neighbours have regarding the environment and issues around sustainability. In a very real sense, it takes into account the realities of how neighbour law functions within a bigger social order. SAGEART, in his turn, writes that such a preventative measure is favourable because it is better to prevent nuisances that pose specific risks to the environment than to grant a remedy *ex post facto*.[55] It would therefore be incredibly interesting to see how this provision will play out in future, especially if we accept normatively that private property rules and constructs must be mindful and structured in such a way that the broader goals of ensuring health, safety and environment are key to understanding how the private property rules are interpreted. SCOTFORD and WALSH posit that "*property lawyers must take seriously environmental regimes and their public law dimensions, just as environmental lawyers must engage with the doctrinally and theoretically rich property law landscape within which environmental controls operate.*"[56] These authors therefore call for a symbiotic relationship between property rights and environmental regulation.[57]

---

53 My thanks to K. DE SCHEPPER for highlighting this point.

54 M. DEGROOTE, "Neighbor relations in the new Belgian property law" 2021 (10) *EPLJ*, 66-80 at 67.

55 V. SAGEART, "The background and general principles of the new Belgian property law" 2021 (10) *EPLJ*, 3-25 at 24.

56 E. SCOTLAND and R. WALSH, "The symbiosis of property and English environmental law – Property rights in a public law context" (2013) 76 *MLR*, 1010-1045, 1011.

57 E. SCOTLAND and R. WALSH, "The symbiosis of property and English environmental law – Property rights in a public law context" (2013) 76 *MLR*, 1010-1045, 1015.

In South African law, there have been some fascinating developments that have taken place in the context of the doctrine of public nuisance that impact on the interplay between principles of nuisance law and the environment. South African law took over the English-law notion of public nuisance mostly in cases where normal or ordinary nuisance affected or caused discomfort for the public at large. The idea also being that public nuisance could be used – as in English law – as a way to protect the public against environmental degradation. However, if one looks at the cases in South Africa purportedly adopting this idea of public nuisance, it is clear that a different class of cases evolved early on in South Africa. This class essentially consisted of residents of fairly well established, often white, neighbourhoods complaining about informal settlements, mostly inhabited by black, poor communities resulting in public nuisance. VAN DER WALT makes the argument that in these cases where the public nuisance doctrine was used, it is highly suspect, and reminiscent of apartheid-style forced removals, where occupiers were often "evicted" summarily from land using common law constructs.[58] The added mischief in the constitutional dispensation of allowing this permutation of public nuisance would of course be the by-passing of eviction legislation using a common law construct like nuisance law. Therefore, VAN DER WALT argues that "*in circumstances where current landowners attempt to prevent housing developments in their vicinity, ... greater caution is required – their wish to have their neighbourhoods undisturbed by new (lawful but possibly troublesome) developments cannot be protected as of right in a country plagued by historical injustices resulting in forced removals and continuing massive homelessness.*"[59]

That is not to say that there may not be room to develop the doctrine of public nuisance as an effective remedy to prevent instances where the public safety, health and/or environment are at stake, but it does seem unlikely in the South African context. Even barring the instances where it is not favourable to use the remedy as argued by VAN DER WALT above, and legitimate reasons can therefore be advanced to avoid its use in those contexts, it is also important to recognise that in most of the instances where public safety, health and the environment are at stake in South Africa, it is regulated by legislation, and the need for the common law of nuisance to play any real or significant role becomes somewhat redundant. For instance, in the context of the environment, South Africa has various pieces of legislation that has been put in place to give effect to Section 24 of the Constitution, which is South Africa's environmental right under the Constitution. The National Environmental Management Act 107 of 1998 (NEMA) is South Africa's framework environmental legislation.[60] There

58 A.J. VAN DER WALT, *The law of neighbours,* Juta, Cape Town 2010, p. 307.

59 A.J. VAN DER WALT, *The law of neighbours,* Juta, Cape Town 2010, p. 308.

60 I. CURRIE and J. DE WAAL, *The Bill of Rights Handbook*, Juta, Cape Town, 6 ed 2013, pp. 528-529.

are also many other pieces of legislation (so-called specific environmental management Acts) that have been enacted in South Africa to give effect, broadly speaking, to Section 24 of the South African Constitution, namely: the Environment Conservation Act 73 of 1989; the National Water Act 36 of 1998; the National Environmental Management: Protected Areas Act 57 of 2003; the National Environmental Management: Biodiversity Act 10 of 2004; the National Environmental Management: Air Quality Act 39 of 2004; the National Environmental Management: Integrated Coastal Management Act 24 of 2008; and the National Environmental Management: Waste Act 59 of 2008. Furthermore, in terms of Section 32(1) of NEMA, any person or group of persons may seek appropriate relief in respect of any breach or threatened breach of any provision of this Act, including a principle contained in Chapter 1, or any other statutory provision concerned with the protection of the environment or the use of natural resources. The section therefore provides the *locus standi* for anyone wishing to make a claim that the conduct or activities of a neighbour causes excessive harm or environmental degradation, to do so in terms of this provision. It would therefore be unnecessary to use the doctrine of public, or even private, nuisance in the quest to protect the environment in the South African context.

IV. CONCLUDING REMARKS

It is impossible to determine *a priori* how any provision aimed at ensuring reform will fare. Only time will tell. What is clear is that the new provisions in the Belgian Civil Code aimed at regulating nuisance law are aimed at providing greater clarity about when conduct on neighbouring property amounts to nuisance and what the consequences of such conduct are likely to be. In this regard, this chapter has shown that the position espoused in the new Belgian Civil Code accords with the starting points in nuisance law in a number of other jurisdictions including South Africa.

An interesting, and perhaps more novel, addition to the new Belgian Civil Code is the provision that aims to broaden the scope of the sustainability duty related to the use of (neighbouring) land. Ensuring that environmental considerations are brought into the realm of neighbour law is imperative and should be welcomed in any jurisdiction. Regarding the interplay between existing neighbour law principles and environmental considerations, some interesting questions have arisen in the South African law context as shown in the chapter. It became clear that not all the (initial) jurisprudential developments in South Africa in this regard were favourable. It is also not clear that a private law mechanism – undergirded in private or public nuisance – to ensure environmental protection will necessarily be used, given the plethora of legislation that exists in South Africa in this context. Nonetheless, it remains to be seen whether provisions of this nature will be utilised effectively in Belgian law to prevent the kind of harms to the environment and public health that it seeks to achieve. It will certainly provide an additional mechanism in private law to take greater care of property so as not to impact negatively on neighbouring properties by causing threats in relation to safety, health, or pollution.

SUSTAINABILITY AS A RULE OF CONDUCT IN THE RECODIFICATION OF PROPERTY LAW

Dorothy GRUYAERT
Assistant professor, KU Leuven and KULAK

I. INTRODUCTION: THE EMERGENCE OF SUSTAINABILITY IN PRIVATE LAW RELATIONS

1. In recent times, the call for sustainability rises as the global problem of climate change becomes more and more urgent. Gone are the days when sustainable development was perceived to be merely a matter of public law, i.e. a political stance or ambition of public authorities. Nowadays, there is an increasing pressure on companies and private individuals to take on their responsibilities and to limit activities that might harm the environment. There is an abundance of regulatory instruments aiming for such behavioural change, for example, within the Green Deal of the European Commission.[1] An interesting example at a national level can be found in a recent decision of the Flemish Council for Permit Disputes in the petrol station case.[2] The Council approved the refusal of a building permit for a petrol station that did not provide for carbon neutral options. The Council also stated:

---

1 Communication from the Commission to the European Parliament, the European Council, the Council, the European Economic and Social Committee and the Committee of the Regions, *The European Green Deal*, COM/2019/640 final. This has led to a lot of sustainability legislation, e.g. Directive (EU) 2022/2464 of the European Parliament and of the Council of 14 December 2022 amending Regulation (EU) No 537/2014, Directive 2004/109/EC, Directive 2006/43/EC and Directive 2013/34/EU, as regards corporate sustainability reporting *OJ L* 322, 16 December 2022; Proposal for a Directive of the European Parliament and of the Council on the energy performance of buildings, COM/2021/802 final.

2 Council for Permit Disputes 22 April 2021, no. RvVb-S-2021-0923, *Amén.* 2022 (reflection A. VANDAELE), vol. 3, 224, *TMR* 2021, vol. 4, 380, note H. SCHOUKENS, *TROS* 2022, afl. 105, 35, note S. DE MEUE; Council for Permit Disputes 9 December 2021, no. RvVb-A-2122-0276, *Amén.* 2022 (reflection A. VANDAELE), vol. 3, 224, *TROS* 2022, vol. 105, 35, note S. DE MEUE.

> "Climate goals not only require efforts from the municipality as an organisation, but also efforts from its citizens and companies who are vested or want to be vested on its territory."

Beyond sustainable development as a key organizing principle[3] for policy decisions and regulations, property right holders are asked to take up responsibility and to consider the environment and the interests of others. This is reflected *inter alia* in more and more environmental regulations that limit the rights of individuals. Graham puts it aptly as follows:

> "Reforming law to address the climate crisis involves greater regulation of private interests to pursue the global goal of sustaining organised human societies and thus addressing conflict between individual freedoms and collective exigencies."[4]

With regard to property law, environmental regulations limit the freedom of the private individual *inter alia* to produce and construct respectively movable and immovable goods to reduce their ecological impact.[5] Apart from specific public regulations that have an impact on private individuals, the branches of private law itself can also be used to protect the environment. Property law in particular is a field of law that has a lot of potential for environmental protection, since property law determines the allocation of and our relationship with goods.[6] Property rules are therefore a crucial component in the system of regulation.[7] An important example in the context of this book is the protection of natural resources by qualifying them as commons, not capable of appropriation (see below).

2. The potential of property law for sustainable development extends even further. Property law not only governs the rights, but also the obligations that legal subjects have in relation to goods. That leaves a window of opportunity for the implementation of sustainable behaviour in property law. The question arises whether, in current times, property right holders should not *always* consider

---

3 J. Robbie and E. Van Der Sijde, "Assembling a sustainable system: exploring the systemic constitutional approach to property in the context of sustainability", *Loyola Law Review* 2020, vol. 66, (553) 555.

4 N. Graham, "Teaching private law in a Climate Crisis", *University of Queensland Law Journal*, vol. 40, no. 3, 2021, (403) 403.

5 See also the other examples mentioned by M. Habdas in her contribution to this book.

6 P. Lequet, *L'ordre public environnemental et le contrat de droit privé*, Paris, LGDJ, 2022, 6.

7 D. Grinlinton and P. Taylor, "Property Rights and Sustainability: Toward a New Vision of Property" in D. Grinlinton and P. Taylor (eds.), *Property Rights and Sustainability: The Evolution of Property Rights to Meet Ecological Challenges* in *Legal Aspects of Sustainable Development*, vol. XI, Leiden, Martinus Nijhoff Publishers, 2011, (1), 9; J. Robbie, "Moving Beyond Boundaries in the Pursuit of Sustainable Property Law" in B. Akkermans and G. Van Dijck (eds.), *Sustainability and Private Law*, The Hague, Eleven International Publishing, 2020, (59) 73.

the impact of their behaviour on their environment and on future generations? This article will look into this opportunity of "sustainability as a general rule of conduct" to tackle the rising concerns about the decisive impact of human activity on the environment and on the possibilities for future generations to meet their own needs.

The aim of this article is to analyse recent recodifications of property law to see whether these law reforms reflect this idea of sustainable behaviour in a property law context. Some recent private law reforms approach the protection of the environment merely from the field of liability law.[8] Other legal systems do include ecological protection in their property law. This article aims to provide an overview of the recent property rules that have the potential to impose a sustainable behaviour on private individuals. The research question is: What specific rules to enhance sustainability are included in the recodification of property law and does this amount to a general rule of conduct? The main emphasis will be on the recent property law reform in Belgium, which has been in force since 1 September 2021, which we will compare with the law reform in other legal systems, such as Québec, the Netherlands and France. In Chapter III, we also discuss the recent law reform in China and the introduction of the "green principle" as a rule of conduct in the Chinese Civil Code (2020). However, due to language constraints, the reader should consider this as a high-level comparison based on the limited sources available in English.

II. THE RISE OF SUSTAINABLE BEHAVIOUR IN PROPERTY LAW REFORMS

A. THE USE OF COMMONS

3. A first indication of the fact that recent property law reforms expect legal subjects to act in a sustainable way can be found in the rules on the commons. Common objects are resources that belong to or affect the whole of a community, including natural materials such as air and running water. Commons are in principle excluded from private ownership not linked to the model of appropriation and their use is common to all.[9] An example of a legal ground for the use of commons in the property law reform movements is the Civil Code of Québec. According to Article 913, paragraph 1 of the Québec Civil Code, certain things may not be appropriated; their use, common to all, is governed

8 See e.g. Art. 6:535 (2) Hungarian Civil Code: "*A person who causes damage by his activity endangering the human environment shall be liable according to the rules on liability for hazardous operations.*"

9 G. Hardin, "The Tragedy of the Commons: The population problem has no technical solution; it requires a fundamental extension in morality", *Science* 1968, vol. 162, 1243-1248.

by general laws and, in certain respects, by the Civil Code. However, water and air not intended for public utility may be appropriated if collected and placed in receptacles (Art. 913, para 2 Québec Civil Code).

Belgian property law also contains an explicit legal provision on the commons. According to the old Belgian Civil Code, which remained into force until 31 August 2021, common objects belong to no one, and their use is common to all. Their use is governed by police laws (Art. 714 old Belgian Civil Code). From a historical perspective, commons were considered to be abundant and therefore everybody had free access and use.[10] In recent times, there is however a growing concern and awareness that our natural resources are limited.

4. Against this background, the recent Belgian property law reform[11] took it one step further and explicitly provides that commons should be used sustainably. Article 3.43, paragraph 1 of the Belgian Civil Code now stipulates that:

> "Common objects cannot be appropriated in their entirety. They do not belong to anyone and are used *in the public interest, including the interest of future generations*. Their use is common to all and is governed by special laws." (own emphasis)

The importance of this legal innovation should not be underestimated. The Belgian legislator explicitly refers to the interest of future generations as a guiding principle to judge upon the use of common objects. Private individuals should behave in a sustainable way when making use of common objects. The use of commons does not only concern the user's private interest, but also the interest of future generations.[12] In the explanatory memorandum, the legislator argues that this attention to the interests of future generations is in response to climate change and the growing ecological and social awareness of the public.[13]

---

10 H. De Page and R. Dekkers, *Traité élémentaire de droit civil belge*, V, *Les principaux contrats usuels, Les biens*, Brussels, Bruylant, 1975, 537: "*On désigne sous ce nom* [res communes] *certaines choses qui ne sont pas susceptibles d'appropriation exclusive, et qui d'ailleurs,* par leur abondance, *se prêtent constamment à l'usage de tous.*" (own emphasis). See also: F. Barriere, 'Turbulence over Wind Turbines: *Res Communis* under the Spotlights", *ERPL* 2012, vol. 44, (1149) 1154; G. Hardin, "The Tragedy of the Commons: The population problem has no technical solution; it requires a fundamental extension in morality", *Science* 1968, vol. 162, 1243-1248.

11 See for an overview of the Belgian property law reform: V. Sagaert, A. Appelmans, S. Baeyens, G. Degeest, M.-L. Degroote, B. Maeschaelck and B. Verheye, "Act of 4 February 2020 containing Book 3 "Property" of the Civil Code Belgian Official Gazette 17 March 2020", *European Property Law Journal* 2021, vol. 10, no. 1, 108-176. https://doi.org/10.1515/eplj-2021-0009.

12 See also U. Mattei and A. Quarta, *The Turning Point in Private Law. Ecology, Technology and the Commons*, Cheltenham/Northampton, Elgar, 2019, 48.

13 *Parl.St.* Kamer 2019-20, no. 173/2, 5.

The legislator also refers to the current times of possible scarcity and the growing concern about ecology and environment in our society.[14]

5. Although the Dutch Civil Code does not contain a legal provision on the use of commons, some scholars do advocate for a more sustainable use of water, a very valuable common object, in the interest of future generations.[15] Additionally, Article 5:39 of the Dutch Civil Code states that, with regard to the private use of water, a parcel owner may not cause harm to the owners of surrounding parcels by changing the course, the amount or the nature of the water that is flowing over his parcel or the groundwater or by using the water that is on his parcel but is physically connected to the water on someone else's parcel. The same is true for an owner who uses public or running water from an adjacent parcel (Art. 5:40 Dutch Civil Code). The owner of a higher piece of land always has a responsibility towards the owner of the lower piece of land with regard to the water that runs from his land to the lower land.[16] In the United States as well, there is case law where the private interest of an owner to use groundwater cannot supersede the common interest of the community.[17]

The Québec Civil Code also contains a specific division with rules on the use of water. According to Article 980 Québec Civil Code, an owner who has a spring on his land may use it and dispose of it. He may, for his needs, use water from the lakes and ponds that are entirely on his land, taking care to preserve their quality. Article 981 Québec Civil Code stipulates that a riparian owner may, for his needs, make use of a lake, the headwaters of a watercourse or any other watercourse bordering or crossing his land. As the water leaves his land, he shall direct it, not substantially changed in quality or quantity, into its regular course. No riparian owner may by his use of the water prevent other riparian owners from exercising the same right. A private land owner should thus consider the

---

14 *Parl.St.* Kamer 2019-20, no. 173/001, 108.

15 O. Spijkers, "Equity across Generations in International and Domestic Water Law" in T. Cottier, S. Lalani and C. Siziba (eds.), *Intergenerational equity: environmental and cultural concerns*, Leiden/Boston, Brill Nijhoff, 2019, (90) 90: *"If we care about the plight of future generations, it is necessary for the present generation to use these freshwater resources sustainably, in a way that does not compromise the ability of future generations to benefit from the same resources. There are different ways to give substance to this obligation of sustainable use."* Sustainable water use management does not only entail obligations for public authorities, but also for citizens, as is shown by a.o.: L. Dai, R. Wörner and H.F.M.W. Van Rijswick, "Rainproof cities in the Netherlands: approaches in Dutch water governance to climate-adaptive urban planning", *International Journal of Water Resources Development* 2018, vol. 34, no. 4, 652–674.

16 B. Akkermans, "Sustainable Ownership – new obligations towards achieving a sustainable society", *EPLJ* 2021, vol. 10(2–3), (277) 279.

17 A. Di Robilant, "Abuse of Rights: The Continental Drug and the Common Law", *Hastings Law Review* 2010, vol. 61, (687) 722, with reference to *Katz* v. *Walkinshaw*, 70 P. 663, 663-64 (Cal. 1902): *"In short, the members of the community, in the case supposed, have a common interest in the water. It is necessary for all, and it is an anomaly in the law if one person can for his individual profit destroy the community, and render the neighborhood uninhabitable."*

rights of others when making use of the water. According to Article 982 Québec Civil Code, unless it is contrary to the general interest, a person having a right to use a spring, lake, sheet of water, underground stream or any running water may, to prevent the water from being polluted or depleted, require the destruction or modification of any works by which the water is being polluted or depleted. Although the Québec Civil Code does not refer to the interests of future generations, it is clear that water should be used in a sustainable way, taken into account not only the user's private interest, but also the general interest and the impact on the environment.

6. The rules on water show that sustainable behaviour, i.e. being mindful of the interests of others, including the future generations, starts by considering the environment at a microlevel. Therefore, the rules on neighbour law and nuisance offer important opportunities to introduce sustainability into property relations between individuals. Not only the use of commons, but the use of property in general must be done with due observance of its impact on the surrounding properties and the environment. This will be further elaborated on in the following section.

B. LIMITATIONS TO PROPERTY RIGHTS THROUGH GOOD NEIGHBOURHOOD RELATIONS

7. The recent Belgian property law reform in particular shows the potential of neighbour law to contribute to sustainable development. During the recodification of the Belgian Civil Code, sustainability made its appearance in the rules on overhanging branches, a classic example of nuisance. The new rules on "unlawful" plants, i.e. branches or roots that are in violation of the legal distance rules to the plot boundaries, can be found in Articles 3.133 and 3.134 of the Belgian Civil Code. These Articles provide that a neighbour may demand to trim or to uproot the trees or plants planted at a shorter distance, unless if the judge considers this to be an abuse of rights. This is in line with Dutch law, where a claim for grubbing (Art. 5:42 Dutch Civil Code) or cutting (Art. 5:44 Dutch Civil Code) trees or plants may constitute an abuse of rights.[18]

The renewed Belgian legal provisions further establish that, in making the decision on whether or not there is an abuse of rights, the judge "*shall take into account all circumstances of the case, **including the public interest***" (Art. 3.133, para 2 and 3.134, para 1 Belgian Civil Code – own emphasis). A judge can thus take into consideration other interests than the private interests of the parties concerned. In that way, a claim to remove trees or plants can be

18 S.E. Bartels and A.A. Van Velten, *Zakenrecht: Eigendom en beperkte rechten* in *Asser-serie*, 5, Deventer, Kluwer, 2017, 175, no. 149 and 178, no. 151.

regarded as contrary to the public interest.[19] Adding the words "*including the public interest*" was a clear political choice from the Belgian legislator driven by sustainability considerations. The explanatory memorandum contains the following argumentation:

> "Especially today, one cannot ignore the functions that plants fulfil in the public interest. This includes, not exhaustively, the interests of the environment, the landscape value, and heritage value."[20]

> "Moreover, one cannot ignore the functions that plants fulfil in the public interest. When a tree dies, this has not only consequences for its owner, but also for the public interest. This includes, not exhaustively, the interests of the environment, the landscape value, and heritage value. Therefore these provisions contain that a judge, when deciding upon the request for removal, will take the general interest into account."[21]

The Belgian legislator recognized considerations of sustainability as an inherent component of the public interest and created the possibility to raise the following argument in court: It constitutes an abuse of rights when a private individual invokes his/her right to the cutting of trees while this causes disproportionate harm to the environment. When conducting the abuse of rights balancing test, a judge naturally considers *all* circumstances of the case. By explicitly adding the public interest to this test, the Belgian legislator paved the way for sustainability arguments. Courts must take the public interest into account when judging upon the protection of property rights under nuisance law. This is an important legislative innovation, since the Belgian *Cour de Cassation* recently took an opposite stance under the old regime and ruled that:

> "When a private person invokes a right against another private person, the judge may not assess the proportionality of the exercise of that right in the light of the public interest distinct from their respective private interests."[22]

The same position was taken by the French *Cour de Cassation* which rejected the sustainability argument in favour of the private interest of a neighbour and his perpetual right to claim for grubbing or cutting the trees or plants.[23] In the

---

19 V. Sagaert, *Goederenrecht* in *Beginselen van Belgische Privaatrecht*, Mechelen, Kluwer, 2021, 152.

20 *Parl.St.* Kamer 2019-20, no. 173/002, 7.

21 *Parl.St.* Kamer 2019-20, no. 173/002, p. 9.

22 Cass. 22 October 2021, C.20.0265.F/3, *JT* 2022, vol. 6885, 76, note F. Glansdorff, *JLMB* 2022, vol. 3, 106, *Rev.not.b.* 2022, vol. 3167, 47, note J. Van Boxstael, *RW* 2021-22 (summary), vol. 28, 1105, note D. Gruyaert and *TMR* 2022, vol. 2, 270, note.

23 Cass.fr. 31 May 2012, no. 11-17313, *Recueil Dalloz* 2012, no. 32, 2128, note B. Mallet-Bricout and N. Reboul-Maupin. See also: V. Sagaert, "Property Law, Contract Law and Environmental Law: Shaking Hands with the (Historical) Enemy" in S. Demeyere and V.

meantime, Belgian case law has acknowledged that the public interest should be taken into account because of the importance of trees for the environment.[24] Private nuisance cases raise this relationship between private (individual) interest and the collective (or public) interest.[25] For other examples of how neighbour law can promote sustainable behaviour, other than the prohibition of abuse of rights in claiming for the cutting of plants, we refer to other contributions in this book.[26]

C. GENERAL DUTY TO CONSIDER THE ENVIRONMENT: OWNERS AS STEWARDS

8. Next to such specific obligations that limit the use of property for the sake of sustainable development, referred to in the previous section, we have identified a broader potential in the property law reforms for sustainability to determine property relations. Hereinafter, some examples from different legal systems are set out to illustrate the role sustainability has to play in how property right holders may behave.

In their Land Rights and Responsibilities Statement of 22 September 2022, which exists by the virtue of the Land Reform Act (2016), the Scottish Ministers explicitly recognized the importance of social and environmental factors in the regulation of land.[27] Most interestingly, the fourth principle of this Statement urges private owners to take their share of responsibility:

> "The holders of land rights should exercise these rights in ways that take account of their responsibilities to meet high standards of land ownership, management and use. Acting as the stewards of Scotland's land resource *for future generations* they should contribute to wider public benefit, sustainable growth and a modern, successful country." (own emphasis)

Private owners are expected to behave in such way that the rights of future generations are not compromised. The Scottish government is currently working

---

SAGAERT (eds.), *Contract and Property with an Environmental Perspective* in *Property Law Series*, X, Antwerp, Intersentia, 2020, (1) 6, no. 9.

24 Justice of the Peace Lier 13 June 2023, unpublished. See also: Justice of the Peace Luik (II) 16 February 1976, *Rev.not.b.* 1976, (549) 552; Court of First Instance Antwerp 10 June 2002, *TBBR* 2004, 221; Justice of the Peace Fontaine-L'Evêque 28 February 2008, *T.Vred.* 2009, 475.

25 M. LEE, "The public interest in private nuisance: collectives and communities in tort", *Cambridge Law Journal* 2015, vol. 74(2), (329) 329-330.

26 See in particular the contribution of Z-Z BOGGENPOEL-TEMMERS, but also A. CHAIGNEAU's contribution on land burdens.

27 Available at: www.gov.scot/publications/scottish-land-rights-responsibilities-statement-2022/. This Statement is a revision of the first edition of 27 September 2017. See also: J. ROBBIE, "Moving Beyond Boundaries in the Pursuit of Sustainable Property Law" in B. AKKERMANS and G. VAN DIJCK (eds.), *Sustainability and Private Law*, The Hague, Eleven International Publishing, 2020, (59) 73.

on a Land Reform Bill that will oblige owners of large-scale landholdings to prepare and publish land management plans.[28] Owners must – amongst others – demonstrate how the land will be used and managed so as to meet requirements (to be set out in the Land Rights and Responsibilities Statement codes/protocols) for sustainable management.

Other legal systems also reflect a growing attention in their legislation for sustainable behaviour in private law relations. In this regard, Article 13.2 of the Ukrainian Civil Code stipulates that "[w]*hen implementing the rights person shall refrain from actions which could, violate the rights of other persons, cause environmental damage or to cultural heritage.*"[29]

In the new Argentinian Civil and Commercial Code of 2015 (Law 26994 – "CCC"), land owners play a significant role in securing the sustainability of the environment.[30] The law reform includes limitations to individual rights over things in order to protect a sustainable environment. Article 14 CCC stipulates that the exercise of individual rights must not be abusive and must be compatible with rights that have a collective impact. Individual owners should not affect the functioning or sustainability of, amongst others, ecosystems of flora, fauna, biodiversity and water (Art. 240 CCC).

In France, the Environmental Charter explains the rights, but also the obligations that each individual has with regard to the environment.[31] Each individual has the right to live in a balanced and healthy environment (Art. 1), to have access, under the conditions and limitations set out by the law, to information with regard to the environment held by the authorities and to participate in the development of public decisions affecting the environment (Art. 7). However, each individual also has the duty to take part in the preservation and improvement of the environment (Art. 2), to prevent, under the conditions set out by the law, any harm that they could cause to the environment or alternatively, limit the consequences (Art. 3) and to contribute to the repair of the damages caused to the environment, under the conditions set out by the law. In interpreting these Articles, the French *Conseil constitutionnel* has recognized that *all* private individuals have a duty of care towards the impact their behaviour might have on the environment.[32]

---

28 See the Scottish government's consultation paper: www.gov.scot/publications/land-reform-net-zero-nation-consultation-paper/.

29 https://cis-legislation.com/document.fwx?rgn=8896.

30 J. Marotta and A. Parisi, "Private and public intermingled: the changes in the Family and Property Law of Argentina", *Journal of Civil Law Studies* 2020, vol. 13, (383) 402.

31 Loi constitutionnelle no. 2005-205 du 1er mars 2005 relative à la Charte de l'environnement (JORF no. 0051 du 2 mars 2005 page 3697), https://www.legifrance.gouv.fr/loda/texte_lc/JORFTEXT000000790249/2019-08-13/.

32 Cons.const. 8 April 2011, no. 2011-116, www.conseil-constitutionnel.fr/en/decision/2011/2011116QPC.htm, no. 5: "*Considering, secondly, that Articles 1 and 2 of the Environmental Charter provide that: "Every person has the right to live in a balanced environment that respects health. – Every person has the duty to participate in the preservation and improvement of the environment"; that compliance with the rights and duties set out in general terms under these Articles is a requirement not only for public bodies and the*

D. CONCLUSION: OWNERS AND THEIR SOCIAL RESPONSIBILITY

9. The recent recodifications of property law address sustainability more on a limited and one-off basis. A good example is the reference to the interest of future generations in Article 3.43 of the Belgian Civil Code on the use of commons. However, the many limitations on the right of ownership that had already been developed and led to the socialisation of ownership also have the potential to foster sustainable development.[33]

10. In western legal systems, much of the legal debate about property law is framed around rights, not obligations.[34] Nevertheless, the fact that private property has largely been thought of through the prism of individualism cannot mask the social function of property and its more collective origins.[35] Due to the historical origins of our modern concept of property, the right of ownership is considered to be a perpetual, absolute and exclusive property right.[36] However, this idea of property as a means for economic growth and prosperity gradually evolved towards a more social and less individualistic interpretation.[37] A clear example is Article 14(2) of the German Constitution: "*Property entails obligations. Its use shall also serve the public good.*"[38] In the recodification of the Belgian Civil Code, the Belgian legislator chose to adopt a more functional definition of ownership.[39] In Québec law, the absolute conception of ownership

---

administrative authorities within their respective areas of competence but also for all persons; that it follows from these provisions that every person is under an obligation to exercise care that no damage to the environment results from his actions."

33 See also B. Grimonprez, "Le droit de propriété à l'ère du changement climatique", *Sciences de l'Homme et de la Société* 2019, ID: 10670/1.sbxvgi, 5.

34 See also A. McHarg, B. Barton, A. Bradbook and L. Godden, *Property and the Law in Energy and Natural Resources*, Oxford Scholarship Online, 2010, 12.

35 Y. Emerich and F.P. Rivard, "La résurgence des communs en droit des biens contemporain: étude sur les cohabitats écologiques et les ruelles vertes", *Revue générale de droit* 2020, vol. 50/1, 245.

36 Art. 544 French Civil Code; Art. 5:1 Dutch Civil Code; Art. 544 old Belgian Civil Code. See more extensively: D. Gruyaert, *De exclusiviteit van het eigendomsrecht* in *Property Law Series*, IV, Antwerp, Intersentia, 2016, 147 et seq.

37 B. Akkermans and G. Van Dijck (eds.), *Sustainability and Private Law*, The Hague, Eleven International Publishing, 2020, 186 p.

38 "Property obliges" was already included in Art. 153 of the Weimar constitution (1919), see: U. Mattei and A. Quarta, *The Turning Point in Private Law. Ecology, Technology and the Commons* (Cheltenham/Northampton: Elgar 2019), 25.

39 Art. 3.50 Belgian Civil Code: "*The right of ownership directly grants to the owner the right to use, enjoy and dispose of the object. The owner has the fullness of powers, except for the limitations imposed by laws, regulations and the rights of third parties.*" See also *Parl.St.* Kamer 2019-20, no. 173/1, 126.

from the Napoleonic Code, was already abandoned in the recodification of property law in 1991.[40]

11. In light of sustainable development, the balancing function of property law shows its merits to protect ecological and social factors.[41] An example was again found in the recent recodification of the Belgian Civil Code. The fact that an owner may not abuse his right of ownership now implies, at least in overhanging branches litigation, that the owner should also consider the public interest. This indicates a change of perspective where property law is not only about private interest and wealth creation, but where the content of property rights depends on both the private interests and the public interest involved.[42] Also since the recodification in 1991 and the new conception of individual ownership, some scholars state that Québec law must now take into account, or even give precedence to, collective and general interests rather than prioritizing the interests of individuals and private owners.[43]

12. This inherent limitation of ownership that obliges an owner to consider other interests than its own private interest fits in seamlessly with the principle of sustainable development. The promotion of self-interest and the creation of wealth, which were both at the heart of property law in the early 19th century, have to make way for the public interest.[44] An unlimited exercise of the right of ownership risks to result in the degradation of the environment.[45] According to the recent legal doctrine, restrictions to the right of ownership must ensure the economic, social and ecological function of property.[46] Some authors add the idea that a social function is recently being replaced by one that refers to ownership as fulfilling an ecological function, where there is a duty to secure sustainability.[47]

---

40 Art. 947, para 1 Quebec Civil Code: "*Ownership is the right to use, enjoy and dispose of property fully and freely, subject to the limits and conditions for doing so determined by law.*"

41 See also T.W. Frazier, "Protecting ecological integrity within the balancing function of property law", *Environmental Law* 1998, vol. 28(1), (53) 62.

42 A. Chaigneau, "Des droits individuels sur des biens d'intérêt collectif, à la recherche du commun", *RIDE* 2014, vol. 3, 335. F. ORSI, *Dictionnaire biens communs*, Paris, PUF, 2017, 547; B. Grimonprez, "Le droit de propriété à l'ère du changement climatique", *Sciences de l'Homme et de la Société* 2019, ID: 10670/1.sbxvgi, 9.

43 G. Gidrol-Mistral, "Quebec Private Law, Destined to Preserve the Environment?" in S. Demeyere and V. Sagaert (eds.), *Contract and Property with an Environmental Perspective* in *Property Law Series*, X, Antwerp, Intersentia, 2020, (125) 126.

44 A. Chaigneau, "Des droits individuels sur des biens d'intérêt collectif, à la recherche du commun", *Revue internationale de droit économique* 2014, vol. 3, 335-350.

45 V. Sagaert, "Property Law, Contract Law and Environmental Law: Shaking Hands with the (Historical) Enemy" in S. Demeyere and V. Sagaert (eds.), *Contract and Property with an Environmental Perspective* in *Property Law Series*, X, Antwerp, Intersentia, 2020, (1) 9, no. 13.

46 A. Parise, "Preliminary Reflections on Paradigms, Ownership, and Ecology" in B. Akkermans and G. Van Dijck (eds.), *Sustainability and Private Law*, The Hague, Eleven International Publishing, 2020, (17) 17.

47 A. Parise, "Preliminary Reflections on Paradigms, Ownership, and Ecology" in B. Akkermans and G. Van Dijck (eds.), *Sustainability and Private Law*, The Hague, Eleven International Publishing, 2020, (17) 28.

These findings, and in particular the emergence of a more general duty for owners to take into account sustainability concerns (see section C), raise the question whether sustainability amounts to an open norm or a general rule of conduct in private law, in particular for owners, to act in a sustainable way. This will be further elaborated on in the next chapter. We start our analysis with a comparison with Chinese law where the legislator took the clear stance in 2020 that every individual should behave sustainably in civil legal transactions or relations.

III. SUSTAINABILITY AS A GENERAL RULE OF CONDUCT

A. THE "GREEN PRINCIPLE" UNDER THE CHINESE CIVIL CODE (2020)

a. *Ecologization of private law*

13. The introduction of ecological norms in the recent Chinese law reform, i.e. the "greening" or "ecologization"[48] of the Chinese Civil Code, provides a nice example of how the law may impose environmental considerations as a general limitation to the exercise of property rights.[49] Although the political and legal context, in particular with regard to ownership regulations, are different from Western legal systems, the Chinese example still shows how a Civil Code of the 21st century could look like in terms of sustainability.[50] The Chinese legislator has adopted a new rule that acknowledges the importance of sustainable development and combatting environmental degradation.[51] Article 9 of Book I, Chapter I (General Provisions) of the Chinese Civil Code stipulates that:

> "When conducting a civil activity, a person of the civil law shall act in a manner that facilitates conservation of resources and protection of the ecological environment."

---

48 M. Zhu, "The ecologization of the Chinese Civil Code", *Pravovedenie* 2020, vol. 64 (4), https://doi.org/10.21638/spbu25.2020.405, 511.

49 We only discuss the application of the general green principle in the property law provisions and leave out the specific rules on contracts (Art. 509.3 – however see below no. 13 – and Art. 558 Chinese Civil Code) and tort law (Art. 1229-1233 and Art. 1234-1235).

50 S. De Rey and L. Chen, "Non-monetary relief for breach of contract: a European perspective on Chinese contract law", *Asia Pacific Law Review* 2021, vol. 29:2, https://doi.org/10.1080/10192557.2022.2033086 (325) 334. See also for the peculiarities of the Chinese context: D. Clementi, "Environmental protection through the green principle in the Civil Code of the People's Republic of China", *Comparative Law Review* 2022, vol. 13/2, 37 *et seq.*

51 T. Zhai and Y.-C. Chang, "The Contribution of China's Civil Law to Sustainable Development: Progress and Prospects", *Sustainability* 2019, vol. 11(1), 294, http://dx.doi.org/10.3390/su11010294, 6.

This so-called "green principle" requires private actors to contribute to resources conservation and environmental protection in civil activities.[52] It is legally binding on private actors in all civil activities, including exercising civil rights, performing civil obligations, and bearing civil liabilities. However, as a basic principle of civil law, Article 9 of the Chinese Civil Code is more of a guideline, and cannot be applied directly as the basis for trial cases.[53] The law does not mention clear sanctions for when a person is not acting in a sustainable manner, but this general principle is placed on the same level as the principles of good faith, equality, reasonableness, etc.[54] The green principle represents a value that courts can take into account, namely that the public interest in some instances is more important than individual rights.[55] It provides guidelines for the application of law, legal interpretation and choice in case of conflict of interest in judicial practice.[56]

14. Judges can use Article 9 of the General Provisions to moderate the absolutism of ownership protection and avoid the abuse of freedom by rights holders to bring about the consequences of environmental degradation.[57] The implementation of this basic principle further depends on the specific rules that were also enacted in the new Chinese Civil Code.[58] An example of such specific implementation of the green principle in property law is Article 286 Chinese Civil Code that deals with apartment buildings. This Article provides that the relevant acts of unit owners shall meet the requirements of safeguarding resources and protecting the ecological environment. According to legal scholarship, this could mean, for example, that an apartment owner may not irresponsibly waste water and electricity.[59]

---

52 T. Zhai and Y.-C. Chang, "The Contribution of China's Civil Law to Sustainable Development: Progress and Prospects", *Sustainability* 2019, vol. 11(1), 294, http://dx.doi.org/10.3390/su11010294, 1.

53 T. Zhai and Y.-C. Chang, "The Contribution of China's Civil Law to Sustainable Development: Progress and Prospects", *Sustainability* 2019, vol. 11(1), 294, 294, http://dx.doi.org/10.3390/su11010294, 5.

54 I. Szpotakowski, "The new Chinese civil code and its contribution to sustainable development", *Transformacje Prawa Prywatnego* 2020, vol. 3, www.researchgate.net/publication/344440457_The_New_Chinese_Civil_Code_and_its_contribution_to_Sustaina ble_Development, 233.

55 J. Herbots, "Chinees contractenrecht in een notendop" in X., *Recht in beweging*, Oud-Turnhout, Gompel&Svacina, 2019, (201) 210.

56 J. Zheng, "Integration of Public and Private Law in the New Era – The Green Principle of the Chinese Civil Code", *US-CHINA Law Review* 2022, vol. 19/7, (281) 296.

57 J. Zheng, "Integration of Public and Private Law in the New Era – The Green Principle of the Chinese Civil Code", *US-CHINA Law Review* 2022, vol. 19/7, (281) 288. The green principle can e.g. limit the owner's right to remove illegally occupied items when it concerns trees.

58 J. Zheng, "Integration of Public and Private Law in the New Era – The Green Principle of the Chinese Civil Code", *US-CHINA Law Review* 2022, vol. 19/7, (281) 285.

59 M. Zhu, "The ecologization of the Chinese Civil Code", *Pravovedenie* 2020, vol. 64 (4), https://doi.org/10.21638/spbu25.2020.405, 518. See also: D. Clementi, "Environmental protection

A usufructuary shall also abide by the provisions of laws on the protection, rational exploitation, and utilization of resources and the protection of the ecological environment. The owner may not interfere with the exercise of such rights by the usufructuary (Art. 326 Chinese Civil Code). This Article could give an owner of agricultural land the right to sue its peasants should they fail to properly preserve the productivity of the soil.[60] Similarly, Article 346 of the Chinese Civil Code stipulates that the right – granted by the State – to use a lot of land for construction purposes shall be created in conformity with the requirements for conservation of resources and protection of the ecological environment, and in compliance with the provisions of laws and administrative regulations on the planned use of the lot, and may not impair the rights to usufruct already created thereon.[61]

A last example from property law mentioned here is Article 942 Chinese Civil Code. A property management service provider shall, for any violation of the relevant laws and regulations on public security, environmental protection, fire protection, and the like, in the property, in a timely manner, take reasonable measures to stop the violation, make a report to the competent departments, and render assistance in its handling.

15. Apart from environmental considerations that limit the exercise of property rights (*supra*, no. 14), the Chinese Civil Code also considers sustainability as an essential value of contemporary Chinese society that impacts other fields of law.[62] It is also considered as a basic principle of contractual execution, similar to the principle of good faith.[63] Article 509, para 3 Chinese Civil Code requires that the parties to a contract shall avoid wasting the resources, polluting the environment, or damaging the ecology in the course of performance of the contract. It is up to the civil judges to evaluate whether the execution of a contract causes resource waste, environmental pollution or ecological degradation. Some Chinese legal scholars argue that the green principle should not only be taken into account in contract execution, but also in rules regarding validity and interpretation of contracts.[64]

---

through the green principle in the Civil Code of the People's Republic of China", *Comparative Law Review* 2022, vol. 13/2, (37) 50.

60 M. Zhu, "The ecologization of the Chinese Civil Code", *Pravovedenie* 2020, vol. 64 (4), https://doi.org/10.21638/spbu25.2020.405, 518.

61 The land use for real estate purposes is separated from the right of ownership of the land which belongs to the State, see: D. Clementi, "Environmental protection through the green principle in the Civil Code of the People's Republic of China", *Comparative Law Review* 2022, vol. 13/2, (37) 51.

62 S. De Rey and L. Chen, "Non-monetary relief for breach of contract: a European perspective on Chinese contract law", *Asia Pacific Law Review* 2021, vol. 29:2, https://doi.org/10.1080/10192557.2022.2033086 (325) 333.

63 M. Zhu, "The ecologization of the Chinese Civil Code", *Pravovedenie* 2020, vol. 64 (4), https://doi.org/10.21638/spbu25.2020.405, 519.

64 T. Zhai and Y.-C. Chang, "The Contribution of China's Civil Law to Sustainable Development: Progress and Prospects", *Sustainability* 2019, vol. 11(1), 294, http://dx.doi.org/10.3390/su11010294, 12.

Examples from Chinese case law, which is at the moment still very limited, show that the green principle could lead, for example, to non-performance of taxi-management contracts when the vehicles are energy-inefficient and highly polluting. In general, Chinese scholars find that Chinese judges are relatively open to adjusting contractual arrangements to meet the requirement of sustainability.[65] However, it seems that judges are especially willing to consider ecological considerations in contractual disputes when there is government regulation involved to which the contract should be adopted.[66]

b. *Evaluation of the "Green Principle"*

16. Since the Chinese case law is still very recent and limited, it is yet to be seen how the green principle will be implemented in legal practice and enforced by the courts.[67] In any event, the clear choice of the Chinese legislator to implement a green principle has an important symbolic value in the call for a more sustainable society. It is a typical example of the fusion of public law and private law.[68] The Chinese legislator preferred the legislative approach to a strict judicial interpretation approach, because pressing environmental problems and an urgent need for a timely and effective response to those problems necessitates a new specialized rule in civil law.[69]

However, as the name suggests, the green principle focuses on ecological sustainability, and not so much on social justice. This has its downside.[70] The green principle aims to promote public interests, such as the protection of public health and welfare from environmental harm.[71] Nevertheless, some authors

---

65 M. Zhu, "The ecologization of the Chinese Civil Code", *Pravovedenie* 2020, vol. 64 (4), https://doi.org/10.21638/spbu25.2020.405, 521.

66 This finding is based on the examples given by M. Zhu, "The ecologization of the Chinese Civil Code", *Pravovedenie* 2020, vol. 64 (4), https://doi.org/10.21638/spbu25.2020.405, 520.

67 S. De Rey and L. Chen, "Non-monetary relief for breach of contract: a European perspective on Chinese contract law", *Asia Pacific Law Review* 2021, vol. 29:2, https://doi.org/10.1080/10192557.2022.2033086 (325) 334; J. Ouyang, "Unleashing the Green Principle in the Chinese Civil Code", to be published; J. Zheng, "Integration of Public and Private Law in the New Era – The Green Principle of the Chinese Civil Code", *US-CHINA Law Review* 2022, vol. 19/7, (281) 286.

68 J. Zheng, "Integration of Public and Private Law in the New Era – The Green Principle of the Chinese Civil Code", *US-CHINA Law Review* 2022, vol. 19/7, 281.

69 T. Zhai and Y.-C. Chang, "The Contribution of China's Civil Law to Sustainable Development: Progress and Prospects", *Sustainability* 2019, vol. 11(1), 294, http://dx.doi.org/10.3390/su11010294, 5.

70 Middle-class environmental interests typically trump the interests of the poor and marginalized, too often leading to an exclusionary sustainability of privilege rather than a sustainability of inclusion, see: S.D. Campbell, "Sustainable Development and Social Justice: Conflicting Urgencies and the Search for Common Ground in Urban and Regional Planning", *Michigan Journal of Sustainability*, 2013, vol. 1, http://dx.doi.org/10.3998/mjs.12333712.0001.007, 75.

71 M. Zhu, "The ecologization of the Chinese Civil Code", *Pravovedenie* 2020, vol. 64 (4), https://doi.org/10.21638/spbu25.2020.405, 513; T. Zhai and Y.-C. Chang, "The Contribution

plead that the term "ecological environment" is not strictly limited to ecology as such but includes the living environment.[72]

17. An important constatation is that under Chinese law, the green principle is considered to be a separate basic principle of civil law, next to and different from the good faith principle.[73] As in other legal systems, such as Belgian law, the good faith principle has three different functions under Chinese law.[74] It is a basic principle to balance interests between parties and between parties and society. It requires private actors to keep their word and to abide by the contract, but the principle of good faith also has an interpretative role. It is a guiding principle to fill the gap and help to interpret laws and contracts in a way that is in line with social and economic changes. Some legal scholars were in favour of including sustainability in the interpretation of the principle of public order and moral and/or good faith.[75] Nevertheless, adopting a separate green principle makes sustainability more visible than when the notion of (ecological) sustainability would have been implemented in the guiding principle of good faith.

B. CHALLENGES AND OPPORTUNITIES FOR SUSTAINABLE BEHAVIOUR AS A SEPARATE BASIC PRINCIPLE OF CIVIL LAW

18. The choice for sustainability as a general rule of conduct provides some legal challenges. From a policy perspective, it is the question to individual autonomy and freedom and the acceptable level of limits to that freedom.[76] First, it is not easy to define what "sustainable" behaviour is. Critics might even state that is impossible to define sustainability in legal relationships. One could decide

---

of China's Civil Law to Sustainable Development: Progress and Prospects", *Sustainability* 2019, vol. 11(1), 294, http://dx.doi.org/10.3390/su11010294, 6. See also: D. Clementi, "Environmental protection through the green principle in the Civil Code of the People's Republic of China", *Comparative Law Review* 2022, vol. 13/2, (37) 46.

72 J. Zheng, "Integration of Public and Private Law in the New Era – The Green Principle of the Chinese Civil Code", *US-CHINA Law Review* 2022, vol. 19/7, (281) 297.

73 Art. 509 Chinese Civil Code states: *"Each party shall fully perform its own obligations as agreed. The parties shall abide by the principle of good faith, and perform obligations of notification, assistance, confidentiality, etc. in accordance with the nature and purpose of the contract and the usage of trade. In performing a contract, the parties shall avoid wasting resources, polluting the environment, and compromising ecology."*

74 J. Fu, *Modern European and Chinese Contract Law. A Comparative Study of Party Autonomy*, Tilburg, Tilburg University School of Law, 2010, 41.

75 See the references mentioned in: T. Zhai and Y.C. Chang, "The Contribution of China's Civil Law to Sustainable Development: Progress and Prospects", *Sustainability* 2019, vol. 11(1), 294, http://dx.doi.org/10.3390/su11010294, 5, footnotes 27-31.

76 J. Zheng, "Integration of Public and Private Law in the New Era – The Green Principle of the Chinese Civil Code", *US-CHINA Law Review* 2022, vol. 19/7, (281) 282 en 294.

to limit it, as it has been done under Chinese law, to the duty to act in accordance with the necessity of resource conservation and environmental protection. Some authors claim that the meaning of "sustainability" needs to be scientifically justified by environmental experts and verified with objective proof, unlike other civil law principles. It cannot merely depend on judicial discretion.[77] That brings up another problem.

19. Creating sustainability as a rule of conduct in private law brings along the risk of legal uncertainty when it is up to the courts to decide whether or not the parties to a specific case or civil activity acted sustainably. If such principle is to be accepted, as under Chinese civil law, a judge must measure the environmental impacts of different legal propositions of opponent parties. The application of the green principle in China leaves space for discretion and ground for uncertainty.[78] It is, for instance,not defined what is meant with "conservation of resources" and what kinds of action could violate such an obligation.[79] The application of the green principle largely depends on the interpretation by the courts.

However, this objection should be nuanced. A degree of uncertainty is inherent to general principles of private law. It is for instance difficult (even impossible) to define public interests in the abstract, or to distinguish public from private, collective from individual, in any neutral or universal way.[80] Those general principles of law are uncertain, because they do not refer to the concrete rights and obligations of the parties, leaving the precise outcome of the application of such principle to a concrete case unpredictable and uncertain.[81] Open norms, such as good faith, are used for interpretation where the law fails to govern specific rules and are indeed subject to the discretionary power of the judge. At the same time, this is also an opportunity for the open norm to be contextualised. Indeed, the application of an open norm, such as sustainability as a rule of conduct, will depend on the circumstances.[82] As is the case with the principle of good faith, the benchmark is what a reasonable, careful and

---

77 M. Zhu, "The ecologization of the Chinese Civil Code", *Pravovedenie* 2020, vol. 64(4), https://doi.org/10.21638/spbu25.2020.405, 511.

78 J. Zheng, "Integration of Public and Private Law in the New Era – The Green Principle of the Chinese Civil Code", *US-CHINA Law Review* 2022, vol. 19/7, (281) 295.

79 T. Zhai and Y.-C. Chang, "The Contribution of China's Civil Law to Sustainable Development: Progress and Prospects", *Sustainability* 2019, vol. 11(1), 294, http://dx.doi.org/10.3390/su11010294, 6; J. ZHENG, "Integration of Public and Private Law in the New Era – The Green Principle of the Chinese Civil Code", *US-CHINA Law Review* 2022, vol. 19/7, (281) 295.

80 M. Lee, "The public interest in private nuisance: collectives and communities in tort", *Cambridge Law Journal* 2015, vol. 74(2), (329) 331.

81 J. Fu, *Modern European and Chinese Contract Law. A Comparative Study of Party Autonomy*, Tilburg, Tilburg University School of Law, 2010, 36.

82 The same is true for the green principle: J. Zheng, "Integration of Public and Private Law in the New Era – The Green Principle of the Chinese Civil Code", *US-CHINA Law Review* 2022, vol. 19/7, (281) 286.

forward-looking person *in the same circumstances* would have done. Moreover, a discretionary power of the judge must not be equated with arbitrariness. Judges always need to objectively motivate their decisions. Courts are used to applying general principles in new contexts, ensuring that principles of law are correctly applied, resolving disputes in a nuanced way.[83]

20. Another criticism comes down to the lack of enforceability of "sustainable behaviour" as a legal principle. The obligations we hold towards other members of the community and/or future generations risk to be, as a matter of principle, moral, not enforceable in law.[84] That being said, the main goal of such a general and guiding rule of conduct is to try changing the behaviour of individuals. It is not always necessary to enforce the law in order to give it effect. Making a statement through law or private contracts may alone change our social norms and behaviour.[85] If the principle of sustainability succeeds in changing behaviour, it is of less importance whether it is also legally enforceable or whether or not damages for non-compliance are due. Just as the principle of good faith, the principle of sustainability might not be legally enforceable, and yet binding. It comes down to an *Obliegenheit*.[86] Very general principles can lead to very concrete obligations, based on the concrete circumstances, imposing a precise conduct on the parties involved.[87]

21. Because of these constraints, and although it is not what the Chinese legislator opted for (*supra*, no. 15), one could consider to include the notion of sustainability in today's interpretation of existing legal principles, such as the principle of good faith.[88] These general standards are themselves subject to

83 Bradbook considers this a major advantage of court intervention in general. See A. Bradbook, "The Role of the Common Law in Promoting Sustainable Energy Development in the Property Sector" in A. McHarg, B. Barton, A. Bradbrook and L. Godden, *Property and the Law in Energy and Natural Resources*, Oxford Scholarship Online, 2010, (391) 410.

84 B. Akkermans, "Sustainable Ownership – new obligations towards achieving a sustainable society", *EPLJ* 2021, vol. 10(2-3), (277) 291.

85 K.P. Mitkidis, "Sustainability clauses in international supply chain contracts: regulation, enforceability and effects of ethical requirements", Nordic *Journal of Commercial Law* 2014, vol. 1, [i]-30, 26. This author calls this phenomenon the expressive function of law. See also: D. Clementi, "Environmental protection through the green principle in the Civil Code of the People's Republic of China", *Comparative Law Review* 2022, vol. 13/2, (37) 55.

86 M. Fontaine, "Obliegenheit, incombance?" in X., *Liber amicorum Hubert Claassens. Verzekering: theorie en praktijk* (Antwerp: Maklu, 1998), (151) 154.

87 S. De Rey and L. Chen, "Non-monetary relief for breach of contract: a European perspective on Chinese contract law", *Asia Pacific Law Review* 2021, vol. 29:2, https://doi.org/10.1080/10192557.2022.2033086 (325) 334.

88 For the principle of good faith, see: S. Grundmann and M. Grochowski, "The Creation of Norms: An Evolutionary View on European Contract Law" in S. Grundmann and M. Grochowski (eds.), *European Contract Law and the Creation of Norms* in *European Contract Law and Theory, 5*, Antwerp, Intersentia, 2021, (3) 11.

dynamic evolution.[89] The principle of good faith could thus serve as a vehicle to foster new values cherished by the parties at a certain moment in time.

Other general principles of law can also be interpreted in such way that they include sustainable behaviour. That is for instance the case for the interpretation of "public interest" in the Belgian overhanging branches litigation (*supra*, no. 7). As set out above (*supra*, no. 11) sustainability in property law aims to promote public interests, such as environmental protection, rather than individual liberty.

The question also arises whether sustainability is not merely part of the public order. As Malaurie described it, like every other open norm or general principle of law: "*L'ordre public est un dans sa définition; il est multiple dans ses applications.*"[90] The ecological crisis calls for a specific public order, one that protects the environment. The recodification of the Belgian Civil Code has even led to a new definition of the public order. According to this revision "*Is considered to be of public order, the legal rule that affects the essentials interests of the state or community or that determines, in private law, the legal foundations on which the society is built, such as the economic order, the moral order, the social order* ***or the environmental order.***" (Art. 1.3, para 4 Belgian Civil Code – own emphasis)

However, the added value of a separate principle of sustainability is not only the symbolic value (*supra*, no. 16), but also the emphasis on the intergenerational aspect of sustainable behaviour.[91] Every legal subject should be aware of the impact of his/her behaviour not only on their environment, but also on the interest of future generations.

IV. CONCLUSION

22. The promotion of social and environmental objectives primarily belongs to the States' responsibility. However, it is clear that sustainable development is more than a key organizing principle for policy decisions and regulations. It also affects private owners in their private relationships. The social dimension of ownership already challenged the absoluteness of ownership and the sovereignty of private legal subjects. Since decades, property law no longer focuses solely on the rights of individuals, but also emphasizes obligations and social

---

89 S. Grundmann and M. Grochowski, "The Creation of Norms: An Evolutionary View on European Contract Law" in S. Grundmann and M. Grochowski (eds.), *European Contract Law and the Creation of Norms* in *European Contract Law and Theory, 5*, Antwerp, Intersentia, 2021, (3) 12.

90 P. Malaurie, *L'ordre public et le contrat. Etude de Droit civil comparé France, Angleterre, U.R.S.S.*, Reims, Matot-Braine, 1953, no. 1. See also P. Lequet, *L'ordre public environnemental et le contrat de droit privé*, Paris, LGDJ, 2022, 11.

91 G. Alexander, *Property and Human Flourishing*, Oxford, Oxford University Press, 2018, 119; B. Akkermans, "Sustainable Ownership – new obligations towards achieving a sustainable society", *EPLJ* 2021, vol. 10(2–3), (277) 289.

responsibilities. Individual autonomy remains broad but it is not to be taken for granted. One may thrive own goals, but only with respect for the rights of others. This leads to important opportunities to implement sustainability in private law relations. As Minghze ZHU puts it clearly:

> "Experience with the socialization of private law has already taught civil lawyers how to preserve the notion of private autonomy while still, for the collective good, imposing some restrictions on individual choice. If the threat to autonomy is a devil, it is the devil we know only too well."[92]

In current times, the importance of sustainable development imposes new restrictions on property rights. This chapter has shed light on the question whether the recodification of property law in different legal systems has created a new open norm, a general rule of conduct for legal subjects to behave sustainably. Such sustainable behaviour is exactly what the Belgian legislator imposes for the use of commons. Article 3.43 Belgian Civil Code explicitly stipulates that common objects should be used in the public interest, including the interest of future generations. The Chinese Civil Code even introduced a "green principle" throughout the rules of private law. Others will claim that we do not need such general rule of sustainability and that it is included in the dynamic interpretation of other general principles of law, such as good faith. In any event, whether sustainability is considered as a separate rule of conduct or not, what matters is the recognition at law that sustainability requires the owner to take not only his own interests into account, but also the interests of those around him and those that come after him.[93]

92 M. ZHU, "The ecologization of the Chinese Civil Code", *Pravovedenie* 2020, vol. 64(4), https://doi.org/10.21638/spbu25.2020.405, 514.

93 B. AKKERMANS, "Sustainable Ownership – new obligations towards achieving a sustainable society", *EPLJ* 2021, 10(2–3), (277) 279.

CONDOMINIUM LAW AND THE ENERGY TRANSITION

A Case Study of Rooftop Solar PV under Dutch law*

Sjoerd KALISVAART
Junior associate, Pels Rijcken & Drooglever Fortuijn N.V.
PhD candidate, University of Groningen, LL.M.

Yassine HASNAOUI
PhD Candidate and lecturer, University of Groningen, LL.M.

I. INTRODUCTION

A significant portion of the Dutch building stock consists of condominium complexes.[1] Participation of condominium owners in the energy transition is slow.[2] In this paper, it is argued that causes for reluctance on the part of condominium owners can be found in the lackluster interplay between Dutch condominium law and Dutch energy law. We will illustrate this by categorizing limitations under energy law and condominium law to the installation of rooftop solar photovoltaics (PV) and we will explore possible (regulatory) solutions. In so doing, we lay bare the lacking interplay between a primarily national private law-based body of rules (condominium law) *vis-à-vis* a primarily European public-law based body of rules (energy law), as well as friction between the overarching collective aims of the energy transition and the individualistic nature of both regulatory regimes.

We start our discussion with an overview of the overarching goals, aims and impetus of condominium law and energy law (part II). We then analyze the interplay between both regulatory systems based on the discussion of a (fictitious) case (part III).

---

* Research on this chapter was finished on 16 January 2024. Subsequent legislative developments have not been included in this chapter.

1 Around 36,5% of the Dutch building stock concerns multi-unit houses, i.e. condominiums, gallery homes, as well as homes with commercial spaces, see: https://opendata.cbs.nl/statline/#/CBS/nl/dataset/82550NED/table?fromstatweb.

2 B. HOOPS *et al.*, "Verduurzaming van kleine appartementengebouwen" (2022), *WPNR* 7393, p. 876.

II. SETTING APART CONDOMINIUM LAW AND ENERGY LAW

Condominium law and energy law are two distinctively different fields of law, as regards *inter alia* the origin of the rules (national or European), the rigidity of the body of rules, and the aim of the rules. In this part, we highlight the core elements of condominium law and energy law.

A. CONDOMINIUM LAW

The genesis of Dutch condominium law can be found in the post-war housing crisis of the 1950s. The large-scale destruction of housing during the Second World War, especially in Rotterdam, combined with the sudden population boom after the end of the war resulted in a severe lack of available housing.[3] Multi-unit buildings were seen as an efficient way to resolve this shortage. This new emphasis on condominiums required a robust legal regime that enabled individual ownership of a share of a building. The first Condominium Act went into force in 1954 and has since been integrated in the Dutch Civil Code (DCC).[4]

The owner of a building can split their property right of that building into condominium rights. A condominium right is defined in Article 5:106 DCC as a share in the ownership of the whole building, and the right to the exclusive use of a part of that building. This means the Dutch condominium system is unitary in nature, unlike many other jurisdictions.[5] There is only one property right, and every condominium "owner" has a share in that property right. This also means a condominium "owner" merely has a right to the exclusive use of a designated part of the building. This system differs from dualistic jurisdictions such as Belgium, where condominium ownership is true ownership of the condominium, and only the truly common parts of the building, such as a stairwell, are jointly owned.[6]

The significance of the joint ownership is, however, limited in practice. Article 5:117 DCC states that it is not possible to exercise the right of disposal with regards to the condominium complex while it is divided into condominium rights. At the same time, the condominium rights can be disposed of without permission from the other owners. This means that it is impossible to transfer

---

3 C.N. Siewers, *Balans in het appartementsrecht*, Wolters Kluwer, Deventer 2022, para 2.1.1.

4 C.N. Siewers, *Balans in het appartementsrecht*, Wolters Kluwer, Deventer 2022, para 2.1.2.

5 C. van der Merwe, *European Condominium Law*, University Printing House, Cambridge 2015, p. 5.

6 R. Timmermans, "Het toepassingsgebied van de appartementswet en het ontstaan van de Vereniging van Mede-eigenaars" in V. Sagaert and G. Rommel (eds.), *Appartementsrecht*, die Keure, Brugge 2008, pp. 9-15.

ownership of the building or vest a real property right on the condominium building during the division, but it is possible to transfer or vest a real property right on the condominium rights themselves. Under the *prior* tempore rule, however, real property rights established before the division are respected during the division.

Conceptually, the communal nature of condominium ownership and administration is born out of necessity. After all, the physical reality of a condominium complex is that multiple people share one building. Said building must be maintained. Conversely, condominium rights confer rights to use specific parts of the building exclusively, which – while not technically property in a conventional sense – fulfil many of the same functions as property. Condominium law was introduced in the DCC with the express intent to enable something akin to ownership of a part of a building. Ownership is characterized in Article 5:1 DCC as the right of an owner to do whatever he likes with his property, without interference from others, insofar as the use of his property does not infringe on the rights of others or violates written or unwritten rules of law. As such, condominium law seeks to strike a balance between the necessity of cooperation between the owners and the protection of the private interests of the individual owners.

The Dutch legislator intentionally left a lot of room for legal practice to develop the substantive rules of condominium.[7] As a result, book 5 of the Dutch Civil Code establishes formal rules regarding the division of a building into condominium rights and how to end the division. Rules of a more substantive nature are laid down in the notarial deed of division, and subsequent condominium regulations, which in turn need to contain provisions on, among other things, the way the costs of maintaining the condominium complex are split amongst the owners and rules on the use of the common areas.[8] Additionally, the division regulations can contain restrictions on the use of the exclusive use areas as well.[9] To aid in this process, legal practitioners have drafted a series of model regulations that are often applied when dividing a building into condominium rights.

The emphasis on collective ownership in the Dutch condominium regime echoes throughout the DCC. Most parts of a condominium building are communal: not only the stairwell but all exterior walls and windows, the roof, the interior load-bearing walls, wiring, pipes and many other parts.[10] This, in turn, means individual owners cannot unilaterally make decisions that affect communal parts. Instead, decisions have to be made democratically within the *Vereniging van Eigenaars* (owners' association, OA).[11] The OA is a legal

7 C.N. Siewers, *Balans in het appartementsrecht*, Wolters Kluwer, Deventer 2022, para 2.1.3.
8 See Art. 5:112 DCC.
9 See Art. 5:112 para 4 DCC.
10 See, e.g., Art. 11.1 of Model regulation 2017.
11 See Art. 5:127 DCC.

entity that is established with the division of a building into condominium units.[12] Condominium owners automatically become members of the OA, and membership of the OA is limited to those owners.[13] The OA does not own any part of the building, as the property right of the building is held by the joint owners. However, as a legal person the OA does have its own patrimony.

The OA has two primary aims. The first aim is serving the interests of the joint owners.[14] The scope of this aim is very broad. An example of this is the so-called service flats, which are condominium complexes that also offer medical care, typically aimed at elderly people that are still capable of living independently but require regular medical care and some amount of supervision. Interests that affect most, but not all, of the condominium owners can still fall within the scope of the OA's competence.[15]

The second aim of the OA is the administration of the condominium complex.[16] Administration in this context encompasses all acts aimed at the normal maintenance and normal use of the condominium complex and associated assets. Large-scale renovations, as well as the exercise of the power of disposal fall outside the authority of the OA and require the unanimous approval of all condominium owners.[17]

Under the DCC, decision-making within the OA follows a simple majority rule of 50% of the votes plus half a vote.[18] In practice, division regulations typically mandate a supermajority requirement of two thirds of the votes with a quorum of two thirds of the total eligible voters present for certain impactful decisions, such as large expenditures or long-term contracts.[19]

During the lifetime of a condominium complex, the desire can arise to amend the foundational rules laid down in the deed of division. The DCC prescribes a special procedure for such an amendment, laid down in Article 5:139 DCC. There are two options: amendment by unanimous vote, or amendment through a supermajority of 80% of the votes and the cooperation of the board of the OA. The Dutch Supreme Court decided in a recent case that the latter option, i.e. amendment with a supermajority, cannot be used if the amendment entails an exercise of the right of disposal.[20]

To summarize, the Dutch Civil Code strikes a balance between the collective interests of all owners and the individual interests of each owner. Matters relating to the administration of the building or matters that affect the interests of the

12 See Art. 5:112 para 2 DCC.
13 See Art. 5:127 para 1 DCC.
14 See Art. 5:112 para 2 DCC.
15 J.H. Beekhuis, *Appartementseigendom*, Kluwer, Deventer 1974, p. 237.
16 See Art. 5:126 para 1 DCC.
17 C.N. Siewers, "Beheer en beschikken in het appartementsrecht" (2021), *WPNR* 7351, pp. 981-982.
18 See Art. 5:127 para 1 DCC.
19 An example of this can be found in Art. 56.1 of Model Regulation 2017.
20 HR 24 February 2023, ECLI:NL:HR:2023:286, r.o. 3.4.3.

joint owners, can be decided democratically within the OA. This also means owners can be held to pay for maintenance regardless of their vote. Matters that affect the exclusive use areas of an owner fall within the purview of the owner and matters that fundamentally affect the division can only be decided upon with unanimity.

This traditional conception of a condominium clashes with the evolving role buildings play in modern society. The European Union and the Dutch government seek to reduce the emission of greenhouse gasses through the retrofitting of existing buildings. This is already a challenge when it comes to single-owner buildings, but the division of power within a condominium complex is especially problematic as the scope of the OA's power is limited to the administration of the complex, which is typically understood as reactive maintenance. Energy-efficient retrofitting will however require proactive works to be performed. It is unclear to what extent the OA can play a role in this process.

One aspect of the energy transition is the production and consumption of self-generated electricity, typically through the use of photovoltaic panels. As previously established, the roof of a condominium complex is a part of the common use areas. Condominium owners are therefore in principle not allowed to place their own solar panels on the shared roof but require permission from the other owners. Furthermore, if the condominium owners intend to produce and sell or consume electricity together, the OA seems well-suited to play a coordinating role in this process. It is however unclear to what extent these activities fall within the scope of the OA's powers. We will discuss the legal aspects of the installation and operation of solar PV panels on the roof of a condominium complex in part III.

B. ENERGY LAW

Contrary to condominium law, energy law does not seek to govern ownership. Rather, energy law relates to "*the allocation of rights and duties concerning the exploitation of all energy resources between individuals, between individuals and the government, between governments and between states*" and thus operates in three distinct dimensions.[21] In the context of this paper, we will focus on the (semi-)horizontal dimension of energy law, meaning the rules governing the relationship between individual energy consumers and their suppliers and (public) grid companies, respectively.

Large parts of Dutch energy legislation originate from several European legislative packages, which include the subsequent Electricity Market Directives

21 A.J. Bradbrook, "Energy Law as an Academic Discipline" (1996) 14(2) *JERL* 194; M.M. Roggenkamp, c.s. (red.), *Energy Law in Europe*, OUP, Oxford 2016, p. 7.

(EMD; the most recent being Directive (EU) 2019/944[22]) and accompanying Electricity Market Regulations (EMR; the most recent being Regulation (EU) 2019/943[23]), as well as the Renewable Energy Directives (RED; the most recent being Directive (EU) 2018/2001[24]). Energy legislation is, however, not fully harmonized, as these Directives leave Member States with a certain margin of appreciation, especially regarding the rules governing the (distribution) system and the treatment of final customers (i.e. a customer purchasing electricity for own use[25]), often reflecting (historical) domestic policy considerations.[26]

Following the process of market liberalization, energy supply and consumption have become largely individualistic in nature, i.e. a significant portion of the European energy law *acquis* governs the relationship between energy suppliers and their final customers, as well as the relationship between the final customers and their grid companies (often a distribution system operator; DSO).[27] Within this individual contractual nexus, emphasis is placed on the assignment of rights to individual energy customers and assignment of (information) duties to their contractual counterparts (e.g. grid companies and supply undertakings). This includes the right of free supplier choice, right of universal service (i.e. the right for household customers to uninterrupted supply of electricity of a certain quality at competitive, easily and clearly comparable, transparent and non-discriminatory prices) and the right to self-produce and -consume electricity in an individual setting (i.e. to become "active customers" and/or "renewables self-consumers").[28]

Historically, less emphasis has been put on the production and/or consumption of electricity in collective settings. Over the past decade, energy flows in the electricity system have grown increasingly bidirectional, meaning electricity is both consumed and produced by a myriad of professional and non-professional actors, including conventional generators, energy cooperatives and final customers.[29] The (regulatory) focus is thus shifting towards the express

---

22 Directive (EU) 2019/944 of the European Parliament and of the Council of 5 June 2019 on common rules for the internal market for electricity and amending Directive 2012/27/EU (recast) [2019] OJ, L 158/125 (EMD).

23 Regulation (EU) 2019/943 of the European Parliament and of the Council of 5 June 2019 on the internal market for electricity (recast), *OJ* 2019, L 158/54 (EMR).

24 Directive (EU) 2018/2001 of the European Parliament and of the Council of 11 December 2018 on the promotion of the use of energy from renewable sources (recast), *OJ* 2018, L 328/82 (RED).

25 Art. 2(3) EMD.

26 Cf. COM(88) 238 final, p. 5, 13, 68; COM(94) 659 final, p. 11; COM(2006) 105 final, p. 7; COM(2015) 339 final, pp. 11-12.

27 Cf. S. Pront-van Bommel, *De consument en de andere kant van de energiemarkt*, Universiteit van Amsterdam, Amsterdam 2010, p. 18-59; A. Duterque, "The liberalization of EU energy markets: A consumer's perspective", *EUCML* (2013) 2, pp. 83-88.

28 Art. 2(3) and (8), 4, 10(1), 15(1-2), and 27(1) EMD, and 2(14) RED.

29 D. Parra and R. Mauger, "A new dawn for energy storage: An interdisciplinary legal and techno-economic analysis of the new EU legal framework" (2022), *Energy Policy* 171, p. 113262.

recognition of collective forms of market participation, as evidenced by the 2018 *Clean Energy for all Europeans*-package (CEP).[30] Collective forms of market participation fall under the umbrella term "community energy" and are thought to allow end consumers to share in the benefits of the energy transition at low costs.[31] Furthermore, community energy allows for the management of the electricity system on a more local scale, which is thought to assist in effective grid management and tackling net congestion.[32] The CEP facilitates community energy through roughly (i.) the recognition of (incorporated) "energy communities", as well as (unincorporated) collectives of "active customers", and (ii.) the introduction of modalities for decentralized energy exchange (e.g. P2P-trading, collective self-consumption, and energy sharing).

1. Collectives as individual actors within European energy law

European energy law assigns rights and obligations on the basis of the classification of actors as either "final customers", "household customers", "active customers" (EMD), and "renewables self-consumers" (RED).[33] The classification as active customer or renewables self-consumer is especially relevant from a community energy perspective. Active customers (or renewables self-consumers) can roughly be defined as final customers (of electricity) who consume, store or sell self-generated (renewable[34]) electricity and/or participate in flexibility or energy efficiency schemes, provided that those activities do not constitute their primary commercial or professional activity. This classification requires both an objective (participation in certain activities) and partly subjective (purpose of the transaction) assessment.

Importantly, the definition of active customer includes certain unincorporated[35] groups of jointly acting final customers and treats such groups as a single active customer.[36] The RED requires such groups to be located in the same building or multi-condominium block, whereas the EMD sets no further conditions to treatment of such groups as a single active customer.[37] Where the above conditions are met, European energy legislation treats such

30 Cf. cons. 66-67 RED II and cons. 43-47 EMD IV.

31 Cf. cons. 43 EMD.

32 Cf. H. Yazdani, M. Doostizadeh and F. Aminifar, "Unlocking the value of flexibility of behind-the-meter prosumers: An overview of mechanisms to esteemed trends", *The Electricity Journal* (2022) 35, p. 107126; S. Lavrijssen and A.C. Parra, "Radical Prosumer Innovations in the Electricity Sector and the Impact on Prosumer Regulation", *Sustainability* (2017) 1207, pp. 1-21

33 Art. 2(3), (4), and (8) EMD, and 2(14) RED.

34 Only the RED requires electricity to be produced from renewable sources.

35 Where groups are incorporated, they form an individual active customer (or renewables self-consumer).

36 Art. 2(8) and (15), and 15(2)(a) and (b) EMD, *jo.* 2(14) and (15), and 21(2)(a) RED.

37 Art. 2(8) EMD and 2(15) RED.

unincorporated groups as it would treat individual active customers and renewables self-consumers. Member States may opt, however, for differential treatment of (unincorporated) collectives, if proportionate and duly justified.[38] Such rules might relate to applicable tariffs and charges in relation to electricity consumption of electricity produced outside of the consuming party's premises, and/or conditions for participation in certain energy activities, so long as access to the aforementioned rights is maintained for these groups.[39]

Where collectives of active customers and/or final customers are incorporated, they – in principle – classify as an individual active customer, but could potentially classify as either a "citizen energy community" (CEC; under the EMD) or a "renewable energy community" (REC; under the RED) as well.[40] The European Commission (EC) envisions an important role for energy communities in a decentralized and sustainable energy system and will likely expand upon the current rules in future.[41] The definitions of CECs and RECs are largely similar, when it comes to the required governance structure ("open and voluntary"), ownership and control ("participation" and "effective control" by citizens, local authorities and (non-energy) smaller businesses), and purpose ("to generate social and environmental benefits" rather than financial profits).[42] Furthermore, both types of energy communities have a right to exercise energy activities, including generation, distribution, supply, aggregation, consumption, sharing, storage of energy and provision of energy-related services.[43] The definitions diverge, however, when it comes to conditions relating to geographical scope (broad access or access only for those situated in the direct proximity of the production unit(s)), the sourcing of energy production (non-renewable or renewable), access of membership (restricted or broadly accessible), autonomy in decision making (full autonomy or decision-making by limited members/shareholders) and effective control (effective control by SMEs in the proximity of the project possible or effective control by medium and large enterprises forbidden).[44] These differences are characteristic of the different aims of the respective directives.[45] When it comes to the actual assignment of

---

38 Art. 2(8) and 15(2)(a) and (b) EMD, and 2(15) and 21(2)(a) RED.

39 Art. 21(2)(a) and (4) RED, and 15(3) EMD.

40 Art. 2(11) and 16 EMD, and 2(16) and 22 RED.

41 Cf. cons. 43-47 EMD.

42 A. Caramizaru and A. Uihlein, *Energy communities: an overview of energy and social innovation*, EUR 30083 EN, Publications Office of the European Union, Luxembourg 2020, ISBN 978-92-76-10713-2, doi:10.2760/180576, JRC119433, p. 7.

43 *Ibid.*, p. 8.

44 *Idem.*

45 L. Diestelmeier, "'Energiegemeenschappen': een decentrale oplossing voor de energietransitie?" (2021) 3 *NTE* pp. 109-112; E. Tarpani *et al.*, "Energy Communities Implementation in the European Union: Case Studies from Pioneer and Laggard Countries" (2022) 14 *Sustainability*, pp. 3-5; A. Grignani *et al.*, "Community cooperative: A new legal form for enhancing social capital for the development of renewable energy communities in Italy" (2021) 14 *Energies*, pp. 1-2.

rights to the aforementioned energy communities, the directives remain largely similar.

2. *Rights of active participation in the energy markets*

Current (and future) EU legislation explicitly provides for the horizontal exchange of electricity. The current (and future[46]) legislative framework recognizes so-called collective self-consumption (CSC)[47], peer-to-peer trading (P2P-trading)[48], and energy sharing.[49] The common element within these modalities of horizontal energy exchange is that they take place in a horizontal setting, meaning that final customers contract each other directly or via a (professional) facilitating third party, such as an energy supplier, an energy community or a different (unclassified) entity.

Self-consumption entails the immediate consumption of electricity at the location of production (i.e. consumption takes place before the electricity is fed into the grid).[50] CSC – although not defined under the CEP – appears to entail the self-consumption of electricity within a group of jointly acting final customers. In such a situation, energy production and consumption take place behind different CPs and energy is thus fed into the distribution grid (uptake) before it is extracted by the final customer (offtake). Any such transfer of electricity via the distribution grid would normally qualify as supply, and thus warrant compliance with the discussed broad set of requirements for supply to end consumers.

CSC, however, requires that end consumers be treated identically to self-consuming end consumers. In order to bridge the differences between CSC and individual cases of self-consumption, it has thus been repeatedly suggested to digitally link the metering devices at the point of production and the point of consumption to offset consumption with production elsewhere.[51] This approach

---

46 See the Proposal for a Regulation of the European Parliament and of the Council amending Regulations (EU) 2019/943 and (EU) 2019/942 as well as Directives (EU) 2018/2001 and (EU) 2019/944 to improve the Union's electricity market design, COM(2023) 148 final (EMD-proposal).

47 Art. 2(15) and 21(2)(a) RED II, and Art. 2(8) and 15(2) EMD IV, respectively.

48 Art. 2(18) RED II.

49 Art. 21(4) RED II, and 16(3)(e) EMD IV. See also the proposed Art. 2(10a), and 15a under the EMD-proposal, pp. 42-44.

50 Cf. T. Capper *et al.*, "Peer-to-peer, community self-consumption, and transactive energy: A systematic literature review of local energy market models" (2022) 162 *Renewable and Sustainable Energy Reviews*, pp. 4-5.

51 H. de Heer, L. Fiorini, A. van der Veen and E. Winters, *Collectieve zelfconsumptie: een bouwsteen om het maatschappelijk draagvlak voor de energietransitie te vergroten?*, RVO, Den Haag 2022, available via: www.dnv.nl/news/collectieve-zelfconsumptie-220385; B. Fina and C. Monsberger, "Legislation for renewable energy communities in Austria: changes from the legislative draft to the finally enacted law" (2022) 15 *Journal of World Energy Law and Business*, p. 242; A. Buijze *et al.*, *Power to the People*, TNO, Den Haag 2021, p. 18-23, available via: www.uu.nl/sites/default/files/rebo-Power-to-the-People-rapport-TKi-2021.pdf.

makes use of the so-called imbalance settlement process, that – somewhat simplified – requires any offtake of electricity to be accounted for by an identical uptake of electricity at the end of every fifteen minutes (imbalance settlement period).[52] Electricity that is netted within these fifteen minutes, does – in theory – not need to be accounted for.

Organizing CSC as such would bring about a fictitious situation of immediate self-consumption, but differences remain. Member States retain, however, the right to differential treatment of and to levy charges over the consumption of electricity produced outside of the location where consumption takes place.[53] As the directives do not include substantive rules on CSC, Member States have a significant margin of appreciation when implementing these rules.

The above notions of CSC and (conventional) self-consumption are of relevance exclusively to unincorporated collectives of final customers. Where collectives are incorporated – and classify as either a CEC or REC – these collectives are permitted to arrange for the sharing of electricity that is produced by the production units owned by the community, either on their site or sites or offsite.[54] The RED conveys a similar right to energy sharing to renewables self-consumers located in the same building, including multi-condominium blocks, without requiring them to be organized within a REC. As such, the concept of energy sharing is of relevance to both individuals, and unincorporated and incorporated collectives. Current legislation, however, does not provide for clarity as to what energy sharing actually is.

A recent EC-proposal for reforming the energy market[55] (EMD-proposal) looks to further establish and expand the notion of energy sharing. Under this proposal, energy sharing can be defined as "*the self-consumption by active customers of renewable energy either: (a) generated or stored offsite or on sites between them by a facility they own, lease, rent in whole or in part; or (b) the right to which has been transferred to them by another active customer whether free of charge or for a price.*"[56] As such, self-consumption can be understood as the consumption of electricity produced onsite, whereas energy sharing always implies the consumption of electricity produced offsite by themselves or a hired third party and/or another active customer, and thus a transfer of electricity

52 Art. 15(2)(f) EMD, and 5(1) EMR, and Art. 53(1) of Commission Regulation (EU) 2017/2195 of 23 November 2017 establishing a guideline on electricity balancing [2017] *OJ*, L 312/6 (Electricity Balancing Guideline).

53 Art. 15(2)(e) and (3) EMD, and 21(2)(a)(i) and (4) RED.

54 Art. 16(2)(e), and 16(3)(e) EMD, and 21(4), and 22(2)(b) RED.

55 Proposal for a Regulation of the European Parliament and of the Council amending Regulations (EU) 2019/943 and (EU) 2019/942 as well as Directives (EU) 2018/2001 and (EU) 2019/944 to improve the Union's electricity market design, COM(2023) 148 final (EMD-proposal).

56 Art. 2(10a) Market reform-proposal.

via the electricity grid. The exact physical and technological implementation of energy sharing, remains, however, contested.[57]

The EMD-proposal also establishes basic rights for active customers relating to energy sharing. These rights include: (i.) a right to share renewable energy amongst themselves based on private agreements or through a legal entity (e.g. an energy community, facilitating third party or homeowners' association), and (ii.) a right to have the shared electricity netted with their total metered consumption within a time interval no longer than the imbalance settlement period (and without prejudice to applicable taxes, levies and network charges).[58] Furthermore, the proposal establishes several information duties and consumer rights relating to the terms and conditions used for (facilitating) energy sharing.[59] The right to share energy is, however, restricted to electricity produced and consumed within one and the same "bidding zone", i.e. the largest geographical area within which market participants are able to exchange energy without capacity allocation.[60] The Netherlands currently has one single bidding zone.[61]

Energy sharing is antonymous to P2P-trading and conventional forms of energy supply. P2P-trading is a subcategory of supply and constitutes the direct or facilitated sale of renewable energy between market participants under a (self-executing) "smart contract".[62] The different nature of these energy exchange modalities is linked to the treatment of the forms of energy exchange under the grid balancing rules. Energy sharing takes place within the imbalance settlement period and thus – where electricity is in fact shared – does not bring about any unbalances at the end of each settlement period. Energy supply and P2P-trading, on the other hand, by definition bring about an imbalance that needs to be settled by the responsible party, as the supplier takes upon themselves the universal service obligation *vis-à-vis* household customers (and in some cases SMEs).[63] Under this system, the energy supplier must match energy offtake by the final customer with (self-produced) energy uptake (by contracted producers). To this end, suppliers either must become a balance responsible party (BRP) themselves, or contract such a party that takes care of (the large-scale) balancing

57 Cf. A. van der Veen *et al.*, *Multi-supplier models and decentralized energy systems*, DG ENER, Brussels 2023, available via: https://op.europa.eu/en/publication-detail/-/publication/3968b2ee-f2d2-11ed-a05c-01aa75ed71a1.

58 Art. 15a(1)(a), (b), (c), and (d) Market reform-proposal.

59 Art. 15a(1)(c), (e), (f), (h) and (k) Market reform-proposal.

60 The electricity grid can be divided in several bidding zones, see Art. 2(65) EMR.

61 A division into two separate bidding zones is currently under review by the Association for the Cooperation of Energy Regulators (ACER), see: https://www.tennet.eu/nl/nieuws/bidding-zone-review-tsos-onderzoeken-alternatieve-biedzone-indelingen.

62 Art. 2(18) RED, and 2(12) EMD.

63 Art. 2(18) RED, 2(12) and 27(1) EMD, and 5(1) EMR.

of their portfolios.[64] Especially for smaller suppliers, becoming a BRP appears unlikely.

C. COMPARISON AND ANALYSIS

Condominium law and energy law are fundamentally different legal systems. Condominium law, as a part of property law, is concerned with the balancing of the conflicting property interests within a condominium complex and the administration of that complex. It governs the relationship between the condominium owner and their condominium, but also the relationship between the joint owners and the condominium complex as a whole, as well as the relationship between the owners. The emphasis in condominium law is very much on the democratic collective management of the shared condominium complex.

Energy law, on the other hand, is traditionally concerned with the allocation of rights and duties between individuals and between individuals and the state. Historically, the focus of energy law was on individual actors but recently there has been increased attention to the collective generation and consumption of electricity. A key detail is that collective organization under energy law is always voluntary. Individuals are empowered to work together and benefit from their collective efforts, but only on a voluntary basis. This is in sharp contrast to condominium law, where the owners are required to cooperate and can be forced to accept and pay for decisions made by the OA.

The justification for the existence of condominium law is the physical reality of multiple owners living in one building. Those owners will have to cooperate in order to maintain the shared building. The rules of condominium seek to regulate this process by creating rules on the way decisions are made with regards to the maintenance of the shared building, while also protecting the interests of individual owners from undue interference in their condominiums. This makes condominium law, to a large extent, reactive.

III. THE CASE OF INSTALLING ROOFTOP SOLAR PV ON A CONDOMINIUM COMPLEX

Condominium law and energy law pursue different regulatory aims and make use of different legal instruments. In the following part, we apply both fields of law to a concrete case. In the studied case, four condominium owners (each with a 25% share in the condominium complex) are jointly represented by

64 Art. 2(14) and 5(1) EMR.

their homeowners' association and are planning to install rooftop solar PV on the shared roof to produce electricity collectively for the purpose of self-consumption. The condominium owners are connected to the distribution grid via their own individual connection (or transfer) point[65] (CP) and have each contracted individual energy suppliers for their energy consumption. The collective parts of the condominium are also connected to the distribution grid via an individual CP, on which the homeowners' association has contracted a supplier.

The studied case is typical for modern (small-sized) condominium complexes. As condominiums qualify as individual immovable property objects (*Woz-objecten)* under the Dutch Wet waardering onroerende zaken (Valuation of Immovable Property Act; Wwoz), condominium owners are in principle entitled to the construction of individual (private) CPs.[66] In the case of older complexes, the entire complex is often situated behind a single CP.[67] In such cases, total consumption by all condominium owners is pooled and oftentimes divided *pro rata* in line with the agreed upon division of costs in the act of division.[68] In these cases, the homeowners' association forms the final customer and concludes an agreement with an energy supplier on behalf of the condominium owners.[69] One further exception to the general rule that condominium owners are connected to the grid via a private transfer point, can be found in the so-called "campus exception" under the Dutch Electricity Act.[70] Under this exception, landlords are able to request for complexes used exclusively for (PhD-)student housing to be considered a single immovable property object, which would allow the construction of a single collective transfer point.[71] In such cases, the landlord concludes a single energy supply agreement with a supplier and charges their tenants either *pro rata* or on the basis of data collected from individual sub-metering devices installed in the various condominiums, rooms or studios.[72] Both situations fall outside of the scope of this paper.

A potential alternative to collective solar panels on the roof of a condominium complex are individual panels on private balconies. Discussion of this alternative falls outside of the scope of this contribution for a few legal

65 A connection (or transfer) point is the physical point which separates the electricity network and the (private) installation, see Art. 1.1 Begrippencode Elektriciteit. Cf. D. Kuiken and L. Diestelmeier, "Legal Framework for Prosumers in the Netherlands", in M.M. Roggenkamp and C. Banet (eds.), *European Energy Law Report XII*, Intersentia, Brussels 2018, p. 151.

66 Art. 16(c) Wwoz, jo. 23(1) Electricity Act.

67 Cf. *Kamerstukken II* 2022/23, 29 023, no. 383, p. 4.

68 Art. 5:112(1)(a), and 5:113(1) and (2) DCC.

69 Art. 5:126(1) DCC.

70 Art. 1(4) Electricity Act.

71 Cf. *Kamerstukken II* 2016/17, 34 627, no. 3, p. 24-25.

72 The right to install submetering devices is presumably implied under the right of ownership of the landlord. Energy law does, however, expressly provide for rules on the central metering device, see: Art. 16(1)(n) Electricity Act and the Dutch *Meetcode Elektriciteit* (Electricity Metering Code).

and practical reasons. First and foremost, balcony-mounted panels are not truly an alternative to rooftop solar panels. It is possible to fill both the roof and the balconies with solar panels in order to maximize the utilization of the condominium complex. As such, balcony-mounted panels are complementary to rooftop panels. Secondly, the yield of balcony-mounted panels is limited in comparison to rooftop panels, at roughly 66% of the yield of a rooftop solar panel.[73] Additionally, the limited size of most balconies severely limits the amount of panels that can be installed, especially if some use of the balcony for other purposes is to be retained. Furthermore, installing balcony-mounted panels will often alter the outer appearance of the condominium complex. This usually requires prior permission from the AO.[74] This makes them easier to install than rooftop-mounted solar PV panel. In summary, balcony-mounted solar PV panels can be useful but are not a full replacement for rooftop-mounted panels due to their relatively low yield. However, the legal obstacles for installing balcony-mounted panels are less restrictive than those for rooftop-mounted panels, which makes them an attractive alternative if cooperation with the other condominium owners is not feasible.

A. THE PURCHASE OF SOLAR PV PRODUCTION UNITS

1. Introduction

We have identified four key questions relevant to the purchasing and operation of solar PV panels on the roof of a condominium complex under Dutch condominium law. The first aspect is whether or not the AO has the competence to purchase, install and operate the solar panels. Secondly, we will look at the decision-making process owners will have to follow in order to purchase, install and operate solar panels. Thirdly, we will take a closer look at the ownership of the solar PV panels after they have been purchased and after they have been installed. Finally, we will describe the way the costs of purchasing and maintaining, and the benefits of operating the solar PV panels are distributed between the condominium owners.

2. Competence to purchase, install and operate solar PV panels

As previously established, the roof of a condominium complex is typically considered a part of the common parts of a complex and the administration of the roof therefore falls within the scope of the competences of the AO. These

[73] P. Van Beek, "Zonnepanelen op balkon of balustrade laten plaatsen", *Slimster* https://slimster.nl/zonnepanelen/voorbeelden/zonnepanelen-op-balkon/.

[74] See, e.g., Art. 25.1 of Model Regulation 2017.

competences, however, are limited to two tasks: serving and protecting the interests of the joint owners, and managing jointly owned goods. A fundamental question in this context is whether purchasing and installing solar PV panels falls within either of these two categories.

Serving the interests of the joint owners is intended to be interpreted loosely. Even interests that affect most, but not all, owners can fall within the remit of the AO. An example of this is the so-called service flats, which are condominium complexes that also offer medical care, typically aimed at elderly people that are still capable of living independently but require regular medical care and some amount of supervision.

Purchasing solar PV panels for collective energy production will likely fall within the scope of this competence. The panels are intended to be used to the benefit of the owners as they will all share in the proceeds of the operation of those panels. Furthermore, there is no need to consider whether or not the purchasing of solar PV panels falls within the scope of managing the jointly owned goods as the purchased solar PV panels will, at least initially, belong to the patrimony of the AO as a legal entity and not that of the joint owners.

Installing the solar PV panels is a more complicated matter. The installation will require work to be performed on the jointly-owned condominium complex. The question is whether this can still be considered a part of the administration of the jointly owned goods.

The condominium section of the Dutch Civil Code does not provide a definition of administration. However, the section of jointly-owned goods does provide a definition in Article 3:170 DCC: administration encompasses the operation required for the ordinary maintenance and preservation of the jointly held goods, as well as all operations that cannot be postponed without causing damage and all operations that can be useful for the normal exploitation of a common asset. What can be considered as the normal exploitation of an asset depends on the kind of asset in question.[75] In a condominium context, management is understood to include more than just mere maintenance but also the placement of new installations such as collective heating and elevators.[76] As such, the installation of collective solar panels can be considered a part of management as well and fall under the authority of the AO.

Finally, the operation and maintenance of the solar panels can certainly be considered management of the jointly owned goods. As we will describe below, the solar panels become a part of the condominium complex after their installation. Normal use of those solar panels requires regular maintenance and can therefore be seen as management.

---

75 H.H. Lammers, "Art. 3:170" in J. Hijma (ed.), *Groene Serie Vermogensrecht*, Wolters Kluwer, Deventer 2023.

76 S.E. Bartels and A.A. van Velten, *Mr. C. Assers Handleiding tot de beoefening van het Nederlands Burgerlijk Recht. 5. Zakenrecht, Eigendom en beperkte rechten*, Wolters Kluwer, Deventer 2017, no. 465.

3. *Decision making*

Now that we have established the AO's competence to purchase, install and maintain solar PV panels we will take a closer look at the internal decision-making requirements. Before the AO can actually purchase and install solar panels the meeting of the owners will need to make a decision to do so.

In practice, the applicable voting threshold differs from complex to complex. While the Condominium Act prescribes a voting threshold of 50% of the total votes, plus half a vote, most divisions will require a higher percentage of the vote for certain impactful decisions.

For the decision to collectively purchase and install solar PV panels through the AO, Article 56.5 Model Regulation 2017, prescribes a threshold of 2/3rds of the votes present at the meeting and a quorum of 2/3rds of the total number of votes for decisions relating to the placing of new installations, such as solar PV panels. Model Regulations 2006 and 1992 contain similar provisions. Older Model Regulations, namely 1983 and 1973, require a majority of 3/4ths of the votes present at the meeting with a quorum of 2/3rds of the total number of votes.

There is limited room for judicial review of decisions made in the meeting of the AO. Decisions that were made without following the procedural rules prescribed by the DCC or that violate the deed of division, or a legal provision are subject to judicial review.[77] More generally, the DCC prescribes in Article 2:8 that those involved in the organization of a legal person must behave in accordance with the standards of reasonableness and fairness. A decision made within the AO that is not in accordance with these standards is voidable, based on the interplay between the Articles 5:130 and 2:15 DCC. Judicial review in this case is limited to determining whether the AO sufficiently took the interests of all owners into account when making a decision.[78]

4. *Ownership of the solar PV panels*

If the AO decides to purchase and install the solar PV panels on the common use roof of a condominium complex, the AO is the initial owner of those panels. As a legal person, it has its own patrimony. However, once the panels are installed on the roof the ownership shifts from the OA to the joint owners through accession, as the building is the joint property of all condominium owners.[79] This shift

[77] See Art. 2:15 para 1 DCC.

[78] HR 12 juli 2013, ECLI:NL:HR:2013:BZ9145 (*VEB/KLM*), para 4.1.

[79] There are in this case two different ways in which the solar PV panels could accede to the building, Art. 3:4 para. 2 DCC and Art. 5:20 para. 1 under e DCC. See for an overview of the discussion regarding this topic P.J. van der Plank, *Natrekking door onroerende zaken*, Wolters Kluwer, Deventer 2016.

in ownership is generally unproblematic, since the condominium owners and members of the OA are the same people.

Accession does pose a problem when a third party has a limited right in the solar panels, for example a pledge. When the solar PV panels accede to the building, they lose their individual identity and are, as such, no longer capable of being the subject of limited property rights. Existing limited rights will cease to exist as a result.[80]

In some situations, for example when an owner wants to rent solar PV panels from a third party, ownership needs to be retained by the original owner at all times. Article 5:117 para 2 DCC states it is not possible to establish a right of superficies on the condominium complex while it is divided into condominium rights. The only way to establish a right of superficies on a condominium complex is to end the division, establish the right of superficies, and then divide the building into condominium rights once more. This requires the cooperation of all owners and two notarial deeds: one to end the division, and one to redivide the building. As a result, this procedure is very costly and time consuming in practice, usually more expensive than the costs of the solar panels.

5. *Costs and benefits*

Purchasing and operating solar PV panels will incur costs in the form of the upfront costs of buying those panels and the recurring costs of maintenance. In principle, all owners have to contribute an equal part to the costs incurred by the AO insofar as the joint owners are liable for those costs, unless the condominium regulations contain a different division of the costs. In practice, this is usually the case. An example can be found in Articles 8 and 10.1 of Model Regulation 2017, which states the owners must contribute to these costs based on a fractional share. Article 5:113 (1) DCC states that the shares of all owners are equal in size unless the deed of division specifies otherwise. In practice this is usually the case, and the size of the shares is often based on the surface of the exclusive use area of a condominium owner in square meters or the value of the condominiums.[81]

Some – older – Model Regulations exempt owners from contributing to the cost of new installations if they do not benefit from that installation in any way. Article 52(8) Model Regulation 2006 states that a decision to place new installations must contain a division of the costs of that installation, which can deviate from the regular fraction. Where Model Regulation 1992 or Model

80 S.E. Bartels and A.I.M. van Mierlo, *Mr. C. Assers Handleiding tot de beoefening van het Nederlands Burgerlijk Recht. 3. Vermogensrecht algemeen. Deel IV. Algemeen goederenrecht*, Wolters Kluwer: Deventer 2021, no. 66.

81 S.E. Bartels and A.A. van Velten, *Mr. C. Assers Handleiding tot de beoefening van het Nederlands Burgerlijk Recht. 5. Zakenrecht, Eigendom en beperkte rechten*, Wolters Kluwer, Deventer 2017, no. 430.

Regulation 1973 is applied, owners are not at all required to contribute to the costs if they do not benefit from the new installation.[82]

The solar PV panels will not only incur costs but also generate benefits. The model regulations specify that the condominium owners are entitled to the proceeds generated from the AO's assets and all other benefits that belong to the joint owners based on the previously mentioned fractional share.[83]

This division of benefits can be challenging when it comes to the electricity generated by the PV panels. In our case, each of the four owners would be entitled to 1/4th of the total electricity generated by the panels. There are several ways the electricity can be divided between the condominium owners. One possibility is connecting the solar panels to the condominiums directly, meaning that each owner is connected to their own solar panel. This can be problematic for a fair division of the electricity, however. If there are differences in the output of each solar panel some owners could receive more electricity than they are entitled to according to their fractional share. Another possibility is the use of a solar electricity divider, a system which automatically balances the distribution of the generated electricity between the owners, ensuring each owner gets the electricity they are entitled to.[84]

In our case, the solar PV panels are connected directly to the electricity grid. This means the owners cannot benefit directly from the generated electricity as there is no direct connection between the solar panels and the condominiums. Instead, the energy is sold, and the generated revenue is divided between the owners based on their fractional share.

6. *Summary*

The management of a condominium complex under Dutch law is characterized by a high degree of communality and democracy. The administration of the complex is done by the Owners' Association, which in turn is governed through a democratic decision-making process.

The purchase and installation of solar PV panels fits within the scope of the OA's competences, as the joint owners benefit from these panels. In order to purchase the panels, the owners will need to make a formal decision within the meeting of the owners, typically with a three-fourths or two-thirds majority vote. If such a decision is made, the board of the OA can purchase the panels and have them installed, after which the panels accede to the condominium complex and become the property of the joint owners. As administrator of the condominium complex the OA is still responsible for the maintenance of these

82 Art. 38(8) Model Regulation 1992, and 37(8) Model Regulation 1973.

83 See, e.g., Art. 9 MR 2017.

84 See Lens Energie, *Herman de zonnestroomverdeler en andere oplossingen voor meergezinswoningen*, https://lens-energie.nl/blog/herman-de-zonnestroomverdeler/.

panels, however. The owners are required to pay the costs and are entitled to the revenue generated by the panels based on a fractional share, usually based on the surface area of their exclusive use area or the value of their condominium.

B. MANAGEMENT AND OPERATION OF PRODUCTION UNITS *DE LEGE LATA* AND *DE LEGE FERENDA*

The management and operation of (electricity) production units is strictly regulated under European (and Dutch) energy law. The Dutch "*Elektriciteitswet* 1998" (Electricity Act) forms the primary body of Dutch energy law. The Electricity Act largely follows the EU directives but also reflects certain national policy decisions, for example with regard to the applicability of customer protection rules, and (distribution) grid management. The CEP is not yet implemented under the Electricity Act. Rather, the Dutch government opted to involve the implementation of the CEP in a broader revision of Dutch energy legislation under the proposal for an "*Energiewet*" (Energy Act Proposal).[85] This legislative proposal aims to combine and modernize Dutch electricity and gas regulation, to facilitate (energy) sustainability, and to implement European (energy and climate) legislation.[86] Although the proposal strives to stick more closely to EU rules, it maintains the specific characteristics of the Dutch electricity market (regulation).

The Dutch Electricity Act assigns rights and obligations on the basis of the classification as either a "customer" (*afnemer*) or "supplier" (*leverancier*). Energy users with a connection to the grid qualify as customers, and have certain rights, which are expended in the case of a small-sized connection point (with a maximum capacity below 3*80 Ampère; small-sized customers).[87] This classification is objective and does not consider whether electricity is consumed for domestic or commercial aims, but rather links rights to the possession and size of a connection point. Suppliers are organizational units that sell electricity to customers.[88] Again, it is not necessary to establish whether electricity is supplied for a commercial or non-commercial purpose. Customers enjoy a right to produce renewable energy and the (mirrored) obligation for suppliers to accept an offer for the reversed supply of electricity by their customers, but also includes several consumer law-type rules aimed at restoring the contractual balance between suppliers and customers, especially for small-sized customers.[89] The

85 *Kamerstukken II* 2022/23, 36378, no. 1-2.
86 *Kamerstukken II* 2022/23, 36378, no. 3, pp. 4-5, 11-13.
87 Art. 1(1)(c), and 95a(1) Electricity Act.
88 Art. 1(1)(f) Electricity Act.
89 Art. 95c(2) Electricity Act. Provisions in energy supply agreements pertaining to restricting a small-sized customer's right to produce renewable electricity are void, see: Art. 95c(1) Electricity Act. Cf. Art. 95a *et seq.* Electricity Act.

right to produce electricity is linked to the right to self-consumption of produced electricity "behind the meter", albeit implied.

The communal purchase of rooftop solar PV implies the collective management and operation of the acquired production units. In the studied case, both the individual condominium owners and the OA are connected to the grid via an individual (small-sized) connection point and as such classify as (small-sized) customers. As such, these individual entities have a right to produce electricity, notwithstanding the limitations under condominium law to the production of electricity by individual condominium owners. Under this system, even in the case of communal ownership of the production units, production units must be linked to individual connection points and the electricity produced can only be self-consumed behind that connection point and be sold to the supplier connected to that particular connection point. This severely limits the possibilities for the collective management of production units.

This situation is aggravated further by the fact that the main "benefits" of self-production concern self-consumption and the application of the so-called "net-metering scheme" (*salderingsregeling*). Under the net-metering scheme, energy suppliers are required to net the total electricity that is fed into the electricity grid by an active customer with the total electricity consumed by that same customer on a connection point, or more specifically, on an allocation point.[90] If electricity production exceeds consumption, suppliers must treat their customers as if no consumption took place and are held to compensate the customer for a reasonable amount (in €/kWh) for electricity produced in excess of the consumed amount.[91] This compensation is, however, usually significantly below market value (in €/kWh) of supplied electricity. If electricity production remains lower than electricity consumption, active customers are charged and taxed over an amount equal to the difference between consumption and production. The net metering scheme thus renders identical the €/kWh-ratio of reverse supply and the €/kWh-ratio of supplied electricity. To benefit fully from the net-metering scheme, it thus seems necessary to link individual production units to the individual connection points of the respective condominium owners, which can create issues under condominium law, i.e. the OA would have to decide on private use of collective areas.

The Dutch government has thus far largely refrained from entertaining community energy projects within energy legislation. Rather, government action in this field has primarily taken the form of financial and/or fiscal support schemes, included under the initial *"Postcoderoosregeling"* (Postal-zip-code-

90 Art. 31c(1) Electricity Act. The Electricity Act allows for the construction of multiple allocation points per connection point, on which different electricity suppliers can be contracted, see: Art. 2.4 through 2.9 Netcode Elektriciteit (Electricity Network Code).

91 Art. 31c(3) Electricity Act.

regulation; PCR) and current "*Subsidieregeling coöperatieve energieopwekking*" (Regulation on cooperative energy generation; SCE) for smaller cooperative projects, and the *Subsidieregeling Stimulering duurzame energieopwekking* (*Regulation on sustainable energy production*; SDE[92]) for larger and individual projects.[93] These support schemes seek to bridge the revenue gap between existing technologies and newer, sustainable technologies to stimulate progress in the energy and climate transition(s).[94]

The SCE is a subsidy for the exploitation of production units, rather than a subsidy for the purchase of production units.[95] Its predecessor – the PCR – was a tax-reduction scheme.[96] Under the SCE, the subsidy amount is calculated through a complex formula that takes into account (i.) the normalized averaged costs of production for the used type of production unit, (ii.) the €/kWh-ratio[97] for the reversed supply of electricity produced by the communal production unit(s), (iii.) the value of guarantees of origin (GoOs) generated by the production unit(s), (iv.) the average market price in the Netherlands for the supply of electricity (in €/kWh), and (v.) possible corrections and other factors.[98] Eligibility of produced electricity is capped on a yearly basis, with room for banking of unused capacity.[99] The SCE, thus, does not involve an actual transfer of electricity among individual final and/or active customers. Electricity is transferred to a supplier by the OA or cooperative and the profits are shared between the members of the collective.

Domestic energy users, if organized within a collective, may make use of the SCE, which replaced the (since deprecated) PCR. The accessibility of the SCE is limited to OAs and cooperatives that focus or co-focus on generating renewable energy, provided several conditions are met.[100] This includes the condition that the individual condominium owners must each have their own (small-sized)

---

92 Besluit van 16 oktober 2007, houdende regels inzake de verstrekking van subsidies ten behoeve van de productie van hernieuwbare elektriciteit, hernieuwbaar gas en elektriciteit opgewekt door middel van warmtekrachtkoppeling (Besluit stimulering duurzame energieproductie), available in consolidated version via: https://wetten.overheid.nl/BWBR0022735/2022-03-26.

93 The PCR was in place until 1 April 2021: Regeling verlaagd tarief voor collectieve opwek, see: Wet van 18 december 2013 tot wijziging van enkele belastingwetten en andere wetten (Belastingplan 2014), *Stb.* 2013, no. 565. The PCR was replaced by: Regeling van de Minister van Economische Zaken en Klimaat van 27 februari 2021, no. WJZ/20120093, tot vaststelling van een regeling voor de verstrekking van subsidie voor het lokaal en gezamenlijk opwekken van hernieuwbare elektriciteit, *Stcrt.* 2021, no. 11080 (SCE), available (in consolidated version) via: https://wetten.overheid.nl/BWBR0044882/2023-01-01.

94 Cf. L. Diestelmeier and D. Kuiken, "Legal Framework for Prosumers in the Netherlands", in: M.M. Roggenkamp and C. Banet (eds.), *European Energy Law Report XII*, Intersentia: Brussels 2018, p. 158-161; *Kamerstukken II* 2022/23, 36378, no. 3, p. 20.

95 *Ibidem*, p. 13.

96 Cf. Diestelmeier and Kuiken 2018, pp. 159-161.

97 Both for electricity actually fed-in to the grid and for produced electricity remaining on the production location, see: Art. 6(1) SCE.

98 Art. 3(1), 5(2), 6(1), and 8(1) and (4) SCE.

99 Art. 4(1), 10(1), and 11(1) SCE.

100 Art. 2(1), and 31 through 39 SCE.

connection point to the electricity grid.[101] The studied case fits these conditions. Furthermore, electricity must be fed into the grid via a dedicated allocation point, meaning no self-consumption can take place before electricity is fed into the grid.[102] Through the SCE, final customers involved in a collective can profit from participation in community energy projects roughly to the same degree as they would profit from installing their own production units and the application of the net-metering scheme. OA-involvement in the SCE remains, however, minimal. Out of the 664 current projects (up until July 2023), only 4 projects concerned OAs, despite efforts from the Dutch government to take away barriers to participation.[103]

Dutch energy law offers no possibilities for the factual horizontal exchange of electricity, despite this being prescribed by the CEP. The Electricity Act treats the exchange of electricity between two separate connection points as "supply", meaning that the OA would qualify as a supplier and would consequently fall within the ambit of the strict customer protection regime of Articles 95a, *et seq.* of the Electricity Act.[104] This regime imposes upon the supplier several information duties and contractual obligations, the obligation of universal supply, and prescribes a supply permit for supplying electricity to small-sized final customers.[105] Furthermore, the OA would be faced with the aforementioned balancing responsibility under the EMR and thus be held to designate a balance responsible party (BRP) for the management of its portfolio.[106] Although the possibility of exemption of these requirements existed for a while under the Decree on experiments on decentralized energy production (*Experimentenbesluit decentrale elektriciteitsopwekking;* Experiments Decree[107]), only a limited number of experiments concerned a condominium setting.[108] This is likely due to the technical nature of the exemptions under the Experiments Decree, for example, an exempted OA would be tasked with managing a project (electricity) grid.[109] The exchange of collectively produced electricity between

101 *Stcrt.* 2021, no. 11080, p. 16-17.

102 Art. 29(2) SCE.

103 Cf. *Stcrt.* 2022, no. 5442, p.3; *Stcrt.* 2022, no. 31822, pp. 2-3; *Kamerstukken II* 2022/23, 31239, no. 367, pp. 3-6. An overview of current projects is available via: https://www.rvo.nl/subsidies-financiering/sce#sce-projecten-in-beheer.

104 Cf. B. Hoops *et al.* 2022, pp. 878-879.

105 See specifically Art. 95a, 95b, and 95m Electricity Act. Following the energy crisis, the conditions for the grant of a supply permit have become even more onerous, see: *Stb.* 2018, 231; *Stcrt.* 2022, no. 26273.

106 Art. 5(1) EMR.

107 Besluit van 28 februari 2015, houdende het bij wege van experiment afwijken van de Elektriciteitswet 1998 voor decentrale opwekking van duurzame elektriciteit, *Stb* 2015, 99; *Kamerstukken II* 2020/21, 31239, no. 335.

108 Cf. Rb, Zeeland-West Brabant 20 juli 2023, ECLI:NL:RBZWB:2023:5098, cons. 4.3.

109 The Experiments Decree leaves room for exemptions of certain grid operating rules and management rules, enshrined in the Art. 16 and 93 of the Electricity Act, see Art. 2(1) Experiments Decree.

the OA and its members thus likely constitutes too large an administrative (and financial) burden to render such activities viable. As such, it must be concluded that the current energy law framework does not facilitate the management and exploitation of communal energy production units by OAs.

The Dutch parliament is currently considering a proposal for an "Energy Act"[110], which seeks to bring energy legislation in line with the CEP. Several important concepts related to decentralized energy exchange are, however, missing in the legislative proposal.[111] The Energy Act Proposal – as it currently stands – only provides for a regime for peer-to-peer-trading of electricity, either directly or indirectly via a facilitating third party (P2P-trader). CSC and energy sharing are both not included in the proposal.[112] As such, more novel options for the non-commercial horizontal exchange of energy "behind the meter" do not seem likely to be implemented in the Dutch context any time soon. Furthermore, the current proposal only allows for the classification of unincorporated collectives of commercial energy customers as a single customer.[113] Finally, the proposal defines energy communities (closely following the EMD-text), without providing for substantive rules on said energy communities yet.[114] Following the EU EMD-proposal mentioned in the previous part, the Dutch government has since noted that rules on energy sharing will be implemented via a separate legislative act, which will likely be introduced after adoption of the EMD-proposal.[115] It is unclear whether a proposal for rules on energy sharing will be integrated with the proposal for an Energy Act.

The concept of P2P-trading under the Energy Act Proposal follows the CEP – specifically the RED – closely.[116] P2P-trading is treated as conventional "supply" with limited carve-outs, depending on the trading actors involved, as well as the commercial or non-commercial nature and scale of trading.[117] In principle, active customers (or energy communities) are not held to obtain a supply permit where the supply of electricity to other customers does not form their primary commercial activity, and the amount of kWh supplied does not exceed the amount of kWh consumed by the active customer over the course of a year.[118] Importantly, the Energy Act Proposal does not exempt traders from

110 *Kamerstukken II* 2022/23, 36378, no. 1-2.

111 Cf. S.T. Kalisvaart, "Energiedelen, peer-to-peer-handel en collectief zelfverbruik" (2023) *NTE* 2/3, pp. 72-74.

112 The Energy Act Proposal does, however, provide for the possibility of issuing regulations relating to energy sharing, see Art. 2.2(3) Energy Act Proposal.

113 Art. 1.1, and 1.5(2) Energy Act Proposal.

114 Art. 1.1, and 2.4 Energy Act Proposal. More substantive rules are set to be included in an accompanying governmental decree, see Art. 2.4(3) Energy Act Proposal.

115 Fiche 6 bij: *Kamerstukken II* 2022/23, 22112, no. JB, p. 5, available via: www.rijksoverheid.nl/documenten/publicaties/2023/03/14/fiche-6-verordening-ter-verbetering-van-het-eu-elektriciteitsmarktontwerp; *Kamerstukken II* 2022/23, 36378, no. 5, pp. 7-8.

116 Art. 1.1 Energy Act Proposal. Cf. Art. 2(18) RED.

117 Art. 2.17(2), and 2.31 Energy Act Proposal.

118 Art. 2.17(2)(a) and (b) Energy Act Proposal.

the obligation of universal supply. This limits the room for small-scale P2P-trading of electricity, as the active customer would have to provide in full for the electricity demand of the contracted energy consumer on their connection point. As such, the trading active customer is in principle faced with balancing responsibilities, of which he is only exempted when participating in facilitated P2P-trading.[119] In those cases, balancing responsibilities lie with the P2P-trader involved.

For the studied case, the envisaged regulation of P2P-trading does not properly facilitate the direct horizontal exchange of collectively produced electricity, as production of electricity should be situated behind different allocation points, that will be linked to the connection points of the respective condominium owners. In that case, the OA would be held to source the entire electricity demand of the respective condominium owners, and would have to negotiate a (likely costly) BRP. The possibility of facilitated P2P-trading remains, however, more likely, as this allows for outsourcing the more stringent obligations under energy law to a professional party. Such a system would, however, not amount to the collective exploitation and consumption of production units, but rather would amount to a situation of (conventional) supply of electricity against a cheaper rate. It must thus be concluded that the Dutch legislator is set to maintain a conservative approach, in which horizontal exchange of electricity is aligned with conventional energy supply as much as possible and more novel arrangements are shunned/ignored/postponed.[120]

IV. CONCLUSION

The energy and climate transitions necessitate the greening of Dutch building stock. In this chapter, we discussed different legal obstacles to the further participation of condominum buildings in the energy transition. Current and future legislation do not provide for easy, profitable, and viable options for the collective management and operation of solar PV production units within a condominium context.

On the one hand, this is caused by distinct differences in nature of the respective energy and condominium rules. Where condominium law purports to safeguard the collective interests involved in the condominium complex, energy law seeks to strengthen individual final customers in relation to their contractual counterparts. Even where condominium law allows for the collective purchase and exploitation of production units, energy law assigns final customers the right

119 Art. 2.40(1) Energy Act Proposal.

120 This likely stems from the focus on the protection of final customers of electricity, which only gained in importance after the energy crisis of the past winter period, cf. *Kamerstukken II* 2022/23, 36378, no. 5, pp. 5-7.

to freely choose a supplier (to opt out) and thus values individual rights over the collective "greener" alternative.

On the other hand, some obstacles can be traced back to a perceived reluctance on account of the Dutch government in facilitating community energy projects as full alternatives to contractual arrangements within the energy market. Despite EU legislation to the contrary, current and future Dutch energy legislation does not facilitate the sharing of collectively produced electricity. Future legislation only provides for P2P-trading as a subcategory for conventional supply, with very limited carve-outs. It refrains from entertaining novel arrangements for the horizontal exchange of electricity, such as CSC or energy sharing. Rather, draft legislation sticks closely to the conventional supplier "roles" within the market and expects new market actors, such as (collectives of) active customers, to meet similar conventional normative requirements under law. Legislation must adapt to meet the specific challenges for condominium complexes posed by the energy and climate transitions.

PRIORITY RULE UNDER PRESSURE?

A Contribution on the Priority Rule, Change in Priority, the Principle of Reasonableness and Fairness and the Abuse of Rights – All in Light of the Achievement of Sustainability Goals

Ellen MAATHUIS*
Lecturer and PhD candidate, Radboud University Nijmegen

I. INTRODUCTION

If the various contributions in Dutch literature are to be believed, several principles of (Dutch) property law stand in the way of achieving sustainability goals.[1] For instance, the "principle of exclusivity" would be a problem in light of the sharing economy: after all, the sharing economy – in line with its name – is all about "sharing" rather than "excluding".[2] Another example of a problematic principle can be found in the context of the circular economy. With regard to the transition to a (more) circular economy – in particular where the product-as-a-service model is concerned – the "principle of unity" is regularly found to be a serious obstacle (or, at least, unfavourable).[3]

* This contribution was completed in June 2023. Later developments were not taken into account.

1 For an overview and further references, see: S.E. BARTELS & E.E. MAATHUIS, "Duurzaamheidsambities en goederenrechtelijke spanning" (2022) 50 *NTBR*, 1–21.

2 B. AKKERMANS, "Duurzaam goederenrecht: naar een herijking van ons goederenrechtelijk stelsel?" (2018) 4 *TPR* 2018, (1437) 1462; B. AKKERMANS, *Sustainable Property Law. Reckoning, Resilience, and Reform*, Eleven, Den Haag 2022.

3 See, among others: A.M. SCHMIDT, "Diensten in de circulaire economie en enkele mogelijke privaatrechtelijke belemmeringen" (2017) 120 *Milieu & Recht*, 1–13; B. LEGGER, "De circulaire economie en het product als dienst-model in het Nederlandse goederenrecht" (2018) 3–4 *TvZ*; R. WESTRIK, "Circulariteit en privaatrecht. Een nieuw eigendomsconcept of een Circulariteitswet?" (2022) 7354 *WPNR*, 21–28; B. HOOPS & B. AKKERMANS, "Goederenrecht en duurzaamheid" (2023) *WPNR* 7407, 330–336.

In this contribution, I focus on another principle: the "principle of priority", also known as "the priority rule". Compared to the principle of unity, less attention has been paid to this principle in light of sustainability ambitions. Nonetheless the priority rule seems to be an obstacle in certain sustainability cases. Hereinafter I first discuss the priority rule as such (II), after which I turn to the possibility of "change in priority" – a possibility that Dutch law provides in so many words (III). Then, using three specific cases, I illustrate the increasing need for change in priority in light of sustainability (IV). After a brief interim conclusion (V), I consider the role that the principle of reasonableness & fairness and/or the doctrine of abuse of rights can play with regard to change in priority in sustainability cases in the final substantive section (VI). I conclude with a brief overview and summary (VII).

II. THE PRIORITY RULE

The priority rule is a well-known and important principle in Dutch property law: property rights that are created earlier in time are awarded stronger protection.[4] In other words: the ranking order of property rights is determined by the order in which they are established. The right established earlier "outranks" the right established later.

Although the priority rule does not appear as a general principle in so many words in the law[5], its validity is undisputed. Meijers – the designer of the Dutch Civil Code (hereinafter: "CC") – was of the opinion that the principle did not need to be enshrined in law, precisely because its validity is already generally recognised.[6] Moreover, the priority rule stems from the well-known *nemo plus*-principle: no one can transfer more rights than he himself has.[7] The party entitled to the prior right can oppose to the party entitled to the later right that the person from whom he acquired the later right no longer had power of disposal over the rights, since these rights had already been transferred to the first party. In addition, the priority rule also follows from the so-called "third-party effect": Property rights apply against everyone and thus, anyone entitled to any right must respect prior property rights concerning the same object.[8]

In short, the priority rule determines the ranking order between property rights: the right established earlier takes precedence over the right established later. However, the principle is not absolute; exceptions are possible. For example,

4 *Prior tempore potior iure.*

5 With regard to registered property, Art. 3:21 (1) CC does stipulate that the order of priority of registrations is determined by the order of registration.

6 Van Zeben, Du Pon & Olthof, *Parl. Gesch. BW Boek 5* 1981, p. 3 (TM).

7 *"Nemo plus iuris ad alium transferre potest quam ipse haberet".*

8 L.M. de Hoog, *De prioriteitsregel in het vermogensrecht (Ars Notariatus nr. 167)*, Wolters Kluwer, Deventer 2018, par. 1.1.

in certain situations and under a number of conditions, parties can modify the ranking order of property rights themselves. This so-called "change in priority" is the subject of the next section.

III. CHANGE IN PRIORITY

A. ARTICLE 3:262 CC

In certain situations, there may be a need to amend the ranking of property rights. It is not always desirable or practical that the prior right takes precedence over the later right. Dutch property law therefore provides – under certain conditions – for the possibility to amend the ranking order between two rights of mortgage[9] (Art. 3:262 para 1 CC) or between a right of mortgage and another limited right (Art. 3:262 para 2 CC).[10] In this contribution I refer to this concept as "change in priority".[11]

For example, in the following situation there may be a need for a change in priority between two rights of mortgage. Party A – the mortgagor – needs additional credit. Party B – A's principal bank and the first mortgagee – is unable and/or unwilling to provide additional financing. A third party – Party C – is willing to provide party A with the credit it needs, but only on condition that it obtains a first, highest-ranking right of mortgage. The need for a change in priority is clear. Based on the priority rule, B's right of mortgage would take precedence, but in order to meet C's condition, the rights of mortgage must switch in rank. An example in which the second paragraph of Article 3:262 CC comes into play, and where there is a need for a change in priority between a right of mortgage and another limited right (specifically a right of superficies), is discussed in the next section (case study 1).

As mentioned earlier, the possibility of change in priority between limited rights exists only under certain conditions. First of all, the change in priority must be set out in a notarial deed, which must then be registered in the public registers. In addition, the party entitled to the prior right – party B in the

---

9 With "right of mortgage" I refer to the Dutch *recht van hypotheek*, as laid down in Art. 3:227 CC.

10 Art. 3:262 CC.
"1. *Bij een notariële akte die in de registers wordt ingeschreven, kan worden bepaald dat een hypotheek ten aanzien van een of meer hypotheken op hetzelfde goed een hogere rang heeft dan haar volgens het tijdstip van haar inschrijving toekomt, mits uit de akte blijkt dat de gerechtigden tot die andere hypotheek of hypotheken daarin toestemmen.*
2. *Met overeenkomstige toepassing van het eerste lid kan ook worden bepaald dat een hypotheek en een ander beperkt recht ten aanzien van elkaar worden geacht in andere volgorde te zijn ontstaan dan is geschied.*"

11 In Dutch this concept is called *rangwisseling*.

situation above – must agree to the change in priority. After all, that party's right gets a lower rank as a result of the change in priority.

B. ANALOGOUS APPLICATION TO THE RIGHT OF PLEDGE

It is important to note that Article 3:262 CC limits the possibility of change in priority to modifications between two rights of mortgage, on the one hand, and between a right of mortgage and another limited right, on the other hand. The Dutch Civil Code does not have a similar provision for the right of pledge.[12] The question as to whether Article 3:262 CC can be applied analogously to the right of pledge has long been the subject of debate in legal literature.[13] With the so-called "*Bowie* judgment" of 2021, this discussion was settled. The Dutch Supreme Court ruled that analogous application of Article 3:262 CC to the right of pledge fits into the system of the law and is in line with the cases regulated by the law – and is therefore possible.[14] In this judgment, the Dutch Supreme Court clearly adopted a so-called "*Quint/Te Poel*-reasoning." This term stems from a judgment from 1959. In the judgment in question, the Dutch Supreme Court stated that in cases not regulated by the law, a solution must be accepted that fits into the system of the law and matches the cases regulated by the law.[15] In the *Bowie* judgment, this solution was the analogous application of Article 3:262 CC to the right of pledge.

---

12 With "right of pledge" I refer to the Dutch *recht van pand*, as laid down in Art. 3:227 CC.

13 See, for example: N.E.D. Faber & N.S.G.J. Vermunt, "Het verleggen van grenzen bij het bepalen van de rangorde van rechten van pand of hypotheek" in: N.E.D. Faber e.a. (eds), *Bancaire zekerheid: liber amicorum mr. J.H.S.G.K. Timmermans*, Kluwer, Deventer 2010; F.E.J. Beekhoven van den Boezem, "Reactie op 'Rangwisseling pandrecht door eigenlijke achterstelling' van mr. R.J. Abendroth in WPNR 2014/7029" (2015) 7072 *WPNR*; B.A. Schuijling, *Levering en verpanding van toekomstige goederen (Onderneming en recht nr. 90)*, Kluwer, Deventer 2016; K.J. Krzeminski, "Een afwijkende rangorde van pandrechten" (2017) 7092 *WPNR*; L.M. de Hoog, *De prioriteitsregel in het vermogensrecht (Ars Notariatus, nr. 167)*, Wolters Kluwer, Deventer 2018, p. 172–177; W.H.M. Reehuis & A.H.T. Heisterkamp, *Pitlo Goederenrecht*, Kluwer, Deventer 2019, nr. 781; C.F.B. Groot Rouwen, "Wijziging van de onderlinge rangorde van pandrechten" (2019) 5 *MvV*; K. Everaars, *Wijziging van beperkte rechten (Onderneming en recht nr. 123)*, Kluwer, Deventer 2021, par. 3.3.2.2.

14 HR 9 april 2021, ECLI:NL:HR:2021:524, *JOR* 2021/193, r.o. 3.1.4: "*Het recht van pand en het recht van hypotheek zijn soortgelijke zekerheidsrechten (art. 3:227 lid 1 BW). Hoewel in de praktijk ook ten aanzien van het recht van pand de behoefte bestaat aan de mogelijkheid tot rangwijziging, is die mogelijkheid niet uitdrukkelijk in de wet neergelegd. Het past in het stelsel van de wet en sluit aan bij de in de wet geregelde gevallen om aan te nemen dat rangwijziging ook ten aanzien van het recht van pand mogelijk is. Het bepaalde in art. 3:262 BW leent zich ten aanzien hiervan voor analoge toepassing.*"

15 HR 30 januari 1959, ECLI:NL:HR:1959:AI1600, *NJ* 1959/548: "*(…) dat in gevallen die niet bepaaldelijk door de wet zijn geregeld, de oplossing moet worden aanvaard, die in het stelsel van de wet past en aansluit bij de wèl in de wet geregelde gevallen.*"

IV. CHANGE IN PRIORITY IN THE LIGHT OF SUSTAINABILITY: THREE CASE STUDIES

In this section, I illustrate the increasing need for change in priority in the context of sustainability through three concrete case studies.[16] For each case, I also assess whether the desired change in priority is possible. I discuss the three cases in order of increasing difficulty.

A. CASE STUDY 1: MORTGAGE RIGHT AND RIGHT OF SUPERFICIES[17]

Party A owns a building and would like to equip it with solar panels. A does not have the financial means to buy solar panels itself and therefore decides to rent the panels from party B. B is a solar panel operator and is willing to rent out the solar panels on the condition that it obtains a right of superficies. Without a right of superficies, B would lose ownership of its solar panels because they will form a component part of the building (Art. 3:4 *jo.* 5:3 CC)[18] and/or because they are indirectly united with the ground (Art. 5:20 (1)(e) CC).[19] A right of superficies prevents this accession[20] and allows B to remain the owner of the solar panels. In this case study, A has previously established a right of mortgage on the ground, containing the building, for the benefit of principal bank C. Under the priority rule, this previously established right of mortgage takes precedence over the right of superficies yet to be established. This means that in case of execution of the building, mortgagee C can ignore the right of superficies. Executory sale then leads (in principle) to the end of the right of superficies.[21] As a result, accession will take place and B will lose ownership of its solar panels.

16 I have taken the three case studies from: S.E. Bartels & E.E. Maathuis, "Duurzaamheidsambities en goederenrechtelijke spanning" (2022) 50 *NTBR*.

17 With "right of superficies" I refer to the Dutch *recht van opstal* as laid down in Art. 5:101 CC. It is defined in the law as a right in rem to own or acquire buildings, works or plants in, on or above immovable property belonging to another person. An important feature of this right of superficies is that it interrupts the accession of buildings, works and plants.

18 Art. 3:4 CC stipulates that everything that, according to common sense, forms part of a thing, and everything that cannot be separated from the main thing without significant damage, is part of the thing.

19 Under Art. 5:20(1)(e) CC buildings and works that are permanently united with the land either directly or through association with other buildings and works are covered by the ownership of the land.

20 With "accession" I refer to the doctrine of *natrekking* (either based on Art. 3:4 jo. 5:3 CC or Art. 5:20 (1)(e) CC).

21 This is a result of so-called release (*zuivering*). Art. 3:273 CC stipulates that (among other things) all limited rights the (executory) property sold is encumbered with that cannot be invoked against the seller are extinguished by transfer and payment of the purchase price.

The above example constitutes an unacceptable risk for B. It therefore wants its right of superficies to switch in rank with C's right of mortgage. Article 3:262 (2) CC offers this possibility in so many words: It concerns a change in priority between a right of mortgage and another limited right, namely a right of superficies. In this case, the change in priority is possible under the current law, but only on condition that mortgagee C is willing to cooperate. It is quite plausible that in such a case, mortgagee C would indeed be willing to cooperate in the change in priority. The value of the originally mortgaged property – and thus the value of C's security right – is not diminished as a result of the change in priority. At the time of establishment of the right of mortgage, the solar panels were not part of the building, and did therefore not fall under the right of mortgage. The establishment of the right of superficies, and the change in priority with the right of mortgage, prevents the solar panels from falling under the ownership of the building and thus under the mortgage right. As a consequence, the position of the mortgagee has not diminished. EVERAARS also notes that in general the value of a right of mortgage will not be reduced by a change in priority with a later established right of superficies, because the party entitled to the right of superficies is often obliged to pay retribution to the owner of the building (Art. 5:101(3) CC).[22]

The legal separation of solar panels through a right of superficies is a common practice in the Netherlands. In this practice, it often happens that an older right of mortgage has already been established on the building; after all, the purchase of real estate without mortgage financing is the exception rather than the rule. The situation discussed in case study 1 thus occurs regularly in practice. Therefore, a standard deed has been drafted, which can be used in notarial practice in the Netherlands as a starting point when solar panels need to be separated by establishing a superficies right.[23] It is interesting to note that this standard model takes into account the case discussed in this section. Article 21 of this standard model provides for the change in priority with any previously established right of mortgage.[24] The aforementioned article stipulates that the

---

22 K. EVERAARS, *Wijziging van beperkte rechten (Onderneming en recht nr. 123)*, Kluwer, Deventer 2021, nr. 301.

23 On this standard model, see: A.H.G. WILOD VERSPRILLE & M. WEVER, "Verduurzaming in de notariële praktijk: het standaardmodel opstalakte zonnepaneleninstallatie" in: L.C.A. VERSTAPPEN & F.J. VONCK (eds), *Duurzaam Wonen (Preadviezen KNB)*, SDU, Den Haag 2019.

24 The standard model can be downloaded from: knb.nl. Said Article reads – in Dutch – as follows:
"*Ter uitvoering van de in de considerans onder (c) omschreven overeenkomst komen de Hypotheekhouder Onroerende Zaak, Eigenaar en Opstaller hierbij overeen als volgt:*
(a) de Hypotheekhouder Onroerende Zaak stemt in met de vestiging van het Opstalrecht en verklaart bekend te zijn met de daarop van toepassing zijnde voorwaarden en bedingen;
(b) het Hypotheekrecht Onroerende Zaak en het Opstalrecht wisselen in rang, waardoor het Opstalrecht rang neemt vóór het Hypotheekrecht; en
(c) *de Hypotheekhouder Onroerende Zaak onderkent de (rechts)gevolgen van het vorenstaande en verklaart zulks te aanvaarden.*"

mortgagee knows and accepts the consequences of the change in priority. If the mortgagee refuses to cooperate in the change in priority – and thus refuses to sign the deed – the change in priority cannot take place.

B. CASE STUDY 2: LONG TERM LEASE RIGHT[25] AND RIGHT OF SUPERFICIES

The second case study is a bit more complicated. Again, we have a building owner, A. In this case, the building owner also wants to establish a right of superficies, but this time in relation to the installation of an "ATES" (an Aquifer Thermal Energy Storage system). A would like its building to be heated and cooled sustainably, but he wants the ATES operator – party B – to remain the owner of the ATES. This has two advantages for A: he does not have to arrange financing and B, as the owner, is responsible for the maintenance of the ATES. A has previously established a long-term lease right for the benefit of party C. This long-term lease right gives C almost all powers connected to ownership. Since the long-term lease right was established earlier in time than the right of superficies, it ranks above the right of superficies under the priority rule. This means that C can ignore the right of superficies.

Hence, in this case as well, the party entitled to the right of superficies (operator B) and the owner of the building (party A) will want to establish a change in priority. As shown in III, a change in priority is only possible if at least one right of mortgage or one right of pledge is involved in the swap. Here, however, we are dealing with a long-term lease right and a right of superficies. This situation is not governed by Article 3:262 CC (compare III-A) nor does it fall within the scope of the extension given by the Supreme Court in the *Bowie* judgment (compare III-B). It is thus not certain that this change in priority is possible.

In III-B, we saw that in the *Bowie* judgment, the Supreme Court used the *Quint/Te Poel* criterion to answer the question whether Article 3:262 CC could be applied analogously to the right of pledge. I would argue that application of this criterion also leads to the conclusion that change in priority is possible in the situation explained above. The question that needs to be answered in this context is whether this variation on the change in priority fits into the system of the law and is consistent with the cases that are regulated by the law. It has frequently been argued in legal literature that this is the case. I will shortly discuss three arguments that have been brought up in the literature[26]:

---

25 With "long term lease right" I refer to the Dutch *recht van erfpacht* as laid down in Art. 5:85 CC. It is defined in the law as a right in rem that gives the party entitled to the long term lease right the authority to hold and use once else immovable property.

26 I derived this overview of arguments from: K. Everaars, *Wijziging van beperkte rechten (Onderneming en recht nr. 123)*, Kluwer, Deventer 2021, par. 3.3.2.2, to which I refer for a

1. *The possibility of change in priority in situations where there is no right of mortgage involved has simply not been considered*

First of all, a study of the parliamentary history reveals that the need for change in priority in cases other than in respect of a right of mortgage was not considered. The explanatory memorandum explicitly states that Article 3:262 CC meets a need that exists in practice.[27] The legislator probably did not realise at the time that a similar need might exist in respect of other limited rights. In any case, the possibility of change in priority in case of other limited rights was not discussed – and thus not explicitly rejected.

2. *Article 3:262 CC is not a deviation from the system of the law, but a confirmation of it*

Secondly, it has been argued that the possibility of a change in priority offered by Article 3:262 CC confirms the system of the law. Under the system of Article 3:98 CC, the content of any limited right can be changed.[28] It is true that the rank of a limited right is not part of the content of the limited right, but it is an important characteristic of the limited right. The rank of a limited right is therefore closely related to the content of a limited right. Change in priority should therefore be treated in the same way as change in content of a limited right. Following this argument, both are possible under Dutch law.

3. *German law offers the possibility of change in priority in respect of all limited rights*

Finally, a glance across the border towards our eastern neighbours also leads to an argument. German law, like Dutch law, is based on the priority rule. Change in priority is then possible under German law in respect of all limited rights resting on immovable property (Art. 880 BGB).

Based on the above arguments – and certainly in light of the *Bowie* judgment – it must be assumed, in my opinion, that change in priority between a long term lease right and a right of superficies is possible, as it fits within the system of the law and is in line with the cases regulated by the law. However, it should be borne in mind that in this case, the cooperation of party C (as the party entitled to the prior right) is required. If it refuses its cooperation, the change in priority cannot take place.

more extensive discussion of the arguments and for further references.

27 Van Zeben, Du Pon & Olthof, *Parl. Gesch. BW Boek 5* 1981, p. 811 (T.M.).

28 On multilateral modification of the content of a limited right by the parties, see: K. Everaars, *Wijziging van beperkte rechten (Onderneming en recht nr. 123)*, Kluwer, Deventer 2021, par. 3.2.

C. CASE STUDY 3: LONG TERM LEASE RIGHT, DIVISION INTO APARTMENT RIGHTS[29] AND RIGHT OF SUPERFICIES

This final case study focuses on a long-term lease right which is divided into apartment rights.[30] After the division, all apartment rights are transferred to different flat owners. Again, in connection with the installation of a sustainability system – for example, the solar panels from case study 1 or the ATES from case study 2 – a right of superficies must be established.

Akkermans, Mertens and Van der Vleuten note that several (junior) civil-law notaries have suggested that change in priority should be possible in this situation.[31] In that case, the right of superficies would have to change in priority with the divided long-term lease right. We would "act as if" the right of superficies had been established first, before the long-term lease right, which was then divided into apartment rights. The division of the long-term lease right into apartment rights then does not affect the "previously" established right of superficies. Based on the arguments set out under case study 2, it can be argued that the change in priority between the long-term lease right and the right of superficies should also be possible in this situation. The fact that the long-term lease right that is to change in priority is divided into apartment rights is however an additional difficulty. Akkermans, Mertens and Van der Vleuten state that an easier solution exists for this particular case. According to them, it would be easier if it were made possible to establish a right of superficies on the common parts: the parts of the property involved in the division that are not intended to be used as a separate whole.[32] In the case of solar panels, the right of superficies could then be established on the roof of the building as a common part.

---

29 With "apartment right" I refer to the Dutch *appartementsrecht* as laid down in Art. 5:106 CC. An apartment right, on the one hand, implies a share in the divided property and, on the other hand, entitles the exclusive use of certain parts of the building which, according to their furnishing, are or will be intended to be used as a separate whole (Art. 5:106 (4) CC).

30 According to Art. 5:106 (1) CC, a party entitled to a long term lease right may split its right into apartment rights.

31 B. Akkermans, R.F.H. Mertens & M.C.E. van der Vleuten, "Appartementsrecht. Een rechtsgebied in ontwikkeling" in: L.C.A. Verstappen (ed), *Boek 5 BW van de toekomst. Over vernieuwingen in het zakenrecht (preadviezen KNB)*, SDU, Den Haag 2016, par. 3.1.

32 B. Akkermans, R.F.H. Mertens & M.C.E. van der Vleuten, "Appartementsrecht. Een rechtsgebied in ontwikkeling" in: L.C.A. Verstappen (ed), *Boek 5 BW van de toekomst. Over vernieuwingen in het zakenrecht (preadviezen KNB)*, SDU, Den Haag 2016, par. 3.1. This would require the amendment of Art. 5:117 CC, which stipulates that the divided property cannot be encumbered (in whole or in part) with a limited right (other than a right of easement).

V. INTERIM CONCLUSION

So far, we have seen that the priority rule entails that previously established limited rights rank higher than later established limited rights. Article 3:262 CC allows parties to amend the ranking order between two rights of mortgage and between a right of mortgage and another limited right – under a number of conditions. The scope of Article 3:262 CC was further expanded in the *Bowie* judgment in 2021: the article can be applied analogously to the right of pledge.

In light of sustainability, the need for change in priority – also outside the cases regulated by Article 3:262 CC and the *Bowie* judgment – is increasing even further. This rising need for change in priority shows that the priority rule is, to some extent, under pressure. In any case, more exceptions to the rule are emerging. The case studies discussed above showed that the required cooperation of the party entitled to the prior right can be problematic. Although I already indicated – for example under case study 1 – that cooperating in the change in priority does not have to have negative consequences for the party entitled to the prior right, in principle, this party always has the power to refuse its cooperation and can thus thwart the – in light of sustainability desired – change in priority.

In the next section, I address the question whether the cooperation of the party entitled to the prior right is legally enforceable on the basis of the principle of reasonableness and fairness. In addition, the doctrine of abuse of rights as a possible basis will also be briefly discussed.

VI. THE PRINCIPLE OF REASONABLENESS AND FAIRNESS

Within property law, the role of the principle of reasonableness and fairness has long been limited. The principle of reasonableness and fairness constitutes in particular an important standard within the law of obligations. An explanation for the limited role of said standard within property law can be found in the great importance that is attached to legal certainty within property law: the parties, but especially third parties as well, must know where they stand. The use of an open standard such as the principle of reasonableness and fairness would impair this legal certainty.

Nevertheless, the proposition that the principle of reasonableness and fairness also has a place within property law has become widely accepted.[33]

[33] See, for example: J.E. Fesevur, "Redelijkheid en billijkheid in het goederenrecht; de rechter reeds lang op het goede spoor" (2002) 6472 *WPNR*; S.E. Bartels & A.A. van Velten, *Mr. C. Assers Handleiding tot de beoefening van het Nederlands Burgerlijk Recht. 5. Zakenrecht, Eigendom en beperkte rechten*, Wolters Kluwer, Deventer 2017, nr. 2a; H.N. Schelhaas, *Redelijkheid en billijkheid (Monografieën BW nr. A5)*, Wolters Kluwer, Deventer 2017, par. 2.11;

When applying the standard within property law, however, the property law context must be taken into account and, moreover, necessary restraint must be observed. Be that as it may, it is certain that parties must also behave "reasonably" in property law relationships.[34] What this "reasonableness" entails and how exactly this standard should be interpreted remains uncertain and always depends on all specific circumstances of the case.

Given the great social need for sustainability, it is, in my opinion, arguable that the principle of reasonableness and fairness entails that – in certain situations – a party entitled to a prior right cannot refuse to cooperate in a change in priority which is necessary in the context of the installation of a sustainability system (hereinafter also referred to as: "sustainability change in priority"). However, a condition must be that the party entitled to the prior right is little or no worse off as a result of the change in priority. We already saw an example of this in case study 1. The right of mortgage never included the solar panels, so it makes little difference for the security position of the mortgagee that the solar panels remain independent by means of a (fictitiously previously established) right of superficies. In that case, if mortgagee C refuses – without any other good reason – to cooperate, he could be obliged by its counterparty (building owner A) to cooperate in the change in priority by invoking Article 6:248 (1) CC in conjunction with Article 6:216 CC.[35]

Another possible ground for enforcing the cooperation of the party entitled to the prior right can be found in the doctrine of abuse of rights, as laid down in Article 3:13 CC.[36] No power – including the power to refuse cooperation in a change in priority – may be abused. It can very well be argued that the party entitled to the prior right abuses its power to refuse cooperation when he has no (or a negligible) interest in stopping the change in priority, while its counterparty's interest in the change in priority – especially in view of the sustainability goals – is real. In addition, the party entitled to the prior rights

A.A. van Velten, *Privaatrechtelijke aspecten van onroerend goed (Ars Notariatus nr. 120)*, Wolters Kluwer, Deventer 2018, par. 2.6.3; K. Everaars, "Wijziging erfdienstbaarheden", (2019) 1 *TvAR*, par. 3.

34 H.N. Schelhaas, *Redelijkheid en billijkheid (Monografieën BW nr. A5)*, Wolters Kluwer, Deventer 2017, par. 2.11. With regard to various property law relationships, the Dutch Supreme Court has determined this in so many words. See, for example, with regard to the relationship between flat owners among themselves: HR 30 oktober 1998, ECLI:NL:HR:1998:ZC2759, *NJ* 1999/83.

35 Art. 6:248(1) CC stipulates that an agreement has, among other things, the legal consequences arising from the requirements of reasonableness and fairness. Via the mutatis mutandis provision of Art. 6:216 CC, this provision can also be applied to other multilateral property law legal acts – and thus to the situation at hand.

36 Art. 3:13 CC generally provides that powers cannot be invoked insofar as they are abused. Powers may be abused, among other things, if they are exercised for no other purpose than to harm another person, or for another purpose than that for which they were granted, or if – in view of the disproportion between the interest in exercising them and the interest that is harmed by exercising them – one could not reasonably have come to exercise its power.

could also abuse its power when it withholds its cooperation solely to harm its counterparty.

As a side note, I would like to point out that in practice it will – hopefully – not have to get to the point where the cooperation of the party entitled to the prior right has to be enforced by invoking the principle of reasonableness and fairness or Article 3:13 CC. Many banks and companies nowadays state that they pursue (big) sustainability ambitions. In that context, one may expect (and hope) that in the situations mentioned above, they are willing to cooperate with the change in priority, especially in those cases where their own position is hardly, if at all, affected. Refusing to cooperate in a sustainability change in priority will not be in line with their own sustainability ambitions. The principle of reasonableness and fairness (as well as the possible use of Art. 3:13 CC) therefore only applies as an *ultimum remedium*.

In short: both the principle of reasonableness and fairness and the doctrine of abuse of power may provide legal frameworks to enforce an obligation to cooperate in a sustainability change in priority, but in light of sustainability ambitions set by modern banks and companies, it will hopefully not be necessary to take such action.

VII. CONCLUSION

I started this contribution by stating that, according to Dutch literature, several property law principles are an obstacle to achieving sustainability goals. This contribution focused on one of these principles: the priority rule. Using three case studies, I have shown that – in light of the achievement of sustainability goals – it is not always desirable for rights established earlier to outrank rights established later. This puts some pressure on the priority rule and increases the need for change in priority.

The law always requires the cooperation of the party entitled to the prior right in a change in priority. This makes sense: after all, its limited right is given a lower rank. If the party entitled to the prior right refuses to cooperate in the – in the context of sustainability desired – change in priority without a good reason (since its own position is, if at all, hardly affected), cooperation may be legally enforceable. A legal basis for the obligation to cooperate in a change in priority in such cases can be found in the principle of reasonableness and fairness. In addition, it can be argued that refusing to cooperate in such a sustainability change in priority without a good reason constitutes an abuse of power within the meaning of Article 3:13 CC. In practice, things will (hopefully) not have to go that far. Modern banks and companies that are aware of their role in the sustainability process will without enforcement be willing to cooperate in the change in priority in the cases described.

PART III

PROPERTY LAW AND THE COMMONS

ECONOMY VERSUS LAW

The Need to Consider the Environment as a Common Good within the EU

Luna Aristei
Postdoctoral Research Fellow, Department of Law, LUISS Guido Carli University

I. INTRODUCTION

Environment and climate are considered today as "commons". They are derived from the Roman *res communes omnium* of Justinian. Commons cannot be privately owned since their function is important for both individual and social needs. The economic theory of the commons is centred on the objective criteria of (non-)excludability and rivalry, which leads to opportunism: The maximization of personal utility, combined with the knowledge that possible self-limitations may benefit other individuals, leads to the inefficient exploitation of the commodity when there are not coordination mechanisms. In this way, there is a *de facto* risk of increasing individual selfish interests that leads to a premature depletion of resources and compromises the integrity of the system, damaging present and future generations.

However, this "tragedy" – to quote Hardin[1] – can be overcome through market instruments. Indeed, Hardin envisages the intervention of a strong state that coercively imposes rules on access and use of resources, placing distrust in individuals who are incapable of self-management and cooperation among themselves; alternatively, a system of property rights with economic interests can be created. As such, the European emissions trading system seems ideal to solve the commons tragedy, allowing operators to use a certain amount of emissions. This mechanism must be cost-effective compared to resources' price, and for sectors where there is not such cost-effectiveness, a complementary carbon tax can be applied. However, some countries (including Italy) lack a reference category for commons. Therefore, it seems that economics have anticipated the law. If environment and climate are commons from an economic point of view, what kind of goods are they legally speaking? What kind of property rights can

[1] G. Hardin, "The Tragedy of Commons" (1968) 162 *Science*, 1243-1248.

arise? How can the punctual definition of environment and ecosystem contribute to the legal definition of commons? There seems to be a clear need to create a single definition of common goods, at least at the European level, also taking the financial taxonomy as a model to allow a fair regulation of these goods.

II. THE TRAGEDY OF COMMONS

Climate and environment are among those open-access goods that everyone can enjoy. Indeed, they are not attributable to anyone's property. Therefore, since exclusion from their enjoyment is not permissible, they cannot be considered private goods. At the same time, they do not fall into the category of public goods either, because if they did, the use by one individual would be indifferent to the enjoyment by others (as is the case in e.g. broadcasting).[2] However, falling neither under the concept of public good nor private good, environment and climate remain somewhat of a grey area.

Environmental and climate may fall under the Roman law category of *res communes omnium*, translatable into today's common goods.[3] In the second half of last century, common goods were placed alongside economic-social management mechanisms to reconcile the environment and the economy, and thereby the ecosystem protection and the productive interests. Indeed, these goods have to be protected and safeguarded for the benefit of future generations, in accordance with the principle of sustainable development.[4] To date, however, there is not a reference category of these goods in positive Italian law. For instance, in 2007 there was an attempt to define common goods within the so called Rodotà Commission, which, however, turned out to be unsuccessful.[5] The Commission defined these goods as things that express utilities functional to the exercise of fundamental rights as well as to the free development of the person.

---

2 G. Bravo, "Dai pascoli a internet. Un'introduzione alle risorse comuni" (2001) 3 *Stato mercato*, 488.

3 U. Mattei, *Beni comuni. Un manifesto*, Editori Laterza, Bari, 2011, 49. The Author considers commons as last generation fundamental rights. See also: E. Ostrom, *Governing the Commons. The Evolution of Institutions for Collective Action*, Cambridge University Press, Cambridge, 1990, 294 p.; T. Dietz, E. Ostrom and P.C. Stern, "The Struggle to Govern the Commons" (2003) 302 *Science*, 1907.

4 The principle of sustainable development was introduced in 1987 with the Our Common Future report by the Brundtland Commission. Sustainable development means development that can meet the needs of present generations without compromising the ability of future generations to meet their own needs. Thus, a balance must be ensured between economic growth and environmental protection to grant generational equality.

5 The Commission on Public Goods (so called Rodotà Commission) operated from June 2007 to February 2008. For more information U. Mattei, E. Reviglio and S. Rodotà (eds), *Invertire la rotta: idee per una riforma della proprietà pubblica*, Il Mulino, Bologna, 2007, 386 p.; P. Rescigno, *I beni pubblici: dal governo democratico dell'economia alla riforma del Codice Civile*, Accademia Nazionale dei Lincei, Roma, 2010, 491 p.

As an example, the Commission identified natural resources (e.g., rivers, waters) as commons, characterized by a critical situation due to their scarcity, excessive depletion and lack of legal guarantees. Thus, a characteristic of commons is that they cannot be privately owned since their function is important for both individual and social needs. Additionally, commons are goods accessible to all that require special protection because of their usefulness, which is expressed in relation to the exercise of fundamental rights and to the development of the person, with no relevance of their exchange value. For these reasons, common goods are excluded from commerce and have to be managed with public governance tools to guarantee the protection of constitutional interests and values. The Italian Supreme Court stressed the limit of the dichotomy between public and private goods based on ownership, leaving out their classification by function and interests pursued. So, if an asset (such as the environment) turns out to be intended for the realization of the welfare state, it should be considered a common good if it is aimed at the realization of interests which are shared by all citizens, regardless of ownership.[6] However, as already mentioned, the attempt to create a legal category of such assets turned out to be unsuccessful.

Even in the European Union there is no single definition of commons. They are not even regulated by the treaties (TEU and TFEU). In 2016, an attempt was made to create an EU Economy for the Common Good, i.e. an economy with a holistic approach close to the core values of the solidarity-based, circular, sharing, functionality-oriented, resource-based and blue economy.[7]

In any case, while from a legal perspective there is no definition of commons, the economic theory identifies four categories of goods, including commons, based on two variables: excludability and rivalry. Excludability refers to whether a consumer can be excluded from the enjoyment of a good because of its use by others. Rivalry means that the available amount of a good for one consumer diminishes because of its use by others. Based on economic classification there are: private goods, which are both rival and excludable (such as a book); club goods, which are non-rival but excludable (such as toll roads); common goods, which are rival but not excludable (like fish resources or the environment); public goods, which are neither rival nor excludable (such as street lighting). So, while the economic classification (public, private, club and commons goods) focuses on the characteristics of the goods apportioned between excludability and rivalry, the legal classification (private, public and commons) focuses on the destination of the good (precisely private, public and common), both neglecting the subjective criterion of the ownership of the good.[8]

---

6 Cass., Sez. Un., 14 febbraio 2011, no. 3665 and 3813.

7 Economic and Social Committee Opinion ECO/378 of 17 September 2015 on the Economy for the Common Good: a sustainable economic model geared towards social cohesion [2015].

8 G. Fidone, "Beni comuni in senso giuridico e commons in senso economico: un confronto tra due categorie non coincidenti" (2018) *ApertaContrada* www.apertacontrada.it/2018/03/07/

Economically, commons are non-excludable since everyone can access them (think eg. of fish resources), but they are rivalrous because if an individual takes some resources, he/she precludes those who come after him/her from doing the same. Commons thus lead to opportunism: The incentive to maximize personal utility, combined with the knowledge that possible self-limitations may benefit other individuals, leads to inefficient exploitation of the good when there is no provision for a suitable coordination. In game theory, this is the so-called *prisoner's dilemma*: Rational individual decisions lead to inefficient and undesirable social consequences.[9] For example, HARDIN, in "The tragedy of commons"[10] poses the example of flocks. Each herder of a flock is compelled to increase the number of his/her animals based on a rational calculation to equalize costs and benefits; at the same time, each animal produces an individual economic benefit while the loss and degradation of pasture resulting from increased exploitation will be divided among all users. Hence, the benefits are internalized, the costs (negative externalities) are not. This is the reason why in economic theory there is the need to internalize the externalities. Indeed, for any action, there are two types of costs, internal and external. Internal costs are costs that the individual bears directly and that are taken into consideration when making personal choices; external costs, on the other hand, fall on others and are borne by society. Indeed, externalities consist of the mismatch between the costs borne by the one who makes use of the resources and those sustained by the community. Externalities are further divided into positive and negative ones, depending on whether they benefit other individuals or not.

If we consider climate change, those who emit greenhouse gases suffer the environmental consequences (i.e. more polluting air) but not the costs (the externalities). Indeed, the polluters bear a private cost but not the social cost resulting from the damage caused by their actions: The producing company does not consider the harm it does to the community (so-called marginal harm) by maximizing its profit and by matching its marginal benefit (benefit recorded by the firm) with the marginal cost it incurs (cost associated with increasing production or service delivery). In such cases, if the costs exceed the benefits, the enterprise will necessarily change its actions. Thus, there are externalities when the environmental/social costs of the activity are both private and public, while the revenues are only for the entrepreneur; on the contrary, climate abatement actions produce diffused revenues but centralized costs.[11]

---

beni-comuni-in-senso-giuridico-e-commons-in-senso-economico-un-confronto-tra-due-categorie-non-coincidenti/ accessed 09.11.2023.

9 R. AXELROD, *The Complexity of Cooperation. Agent-Based Models of Competition and Collaboration*, Princeton University Press, Princeton, 1997; D.G. BAIRD, R.H. GERTNER and R.C. PICKER, *Game Theory and the Law*, Harvard University Press, Harvard, 1998, 248 p.

10 G. HARDIN, "The Tragedy of Commons" (1968) 162 *Science*, 1243-1248.

11 M. CAFAGNO, "La cura dell'ambiente tra mercato ed intervento pubblico. Spunti dal pensiero economico" in D. DE CAROLIS, E. FERRARI and A. POLICE (eds), *Ambiente, attività amministrativa e codificazione*, Giuffrè Editore, Milano 2006, 199.

Hence, to conclude, commons may bring to increasing individual selfish interests and to premature depletion of resources, compromising the integrity of the ecological system to the detriment of present and future generations. However, exploitation cannot be curbed by merely conservative policies since consumption is preliminary and indispensable to economic and/or human development.[12] This is the reason why HARDIN talked about *the tragedy of the commons*, which is surmountable, however, through market instruments.

III. NO MORE TRAGEDY. THE SYSTEM OF PROPERTY RIGHTS

For HARDIN, the undivided ownership of the commons leads everyone to make unlimited and uncontrolled use of them, resulting in overconsumption and the depletion of resources.[13] Indeed, the individual consumer who makes limited use of a common good tends to believe that his/her activity is without consequences; instead, the sum of individual actions leads to the depletion of common goods as a result of the cumulative effect of the initiatives of many that, if taken in isolation, produce low outcomes. So, the human-environment relationship varies depending on whether the individual decides to pursue his/her own interests, putting profit before any other value, or decides to safeguard a common good, as envisioned by economist Adam SMITH.[14]

However, the knowledge that a cooperation between individuals will produce a collective benefit is not sufficient for the behaviour to be implemented. This is one of the reasons why some countries have not signed international agreements to reduce climate-changing emissions, acting in an opportunistic way hoping that others will comply with the constraints of cooperation.[15]

---

12 G. HARDIN, "The Tragedy of Commons" (1968) 162 *Science*, 1243.

13 N. GEORGESCU-ROEGEN, *The Entropy Law and the Economic Process*, Harvard University Press, Harvard, 1971, 457 p.; H.E. DALY and J. FARLEY, *Ecological Economics: principles and applications*, Island Press, Washington, 2003, 488 p.

14 A. SMITH, *An Inquiry into the Nature and Causes of the Wealth of Nations*, Liberty Found, Carmel, 1982, 468 p.

15 E.g. the United States has not ratified the 1997 Kyoto Protocol, despite being among the countries with the largest emissions. The United States promised a simple review of their environmental policies and an implementation of scientific research and technological innovation. In addition, in 1997 the U.S. Senate passed a resolution that made ratification of the Protocol conditional to similar emission reduction commitments from developing countries, such as India, China, Mexico, South Korea and Brazil. Therefore, although the U.S. believed that the Protocol could provide collective benefits by playing the role of regulating energy supply and demand in markets, it did not ratify the Protocol; as a result, the U.S. was able to continue to pollute unconstrained by relying on other countries (those that had ratified Kyoto) making commitments. C. CLINI, "Riflessioni dopo la conclusione all'Aja della VI Conferenza delle Parti firmatarie della Convenzione quadro sui cambiamenti climatici (COP6)", (2001) 1 *Rivista giuridica dell'ambiente*, 176; S. LAVALLÉE – J. SOHNLE – H. TRUDEAU, *Droit international de l'environnement*, Éditions Yvon Blais, Cowansville, 2012.

In this regard, HARDIN, considering the Hobbesian Leviathan, envisions the intervention of a strong state that coercively imposes rules for access to and use of resources, placing great distrust in private individuals, who are incapable of self-management and cooperation amongst themselves.[16] As an alternative to the regulatory state, HARDIN proposes the creation of a system of property rights over the asset, with consequent economic interests to protect it. In both cases, however, these are property-related hypotheses: In the first case, public authority gives rise to public rights; in the second case, by privatizing the use of resources, there is the creation of private rights over the commons.[17]

However, the introduction of public limits on access to and use of environmental resources is not sufficient, as private instruments are also needed to change the human approach. This is because if an individual has an economic interest in protecting the environment, he/she will be motivated to protect it by preventing its overexploitation or damage.

The traditional market model was the command-and-control one, which involved the use of authoritative instruments by public authorities against polluters, leaving no room for flexibility. It was the authority that pre-emptively imposed regulatory and legal constraints on those who caused externalities, with possible imposition of fines. In this market model, the public sector was rarely able to diversify obligations or standards according to different environmental conditions. Furthermore, the imposition of command-and-control measures tended to flatten incentives. Indeed, a standard that specifies both outcomes and ways to achieve them cancels the individual's interest in independently seeking innovative solutions, disincentivizing the search for better environmental protection than the predetermined ones.[18] Instead, the goal must be to internalize the costs arising from activities. So, the command-and-control system is static, and it does not adapt to changing economic positions and environmental contexts. This leads, inevitably, to evasive behaviour, partly because of information asymmetry, and to environmental degradation.

So, over the years, the command-and control model has been shown to have excessive centrality and rigidity as well as substantial information asymmetries.[19] Given these limitations, both the EU and national legislators have attempted to improve and make the model more flexible (e.g. by allowing the use of flexible

16 A re-elaboration of Hobbes' theory was done by William Ophuls, an American ecologist and political scientist in W. OPHULS, *Ecology and the politics of scarcity revisited*, W H Freeman & Co, New York, 1992, 379 p.

17 V. JACOMETTI, "Rivalutazione degli strumenti proprietari a tutela dell'ambiente: tradable pollution rights e emissions trading" (2003) 2 *Rivista giuridica dell'ambiente*, 283.

18 W.J. BAUMOL and W.E. OATES, *The Theory of Environmental Policy*, Cambridge University Press, Cambridge, 1988, 272 p.

19 S. NESPOR, "I contratti ambientali una rassegna critica" (2003) 2 *Diritto pubblico comparato ed europeo*, 962.

terminologies such as "good water quality")[20] establishing a new market approach based on the use of incentive instruments for more environmentally friendly and sensitive behaviour. Several experts have examined the new mechanisms, including Garret HARDIN who has argued that unrestricted, uncontrolled, and unlimited access to ecological resources is the main cause of environmental damage.[21] The need to introduce market instruments that integrate environmental aspects[22] also emerges from the European Commission Communication on environmental policy in Europe (No. 576 of 2000). The Communication states that economic efficiency requires private and social costs to be equivalent at the marginal level. More specifically, resources must be used efficiently and the costs arising from their use must be the same for both the individual and society.

Hence, economic instruments[23] can remedy market failures with cost-efficient results by providing flexibility to firms, incentivizing their technological innovation and supporting employment.[24] Such a market model also enables environmental management coherent with the principle of sustainable development by integrating social, environmental and economic aspects.

The progenitors of economic instruments for reducing pollutant emissions into the environment are PIGOU and COASE, who theorized mechanisms based on the polluter-pays principle.[25] PIGOU[26] suggests using taxation that is equal to the (social) cost of the damage caused to disincentivize pollution: the public authority sets the level of taxation by imposing costs on firms that fail to meet the set standards. To be efficient, this tax should correspond to the marginal external cost of correcting the negative externality, since firms must also include the cost of pollution into their production. Consequently, the idea being that with the imposition of such a tax, the final product will fully reflect the costs required to produce it.

On the other hand, the mechanism envisioned by COASE[27], later demonstrated by DALES[28] and MONTGOMERY[29], is based on imposing a limit on

---

20 A. CROSETTI – R. FERRARA – F. FRACCHIA – N. OLIVETTI RASON, *Introduzione al diritto dell'ambiente*, Edizioni Laterza, Roma, 2018, 207 p.

21 G. HARDIN, "The Tragedy of Commons" (1968) 162 *Science*, 1243-1248.

22 European Environment Agency Technical Report, no. 8, 2005 Market-based instruments for environmental policy in Europe; European Commission COM(2007) 140 final of 28 March 2007 Green paper on market-based instruments for environment and related policy purposes [2007].

23 Like carbon taxes or the emission trading system.

24 European Commission Communication COM(2005) 525 final of 20 October 2005 European values in the globalised world [2005]; European Commission green paper COM(2007) 140 final of 28 March 2007 on market-based instruments for environment and related policy purposes [2007].

25 The polluter-pays principle affirms that those responsible for pollution should bear the costs of the measures necessary to eliminate and reduce it in order to comply with what public authorities dictate.

26 A.C. PIGOU, *The Economics of welfare*, Palgrave Macmillan, London, 1932, 837 p.

27 R.H. COASE, "The problem of social cost" (1960) 3 *The Journal of Law and Economics*, 1-44.

28 J.H. DALES, *Pollution, Property and Prices: an essay in policy making and economics*, University of Toronto Press, Toronto, 1968, 136 p.

29 W.D. MONTGOMERY, "Markets and Licences and Efficient Pollution Control Programs" (1972) 5 *Journal of Economic Theory*, 395-418.

production by granting limited access to a resource characterized by scarcity. It is then up to market actors to determine who can access it through tradable permits.

Pigouvian and Coaseian economic instruments lead to the same result, although they involve different practices; for example, in Pigou's tax-based approach it is the state that benefits from the tax revenue, whereas in Coase's restriction system the economic benefit of higher prices goes to the producer. Therefore, a preference arises for the use of Coase's flexible market mechanisms. Indeed, according to Coase, a market based on command-and-control could not solve the problem of externalities because it could not raise enough economic resources to ensure effective environmental protection. Coase predicts that if there are property rights over the environment, assuming that there are no transaction costs and allowing individuals to maximize their profits through selfish behaviour, a socially optimal equilibrium point will be reached through negotiations among individuals (the so-called Paretian optimum).[30] Indeed, as long as some form of negotiations can be established between those who hold property rights and those who do not, the market will automatically move towards the optimal level of economic activity, regardless of the individual who holds the rights.[31] So, according to Coase's theory, the state should merely allocate property rights, not playing a central role, since it is the market that independently reaches the optimal level of pollution and production activity. So, according to Coase's theory, emission rights are thus property rights that can be transferred in a market maximizing the social benefit.

However, this seemingly efficient model is not without difficulties when it comes to its implementation. First, to implement such a market mechanism requires perfect competition, which is not applicable in the case of the environment because there are the externalities that offset the achievement of competitive equilibrium. In addition, perfect information would be required for everyone in the market, whereas information is mainly held by the operators subject to regulation who have an interest in maintaining information supremacy. Finally, there is the presence of various real-world situations that can occur in the market, making it difficult to identify all the actors involved in a timely manner.

In any case, both Pigou's (i.e. an environmental tax, aimed at incentivizing or disincentivizing certain behaviours) and Coase's instruments have a significant public impact. The latter is also called "cap-and-trade mechanism" that provide a cap – threshold target – and defer to market dynamics the allocation of resources-target among operators, creating an artificial market. It is

---

30 H. Siebert, *Economics of the Environment*, Springer-Verlag, Berlin-Heidelberg-New York 2008, 99.

31 C.D. Malagnino, *L'ambiente sistema complesso. Strumenti giuridici ed economici di tutela*, CEDAM, Padova, 2007, 10.

then up to the public sector to monitor the overall price of emissions by adjusting the cap level to ensure that the price of pollution matches the social costs of reductions; this aspect is not included in the Pigouvian tax system. Instead, such public impact is very limited in voluntary market instruments through which operators' direct consumer choices toward virtuous products or entrepreneurs (think of environmental certifications of products such as eco-label[32] or of production systems such as EMAS[33]).

In any case, the economic system theorized by Coase has had considerable success in environmental regulation (such a model is the one theorized by the Kyoto Protocol and the EU ETS). Under this market-based instrument, as opposed to command-and-control, parties are free to determine the best method for achieving the common goal of reducing climate-changing emissions; indeed, polluters can decide, based on their own facilities and activities, what might be the best and most efficient way to meet their obligations, thereby reducing abatement costs for themselves and for society. The price is then determined according to market dynamics. Such a trading system ensures a considerable exchange of information among market participants, while pushing states to implement their own production by not just setting a cap on climate-changing emissions. This nullifies the costs arising from statutory and regulatory requirements, incentivizing operators to achieve increasingly ambitious goals through self-regulation and evolution.[34]

Participating in such a market system requires a permit to emit greenhouse gases and an allowance that defines the number of permitted emissions.[35] The first is issued at the beginning of the activity, while the second allows the emissions allocated to the individual company to be traded on the market.

The allowance trading system can be based on a baseline-and-credit or on a cap-and-trade approach. In the baseline-and-credit model a reference scenario (baseline) is set on the level of emissions that would occur in the absence of a

---

32 Eco-label was introduced by Regulation (EC) No. 880/1992. The label is applied to those products that have been subjected to an articulated analysis of the environmental impacts of their entire life cycle and that have thus shown to comply with environmental requirements that are stricter than those established by law. This allows for a rating of environmental excellence.

33 EMAS was introduced by Regulation (EC) No. 1836/1993. This certificate enables organizations to periodically monitor and implement their environmental performance by updating the public on the pursuit of their objectives. It is a certificate concerning production facilities and not products.

34 G. Bazzani, "Teorie del denaro e carbon trading. Il frame dell'azione sociale per fronteggiare il riscaldamento globale" (2019) 16 *JURA GENTIUM: La crisi dei paradigmi e il cambiamento climatico* 1, 78.

35 Emission allowances can be allocated through two different methods: grandfathering and auctioning. In the first case, allowances are distributed for free based on historical emissions, allowing operators who have emitted large amounts of GHGs in the past to receive more permits. With auctioning, on the other hand, the distribution of permits is by auction, with allowances allocated to the highest bidder.

regulatory system. For each reduction that is made, a credit is issued that the company can use for its own business or sell to another company who has exceeded the predetermined baseline level. However, this mechanism does not set a fixed limit or cap on emissions. This poses a problem in the event of new market entries. Furthermore, the system also provides trading of emissions that have already occurred and been certified in offsets (credit units).[36]

The other model is the cap-and-trade approach under which a maximum emission (cap) is set by the state. An example is the European Emission Trading System (EU ETS) set by directive 2003/87/EC.[37] Based on this cap, emission rights are then allocated to licensed facilities, which are allowed to emit as much as they hold rights. Unlike the baseline-and-credit system, this mechanism sets a lower cap on emissions than if the mechanism itself did not apply. Cap-and-trade echoes the parameters of Coase's theorem, while differing from it by not issuing property rights over air (quality), but rather allowances to pollute within predetermined limits. Then, once the allowances to emit are distributed, they can be traded on the market. Indeed, in general, individual operators aim to maximize interests by deciding whether it is more profitable for them to invest in their enterprises making them more sustainable or to buy certificates on the market. In particular, each operator compares its allowances distributed by the national authority with its actual emissions in a given time frame. If emissions exceed the available quantity, the company will have to purchase additional allowances on the market. This purchase will result in additional expenses for the operator, who will become less competitive in the market, being forced to raise prices of finished products. Conversely, the virtuous firm that has emitted less than allowed can sell certificates or retain them for future use (if allowance banking is planned). The latter will bring about economic advantage/ increased profit, making it more competitive in the market. So, it is up to operators to choose the more cost-effective action (innovating their company by making it more green or buying emission credits on the market); this is why the price associated to emission allowances has a fundamental role to incentive a greener behavioural change. Thus, to create an efficient allowance trading market, it would be necessary to create a system with as much perfect competition as possible, as envisioned by Coase, with no market actor being able to influence the price. Regarding prices, the amount of the fines (in case of non-compliance) should also not be underestimated. If the penalty to be paid by the operator that

---

36 This system is used in two of the Kyoto Protocol's mechanisms: Joint Implementation, whose credits are Emission Reduction Units or ERUs, and Clean Development Mechanism, whose credits are called Certified Emission Reductions or CERs. These two mechanisms are now unified into the Sustainable Development Mechanism.

37 Council Directive 2003/87/EC of 13 October 2003 establishing a scheme for greenhouse gas emission allowance trading within the Community and amending Council Directive 96/61/EC [2003] OJ L 275.

fails to comply is less than the price of the right to emit, the company will tend not to comply with the reduction obligations, having an economic advantage.

So, in such cap-and-trade mechanisms the state plays a marginal role, as the operators are the real players. By providing a quantitative limit on emissions, these become economic goods with a market price. Operators, therefore, can pollute if they have a permit issued directly by the state authority or if they have purchased the allowance on the market. To ensure the proper functioning of the market, it is necessary to extend the system to as many operators as possible to ensure liquidity and allowances trading, while avoiding excessive fragmentation that would lead to higher system management costs. In this way, the public authority intervenes in the existing market by rewarding the most virtuous behaviour and contributing to pricing, as well as providing for a new Coasian-style market mechanism. In any case, cap-and-trade mechanisms have to be cost-effective compared to resources' price; Where there is not such cost-effectiveness, a complementary carbon tax can be applied.

So, while aware of the failure of a standards-based command-and-control mechanism, the state regulates indirectly by setting up a rigid system, the artificial carbon market, but at the same time leaves flexibility to individual operators to choose what actions to take.[38] However, stricter state regulation of the market is still needed, as it is unable to define and regulate itself to be efficient. In addition, state intervention is necessary to protect environmental resources that would otherwise be disregarded, as companies generally do not intend to deal voluntarily with the negative externalities on the environment generated by their activities.

The combination of emissions allowance marketization and environmental protection has been translated by the doctrine as the carbon trading dogma, indicating that even though the climate crisis leads to market failure, the environment cannot be protected unless market logic is used.[39] It sounds like a paradox, but the economic value of the carbon market should not be underestimated.[40]

To conclude, as Georgescu-Roegen affirmed in 1971[41], it is necessary to connect production and economic activity to the consumption of natural resources, emphasizing their exhaustibility and finiteness. An attempt to combine growth, economic profit and environmental conservation protecting commons has been made with the cap-and-trade market model, but the need to

38 M. Clarich, "La tutela dell'ambiente attraverso il mercato" (2007) 1 *Diritto pubblico*, 239.

39 E. Leonardi, "Carbon Trading Dogma. Presupposti teorici e implicazioni pratiche dei mercati globali di emissioni di gas climalteranti" (2019) 16 *Jura Gentium*, 1.

40 Robert Fletcher estimates about $10 trillion by 2030. See: R. Fletcher, "When Environmental Issues Collide: Climate Change and the Shifting Political Ecology of Hydroelectric Powder" (2010) 5 *Peace and conflict review*, 14.

41 N. Georgescu-Roegen, *The Entropy Law and the Economic Process*, Harvard University Press, Cambridge 1971, 457 p.

define what the commons precisely are, still remains. The taxonomy that will be discussed in the next section can be considered a normative model for trying to solve this issue.

IV. THE FINANCIAL TAXONOMY AS A MODEL?

As seen above, to overcome the *tragedy* of commons there is the need to define market instruments. However, a regulatory framework is needed to define what is a common good. A virtuous example is the so-called sustainable taxonomy, established in the EU with regulation 2020/852/EU.[42] This tool has the peculiarity of identifying the conditions and criteria under which an investment or financial product contributes to EU sustainable goals, being able to mobilize sustainable finance and ensure a high level of financial stability. Indeed, the absence of a unified taxonomy leads to excessive market fragmentation and barriers to cross-border capital flows, due to the existence of different national taxonomies that lead to excessive cost increases.[43]

At the same time, such a taxonomy creates comparability between products, standards, brands, and jurisdictions giving the possibility to market participants to invest more easily and confidently in sustainability. This taxonomy is now focused only on climate change adaptation and mitigation while, in the near future, it will be expanded to embrace all ESG factors including the environmental goals set by Agenda 2030, together with social and governance goals; these latter are currently difficult to determine due to the divergence among different non-financial rating agencies and because of the varying materiality of the indicators used.[44]

The taxonomy is fundamental to increase transparency, providing clarity on the notion of sustainable investment, ensuring greater consistency, reducing fragmentation and implementing the functioning of the market. In addition, perfecting transparency will contribute to a reduction of information asymmetries between market participants, increasing the reliability of financial

---

42 Council Regulation 2020/852/EU of 18 June 2020 on the establishment of a framework to facilitate sustainable investment, and amending Regulation (EU) 2019/2088 [2020] OJ L 198.

43 Technical Expert Group on Sustainable Finance, "Taxonomy pack for feedback and workshops invitations December 2019" (2019). Even before the EU, several authors underlined the need for a green financial taxonomy. See O. Schmid-Schonbein and A. Braunschweig, "EPI-Finance 2000. Environmental Performance Indicators for the Financial Industry"[2000] https://firstforsustainability.org/media/EPI%20Finance%20 2000.pdf, accessed 26.05.2023; J. Keeble, S. Topiol and S. Berkeley, "Using Indicators to Measure Sustainability Performance at a Corporate and Project Level" (2003) 44 *Journal of Business Ethics*, 149; B.J. Richardson, "Climate Finance and its Governance: Moving to a Low Carbon Economy Through Socially Responsible Financing?" (2009) 58 *International & Comparative Law Quarterly*, 626.

44 A. Del Giudice, *La finanza sostenibile*, G. Giappichelli Editore, Torino, 2019, 68.

ESG products and investor confidence. These characteristics will undoubtedly contribute to the integration of sustainability into risk management, fostering the growth of the EU financial market. Indeed, providing transparency to economic actors and investors on which activities are green enables them to reduce costs and to make informed investments in sustainable projects and activities. The use of an EU taxonomy contributes also to the implementation of green investment safety within and outside the EU (by also applying the taxonomy to EU investors investing globally), providing investors with easier access to these products and protecting integrity and trust in the sustainable finance market.

In addition to these immediate benefits, having a universal taxonomy leads to several indirect positive environmental effects through increased investment in activities and sectors related to, for example, energy efficiency or renewable energy. Such a taxonomy will also benefit banks and insurers, who will be able to identify green activities more easily by including sustainability in their investment decisions together with corporations (which will change their activities to attract more investment) and end consumers, who will be able to compare products more effectively thanks to easier access to sustainability criteria and greater transparency.

To enable a full acceptance and integration of the taxonomy, it will be developed in stages. The first regulation approved is 2020/852/EU on climate change mitigation and adaptation. Sustainable investment is defined in Article 2(1) as an investment in one or more economic activities that are considered sustainable under the Regulation. Paragraph 5 of the same Article also defines climate change mitigation as the process of keeping the global average temperature increase below 2°C and continuing efforts to limit it to 1.5°C above pre-industrial levels, as established by the Paris Agreement; adaptation is then defined in paragraph 6 as the process of adapting to current and future climate change and its effects.

Article 3 of the regulation then indicates the sustainable criteria of economic activities. Indeed, in order to be considered environmentally sustainable, an activity must meet four criteria: it must contribute to one or more of the six objectives set out in the regulation[45]; it must not cause significant harm to another objective (i.e. the do-no-significant-harm principle), meaning that the harm must not outweigh the benefits; it must be carried out in accordance with the minimum safeguards set out in Article 18; it must comply with the technical screening criteria. Thus, an activity must contribute to the pursuit of one of the environmental objectives to be included in the taxonomy, even if it is carried out by a so-called "brown company".[46] In addition, to ensure competition in seeking

45 Climate change mitigation; climate change adaptation; sustainable use and protection of water and marine resources; transition to a circular economy; waste prevention and recycling; pollution prevention and control; ecosystem protection.

46 E.g. a company operating in the oil&gas industry may be considered brown. However, even such a company that normally undertakes non-sustainable activities can pursue sustainability goals (i.e. investing in research and development of new energy sources).

funding for sustainable economic activities, the technical selection criteria should ensure that all relevant economic activities in a specific sector that contribute equally to environmental goals are qualified and treated equally. Of course, the ability to contribute to these goals differs from one sector to another, but within the same sector, activities that make the same contribution should be treated equally.[47]

The aim of the taxonomy is also to incentivize the private sector to invest in low-carbon activities, through increased transparency and disclosure of non-financial information. This may also change productions, prompting companies to improve their environmental performance to attract more investment and face lower capital costs.[48]

So, through this taxonomy, a green label is applied to investments. For this reason, with its Action Plan, the European Commission stated that it would use the already existing mechanism of the EU eco-label to establish a voluntary labelling system on sustainable financial products.[49] In this regard, at the end of 2018, the Directorate-General Environment launched a process to define such a label for financial products, which has not yet been completed. Based on the proposed criteria, the first financial products to be covered by the label were identified in March 2019, along with the label criteria related to operators' activities and investment object.

In the long run, the European Commission has established a platform on sustainable finance (Art. 20, Reg. 2020/852/EU). This is a public-private governance structure that brings together experts and market participants with public sector bodies, such as the European Environment Agency (EEA), the European Investment Bank (EIB), the European Supervisory Authorities (ESAs) and the EU Statistical Office (Eurostat). This platform monitors the development of the taxonomy to ensure that it is gradually expanded and adapted to sustainability, together with the execution of activities to achieve sustainable finance goals. It is important to underline that the platform acts on the principle of transparency advising the EU Commission on future sustainable finance actions. It also provides a central forum for discussion among policymakers and other stakeholders to raise awareness and ensure that sustainability remains a permanent feature of policy design over time.

However, although taxonomy can be seen as the regulatory linchpin for the smooth functioning of a sustainable market, it is not without critiques;

---

47 E.g. in the energy sector, the wind and solar subsectors should be treated equally if the environmental objective is common (to reduce pollutant gases to mitigate climate change). On the other hand, the geothermal energy subsector would be treated differently, as it is not carbon neutral.

48 F. Schütze and J. Stede, "The EU sustainable finance taxonomy and its contribution to climate neutrality" (2021) *Journal of Sustainable Finance & Investment*, 2.

49 European Commission Communication COM(2018) 97 final of 8 March 2018 Action Plan: Financing Sustainable Growth [2018], 5-6.

indeed, sustainable positive consequences may not manifest themselves in the same way in different states. It is also important to underline that even though the same sectors and activities should be treated equally if they have the same characteristics, it could happen that an activity that does not fit even slightly into the taxonomy is excluded.

Anyway, the creation of an EU taxonomy on sustainable finance makes it possible to overcome the problems that had emerged especially in the early periods of the functioning of the EU ETS, during which a wide margin of discretion had been left to individual countries. Using "regulations" (instead of "directives" as in the ETS) as legislative acts to regulate the mechanism allows for a uniform regulatory framework within which state action/initiative is limited and a strengthening of EU economic and financial integration is ensured. As a matter of fact, if the taxonomy had been defined by a directive, the drawbacks of decentralized and bottom-up implementation would have occurred. Centralized regulation, on the other hand, produces transparency and environmental benefits by defining sustainable activities at an early stage; this allows financial flows to be directed towards green practices that can contribute to fight climate change and foster the ecological transition.

However, although there is a clear need to use this regulatory tool in other areas as well and to extend it outside the EU, political interference is likely to be a serious obstacle.[50] Therefore, the extension of this regulatory system must be based on objective criteria that are free from national interference. This is perhaps one of the biggest obstacles to the creation of a comprehensive taxonomy at the European or even global level. However, through constant dialogue between market players, it is possible (as it has already been done for the EU taxonomy on climate mitigation and adaptation) to outline a sufficiently clear regulatory framework to help investors direct their financial flows.

So, despite the heterogeneity of climate protection market instruments and regulatory mechanisms developed at different jurisdictional levels, the creation of a regulatory instrument to define which activities can be considered sustainable is necessary to properly and efficiently direct the huge financial flows circulating in the global economic system. To this end, the European mechanism of the sustainable financial taxonomy appears to be a model that should be followed and expanded to include all the factors characterizing sustainability. This regulatory model would also be particularly efficient because it would allow private individuals to manage their own financial resources within a framework

---

50 For instance, the strongly criticized European Commission's recent decision to include natural gas and nuclear power in the EU taxonomy. Indeed, the inclusion of these sectors has been seen by many as a mere consequence of political-strategic and economic interests of some member States heavily dependent on these energy sources. www.europarl.europa.eu/news/en/press-room/20220701IPR34365/taxonomy-meps-do-not-object-to-inclusion-of-gas-and-nuclear-activities, accessed 26.05.2023.

defined by the public regulator, combining the decision-making power of the public and the market.

By creating such a framework, it will be possible to define more precisely what exactly is meant by the terms "environment" and "climate", at least economically. However, there is still a need for a legal definition of the commons, a category that could be better delineated by a legal tool such as taxonomy. Indeed, this would allow its perimeter to be delineated by indicating which activities and investments protect the environment and climate, although not legally defining them.

V. CONCLUSIONS

The condition of privilege we find ourselves in leads most to perceive and experience resource abundance as the rule and scarcity as the exception, resulting in a misrepresentation of the seriousness of global environmental issues.

The discussion above shows that the lack of a unique legal definition of the commons leads to the so-called "tragedy of the commons", which can be overcome with the use of economic instruments. Such instruments protect commons, not through prescription, prohibition or sanctions, but by ensuring that the costs and benefits of individual choices, including those resulting in effects on the environment, are born by the respective authors. Thus, when the implications of the negative externalities caused on the commons are considered, including economic ones, individuals are discouraged from making undesirable choices, thereby indirectly safeguarding the commons itself.

Indeed, responsible use and enjoyment of common goods often leads to widespread and not visible benefits for the individual, for whom the direct and tangible personal costs and sacrifices are instead conspicuous. At the same time, selfish behaviours are usually associated with immediate individual benefit and indistinct or deferred collective risks; however, these are behaviours that lead to the aforementioned "tragedy". This is why the aspect of management is much more important than that of appropriation when it comes to commons. In particular, the latter is characterized more by a legal perspective, while the former is an economic one, which defines commons based on their rivalry and (non-)excludability. Therefore, it seems that the economy anticipated the law creating a framework that defines the proper use of such goods.

This aspect was also underlined by OSTROM[51] who said that neither the market nor the state can ensure the preservation and conservation of the commons. However, partially deviating from OSTROM's assertion, a regulatory

[51] E. OSTROM, *Governing the commons: The evolution of institutions for collective action.* Cambridge University Press, Cambridge 1990, 294 p.

State is needed for the management of the commons to create a legal regulatory framework that unambiguously defines what a common is and what its best management is. This will inevitably lead to defining "environment" and "climate" in legal terms while also enabling the establishment of property rights that may arise from them. To this end, as stated above, the regulatory tool of the European financial taxonomy should be taken as a model to enable fair regulation of these goods. This will allow the creation of a "commons label" that will identify these goods along with the rights (including property ones) and duties arising from them. Through the creation of such a fair regulation it will be possible to define also the individual and social rights linked to the environment and the climate allowing, in the battle of economy versus law, the latter to win. This is necessary to overcome HARDIN's tragedy while respecting the principle of sustainable development.

LEGAL CONTROL OVER BEHAVIOURAL-GENERATED DATA

Shading Its Non-rivalrous Nature

Stijn Debie
FLOF Research Assistant, Institute for Family Property Law (KU Leuven)

It is often argued that legislators, jurisprudence and scholars need to be more precise about how they are examining behavioural-generated data. This contribution puts the remark to the test and uncovers the need to be precise about the natural persons' legal capacities from which they obtain a certain degree of legal control.

Even where the natural persons' existence and behaviour generates data by itself, only the data encoding this ontological information are concerned by (internal) property and obligation law. To further commodify the ontological information, the appropriated data are continuously interrogated and aggregated with freely accessible market information. During these alternating rivalrous and non-rivalrous phases, non-exclusive rights provide natural persons with legal control over the ontological information encoded in behavioural-generated data. A first type of non-exclusive rights enables a "data subject", at all times and *erga omnes*, to influence the processing of data that encode information reasonably relating to him. A second type concerns statute-based personal rights that enable a "consumer" to reclaim legal control over data generated by the use of connected products and services (*inter partes*). Considering their defensive nature, they do not provide a natural person with active legal control over the usage, storing or asset value of the appropriated dataset (rights *in rem*). Instead, the data holder is obliged to provide a duplicated version from which the receiver can accurately interpret the encoded ontological information. As lawful acquisition of property, (internal) principles of property and obligation law determine the degree of the natural person's active legal control over this duplication. Within Belgian private law, one only has (prospect on) full powers if he retains the technical ability to store the duplication. If a third party is irrevocably provided with the technical control over the duplication, the loss of control over the ontological information is *erga omnes* and *inter partes* protected by non-exclusive rights. Thus, when a natural person has the legal capacity of holder, consumer, and subject of a dataset, its legal control must be understood as a statutory and contractual "bundle" of exclusive and non-exclusive rights.

Nonetheless their scope will further evolve along the ever-evolving data economy, this complementary functioning of exclusive and non-exclusive control rights should suffice to regulate the appropriation of behavioral-generated data wherever and whenever they are repurposed.

I. INTRODUCTION

1. **Unstable commodification and commercialization of data** – Individual consumer preferences and market information are generated by mere consumers' existence.[1] Some online service providers, such as Apple, Google, Meta and Amazon, have the technical ability to appropriate and commodify this information.[2] As this potentially harms consumers' personal autonomy, the European legislator felt compelled to limit the service providers' sovereignty over the processing of appropriated data (syntactic data protection) and the usage of ontological information encoded in their ecosystem (semantic data sharing).[3] Non-exclusive rights particular to (non-)personal data and metadata, alongside standardised data frameworks and guidelines on data protection impact assessment, should enable natural persons, competing service providers and governmental actors to (re)gain technical and economic control.[4]

Since a careful reading of general terms and conditions proves that consumers have exclusive rights over substances of the appropriated data, the acceptance of exclusive rights over data could also enhance their economic position.[5] Moreover, the recognition of data ownership could bestow stability upon the economically unstable technical control of data holders.[6] The European parliament is, however, of the opinion that "*a general approach to assigning rights*

---

1 Recital 15 Regulation on harmonised rules on fair access to and use of data (Data Act) [2023] OJ L, 2023/2854; N. Purtova, "The illusion of personal data as no one's property" (2015), 7, *Law, Innovation and Technology*, p. 109.

2 M. Durovic and F. Lech, "A Consumer Law Perspective on the Commercialization of Data" (2021) *ERPL*, pp. 702 and 705 et seq.; H. Zech, "Information as Property" (2015) *JIPITEC*, p. 192.

3 European Commission (EC), "A European Strategy for data – communication from the commission to the European parliament, the council, the European economic and social committee and the committee of the regions", [2020] COM(2020) 66, https://eur-lex.europa.eu/legal-content/EN/TXT/PDF/?uri=CELEX:52020DC0066, pp. 3 *jo.* 4-14.

4 Referred to as "round-about approach" by S. Geiregat, "The Data Act: Start of a New Era for Data Ownership?" (2022), *SSRN Journal*, p. 49, no. 60.
Hereinafter referred to as "commons-oriented theories".

5 N.M. Banta, "Property interests in digital assets: The rise of digital feudalism" (2016) 38 *Cardozo L. Rev.*, pp. 1105-1134.

6 Therefore referred to as "conservative bottom-up approach" by V. Janeček, "Ownership of personal data in the Internet of Things" (2018) 34 *Computer Law & Security Review*, pp. 1041 and 1044.
Hereinafter referred to as "anti-commons-oriented theories", *cf.* no. 2.

regarding access to and the use of data is preferable to awarding exclusive rights of access and use."[7]

2. **Continuous circulation of information** – Incongruent observations on current and desirable evolutions within the data economy are often depicted by the parable of the blind men: While examining one part of an elephant, every blind man comes to a different conclusion about the researched subject matter. Not able to figure out what they are examining, they keep focussing on their own reality.[8] This parable appears to also hold true within (supra)national private law: While some cannot help but notice that the capturing of data excludes its utility to other stakeholders (rivalrous nature), others focus on socio-economic opportunities following its continuous and non-consumable circulation (non-rivalrous nature).

These rivalrous and non-rivalrous characteristics are shared with objects that are accessible and enjoyable by a plurality of non-individualised persons (*res communes*), such as air water, fauna and flora, electricity, gas and sunlight.[9] As evidenced by emission rights, groundwater, pets, flower bouquets, electricity distribution and solar energy, also these objects can be subjected to market economies. Being part of an entire ecosystem, these individualised objects are therefore more often approached circularly. Take groundwater for example. Although one can exclude others from using the same water by intercepting groundwater in a water well, he cannot overcome its continuous circulation within the hydrological cycle. Because the appropriated water will resume freely accessible to all, its non-rivalrous nature demands sustainability commitments from the appropriator.[10]

3. **Complementary functioning of exclusive and non-exclusive rights over data** – By analogy, holders nor subjects of data can overcome the continuous circulation of ontological information. Firstly, because data are generated by neural networks in our brains, by mere existence and by human interaction (hereinafter "behavioural-generated data"). Secondly, discarded data are more

7 Recital 6, penultimate sentence Data Act.

8 See a.o. D. Obasanjo, "Privacy is Like an Elephant", *Medium Online*, https://shorturl.at/cSTVY (Blogpost, accessed 8.04.2024); T. Jetzek, "The Blind Men and the Elephant: On measuring", https://shorturl.at/diqLY, (LinkedIn Post, accessed 8.04.2024). At the most recent MyData conference in Helsinki (https://2023.mydata.org/), the data economy was often compared to "the sea" as some discuss the health of the fish, some talk about vegetation and other care about the quality of the water, but none of them is able to depict the whole sea.

9 Art. 3.43 CC.

10 Arts. 3.43 and 3.50 CC, interpreted in accordance to Draft Bill No. 54-3348/001, 127, see more extensively F. Vavourakis and M.-L. Degroote, "To whom belongs the water? Someone, no one and everyone appropriating freshwater in the Low Countries", see *infra* 323-350.

often repurposed by other stakeholders ("data life cycle").[11] To ensure public data-driven value growth, data holders (should) engage in the protection of the intrinsic ontological nature of data, on the one hand, and the establishment of dynamic data environments, on the other hand.[12]

This contribution assesses whether and how, in the context of Belgian private law, exclusive and non-exclusive rights can contribute to both socio-economic objectives (IV). This assessment requires a preliminary analysis of the regulatory challenges (II.B) following from the circular usage of behavioural-generated data (II.A). The subsequent section commences with typical situations of technical and economic control (III.A). Hereinafter, the different stakeholders' active legal control over behavioural-generated data is determined (III.B). Lastly, the extent to which non-exclusive rights can enforce technical or economic control upon those holding active legal control is examined (III.C).

II. REGULATORY CHALLENGES

A. CIRCULAR USAGE OF BEHAVIOURAL-GENERATED DATA

4. Layers of information[13] – Both anti-commons- and commons-oriented theories distinguish between data on the one hand, and information encoded in these data on the other hand, to explicate different layers of information.[14] A first layer of information is what one wants to represent with (a combination

---

11 L. Hsu, R.L. Martin, B. McElroy, K. Litwin-Miller and W. Kim, "Data management, sharing, and reuse in experimental geomorphology: Challenges, strategies, and scientific opportunities" (2015) 244 *Geomorphology*, p. 181, fig. 1; J.M. Yun, "The Coming of Age of Open Data", in K. Mathis and A. Tor (eds) *Law and Economics of the Coronavirus Crisis. Economic Analysis of Law in European Legal Scholarship*, Springer, Cham, p. 385, fig. 1; J.M. Wing, "The Data Life Cycle" (2019) *Harvard Data Science Review*, 2019, p. 2, fig. 1.

12 EC, "A European Strategy for data", [2020] COM(2020) 66, p. 1; B. Custers and H. Uršič, "Big data and data reuse: a taxonomy of data reuse for balancing big data benefits and personal data protection", (2016) 6 *International data privacy law*, pp. 4-15; A. Poikola et al., "MyData – An introduction to human-centric use of personal data" (2020) *MyData Global Report 3rd revised edition*, Helsinki, Ministry of Transport and Communications Finland, 2020, pp. 6-11 and 44-54.

13 Obviously, numerous other qualifications and perspectives on information can be found, see a.o. L. Floridi and Routledge (eds.), *The Routledge handbook of philosophy of information in Routledge handbooks in philosophy*, London, Routledge, 2016, p. 1, third alinea; S. Sequoiah-Grayson and L. Floridi, "Semantic Conceptions of Information", *The Stanford Encyclopedia of Philosophy*, https://seop.illc.uva.nl/entries/information-semantic/ accessed 8.04.2024.

14 Commons-oriented theories: N. Duch-Brown, B. Martens and F. Mueller-Langer, "The economics of ownership, access and trade in digital data" (2017) *JRC Digital Economy Working Paper*, pp. 7 et seq.; S. Geiregat, "The Data Act: Start of a New Era for Data Ownership?" (2022), *SSRN Journal*, pp. 4-5, no. 3.
Anti-commons-oriented theories: K. Swinnen, "Eigendom van data? "Reculer pour mieux sauter" [in onder meer Nederland en België]" (2019) *Tijdschrift voor Privaatrecht*, p. 73, no.

of) numbers, letters, symbols or facts,[15] and thus what one actually sees or can use within a digital ecosystem ("semantic layer", to be understood as the "(sub)content of a dataset", hereinafter mostly referred mostly referred to as "(ontological) information").[16] Patterns of characters, such as numbers, letters, symbols and facts, encoding the content layer qualify as the syntactical layer (hereinafter also referred to as "data (sub)set" or "data"). The most direct physical or digital carrier of the code layer structures interactive characters and therefore qualifies as the "structural layer" (hereinafter also "carrier (of data)").[17]

This static view is more often complemented by a circular conceptualisation. According to this latter view, the information encoded in data is "*a system resource comprising not merely individual pieces of information pertaining to identifiable individuals, but an entire 'ecosystem', comprising interconnected but separate elements.*"[18]

5. **Interconnection of informational layers** – The usage of information encoded in behavioural-generated data as a system resource can be illustrated by packaging of, for example, the beverage Coca-Cola.[19] While the brand's trade mark on the packaging informs you about the beverage (e. g. Coca-Cola instead of Pepsi Cola), the branding and product name indicate the employed ingredients (e.g. zero sugar). If the consumer is also interested in the nutritional value of the ingredients, he can either consult the grey-, green- and red-coloured nutrition percentages or examine all ingredients listed above the nutrition values. With his smartphone, the consumer can read out the QR-code on the packaging. Besides additional nutritional information, the newest advertising campaigns, special offers and recycling competitions will be presented to the

---

13; B. Verheye, "Digitale activa in het familiaal vermogensrecht" (2023) 1 *TEP*, pp. 13-14, no. 5; H. Zech, "Information as Property" (2015) *JIPITEC* p. 194.

15 Facts provide a residual category and are to be understood as all objectively perceivable or measurable conditions, see M. Weggeman, *Kennismanagement: de praktijk*, Schiedam, Scriptum, 2000, pp. 34-36.

16 See for example the definition of "personal data" in Art. 6 Regulation (EU) 2016/679 on the protection of natural persons with regard to the processing of personal data and on the free movement of such data [2016] OJ L 119 ("GDPR") and the definition of "data" in Art. 2.1 Data Act.

17 M. Weggeman, *Kennismanagement: de praktijk*, Schiedam, Scriptum, 2000, pp. 34-36.
Not only is this interpretation used by the majority of legal doctrine within both property and personality law, but this interpretation is also shared by authors within information science, see a.o. H.J. Van Meter, "Revising the DIKW Pyramid and the Real Relationship Between Data, Information, Knowledge and Wisdom" (2020) 2 *Law, Technology and Humans*, p. 71; M. Weggeman, *Kennismanagement: de praktijk*, Schiedam, Scriptum, 2000, pp. 34-36.

18 N. Purtova, "The illusion of personal data as no one's property" (2015), 7, *Law, Innovation and Technology*, p. 109.

19 This example is inspired by "the back of a bag of Chips"-example used by M. Fierens during his First Doctoral Seminar, see M. Fierens, *First Doctoral Seminar: In search of a (new) balance between data sharing and data protection in light of semantic interoperability*, KU Leuven Centre for IT & IP Law, 2024, slide 13 https://lirias.kuleuven.be/retrieve/751286 accessed 8.04.2024.

consumer.[20] The barcode, compromising black lines and white spaces of different widths, does not reveal much information to the consumer in turn. Instead, this combination of lines and numbers provides the necessary information to cashiers in supermarkets, order pickers in warehouses and accountants evolved in this purchase process.

While all the aforementioned content layers[21] can be differentiated from its underlying code layers[22], such demarcation of data neglects their interconnectedness within the product providers' data ecosystem. By monitoring the sale of alternative versions of the product, such as Cola zero or Fanta, the ingredients used for the original as well as the alternate versions can continuously be improved. By monitoring individual responses to branding and marketing, Coca-Cola gains individual consumer preferences based on which they can categorise target audiences. By monitoring indirect network effects[23], the Coca-Cola company will gain additional market insights. While competitors (e.g. Lipton Ice-Tea) or smaller entities (e.g. Ritchie Cola) will inevitably attract dissatisfied or underserved clientele, these consumers will at some point go back to consuming beverages manufactured by the Coca-Cola company. This is because of indirect network effects such as the beverages' widespread use, the variety of alternative products (e.g. Coca-Cola zero, Fanta and Sprite), or peer pressure. When these consumers decide to do so, Coca-Cola can further interrogate their consumer behaviour and uncover why they switched products in the first place.

6. Data-driven value growth within platform systems – Within platform systems, participants are even more interdependent in terms of private and public (co-)creation of value. Relying on network effects, service providers of free or low-cost services are only able to reach sufficient consumers if their purchasing behaviour is influenced by, amongst others, peer pressure.[24] Once inscribed, functionalities of platform products and services forces the service user to consume additional services provided on the online platform. This platform

---

20 E. Vincent and A. Kolade, "Persuasive communication: Semiotic analysis of 'Share-a-Coke' advertising campaign" (2019) 7 *World Journal of Innovative Research*, pp. 1-6; I. Kottassova, "Does formula mystery help keep Coke afloat?" (2014) *CNN Online*, https://edition.cnn.com/2014/02/18/business/coca-cola-secret-formula/index.html accessed 8.04.2024; X, "Klantverhaal: Coca Cola – recycle", *Coupontools Online*, https://shorturl.at/pEMN2 accessed 8.04.2024.

21 Respectively used ingredients, nutrition value and allergy-risks as well as campaigns, offers and competitions.

22 Respectively the ingredient declaration, the units and percentages of measurement as well as the branding and the QR-code.

23 A. Basaure, A. Vesselkov and J. Töyli, "Internet of things (IoT) platform competition: Consumer switching versus provider multihoming", (2020) 90-91 *Technovation* 102101, pp. 1-13.

24 Q. Liangfei, Q. Tang, and A. B. Whinston. "Two formulas for success in social media: Learning and network effects", (2015) *Journal of Management Information Systems* 32.4, pp. 78-108.

design does not only enhance the usage of and interactions on the platform but also enables the service provider to capture user interactions.[25] This enables the continuous harvesting of consumer preferences and other market insights. Consequently, providers can keep users' data profiles up-to-date, train algorithms in targeting users with personalised content, optimise existing products and develop new services (*infra* fn. 69). For all these reasons, the intensive relationship is even more dependent on collaborative efforts of all participants.[26]

7. **Public data-driven value growth** – Since the accumulation of service, product and market knowledge is more often used for public interests[27], service providers are left with sovereignty to interrogate, aggregate and share data in the most balanced and appropriate way.[28] After all, product and market wisdom is "*much more complex, uncommon, and not entirely achievable based on mere personal effort*"[29] so that those having experience and knowledge should be left with (even more) technical and economic incentives.[30] Since information and resultant knowledge are even without wisdom both valuable and necessary for most human activity[31], the EC, scholars and practitioners are in search for ways in which ontological information can be shared without exposing product and market know-how (semantic data sharing). Private and public value creation are therefore considered communicating vessels.[32]

25 P. Bernal, *Internet Privacy Rights: Rights to Protect Autonomy*, Cambridge, Cambridge University Press, 2014, 55 et seq; N. Purtova, "The illusion of personal data as no one's property" (2015), 7, *Law, Innovation and Technology*, pp. 109-110.

26 M.S. Lee and I. Soon, "Taking a bite out of Apple: Jailbreaking and the confluence of brand loyalty, consumer resistance and the co-creation of value" (2017) 4 *JPBM* 1 26, p. 352.

27 Vlaanderen Digitaal, *Flemish Data Utility Company Projects*, www.vlaanderen.be/digitaal-vlaanderen/athumi-het-vlaams-datanutsbedrijf/the-flemish-data-utility-company/flemish-data-utility-company-projects#my-professional-data (Webpage).

28 EC, "A European Strategy for data", [2020] COM(2020) 66, p. 3; P. Hummel, M. Braun, S. Augsberg and P. Dabrock, "Sovereignty and Data Sharing", (2018) 2 *ITU Journal: ICT Discoveries*, p. 10.

29 H.J. Van Meter, "Revising the DIKW Pyramid and the Real Relationship Between Data, Information, Knowledge and Wisdom" (2020) 2 *Law, Technology and Humans*, 34, pp. 77.

30 Anti-commons-oriented theory: A. Appelfeld, *Feedback to Data Act proposal on behalf of Royal Philips*, 13 May 2022, feedback ref. F3258758, p. 1 https://ec.europa.eu/info/law/better-regulation/have-your-say/initiatives/13045-Data-Act-amended-rules-on-the-legal-protection-of-databases/F3258758en, accessed 8.04.2024.
Commons-oriented theory: J. Hoffmann and B.G. Otero, "Demystifying the role of data interoperability in the access and sharing debate" (2020) 11 *J. Intell. Prop. Info. Tech. & Elec. Com. L.*, pp. 252-273.

31 H.J. Van Meter, "Revising the DIKW Pyramid and the Real Relationship Between Data, Information, Knowledge and Wisdom" (2020) 2 *Law, Technology and Humans*, p. 70.

32 A. Appelfeld, *Feedback to Data Act proposal on behalf of Royal Philips*, 13 May 2022, feedback ref. F3258758, p. 1; T. Berners-Lee, "Marking the Web's 35th Birthday: An Open Letter" *Medium.com*, https://medium.com/@timberners_lee/marking-the-webs-35th-birthday-an-open-letter-ebb410cc7d42 accessed 8.04.2024; I. Graef, R. Gellert and M. Husovec, "Towards a holistic regulatory approach for the European data economy: Why

B. REGULATING (NON-)RIVALROUS NATURE OF INFORMATIONAL LAYERS

8. Legal protection of intellectual efforts – If the commodification of behavioural-generated data requires intellectual efforts, the commodity is protected by trade secrets and other intellectual property mechanisms.[33] Due to the non-rivalrous nature of the information encoded in the commodity, conflicts between intellectual property and non-exclusive rights are inevitable. A multitude of recitals and provisions of the Data Act therefore stipulate that any intellectual property right is respected by the enacted non-exclusive rights.[34] Commons-oriented theories find these recitals overly absolute and believe the appropriateness and proportionality of the violation of the service providers' intellectual and economic interests are to be assessed.[35] Now that the semantics of generated datasets is more often taken into account (*infra* no. 9), it is argued that service providers can be left with sufficient discretion to assess the most balanced and appropriate way to share information without sharing any know-how (service provider-friendly interpretation of the duty to make available, *cf.* nos. 9, 22 and 25).[36]

the illusive notion of non-personal data is counterproductive to data innovation", (2019) 5 *European Law Review*, pp. 605-621.

[33] See with regard to general principles of intellectual property rights: K. Swinnen, "Eigendom van data? 'Reculer pour mieux sauter' [in onder meer Nederland en België]' (2019) *Tijdschrift voor Privaatrecht*, pp. 74-75, nos. 16-17.
See with regard to the Directive 96/9/EC of 11 March 1996 on the legal protection of databases [1996] OJ L 77, S. Geiregat, "The Data Act: Start of a New Era for Data Ownership?" (2022), *SSRN Journal*, p. 5-6, no. 4; B. Verheye, "Digitale activa in het familiaal vermogensrecht" (2023) 1 *TEP*, pp. 19-20, no. 9.

[34] Recitals 15, 16 30, 82, 101 and Art.s 1.8, 2 (38), 30, 32 and 49.1 (e) Data Act.
Indeed, these provisions do only apply to data generated by using IoT-products and related services but not to data generated through the use of social media or streaming services, nonetheless these services can be linked to the same platform ecosystem, see Recitals 80-81 jo. art. 2(12) Data Act; J. Drexl et al., "Position Statement of the Max Planck Institute for Innovation and Competition of 25 May 2022 on the Commission's Proposal of 23 February 2022 for a Regulation on Harmonised Rules on Fair Access to and Use of Data Research Paper no. 22-05," (2022) *SSRN Electronic Journal*, p. 63, no. 171; S. Geiregat, "The Data Act: Start of a New Era for Data Ownership?" (2022), *SSRN Journal*, p. 49, no. 60.

[35] J. Drexl et al., "Position Statement of the Max Planck Institute for Innovation and Competition of 25 May 2022 Research Paper no. 22-05," (2022) *SSRN Electronic Journal*, pp. 100-105, nos. 277-290; S. Geiregat, "The Data Act: Start of a New Era for Data Ownership?" (2022), *SSRN Journal*, p. 27, no. 25.

[36] See along the same line with regard to art. 35 GDPR Guidelines on Data Protection Impact Assessment (DPIA) and determining whether processing is "likely to result in a high risk" for the purposes of Regulation 2016/679 [2017] 17/EN, WP 248 rev.01, 22p.
Some question the desirability of the large emphasis on the protection of the exclusive *de facto* control position of the data holders, see a.o. W. Kerber, "Governance of IoT Data: Why the EU Data Act will not fulfill its objectives" (2022) *SSRN Journal*, p. 20.

9. Legal protection of ontological nature – Rooted in consumer protection law and inspired by personality law (*infra* no. 19)[37], the Data Act aims to protect the ontological nature of behavioural-generated data. GEIREGAT articulates this focus as follows: "[Though] *the concrete pattern saved on one person's hard disk is not 'the same' pattern as that on someone else's hard disk or on a cloud server,* [t]*hings are different when data is understood on the level of the logical layer, as a pattern wherever it is reproduced. In that sense, only the files saved on the two hard disks and on the cloud server are 'the same' data.*"[38] Along the same line, the American and European Law Institute state that "*only an exact copy of a particular set of data would count as the 'same' data, and even minor modifications would make a set of data a 'different' set of data.*"[39] While examining data and consumer protection law principles, one must be aware of this fictitious equivalence of separate datasets encoding the same information. On the one hand, two completely different datasets can encode the same information (e.g. an encrypted file and the encryption). On the other hand, an exact copy of a dataset can encode completely different information (e.g. the letter "P" can indicate a parking space or refer to 17th letter of the Greek alphabet). A transfer of a dataset without translation, modification or complementation will therefore be useless for or misinterpreted by the receiver (economic consumption). A translation, modification or complementation of the data can in contrast preserve the encoded information (technical consumption).

Like human communication, data are made up in different markup languages, formats, grammar or architectural structure (syntax of data). Data interoperability is therefore to be understood as the standardisation of data syntax, user-interfaces and semantics of the underlying data (e.g. architectural context and used revenue model) to ensure that datasets have the same meaning wherever they are repurposed.[40] Standardised data frameworks, such as GAIA-X and IDAS (European initiatives) and Solid (W3C standard), do provide in markup languages, protocol standards and architectural recommendations. As a result, encoding and decoding rules used within different ecosystems can be aligned.[41] However, ecosystems are only fully interoperable if they are able to automatically interpret the information exchanged meaningfully and accurately in order to produce useful results as defined by the end users of both systems.[42]

---

37 Recitals 7 *jo.* 9 and 34 Data Act.

38 S. GEIREGAT, "The Data Act: Start of a New Era for Data Ownership?" (2022), *SSRN Journal*, p. 5, no. 3.

39 ALI-ELI Principles For A Data Economy- Data Transactions And Data Rights [2021], Principle 3, 34, no. 21-22.

40 M.P. BALL et al., "MyData: Applying human-centric principles to health data" (2020) 29 *Medical Writing*, p. 66.

41 A. BRAUD, G. FROMENTOUX, B. RADIER and O. LE GRAND, "The Road to European Digital Sovereignty with Gaia-X and IDSA" (2021) 35 *IEEE Network*, pp. 4-5.

42 P. DE HERT, V. PAPAKONSTANTINOU, G. MALGIERI, L. BESLAY and I. SANCHEZ, "The right to data portability in the GDPR: Towards user-centric interoperability of digital services" (2018) 34 *Computer law & security review* 2018 2, p. 197.

Going beyond syntactic data protection and technical integration, the understanding that information and knowledge-sharing is preferable to the enforcement of non-exclusive rights *in rem* is beginning to dawn.[43] The Data Act lacks clarifications in this regard. Instead, it stipulates that "[d]*ata generation is the result of the actions of at least two actors, in particular the designer* [..], *and the user of the connected product or related service.* [..] *In order to realise the important economic benefits of data, including by way of data sharing on the basis of voluntary agreements and the development of data-driven value creation by Union enterprises, a general approach to assigning rights regarding access to and the use of data is preferable to awarding exclusive rights of access and use.*"[44] Only because the obligation to make readily available does not concern "*an obligation to store data on the central computing unit of a connected product*"[45], service providers and some scholars argue that the (real-time) translation into a duplicated version of the relevant subset of the data ecosystem (still) suffices (*infra* no. 22).[46] In this view, the obligation to make available condones, and to the current state of technology even requires, a translation, modification or complementation of the relevant characters, alongside metadata necessary to interpret these duplications.[47]

If non-exclusive access rights are interpreted otherwise, they tend to overlap in scope with exclusive rights *in rem (infra* nos. 13-17), so that product and service providers are at risk of having to share "*what they have built up, not only in terms of data, datasets but also IP, trade secrets and valuable know-how as all these may be embedded in the data having to be shared*" (hereinafter "know-how not protected by intellectual property principles").[48] In this case, balanced and proportionate value for all stakeholders involved is *a priori* hampered *(cf. supra* nos. 7-10).[49]

---

43 M. Fierens, *First Doctoral Seminar: In search of a (new) balance between data sharing and data protection in light of semantic interoperability*, KU Leuven Centre for IT & IP Law, 2024, slide 18.
Dissenting: S. Geiregat, "The Data Act: Start of a New Era for Data Ownership?" (2022), *SSRN Journal*, p. 49, no. 60.

44 Recital 6, first three sentences Data Act.

45 Recital 20 Data Act.

46 D. Brouwer, "Making messaging interoperability with third parties safe for users in Europe", https://engineering.fb.com/2024/03/06/security/whatsapp-messenger-messaging-interoperability-eu/, accessed on 8.04.2024; W. Kerber, "Governance of IoT Data: Why the EU Data Act will not fulfill its objectives" (2022) *SSRN Journal*, p. 9.

47 Art. 15(3) and 20 (1) GDPR; Recital 5, 8, 19-21 *jo.* art. 3 (1) Data Act; W. Kerber, "Governance of IoT Data: Why the EU Data Act will not fulfill its objectives" (2022) *SSRN Journal*, p. 9.
See for a service-user friendly interpretation: S. Geiregat, "The Data Act: Start of a New Era for Data Ownership?" (2022), *SSRN Journal*, p. 22, no. 21.

48 A. Appelfeld, *Feedback to Data Act proposal on behalf of Royal Philips*, 13 May 2022, feedback ref. F3258758, p. 2.

49 J. Hoffmann and B.G. Otero, "Demystifying the role of data interoperability in the access and sharing debate" (2020) 11 *J. Intell. Prop. Info. Tech. & Elec. Com. L.*, pp. 252-273; P. Hummel, M. Braun, S. Augsberg and P. Dabrock, "Sovereignty and Data Sharing", (2018) 2 *ITU Journal: ICT Discoveries*, p. 10; S. van Erp, "Management as Ownership of Data" in S.

10. Legal protection of technical or economic efforts – Since non-intellectual property principles approach code layers of behavioural-generated data as mere binary codes[50], commons-oriented theories suspect these principles unfit to regulate the catching and releasing of behavioural-generated data (*supra* no. 1). Instead, being the subject of the information should suffice to acquire legal control.[51] This twofold reasoning prejudices the fundamental right to property and consequently the rules in Member States governing the system of property.[52] The fundamental right to property does first and foremost not entail a right to be(come) an owner but concerns the right to own, use, dispose of and bequeath property in so far as property is lawfully acquired.[53] Appelmans and Verheye prove that a lawful acquisition of active legal control over data requisites some decision-making power over the appropriation of the data in question.[54] Accordingly, one has a right not to own (digital) property that involves debts or economic costs.[55]

In sum, property regimes are meant to protect technical and economic efforts which might lead to know-how not protected by trade secrets and other intellectual property mechanisms. This is why data ownership could bestow stability upon the economically unstable technical control of data holders (*supra* no. 1). As such stability would inevitably benefit platform providers, the accompanying negative socio-economic consequences are already widely

Lohsse, R. Schulze and D. Staudenmayer (eds.), *Data as Counter-Performance – Contract Law 2.0?*, Baden-Baden, Nomos Verlagsgesellschaft mbH & Co. KG, 2020, pp. 77-94.

50 A. Appelmans and B. Verheye, "Digital goods in property law", in B. Akkermans (ed.), *A Research Agenda for Property Law,* Elgar Research Agendas, 2024, p. 198, forthcoming, www.e-elgar.com/shop/gbp/a-research-agenda-for-property-law-9781803924809.html.

51 S. Geiregat, "The Data Act: Start of a New Era for Data Ownership?" (2022), *SSRN Journal*, p. 50, no. 60.
The American and European Law Institutes seems to reason along these lines as well, see *infra* no. 11.

52 J. Drexl et al., "Position Statement of the Max Planck Institute for Innovation and Competition of 25 May 2022 Research Paper no. 22-05," (2022) *SSRN Electronic Journal*, p. 20, no. 46; V. Janecek, "Ownership of personal data in the Internet of Things" (2018) *Comp.L.&S.R.*, p. 1039, no. 3.3; B. Verheye, "Digitale activa in het familiaal vermogensrecht" (2023) 1 *TEP*, p. 11, no. 22.

53 Art. 1 of the Protocol to the European Convention of Human Rights [1950]; art. 17 Charter of Fundamental Rights of the European Union [2000]; Case 44/79, *Liselotte Hauer v Land Rheinland-Pfalz,* ECLI:EU:C:1979:29.

54 A. Appelmans and B. Verheye, "Digital goods in property law", in B. Akkermans (ed.), *A Research Agenda for Property Law,* Elgar Research Agendas, 2024, p. 212, forthcoming; B. Verheye, "Digitale activa in het familiaal vermogensrecht" (2023) 1 *TEP*, p. 33, no. 20.

55 This reasoning adheres to the principle that one cannot be forced to be an owner, or at least not be forced to remain owner. The widespread enactment of the right of succession option or succession waiver exemplifies this principle, see a.o. J.-M. Miricescu, "The Right of Succession Option" (2019) 2 *Annals of the Constantin Brancusi University of Targu Jiu Juridical Sciences Series*, pp. 89-96; D. Muritano, "Chapter 13: Acceptance and waiver of the Succession", in S. Bariatti and C. Villata (eds.) *EU Cross-Border Succession Law,* Cheltenham, UK: Edward Elgar Publishing, 2022, 188-199; I. Titu, "The effects of exercising the right to succession option" (2019) 3, *Annals of the Constantin Brancusi University of Targu Jiu Juridical Sciences Series*, pp. 7-16.

discussed.[56] Not having any legal authority on the rules in Member States governing the system of property ownership, the European Commission advises that "[i]*f a data producer right is to be created as a right in rem* [...], *the allocation of the right (i.e. defining the 'data producer') would be guided by a thorough analysis of all elements relevant for allocating such a right.*"[57]

11. Transcending the (anti-)commons debate: terminology – In their Principles for a Data Economy, the American and European Law Institute avoid such a thorough analysis. Instead, they use a "co-generation approach" that transcends the debate. On the one hand, the technical, economic and intellectual efforts made by the generator of data are recognised. On the other hand, subjects of information are considered co-generators as "*being the subject of the information may, from a legal point of view, even be the strongest form of contribution, depending on the specific link between the information and the legitimate interest in being provided access etc., or requiring desistance, or correction, or an economic share.*"[58]

On account of feasibility assessments, the UNIDROIT Principles on Digital Assets and Private Law only aim to facilitate transactions in digital assets that are capable of being subject to control. The concept of control therefore "[...] *refers to a digital asset where a person can establish that it has (i) the exclusive ability to prevent others from obtaining substantially all of the benefit from the digital asset, (ii) the ability to obtain substantially all the benefit from the digital asset and (iii) the exclusive ability to change the control of the digital asset to another person.*"[59]

In their Final Report on Digital Assets, the UK Law Commission questions whether the concept of "(active) legal control" alone is sufficiently nuanced, refined or sensitive to market specificities to determine adequately and definitively the consequences of complex legal arrangements.[60] Along these lines, Van Erp argues that "*as to data, the degree of ownership we should try to understand is management, as the expression of access, control, portability and erasure.*"[61] Accordingly, non-exclusive rights can be understood as an expression of control over the erasure, duplicability and transferability of the

---

56 See for an overview of warnings K. Swinnen, "Eigendom van data? "Reculer pour mieux sauter" [in onder meer Nederland en België]" (2019) *Tijdschrift voor Privaatrecht*,pp. 168-170.

57 EC, *Commission Staff Working Document On The Free Flow Of Data And Emerging Issues Of The European Data Economy,* [2017] Document 52017SC0002 – SWD/2017/02 final, https://eur-lex.europa.eu/legal-content/EN/TXT/PDF/?uri=CELEX:52017SC0002, 34.

58 ALI-ELI Principles For A Data Economy- Data Transactions And Data Rights [2021], Principle 3(h) and Principle 18, pp. 11 and 134-136.

59 UNIDROIT Digital Assets and Private Law Principle [2023] v. 2(2), p. 5, no. 0.11.

60 UK Law Commission, *Digital assets: final report* in *Law Com No 412*, London, 2023, p. 26, no. 2.69.

61 S. van Erp, "Management as Ownership of Data" in S. Lohsse, R. Schulze and D. Staudenmayer (eds.), *Data as Counter-Performance – Contract Law 2.0?*, Baden-Baden, Nomos Verlagsgesellschaft mbH & Co. KG, p. 93.

ontological information encoded in behavioural-generated data (hereinafter "passive legal control").

In this regard, the concept "behavioural-generated data" is (also) used to refer to any legal effect given to any contribution to the generation of data (*cf. supra* no. 3). Indeed, because the data in question are generated based on individual's actions, behaviour or interactions in dynamic (physical or digital) environments ("behavioural"), not only incentives to make technical, economical and intellectual efforts ("generated") are protected by (private) law: In consequence of these different socio-economic positions, stakeholders derive different legal capacities, such as "subject", "consumer" and "holder" of generated data. Hence, the interdependence of different stakeholders.

III. ACTIVE AND PASSIVE LEGAL CONTROL OVER BEHAVIOURAL-GENERATED DATA

A. TECHNICAL AND ECONOMIC CONTROL

12. Typical situations of factual control – The various "shades" of control rights stakeholders derive from distinct legal capacities more often tend to overlap in scope.[62] Only after elucidating on typical situations of exclusive and shared technical and economic control, the legal anchoring of stakeholders' factual control can be examined.

(i) First typical situation: closed storage – A natural person can retain in technical control over generated multimedia files by storing them on a closed storage space, such as a USB-stick, the hardware of a portable computer or a digital vault. Since the software packages needed to generate these datasets, such as Microsoft Word, are disconnected from other storage spaces, the natural person retains exclusive technical control over the generated dataset.[63] When the natural person wants to share this dataset, he has to use additional services, such as OneDrive and Google Drive or Outlook and Gmail. In accordance with his lasting technical control over the dataset on the service platform, the service provider only acquires license rights over the shared dataset.[64] In order not to be

[62] J. Drexl et al., "Position Statement of the Max Planck Institute for Innovation and Competition of 25 May 2022 Research Paper no. 22-05," (2022) *SSRN Electronic Journal*, pp. 19-20, no. 44-49; S. Geiregat, "The Data Act: Start of a New Era for Data Ownership?" (2022), *SSRN Journal*, p. 9, no. 7.

[63] B. Verheye, "Digitale activa in het familiaal vermogensrecht" (2023) 1 *TEP*, p. 32, no. 20.

[64] Google, "Permission to use your content -License", *Terms and conditions Google services*, https://policies.google.com/terms?hl=en#toc-permission accessed 8.04.2024: *"Your content remains yours, which means that you retain any intellectual property rights that you have in your content. [...] This license doesn't affect your data protection rights – it's only about your intellectual property rights"*; Microsoft, "Permission to use your content -License",

reliant upon the benevolence of the service provider, a service user can encode the dataset on a distributed-ledger technology, such as Blockchain, and ensure his technical and economic control.[65]

When the shared multimedia file is not externally generated but created through platform functionalities (e.g. Google Docs), platform functionalities are decisive to determine the service user's decision-making power over the erasure, duplication and porting of the generated data. Within his Google Drive account, the service user does, for example, possess full technical powers over the generated multimedia files. This technical control, alongside his legal claim on the potential asset value, is anchored within terms of service agreement.[66] Other datasets, such as domain names, visual illustrations or and online avatars, are not generated by the service user. Platform functionalities ensure the service provider's lasting technical control with regard to these datasets. Accordingly, the service user is only provided with license rights over these datasets.[67]

Terms and conditions Microsoft services, www.microsoft.com/en/servicesagreement#2_yourContent, accessed 8.04.2024: *"Many of our Services allow you to create, store or share Your Content or receive material from others. We don't claim ownership of Your Content. Your Content remains yours and you are responsible for it"*.

Along the same line Meta, "Terms of Use – Permissions you give to us", *Terms and conditions Meta Account*, https://help.instagram.com/581066165581870?cms_id=581066165581870, accessed 8.04.2024: *"Nothing is changing about your rights in your content. We do not claim ownership of your content that you post on or through the Service and you are free to share your content with anyone else, wherever you choose. However, we need certain legal permissions from you (known as a "licence") to provide the Service"*.

65 Yuga Labs CC, "Bored Apes Yacht Club Terms and Conditions – Ownership", *Terms and Conditions BAYC*, https://boredapeyachtclub.com/#/terms, accessed 8.04.2024: *"You Own the NFT. Each Bored Ape is an NFT on the Ethereum blockchain* [...]*: at no point may we seize, freeze, or otherwise modify the ownership of any Bored Ape"*.

About security and economic benefits following the tokenization of medical data M. Sadeghi and A. Mahmoudi, "Synergy Between Blockchain Technology and Internet of Medical Things in Healthcare: A Way to Sustainable Society" (2013) *Information Sciences*, 120049, pp. 1-15; M.T. Quasim, F. Algarni, A.A.E. Radwan and G.M.M. Alshmrani, "A blockchain based secured healthcare framework" in *International Conference on Computational Performance Evaluation (ComPE)*, Shillong, India, 2020, pp. 386-391.

66 See with regard to the Google Drive service: Google, "Permission to use your content-License" *jo.* "How to earn money on YouTube" *Algemene voorwaarden Google services*, https://policies.google.com/terms?hl=en#toc-permission en https://support.google.com/youtube/answer/72857?hl=en&ref_topic=9257988&sjid=17360789684747972736-EU (accessed on 13.08.2024): *"Your content remains yours* [...] *If you're in the YouTube Partner Program, you can earn money through YouTube."*

Along the same line: N.M. Banta, "Property interests in digital assets: The rise of digital feudalism" (2016) 38 *Cardozo L. Rev.*, pp. 1105-1134.

67 Google, "Google Content", *Terms and conditions Google services*, https://policies.google.com/terms?hl=en#toc-permission, accessed on 8.04.2024: *"Some of our services include content that belongs to Google – for example, many of the visual illustrations you see in Google Maps. You may use Google's content as allowed by these terms and any service-specific additional terms, but we retain any intellectual property rights that we have in our content"*; Meta, "Terms of Use – Permissions of use", *Terms and conditions Meta Account*, https://help.instagram.com/581066165581870?cms_id=581066165581870, accessed on 8.04.2024: *"You can't sell, license or purchase any account or data obtained from us or our Service. This includes attempts*

(ii) Second typical situation: "derived" data[68] – In accordance with this property law reasoning, terms of service agreements therefore stipulate that the service provider, in his capacity as licensee, has the right to capture data generated by the use of externally generated multimedia files, on the one hand, and data generated by the use of licensed datasets, on the other hand (derived data).[69] Since the user can only end the generation of derived data by deleting (subsets of) the licensed account, he cannot be considered to have technical or economic control over the derived data.

Some service providers aim to share economic control over derived data. The financial platform "CAKE", for example, rewarded users with a monthly share in accordance with the profits gained from the user's anonymised and aggregated financial records.[70] More recently, financial institutions developed in-house data aggregation tools. This forced CAKE to reorient their platform functionalities. The platform now provides financial institutions and enterprises with plug-and-play solutions to integrate their cashback mechanism into their own applications. Nonetheless these cashback mechanisms still ensure that all stakeholders receive a piece of the "cake", users only gather crumbs.[71]

---

to buy, sell or transfer any aspect of your account (including your username); solicit, collect or use login credentials or badges of other users; or request or collect Instagram usernames, passwords or misappropriate access tokens."; Microsoft, "Digital Assets", *Terms and conditions Microsoft services*, www.microsoft.com/en/servicesagreement#2_yourContent, accessed on 8.04.2024: "*Digital Goods may be owned by Microsoft or by third parties. In all circumstances, you understand and acknowledge that your rights with respect to Digital Goods are limited by these Terms, copyright law, and the Usage Rules located at https://go.microsoft.com/fwlink/p/?LinkId=723143".*

68 Terminology derived from ALI-ELI Principles For A Data Economy- Data Transactions And Data Rights [2021], Principle 3, (1) (i).

69 Google, "Google Policies", *Terms and conditions Google services, https://policies.google.com/terms?hl=en#toc-permission*, accessed 8.04.2024: *"operating and improving the services, which means allowing the services to work as designed and creating new features and functionalities. This includes using automated systems and algorithms to analyze your content,* [...] *to recognize patterns in data,* [...] *to customize our services for you* [...] *developing new technologies and services;* Meta, "Terms of Use – Permissions you give to us", *Terms and conditions Meta Account,* https://help.instagram.com/581066165581870?cms_id=581066165581870, accessed on 8.04.2024: "[...] *When you share, post or upload content that is covered by intellectual property rights (such as photos or videos) on or in connection with our Service, you hereby grant to us a non-exclusive, royalty-free, transferable, sublicensable, worldwide licence to* [...] *create derivative works of your content (consistent with your privacy and application settings). This licence will end when your content is deleted from our systems. You can delete content individually or all at once by deleting your account".*
Along the same line Microsoft, "Your Content" and "Reservation of Rights and Feedback", *Terms and conditions Microsoft services,* www.microsoft.com/en/servicesagreement#2_yourContent, accessed 8.04.2024.

70 X, "Cake", *Open Banking Use Cases,* https://openbankingusecases.com/apps/cake-app, accessed 8.04.2024.

71 J. Jonkers, "Cake zet bankingapp voor consumenten stop vanaf februari" (2022) *TechPulse*, https://techpulse.be/nieuws/332341/bankingapp-cake-stopt-vanaf-februari/ (Blogpost), accessed 8.04.2024.

The ongoing development of in-house data aggregation tools exposes first and foremost that interoperability amongst platform services and traditional services, such as financial institutions and governmental service providers, is rather limited. Besides technological challenges (*supra* no. 9), the lack of interoperability is predominantly caused by economic considerations: Traditional (private and public) services aim to evolve in platform systems, allowing them to exclude other stakeholders from exploiting data generated through the usage of their services.[72] As a result, individual consumer preferences are, to the current state of the data economy, mere business assets.[73]

(iii) Shared control over derived data – To enhance the natural persons' technical and economic control over derived data, alternative platform architectures are developed ("personal information management systems" (PIMS), also referred to as "human-centric management systems").[74] By linking one or more (de)centralized storage locations distributed across the internet to a unique user code, a user interface can be set up. Through this interface a natural person can gain granular control over the sharing of data between (de)centralized storage locations, on the one hand, and (de)centralized applications, government services and platforms, on the other hand. The shared data can therefore also concern (interactions with) other persons or goods, such as his residence or his car (so called "data storage spaces for natural persons", also referred to as "personal (data) pods").[75] Such personal storage spaces can be

72 B. Serrure, "KBC-app wordt ook financieel nieuwskanaal" (2021), *De Tijd*, www.tijd.be/ondernemen/banken/kbc-app-wordt-ook-financieel-nieuwskanaal/10354910.html; Podcast De Tijd Vooruit, "Peter Adams, CEO ING België: 'Fintechs zijn partners in innovatie'" www.tijd.be/podcasts/de-tijd-vooruit.html?_sp_ses=04b7689f-9249-4b82-8fb5-6fe08407c790, 7:35-15:34: (Podcast), accessed 8.04.2024; Podcast De Tijd Vooruit, "Johan Thijs (KBC): 'De echte concurrenten van de banken zijn Google, Facebook en Amazon'", https://podtail.com/fr/podcast/de-tijd-vooruit-1/johan-thijs-kbc-de-echte-concurrenten-van-de-banke/ *en* en https://open.spotify.com/episode/5FyteOpicOjqMjb08J0UCh?si=96acb6459aed44f3, 5:20-17:12 (Podcast), accessed 8.04.2024.

73 OECD Directorate for Science, Technology and Innovation (STI), "Exploring the Economics of Personal Data: A Survey of Methodologies for Measuring Monetary Value" (2013), *OECD Digital Economy Papers* 220, 18 et seq.; G. Malgieri and B. Custers, "Pricing privacy – the right to know the value of your personal data" (2018) 34 *Computer Law & Security Review* 2, p. 292, no. 2.

74 M. Attoresi and T. Moraes, *TechDispatch #3/2020 – Personal Information Management Systems*, Luxembourg, Publications Office of the European Union, 2020, pp. 1-4; A. Poikola et al., "MyData – An introduction to human-centric use of personal data" (2020) *MyData Global Report 3rd revised edition*, Helsinki, Ministry of Transport and Communications Finland, 2020.

75 A. Poikola et al., "MyData – An introduction to human-centric use of personal data" (2020) *MyData Global Report 3rd revised edition*, Helsinki, Ministry of Transport and Communications Finland, 2020, p. 53; V. Lähteenoja, "What are "personal data spaces"?" (2023) *Companion Proceedings of the ACM Web Conference 2023*, pp. 1458-1461; S. Verbrugge et. al., "Towards a personal data vault society: an interplay between technological

integrated in hub-and-spoke-[76], federated-[77], or mixed architectures, so that a natural person can be provided with lasting control over the erasure, storing and portability of multimedia, other externally generated datasets and derived datasets.[78] Analogously to tokenised datasets, and only if these systems will bring us in the next stage of the data economy[79], personal storage space-users should be able to commodify, and therefore also monetise, derived datasets, such as self-assembled profiles, retail loyalty cards and datasets about things.[80] Alternative storage architectures built by the Flemish Utility Service will for example provide citizens with technical control over the storing method of data derived from the usage of real estate and professional multimedia files, such as CV's and payrolls.[81]

The scaling of alternative data management systems is currently hampered by economic and technical interoperability challenges, on the one hand, and market dominance of so called "Internet Giants", on the other hand.[82] Meanwhile,

---

and business perspectives" (2021) *60th FITCE Communication Days Congress for ICT Professionals: Industrial Data – Cloud, Low Latency and Privacy (FITCE)*, Vienna, Austria, pp. 1-6.

76 These types of architectures use storage spaces as a central point ("hub") for data exchange with other entities ("spokes"), see more extensively T. Ariyachandra and H.J. Watson, "Which data warehouse architecture is most successful?", *Business intelligence journal* 2006, 11, afl. 1, (4) p. 5, fig. 1; G. Blažić, P. Poščić and D. Jakšić, "Data warehouse architecture classification" in, Opatija, Croatia, IEEE, 2017, p. 1492, no. F.

77 Instead of using one or more storage locations as a central data exchange point, multiple autonomous and independent entities exchange data. This requires interoperability standards amongst the data storage spaces or at least the ability of the receiving data space to adapt its language and protocols to the markup language and protocols used in the original data spaces, see M. Adnan e.a., "Federated learning and differential privacy for medical image analysis", *supra* note 242; R.S. Antunes, C. André da Costa, A. Küderle, I.A. Yari en B. Eskofier, "Federated learning for healthcare: Systematic review and architecture proposal", *ACM Transactions on Intelligent Systems and Technology (TIST)* 2022, 13, afl. 4, pp. 1-23; G. Bent, P. Dantressangle, D. Vyvyan, A. Mowshowitz en V. Mitsou, "A dynamic distributed federated database", Verslag Proc. 2nd Ann. Conf. International Technology Alliance, 2008, pp. 1-8.

78 M. Attoresi and T. Moraes, *TechDispatch #3/2020 – Personal Information Management Systems*, Luxembourg, Publications Office of the European Union, 2020, p. 1 fig. 1 and p. 2, no. II.2 and p. 3, no. II. 6; S. Verbrugge et. al., "Towards a personal data vault society: an interplay between technological and business perspectives" (2021) *60th FITCE Communication Days Congress for ICT Professionals: Industrial Data – Cloud, Low Latency and Privacy (FITCE)*, Vienna, Austria, pp. 1-6.

79 EC, 'A European Strategy for data', [2020], COM(2020) 66, p. 19.

80 A. Poikola et al., "MyData – An introduction to human-centric use of personal data" (2020) *MyData Global Report* 3rd, revised edition, Helsinki, Ministry of Transport and Communications Finland, 2020, pp. 6, 42 and 44-54.

81 Vlaanderen Digitaal, *Flemish Data Utility Company Projects*, www.vlaanderen.be/digitaal-vlaanderen/athumi-het-vlaams-datanutsbedrijf/the-flemish-data-utility-company/flemish-data-utility-company-projects#my-professional-data> (Webpage), accessed 8.04.2024.

82 H. Asri, H. Mousannif, H. Al Moatassime and T. Noel, 'Big data in healthcare: Challenges and opportunities' (2015) *International Conference on Cloud Technologies and Applications (CloudTech)*, Marrakech, Morocco, IEEE, pp. 1-7; S. Dothan, 'Facing Up To Internet Giants'

governmental actors and private service providers do more often opt for the in-house development of proxy/agency systems.[83] Within these systems, nodes[84] or intermediaries anticipate consumers' preferences following their dynamic consent. By lack of personal storage space and accompanied user-interface, the node or intermediary has to make decisions on behalf of the natural person ("cascading consent"). This human-centric generation of data requires less time-consuming supervisory and economic efforts from the natural person. Nonetheless, they still enable the natural person to (re)gain and sustain control over their data.[85]

B. PREREQUISITES TO LAWFULLY ACQUIRE STATUTORY PROPERTY RIGHTS[86]

13. Stabilising exclusive control over individualised and appropriated objects – The simultaneous use of non-individualised objects is in Belgian property law differentiated from exclusive technical or economic control over an individualised and appropriated object (*res proprietas*). If in this case, the (universality of) object(s) is determinable and delineated, the (universality of) object(s) is in its entirety subjected to property rights (specialty and unity principle).[87] The appropriator is in this case authorised to exclude others from

(2023) 320 *Duke Journal of Comparative & International Law, Forthcoming, iCourts Working Paper Series*, pp. 1-36; Interoperable EU Academy, *Enabling the Twin Digital and Green Transition via personal IoT data – The Case of Electric Vehicles*, 8 juni 2023, www.youtube.com/watch?v=RX0vVBhvNis, 27:31-36:50 (Webinar), accessed 8.04.2024.

83 Germany: Deutscher Ethikrat, *Big Data und Gesundheit Datensouveränität als informationelle Freiheitsgestaltung: Stellungnahme*, [2017] Berlin, Deutscher Ethikrat, p. 37, no. 87, and p. 268; Comparative research: M. Fierens, *First Doctoral Seminar: In search of a (new) balance between data sharing and data protection in light of semantic interoperability*, KU Leuven Centre for IT & IP Law, 2024, slide 17; International legal doctrine: P. Hummel, M. Braun, S. Augsberg and P. Dabrock, "Sovereignty and Data Sharing" (2018) 2 *ITU Journal: ICT Discoveries*, p. 5, no. 5.

84 A node is in this contribution understood as an intersection in a linear or dynamic data environment where data is processed, stored, or transmitted. Examples of nodes are for instance computers, servers, printers, routers, or interfaces of human-centric management systems. If such nodes, in accordance to cascading consent, make decisions on behalf of the stakeholders, they are referred to as "proxies".

85 P. Hummel, M. Braun, S. Augsberg and P. Dabrock, "Sovereignty and Data Sharing" (2018) 2 *ITU Journal: ICT Discoveries*, p. 5, no. 5.

86 Jargon used in this part of the contribution is influenced by published and non-published translations of the current Civil Code compiled at the KU Leuven Department of Private Law, see a. o. V. Sagaert, A. Appelmans, S. Baeyens, G. Degeest, M.-L. Degroote, B. Maeschaelck and B. Verheye, "Act of 4 February 2020 containing Book 3 'Property' of the Civil Code Belgian Official Gazette 17 March 2020" (2021) 110 *European Property Law Journal* 1, pp. 108-176.

87 Art. 3.41 *juncto* 3.8 CC; Draft Bill No. 54-3348/001, pp. 25, 104 and 108.

the usage, fruits and revenues of the object (Dutch: *externe exclusiviteit*).[88] If the good is appropriated by different stakeholders, ownership does not externalises itself through technical possession but through the residual right which attracts all legal powers (Dutch: *potentieel volheid van bevoegdheden door de elasticiteit van het eigendomsrecht*).[89] Accordingly, only this stakeholder is the beneficiary of the (residual) asset value of the good (Dutch: *interne exclusiviteit*).[90]

14. Individualised universalities of data as a "good" – Following these recodifications of traditional property principles, a (universality of) dataset(s) are brought within the scope of Belgian property law upon appropriation in its entirety.[91] Because data can be generated out of thin air, the mere generation of data does not suffice.[92] After all, without any technical resources (e.g. axes, ink or chips) data generated by neural networks in our brains, by mere existence and human interaction itself, could have never been encoded on enduring carriers (resp. caves, parchment or portable devices). When a dataset is individualised on a durable carrier, the appropriator is in the ability to exclude other stakeholders from interrogating and aggregating the dataset. Following, this endurance, the individualised code and structured dataset is determinable and delineated.[93] Because the non-rivalrous character of the ontological information, potentially also encoded within another dataset, is irrelevant in this line of reasoning, the (recodified) requirements for transformation are met.[94]

Data is not always generated out of thin air but can also be "seized" from its carrier. This reasoning can be exemplified by Banksy's artworks.[95] In a first case, an artwork painted on a wooden gateway was appropriated in its

88 D. Gruyaert, *De exclusiviteit van het eigendomsrecht* in *Property law series 4*, Intersentia, Antwerp, 2016, pp. 27-31, nos 20-22.

89 Art. 3.14 § 2 *juncto* art. 3.50 CC; Draft Bill No. 54-3348/001, p. 38 and pp. 126-127; D. Gruyaert, *De exclusiviteit van het eigendomsrecht* in *Property law series 4*, Intersentia, Antwerp, 2016, p. 753, nos. 538, pp. 765-780, nos. 544-553, p. 801, nos. 572, p. 806-810, no. 575, pp. 814-815, no. 580.

90 Draft Bill No. 54-3348/001, pp. 104 and 127, with reference to D. Gruyaert, *De exclusiviteit van het eigendomsrecht* in *Property law series 4*, Intersentia, Antwerp, 2016, p. 23, no. 17, p. 115, no. 105, p. 293, no. 235, pp. 343-345, nos. 269-270, pp. 419-420, no. 318, pp. 429-434, no. 326, pp. 445-447, nos. 333 and 335, and p. 766, 545.
Along the same lines B. Rudden, "Things as Thing and Things as Wealth" (1994) 14 *Oxford Journal of Legal Studies* 1, p. 89; M. Storme, "Vertrouwen is goed, dual ownership is beter: elf essentialia bij de invoering van een trustachtige figuur of fiduciaire overeenkomst in het Belgische recht" (1996) *RW* 1996-97, p. 140, no. 11.

91 Draft Bill No. 54-3348/004, 127; B. Verheye, "Digitale activa in het familiaal vermogensrecht" (2023) 1 *TEP*, pp. 13-35, nos. 5-23.

92 B. Verheye, "Digitale activa in het familiaal vermogensrecht" (2023) 1 *TEP*, p. 32, no. 20.

93 B. Verheye, "Digitale activa in het familiaal vermogensrecht" (2023) 1 *TEP*, pp. 31-32, no. 20.

94 Art. 3.11 and 3.56 CC.

95 P.N. Salib, "The law of Banksy: Who owns street art?" (2015) *The University of Chicago Law Review*, pp. 2293-2294; J. Wetherbe, " Missing Banksy Mural Fetches $1.1 Million at Auction" (2013) *LA Times*, https://perma.cc/85FF-HUGS (Newsarticle), accessed 8.04.2024.

entirety through the appropriation of some wooden planks. Only after Banksy's interference, the city recognised the appropriator's property rights. In the second case, Banksy painted an artwork on the side of a store, whereupon the bricks carrying the artwork were removed from the stores' wall. Following an auction at the London Film Museum, the appropriated artwork was legally salvaged. The technical seizure of (subsets of) data are often referred to as the "hacking" of a closed storage space. Accordingly, data can also be "seized" in mutual agreement, and thus transfered upon a third party (*supra* no. 12). The duplication of an ecosystem's subset cannot be equated with a technical seizure or transfer of this dataset (*supra* no. 9).

15. Continuous interrogation and transformation of universalities of data – Individualisable universalities of data are continuously complemented, updated and altered (*supra* no. 6). Preliminary works clarify that as long as the universality is deployed for a common destination, changes in composition nor the interaction with other data universalities do violate the specialty and unity principle.[96] As illustrated above, universalities of data stored on closed storage spaces are deployed for a common destination (*supra* no. 12).

16. Prospect on full powers – While managing a universality of data for a common destination, the data holder has the legal power to exclude third parties from erasing, accessing and porting data.[97] Consequently, debtors, data subjects or consumers can only impose a legal obligation on the part of the data holder (*supra* no. 9). The legal power to exclude third parties from erasing, accessing and porting data is however not accompanied with (prospect on) full powers over the universality.[98] Approaching ownership over data as management is therefore not useful to identify the owner of the data universality. When different stakeholders share technical and economic control over data, the stakeholder with decision-making power to generate data is often

---

96 Draft Bill No. 54-3348/001, 25; E. Dewitte, *Feitelijke algemeenheden in het privaatrecht*, Intersentia, Antwerp, 2017, pp. 480 and 485-486; V. Tweehuysen, *Het uniciteitsbeginsel in het goederenrecht*, Kluwer, Deventer, 2016, pp. 283-295; J.C. Van der Steur, *Grenzen van rechtsobjecten*, Kluwer, Deventer, 2003, pp. 124-145.

97 Interpretation of art. 3.24 CC based on S. van Erp, "Management as Ownership of Data" in S. Lohsse, R. Schulze and D. Staudenmayer (eds.), *Data as Counter-Performance – Contract Law 2.0?*, Baden-Baden, Nomos Verlagsgesellschaft mbH & Co. KG, p. 93.

98 This is not only true from a technical perspective (*supra* no. 12) but also from a legal perspective, see D. Gruyaert, *De exclusiviteit van het eigendomsrecht* in *Property law series 4*, Intersentia, Antwerp, 2017, pp. 42 et seq and 780.
Along the same line B. Rudden, "Things as Thing and Things as Wealth" (1994) 14 *Oxford Journal of Legal Studies* 1, p. 89; M. Storme, "Vertrouwen is goed, dual ownership is beter: elf essentialia bij de invoering van een trustachtige figuur of fiduciaire overeenkomst in het Belgische recht" (1996) *RW* 1996-97, p. 140, no. 11.

identified as the owner of data.[99] This is because he bears costs of labour and materials to "transform" data.[100]

This general consideration provides an interesting starting point but is insufficiently tailored to the circular usage, interrogation and aggregation of behavioural-generated data. Firstly, data are not always generated out of thin air but can also be seized or transfered multiple times. In this hypothesis, the criterion obliges us to trace the original creator of the data and follow the chain of ownership. This is only feasible in distributed-ledger technologies (*supra* no. 12).[101] Secondly, evolving technologies, such as PIMS and proxy/agency-systems, will only provide natural persons with a granular level of control over data generation (*supra* no. 12 (iii)).

Upon attentive analysis of different (de)centralised ecosystems[102], the distinction between technical control over the storage of a demarcable and delineable dataset on the one hand and technical over its carrier on the other hand, provides us with a more nuanced, circular criterion. While the provider of a centralized platform, governmental and private actors in open data ecosystems, and the issuer of cryptoassets all determine how the dataset is structured and its content is presented and used, it is the user who decides where, and thus on which carrier, the data set is stored as a structured whole – whether on a centralized platform or decentralized data pod or when hashed, where the private key is stored. While being in control over the storage of a data set, he also has the power to generate revenues or monetise its market value. Consequently, he also has the power to erase, port and transfer the dataset. In sum, it is the

---

99 A. Appelmans and B. Verheye, "Digital goods in property law", in B. Akkermans (ed.), *A Research Agenda for Property Law,* Elgar Research Agendas, 2024, forthcoming, p. 212; V. Janecek, "Ownership of personal data in the Internet of Things" (2018) *Comp.L.&S.R.*, p. 1048, no. 3.2.4.1; K. Swinnen, "De inpassing van digitale producten in het Belgisch privaatrecht" in (2017) *Preadviezen Vereniging voor de vergelijkende studie van het recht,* p. 262, no. 31.
Along the same line EC, *Commission Staff Working Document On The Free Flow Of Data And Emerging Issues Of The European Data Economy,* [2017] Document 52017SC0002 – SWD/2017/02 final, 34.

100 A. Appelmans and B. Verheye, "Digital goods in property law", in B. Akkermans (ed.), *A Research Agenda for Property Law,* Elgar Research Agendas, 2024, forthcoming, p. 208-211.

101 V. Janecek, "Ownership of personal data in the Internet of Things" (2018) *Comp.L.&S.R.*, p. 1048, nos. 3.2.4.1 jo. 3.2.4.2.

102 This analysis concerns a concise summary of the ongoing doctoral research project on 'Digital Inheritance: Access and Inheritability of Digital Assets' conducted by the RRDI and finds origin in previous research activities such as a lecture held and the lectures attended at the most recent MyData conference in Helsinki (https://2023.mydata.org/), the closed SEMIC workshop 3 on Personal data spaces, the Interoperable EU Academy about Electric Vehicles (www.youtube.com/watch?v=RX0vVBhvNis), the ALI-ELI Webinar on the ALI-ELI Principles for a Data Economy: A New Framework for Innovation and Growth (www.youtube.com/watch?v=QIfG9uPG4pU) and ELI Project Kick-Off Webinar on Succession of Digital Assets, Data and Other Digital Remains (https://europeanlawinstitute.eu/news-events/news-contd/news/eli-project-kick-off-webinar-on-succession-of-digital-assets-data-and-other-digital-remains/).

stakeholder with active control over the storage of the individualised and delineated dataset who has full powers under Belgian law, including the rights to use, enjoy, and dispose of the object (art. 3.50 CC).[103]

Thus, when different stakeholders share technical control, the stakeholder(s) with the technical ability to store data, and thus, claim revenues or the asset value, can be considered the (co-)owner(s) of the data. Hence, the owner of the data carrier, the data holder and the data generator can only be considered the owner of the dataset if they have this (prospect on) full technical powers.

17. **Legal consequences** – Considering the warnings issued by the European Commission and previous research (*supra* no. 10), the consequences of this criterion should be considered.

In terms of the protection of the intrinsic ontological nature of data, on the one hand, and the establishment of dynamic data environments, on the other hand, this criterion leaves sufficient room for balanced and proportionate value generation for all stakeholders involved (often referred to as "socialisation of property", *infra* III.C).[104] After all, exclusive control rights enacted within Book 3 and Book 5 of the Belgian Code Civil do only protect know-how not protected by intellectual property principles (*supra* no. 9). As knowledge even without wisdom is both valuable and necessary for most human activity[105], non-exclusive rights can complement these provisions of internal private law in terms of semantic information sharing. Moreover, the proposed criterion provides a natural person with the freedom to either acquire active legal control or transfer active legal control upon a third party (*infra* no. 22).

In terms of fairness and reasonableness, the natural person can in all the outlined types of situations be the "owner" of the dataset. It goes without saying that the facilitation of the most desirable situations still requires economic and technological evolutions. If we reach the next stage of the data economy, a natural person will be able to take technical control over the storing of derived data and acquire full powers over its economic value. If this technical control is shared with other stakeholders, the data is co-owned. If in contrast the provider of a centralised platform systems, providers of personal data pods, providers of proxies or intermediaries have control over the storing of the derived data,

103 In accordance to "change-of-terms provisions", service providers can modify their arrangements with consumers at any given moment, see D. Horton, "The shadow terms: contract procedure and unilateral amendments", (2009) 57 *UCLA L. Rev.*, pp. 605-667.

104 See along the same line with regard to other (de)material objects D. Gruyaert, *De exclusiviteit van het eigendomsrecht* in *Property law series 4*, Intersentia, Antwerp, 2016, pp. 299-348; U. Mattei and A. Quarta, *The turning point in private law: ecology, technology and the commons* in *Elgar studies in legal theory*, Cheltenham, UK Northampton, MA, USA, Edward Elgar Publishing, 2019, pp. 146-157.

105 H.J. Van Meter, "Revising the DIKW Pyramid and the Real Relationship Between Data, Information, Knowledge and Wisdom" (2020) 2 *Law, Technology and Humans*, p. 70.

it is fair and reasonable to protect their technical and economic efforts (*supra* nos. 7-10 and 12). For the same reason, data as counterperformance is no longer deemed unreasonable by the European Parliament and scholars.[106] The Belgian legislator reasons accordingly: The possessor of an object can retain the fruits and products given to him by the right he possessed on legal or contractual grounds if these fruits or products were acquired in good faith.[107] The restitution regime enacted within obligation law does therefore not apply to the valid mutual or unilateral termination of the contract.[108] As consumer or subject of the content, one can only (re)claim a duplication of the ontological information.

Within platform systems, the possessed good is to be considered the licensed dataset. If, for example, an Instagram-user gains revenues income by advertising, these revenues on the licensed online account are acquired in good faith. For the service provider these "fruits" concern "derived" data. If the usage of the service is free (*supra* no. 6), the generation of derived data does even concern the main counter performance. The retainment of data derived from externally generated datasets is therefore in accordance with Belgian property and obligation law principles. With regard to the licensed datasets, the natural person has the contractual freedom to waive his statutory rights on "fruits". After all, one has a right not to own property that involves debts or economic costs (*supra* no. 10). Moreover, these stipulations protect the service providers' technical and economic efforts so that they cannot be considered unreasonable. The potential unreasonableness of these provisions is remedied by the possibility to export product and service activity in unstructured ZIP-files.[109] Newly

---

106 European Parliament: M. Loos and J. Luzak, "Update the Unfair Contract Terms directive for digital services", European Parliamentary Research Service, 9 February 2021, https://policycommons.net/artifacts/1426506/update-the-unfair-contract-terms-directive-fo r-digital-services/. International legal doctrine: L. Drechsler, "Data As Counter-Performance: A New Way Forward Or A Step Back For The Fundamental Right Of Data Protection?" in *Datenschutz & LegalTech/ Data Protection & LegalTech*, Weblaw.ch, Bern, 2018, pp. 35-43; I. Graef, R. Gellert and M. Husovec, "Towards a holistic regulatory approach for the European data economy: Why the illusive notion of non-personal data is counterproductive to data innovation", (2019) 5 *European Law Review*, pp. 605-621; P. Hacker, "Regulating the economic impact of data as counter-performance: from the illegality doctrine to the unfair contract terms directive" in S. Lohsse, R. Schulze and D. Staudenmayer (eds.), *Data as Counter-Performance: Contract Law*, Londen, Bloomsbury Publishing, 2019, pp. 13-21.

107 Art. 3.29, first and second sentence CC.

108 Arts. 5. 112 *jo.* arts. 5.95, 5.101 and 5. 115-5.124 CC.

109 Google "How to download your data", *Google account Help*, https://support.google.com/accounts/answer/3024190?hl=en, accessed 8.04.2024; Microsoft, 'Respond to personal data export requests (Microsoft account)', *Microsoft terms of service agreement*, https://learn.microsoft.com/en-us/power-automate/privacy-dsr-export-msa, accessed 8.04.2024; Meta, 'Access and download your information', *Meta terms of service agreements*, https://help.instagram.com/181231772500920/?helpref=search&query=download%20information&search_session_id=4fb1e8f55b5cdaa8c3003fd72a74712b&sr=0 and www.facebook.com/help/212802592074644, accessed 8.04.2024.

enacted data portability obligations for service providers can in this regard prove useful.[110]

In terms of harmonization, and although still insufficiently noticed, this criterion is present in various nonbinding initiatives, such as the afore discussed ALI-ELI principles, UNIDROIT Principles and the UK Law Commission Report (*supra* no. 11). Since Article 3.50 CC relies on comparative research on the contractualisation and socialisation of internal ownership[111], this should however not surprise. Because previous research uncovered that several civil and common law systems assign a residual right which attracts all powers, such as a claim on the (residual) asset value, upon the owner of the property[112], the Belgian legislator codified this residual right (*supra* no.13). This residual right is by nonbinding initiatives approached as a "superiour legal title". The UK Law Commission does for example conclude in their Final Report on Digital Assets that "*factual control (plus intention) can found a legal proprietary interest in a digital object* [and] *in certain circumstances such a control-based legal proprietary interest can be separated from (and be inferior to or short of) a superior legal title.*"[113] Accordingly, UNIDROIT conceptualises the highest degree of active legal control as "*the ability to prevent others from obtaining substantially all of the benefit, the ability to obtain substantially all the benefit and the ability to change this control to another person.*"[114] Adhering to concepts of personality and consumer protection law, no such "superior legal title" is conceptualised within the ALI-ELI Principles for a Data Economy. Nonetheless also these Institutes notice that "*'Porting' and 'transfer' are thus closely related, with the main difference being that of perspective, as 'porting' clearly takes the perspective of the recipient exercising a right, while 'transfer' is more neutral and describes an activity of the supplier.*"[115] Upon further exploration of the latter perspective, these Institutes might also consider "transfer" as a superior legal title borrowed from the technical control over the storing of datasets.

C. SOCIALISATION OF ACTIVE LEGAL CONTROL OVER DATA

18. Defensive nature of non-exclusive rights – Due to the substantial enlargement of their scope (*supra* no. 9), data (consumer) protection rights

110 C. Ducuing, T. Margoni, L. Schirru, D. Spajic, T. Lalova-Spinks, L. Stähler, E. Bayamlioğlu, A. Pétel, J. Chu and B. Peeters, "CITIP White Paper on the Data Act Proposal" (2022) www.law.kuleuven.be/citip/en/Publications/citip-whitepaperdataact.pdf, pp. 8 and 27-31.

111 Draft Bill No. 54-1805/001, 127.

112 D. Gruyaert, *De exclusiviteit van het eigendomsrecht* in *Property law series 4*, Intersentia, Antwerp, 2016, pp. 296-297, nos. 237 and 814, 580.

113 UK Law Commission, *Digital assets: final report* in *Law Com No 412*, London, 2023, p. 272, 10.7.

114 5, no. 0.11.

115 ALI-ELI Principles For A Data Economy- Data Transactions And Data Rights [2021], p. 36-37.

have allegedly outgrown their "defensive" nature (*ius excluendi*) so that these statute-based personal rights are licensable and inheritable but not waivable nor transferable *inter vivos*.[116] The Max Planck Institute for Innovation and Competition (MPIIC) dissents by highlighting the importance of the defensive nature of any data (consumer) protection right.[117] Hereinafter, the defensive nature of data (consumer) protection rights will be assessed with regard to a natural person's legal capacity as "data subject" and "consumer".

19. Losing legal control: *qui peut le plus, peut le moins* – While subjective rights enacted within General Data Protection Regulation find their origin in Article 8 of the Charter of Fundamental Rights of the European Union (CFREU) and Article 16(1) of the Treaty on the Functioning of the European Union (TFEU)[118], it is only clarified within the Data Act that the regulation complements and is without prejudice to GDPR, on the one hand, and to Union law which aims to promote the interests of consumers, to ensure a high level of consumer protection, and to protect their health, safety and economic interests, on the other hand.[119] Furthermore, any linkage between enacted non-exclusive rights and these foundational principles of personality and consumer law, as well as any reference to national rules regulating property, lack.[120] We can therefore only assume that these personal rights either protect the natural person in his capacity as (i) "data subject" or (ii) "consumer".

(i) Subjective rights related to the capacity of "data subject-third party" – Assumed that all claims enacted within the Data Act are prerogatives inextricably linked to a natural persons' legal capacity as "data subject", the defensive nature of these prerogatives cannot be disputed. As subjective personality rights, they find their origin in the fundamental need to protect a natural persons' human dignity and personal autonomy.[121] Indeed, since a natural person has the autonomy to commercialise his (moral) personality, and thus create, contractual personal rights, personality rights counterbalance this personal autonomy. These rights do, amongst others, enable the natural person at all times and *erga omnes*

116 S. Geiregat, "The Data Act: Start of a New Era for Data Ownership?" (2022), *SSRN Journal*, abstract and pp. 41-48 and pp. 49-50, no. 60.

117 J. Drexl et al., "Position Statement of the Max Planck Institute for Innovation and Competition of 25 May 2022 Research Paper no. 22-05," (2022) *SSRN Electronic Journal*, pp. 32-35, no. 79-90.

118 Recital 1 GDPR.

119 Recital 5, 7, 9 and 25 Data Act.

120 J. Drexl et al., "Position Statement of the Max Planck Institute for Innovation and Competition of 25 May 2022 Research Paper no. 22-05," (2022) *SSRN Electronic Journal*, p. 20, no. 48; S. Geiregat, "The Data Act: Start of a New Era for Data Ownership?" (2022), *SSRN Journal*, pp. 43-45.

121 N. Debruyne, *Commerciële exploitatie van de menselijke afbeelding, naam en stem*, KU Leuven Faculteit Rechtsgeleerdheid, Leuven, 2021, p. 26, nos. 27, pp. 30-32, no. 32, p. 37, no. 37 and pp. 43-46, no. 43.

to prevent, terminate, undo or sanction an impermissible use of the same data and information (so-called "monistic interpretation of personality rights").[122] The defensive nature of personality rights over personal data are in other words at the root of the commercial use of personal data ("*qui peut le plus, peut le moins*").[123]

(ii) Subjective rights related to the capacity of "consumer-contractual party" – Because the Data Act also concerns "non-personal data", it is difficult to argue that the defensive nature of the enacted non-exclusive rights functions as counterbalance to the commercial use of personal data. Nonetheless, a similar reasoning applies: Because non-personal data does not relate to an identifiable natural person, not his personality but his contractual freedom is protected by non-exclusive rights, namely those protecting non-personal data generated by the use of a connected product or related service.[124] These constraints to a consumers' contractual freedom ensures "absolute" enjoyment of passive legal control ("*qui peut le plus, peut le moins*").[125]

Regulatory consumer protection rights concerning non-personal data generated by the use of a connected product or related service are therefore to be considered statutory constraints to the natural persons' personal autonomy. Not their *erga omnes* opposability but this *raison d'être* confers the personal rights' defensive nature. If interpreted otherwise, the *raison d'être* of the non-exclusive rights over this category of non-personal data is cancelled out.[126] Moreover, by arguing that these non-exclusive rights *in personam* are licensable and inheritable but not waivable nor transferable *inter vivos,* rules governing property in Member States are prejudiced.[127]

---

122 N. Debruyne, *Commerciële exploitatie van de menselijke afbeelding, naam en stem*, KU Leuven. Faculteit Rechtsgeleerdheid, Leuven, 2021, pp. 61-74, nos. 58-69 and p. 77, no. 72.

123 Art. 7 Charter of Fundamental Rights of The European Union; Recitals 4-15 and 26 GDPR; N. Debruyne, *Commerciële exploitatie van de menselijke afbeelding, naam en stem, supra* note 32, pp. 33-82, nos. 34-79, 230-242, nos. 236-252 and p. 492, no. 572-573; N. Purtova, "The law of everything. Broad concept of personal data and future of EU data protection law" (2018) 10 *Law, Innovation and Technology* 1, pp. 49, 62 and 79.

124 Recitals 43 and 61 *jo.* art. 4.13 Data Act.

125 Belgium: art. 5.104. jo. art. 5.142 CC; International legal doctrine: Recital 6 Data Act; J. Drexl et al., "Position Statement of the Max Planck Institute for Innovation and Competition of 25 May 2022 Research Paper no. 22-05," (2022) *SSRN Electronic Journal*, 19-21, no. 44-50; S. Geiregat, "The Data Act: Start of a New Era for Data Ownership?" (2022), *SSRN Journal*, pp. 43-45, nos. 49-42.

126 See along the same line J. Drexl et al., "Position Statement of the Max Planck Institute for Innovation and Competition of 25 May 2022 Research Paper no. 22-05," (2022) *SSRN Electronic Journal*, pp. 32-35, no. 79-90.

127 J. Drexl et al., "Position Statement of the Max Planck Institute for Innovation and Competition of 25 May 2022 Research Paper no. 22-05," (2022) *SSRN Electronic Journal*, p. 20, no. 46; V. Janecek, "Ownership of personal data in the Internet of Things" (2018) *Comp.L.&S.R.*, p. 1039, no. 3.3; B. Verheye, "Digitale activa in het familiaal vermogensrecht" (2023) 1 *TEP*, p. 11, no. 22.

20. Interconnectedness of (fundamental) principles of (internal) private law – The Belgian legislator reaffirms this "interconnectedness" of fundamental principles of (internal) private law. It is first and foremost acknowledged that a natural persons' autonomy still serves as the foundational premise for interpersonal relations among legal subjects, chiefly circumscribed by boundaries of public order.[128] Hereby, it is reaffirmed that a natural person has the personal autonomy to create claims, competences and obligations that can either partially or in their entirety be transferred upon a third party. As a result, not only (intellectual) property and personal claims but also obligations and other bonds of law are included within the natural person's patrimony.[129]

Furthermore, constraints to the natural persons' personal autonomy as boundaries of public order provides adequate counterbalance.[130] In addition to traditional personality rights, data consumer protection rights do now prevent service providers from exploiting their superior bargaining at the expense of a natural persons' autonomy with regard to the object, cause and enforcement of the agreement. The definite waiver or transfer of these non-exclusive rights, for example in terms of service agreement, is therefore null and does not form part of the contractual relationship between the provider and the user.[131] Thus, at least within Belgian private law, these statute-based personal rights are of "absolute defensive nature".[132]

21. Limitations to myriad shades of control rights – Also on supranational level, the "fundamental right to the protection of personal data" cannot be interpreted as a "fundamental right on personal data". Instead, it protects the ontological information that reasonably relates to a natural person whenever it is encoded within a dataset. The obligation to make available can therefore not be interpreted as a legal claim on the usage or storage of a dataset. In both hypotheses, the rules in internal private law governing the system of exclusive control would be prejudiced (*supra* nos. 13-22). (Supra)national statute-based personal rights, such as those enacted within the Data Act, can for the same

128 Draft Bill No. 54-1805/001, p. 10.

129 Arts. 3.41 and 3.35 *jo.* arts. 5.1 and 5.3 CC, to be interpreted as clarified by Draft Bill No. 54-1805/001, p. 10 and Draft Bill, No. 54-3348/001, pp. 46 et seq. and pp. 103-104.

130 Draft Bill No. 54-1805/001, p. 10.

131 Reasoning based on A. Lenaerts, "Over de redelijke mogelijkheid tot kennisname van algemene voorwaarden in contracten met consumenten: wat in geval van ongebruikelijke of buitensporige bedingen?" (2021) 10 *Tijdschrift voor Belgisch Burgerlijk Recht / Revue Générale de Droit Civil*, p. 501, no. 22.
Along the same line J. Drexl et al., "Position Statement of the Max Planck Institute for Innovation and Competition of 25 May 2022 Research Paper no. 22-05," (2022) *SSRN Electronic Journal*, pp. 32-35, no. 79-90.

132 Along the same line J. Drexl et al., "Position Statement of the Max Planck Institute for Innovation and Competition of 25 May 2022 Research Paper no. 22-05," (2022) *SSRN Electronic Journal*, pp. 32-35, no. 79-90.

reason not be interpreted as a seizure of appropriated data. On top, service providers would no longer have incentives to interrogate and aggregate behavioural-generated data so that public data-driven value growth is *a priori* hampered (*supra* nos. 7-10).

Conversely, exclusive rights *in rem* cannot be interpreted as an exclusive *erga omnes* right that "follows" data wherever they are reproduced.[133] Regardless of what exclusive rights holders built up in terms of information, they only have powers over the code dataset deployed for the common destination. If this information and related know-how is not protected by intellectual property rights and becomes in any way freely accessible, they do not have any claim on rectification or erasure. Along the same line of reasoning, exclusive rights *in rem* do not enhance the natural persons' control over the ontological information encoded in appropriated data.

Anti-commons and commons-oriented theories do at least agree upon this line of reasoning.[134] From here on, they seem to examine different aspects of the same subject matter from a fundamental different angle. While commons-oriented theories focus on the free flow of ontological information encoded behavioural-generated data, anti-commons-oriented theories do by no means take into account the content layer of information. To this end, they have developed intellectual property principles. Blinded by the fundamental different rationale of the principles underlying their branches of expertise, they were not able to figure out what they are examining and therefore kept focussing on their own reality (*supra* no. 2). Nonetheless, they can find common ground, namely in the absolute limitations on exclusive and non-exclusive rights' scope. While the residual right on fullness of powers does provide a natural person with a claim on the usage, storing and asset value of the relevant dataset, this right does not provide him with any direct claim on the ontological information encoded in the dataset. Conversely, as holder of non-exclusive rights the natural person has prospect on active legal control over the ontological information wherever and whenever it is reproduced but does not have a claim on the usage or the storing of the dataset encoding this information.[135] Instead, his non-exclusive rights only provide him with passive legal control over the processing of this information.

---

133 S. Geiregat, "The Data Act: Start of a New Era for Data Ownership?" (2022), *SSRN Journal*, 33, no. 33.

134 Anti-commons-oriented theory: see a.o. A. Appelfeld, *Feedback to Data Act proposal on behalf of Royal Philips*, 13 May 2022, feedback ref. F3258758, p. 1; K. Swinnen, "Ownership of data: Four recommendations for future research" (2020) 5 *JL Prop. & Soc'y*, pp. 146-164. Commons-oriented theory: see a.o. EC, "A European Strategy for data", [2020], COM(2020) 66, p. 3-7 and 13; S. Geiregat, "The Data Act: Start of a New Era for Data Ownership?" (2022), *SSRN Journal*, 49, no. 60.

135 Contra: S. Geiregat, "The Data Act: Start of a New Era for Data Ownership?" (2022), *SSRN Journal*, p. 22, no. 21."*it should be left to beneficiary users to determine whether they merely wish to read out their product's data, copy it to a storage medium, or otherwise retrieve it*".

22. Round-about to exclusive legal control over ontological information – Non-exclusive rights do only provide a natural person over two categories of ontological information, respectively information related to him or information generated by the usage of connected products and related services, alongside metadata necessary to interpret the duplicated version.[136] A sufficient sharing of this information concerns a duplication of the relevant characters available in a machine-readable format and, where relevant and technically feasible, also continuously and in real-time.[137] To delineate the relevant characters in legal conflicts, cooperations with experts in the relevant technic and economic ecosystem dynamics can be helpful.[138] Moreover, this claim is not an absolute right: The disclosure of the duplication should support its function in society and be balanced against other fundamental rights, in accordance with the principle of proportionality.[139]

Upon duplication of the ontological information, the natural person cannot be obliged to make technical and economic efforts to store, interrogate and aggregate the duplicated version (*supra* no. 10). Hence, the *raison d'être* of his "right to data portability": It provides the natural person with the possibility to directly port the duplicated version unto the ecosystem of a competing service provider. If the natural persons' technical control over this duplicated version is let alone (*supra* no. 12), internal rules of property law provide him with a residual right which attracts full powers over this duplicated dataset. If also the technical control over this dataset is transferred upon the third party, the natural person

---

136 PURTOVA wonders whether *"everything will fall within the definition of personal data as interpreted by the WP29 and the Court of Justice* [...] *once the onlife world becomes a reality* [so that] *the good intentions will backfire"*, N. PURTOVA, "The law of everything. Broad concept of personal data and future of EU data protection law" (2018) 10 *Law, Innovation and Technology* 1, p. 78.

137 Arts. 3.2 (c), 5. 1 and 33. 1 (c) Data Act.

138 K. SWINNEN, "Ownership of data: Four recommendations for future research" (2020) 5 *JL Prop. & Soc'y*, pp. 154-166.

139 Europe: Recital 4 jo. art. 6 GDPR; Recital 119 Data Act; Germany: Bundesgerichtshof, 12 July 2018, Case III ZR 183/17; Justizministerkonferenz (ed.), *Bericht der Arbeitsgruppe "Digitaler Neustart" der Konferenz der Justizministerinnen und Justizminister der Länder vom 15 mei 2017*, [2017] p. 349; France: Projet de loi pour une République numérique, *Consultation – Article 20 – Mort numérique – Contribution du Conseil supérieur du notariat* www.republique-numerique.fr/projects/projet-de-loi-numerique/consultation/consultation/opinions/section-1-protection-des-donnees-a-caractere-personnel/article-20-personnes-decedees/versions/contribution-du-conseil-superieur-du-notariat-observations-sur-la-mort-numerique-art-20,accessed 8.04.2024; C.-A. FRASSA, *Rapport n° 534 (2015-2016), fait au nom de la commission des lois, déposé le 6 avril 2016*, [2016] pp. 162-165; L. CASTEX, E. HARBINJA, and J. ROSSI, "Défendre les vivants ou les morts? Controverses sous-jacentes au droit des données post mortem à travers une perspective comparée franco-américaine" (2018) 4 *Réseaux* 210, pp. 138-139; Italy: G. RESTA, "La successione nei rapporti digitali e la tutela post-mortale dei dati personali", (2019) 1 *Contratto e Impr.*, pp. 6-7, no. 5; The Netherlands: Ministry of Internal Affairs, (MVBZ), *Data na de dood – juridische aspecten van digitale nalatenschappen*, [2021] pp. 97-110; International legal doctrine on data protection conflict resolutions: R.C. POST, "Data privacy and dignitary privacy: Google Spain, the right to be forgotten, and the construction of the public sphere" (2017) 67 *Duke LJ*, pp. 981-1072.

loses active legal control. This loss of active legal control is counterbalanced by his *erga omnes* and *inter partes* control on the ontological information wherever and whenever it is repurposed.

In sum, defensive access and usage claims do only complement, but are not preferable to, exclusive rights *in rem*. Non-exclusive rights do in this regard align with the fundamental right to property (*supra* no. 10) and consequently the rules in Member States governing the system of property. Recital 6 of the Data Act, however, has sown a great deal of ambiguity in this regard (*cf. supra* no. 1 *jo.* nos. 8-9 and 18-20). Hence, when a natural person has the legal capacity of holder, consumer and subject of a dataset (supra nos. 8-11) , its legal control must be understood as a statutory and contractual "bundle" of exclusive and non-exclusive rights. According to this line of reasoning, only non-exclusive rights are absolute in nature, as they cannot irrevocably be disposed of.[140]

This reasoning establishes that, to the extent that stakeholders' capacities are reduced to their lowest generic terms and their rights are expressed in terms of their lowest common denominators, legal control over behavioral-generated datasets should be understood as a bundle of powers and claims which they can exercise and dispose of regarding the various layers of a dataset.

IV. CONCLUSION

23. Interdependence of stakeholders with regard to private and public value-creation – Even where the natural persons' existence and (consumer) behaviour generates data in itself, property and obligation law principles address this rivalrous good as mere patterns of digital characters. To further commodify the ontological information encoded in data, the appropriated data are continuously interrogated and aggregated with freely accessible market information. During these alternating rivalrous and non-rivalrous phases of the data life cycle, data holders are inevitably confronted with natural persons' (non-)exclusive rights derived from their legal capacities as "contracting parties", "consumers" and "data subjects". Because participants in platform systems are even more

140 Reasoning inspired by D. Horton, "Indecendibility", *California Law Review* (2014) vol. 102, no. 3, pp. 543, 545, and pp. 576-577; B. Verheye, "The Future of the Circular Real Estate Economy", *Tijdschrift voor Privaatrecht* (2019), no. 1, pp. 107, 118-120, no. 7.
Note that the metaphor of "a bundle" does not conceptualise ownership nor legal control over digital assets as legal concepts without any defined structure. It solely references the power to convey, either temporarily or definitively, one or more (sets of) legally protected interests, whether they qualify as a power or a claim.
Along these lines, the reasoning is also inspired by D. Gruyaert, *De exclusiviteit van het eigendomsrecht* in *Property law series 4*, Intersentia, Antwerp (2016), p. 784, no. 556; W.N. Hohfeld, "Fundamental Legal Conceptions as Applies in Judicial Reasoning", Yale L.J., (1913), vol. 23, no. 1., p. 59; L. Katz, "Exclusion and exclusivity in property law", University of Toronto Law Journal, (2008), vol. 58, 275-279; J.H. Merryman, "Ownership and estate (variations on a theme by Lawson)", *Tul.L.Rev.* (1974), vol. 48 p. 927.

interdependent in terms of private and public (co-)creation of value than traditional consumers and product providers, there is growing need to determine the scope of (non-)exclusive rights in accordance to the natural persons' distinctive legal capacities. Therefore, jurisprudence and legal practitioners should be more precise about the natural persons' legal capacities from which they obtain a certain degree of legal control over behavioural-generated data.

24. **Holistic yet conservative Belgian civil law approach** – As contracting party, a natural person can acquire control over the usage, storing and asset value of externally generated and derived data. The Belgian legislator recently clarified that such technical and economic appropriation of rivalrous datasets suffices to appropriate this good in its entirety. If two or more stakeholders share technical control over the dataset, only the stakeholder with technical control over the storing of the appropriated dataset, and thus the prospect on its asset value, can be considered "owner" of the dataset. To avoid reliance on platform functionalities, a natural person can use distributed-ledger technologies or alternative data management systems. The first system provides the natural person with proof of ownership over externally generated datasets. The second system provides control over the erasure, storage, encryption and sharing of derived data. If the latter type of system brings us in the next stage of the data economy, the natural person may also have technical control over the storing of other datasets than multimedia files.

Furthermore, it is uncovered that inscribing to an online service constitutes a valid contractual relationship based on which the natural person can transfer active legal control. Following this transfer of usage rights, the service provider can retain all "fruits" acquired in good faith, for example data derived from the usage of externally generated multimedia files. Moreover, the natural person has the right to waive legal control over data derived from the usage of licensed datasets. This is because one has the (contractual) freedom not to own property that involves debts or economic costs.

25. **Socialisation of active legal control** – Since property regimes only protect technical and economic efforts, the reluctance of natural persons to make time-consuming supervisory and economic efforts, amongst others evidenced by the need for proxy systems, prevent them from acquiring active legal control. Consequently, he does not have legal control over the commodification of ontological information encoded within the appropriated dataset. Hence, the *raison d'être* of a natural persons' non-exclusive rights as "data subject" and "consumer". A first type of non-exclusive rights enables a data subject, at all times and *erga omnes*, to influence the processing of a subset that encode information reasonably relating to him. The second type of non-exclusive rights only concerns a personal right as it enables a consumer to reclaim legal control over a subset that is generated during the use of connected products and services (*inter*

partes). In order not to prejudice rules of Member States governing property regimes and to preserve technical, economic and intellectual incentives for service providers, these access and usage claims cannot be interpreted as "non-exclusive right *in rem*". Moreover, such interpretation would not enhance the natural persons' economic position. Instead, the duty to make available requires a modification of the characters into a duplicated version. Non-exclusive rights are thus not particular to the dataset itself but to the information's ontological, non-rivalrous nature.

26. Socio-economic consequences – The adequacy of (internal) property regimes to regulate the rivalrous nature of data was never actually doubted. Instead, the European Commission and scholars questioned the desirability of the socio-economic consequences. In essence, this contribution argues that the criterion "technical control over the storing of the dataset", and thus the prospect on asset value, may address these concerns and can even support the protection of the intrinsic ontological nature of data, on the one hand, and the establishment of dynamic data environments, on the other hand.

An attentive analysis of platform ecosystems and various data storage architectures reveals that this criterion avoids ownership rights by default for the data generator, the data holder and owners of the data carrier. Simultaneously, the criterion leaves room for other principles of property law, accompanied by intellectual property and obligation law, to protect these stakeholders' technical and economic efforts. Only if these stakeholders also have technical control over the storing of the dataset, the natural person loses prospect on fullness of powers.

This loss of active internal and exclusive legal control is counterbalanced by his *erga omnes* and *inter partes* control on the ontological information wherever and whenever it is repurposed. Upon exercising defensive access and usage rights, the natural person is left with the (contractual) freedom not to hold data. This is because the fundamental right to the protection of personal data does not imply a right "on personal data" and the fundamental right to property does not entail a right "on property". If the natural person does not wish to make technical and economic efforts, he can immediately port the duplicated version upon a third party. If the natural persons' technical control over this duplicated version is let alone, the proposed criterion provide the natural person with prospect on full powers over these duplicated data. If also the technical control over this dataset is transferred upon the third party, the loss of legal control over the ontological information is *erga omnes* and *inter partes* counterbalanced by his non-exclusive rights. Hence, the proposed criterion also leaves sufficient room for principles of personality and consumer protection law.

Last but not least, a comparable reasoning lies at the root of concepts and principles introduced by nonbinding initiatives, such as the ALI-ELI principles for a data economy, UNIDROIT Principles on digital assets and private law and the UK Law Commission Report.

ENVIRONMENTAL COMMONS IN BELGIAN PROPERTY LAW

Vincent JANSSEN
PhD researcher, Institute for Property Law (KU Leuven)

Kato DE SCHEPPER
PhD researcher, Institute for Property Law (KU Leuven)

I. INTRODUCTION: SHARING LAND AND ITS NATURAL RESOURCES

1. **Human dominance and biodiversity loss** – Since several decades, it has been indisputable that climate change seriously threatens the future of our living environment. Nature's carrying capacity is limited and is being put to test more than ever.[1] Mankind and human domination are (the most) important causes of biodiversity loss.[2] Both the market economy and our consumption model have an irreversible impact on the Earth and its biodiversity. Mainly greenhouse gas emissions and, more specifically, the way natural resources, such as air, water, minerals, energy, flora, fauna, marine resources and wildlands are exploited, lead to ecological destabilization and environmental degradation.[3] In a world of finite resources – which are becoming frighteningly scarce – the number and complexity of resource-use conflicts increase as population density continues to rise.[4] More than ever, academics, lawyers and all other legal practitioners

---

1 F.R. SIEGEL, *The Earth's Human Carrying Capacity*, Springer, Cham, 2021, 154 p. Also: A. GORE, *An Inconvenient Truth: A Global Warning*, Paramount Home Entertainment, *s.l.*,2007 (video); A.D. BARNOSKY *et al*, "Has the Earth's sixth mass extinction already arrived?" (2011) 417 *Nature*, (51) 51-57.

2 P.J. CRUTZEN, "Geology of Mankind" (2000) 415 *Nature*, (23) 23.

3 K. BYTTEBIER, *Ethiek van de sociaal-economische ordening*, Intersentia, Antwerp, 2023, 83-141; P.J. CRUTZEN, "Geology of Mankind" (2000) 415 *Nature*, (23) 23: "*Fossil-fuel burning and agriculture have caused substantial increases in the concentrations of 'greenhouse' gases* [...] *reaching their highest levels over the past 400 millennia, with more to follow.*"

4 T.W. FRAZIER, "Protecting Ecological Integrity within the Balancing Function of Property Law" (1998) 28 *Envtl. L.*, (53) 57. In Belgium alone, population will increase from 11.5 (2022) to 12.9 million people by 2070, putting even more pressure on its relatively small living environment. See: FEDERAL PLANNING BUREAU (Belgium), *Demografische*

need to reconsider the access, use and purpose of our (built-up) land, including its natural resources in order to protect and conserve the remaining biologically valuable spaces. Evermore, our economic model needs to be rebalanced with nature.[5]

2. Property law as enemy or guardian of environmental conservation? – In light of this environmental crisis, the law as a social construct plays a quintessential role in driving societal change.[6] While environmental conservation considerations have traditionally been dealt with exclusively by public law, and more particularly, environmental law, today it seems that environmental protection measures transcend the dogmatic *summa divisio* between private and public law.[7] Property law, in particular, seems to become an increasingly significant tool in this regard, as this field of study essentially manages relations between people, on the one hand, and land and its resources, on the other hand.[8] From a traditional viewpoint property law and, more specific, private ownership as one of its fundamental pillars is considered to be an enemy of environmental law.[9] The absolute and exclusive nature of private ownership rights are considered to be irreconciable with nature conservation objectives.[10] In the neo-liberal conception of property law, private ownership, utilitarianism and welfare maximalisation go hand in hand.[11] The current economic order, backed by the property law system, tends to maximize short-term exploitation of resources for profit, without considering sustainable

---

vooruitzichten 2021-2070, Federal Planning Bureau, Brussels, 2022, www.plan.be/uploaded/do cuments/202202080742020.Persp_FLASH_DP21_12568_N.pdf accessed 10.11.2023.

5 Environment Department (Flemish Government), *Beleidsplan ruimte Vlaanderen*, Flemish Government, Brussels, 2018, https://publicaties.vlaander en.be/view-file/28360 accessed 10.11.2023. Also: B. Akkermans, "Duurzaam goederenrecht: naar een herijking van ons goederenrechtelijk stelsel?" (2018) *TPR*, (1437) 1437-1470.

6 A. Hucq, "Code civil et enjeux écologiques: le cas des choses communes" (2022) 7 *TBBR*, (363) 364 (hereinafter: A. Hucq (2022) 7 *TBBR*). Also: B. Akkermans and G. Van Dijck, *Sustainability and private law*, Eleven International Publishing, The Hague, 2020, 186 p.

7 B. Akkermans, B. Hoops, E. Van Der Sijde and B. Verheye (eds.), *Privaatrecht 2050. De weg naar ecologische duurzaamheid*, die Keure, Bruges, 2022, 286; A. Van Lang, "La doctrine environnementaliste doit-elle inévitablement s'inscrire dans la summa divisio?" (2016) 16 *Rev.jur.environ.*, (60) 60-71; J. Van Meerbeeck *et al.* (eds.), *La distinction entre droit public et droit privé*, Anthemis, Limal, 2019,490.

8 See the contribution of D. Gruyaert in this volume, No. 1, v. 6-7 and the references there.

9 V. Sagaert, "Property Law, Contract Law and Environmental Law: Shaking Hands with the (Historical) Enemy" in V. Sagaert and S. Demeyere (eds.), *Contract and Property with an Environmental Perspective*, Intersentia, Antwerp, 2020, (1) 5, No. 8 *et seq* (hereinafter: V. Sagaert, "Shaking Hands").

10 On absolute and exclusive ownership: See V. Sagaert, "Shaking Hands", (1) 2, No. 3, *et seq.*

11 See a.o. B. Akkermans, "Sustainable Property Law: towards a revaluation of our system of property law", in B. Akkermans and G. van Dijck (eds.), *Sustainability and private law*, Eleven International Publishers, The Hague, 2019, 37 *et seq*; D. Grinlinton, "Evolution, adaption, and invention: Property rights in natural resources in a changing world" in D. Freestone (ed.), *Legal Aspects of Sustainable Development*, Brill, Leiden, 2011, (275) 278.

resource management. From a sustainability perspective, this traditional property approach is problematic, since it stimulates an owner to make decisions for his own benefit only. As a result, subject to ownership rights, natural resources, such as for example raw materials, risk being depleted. On the contrary, environmental law is said to be reflecting public interest and community-thinking.[12] However, property rights are not necessarily irreconcilable with environmental protection objectives.[13] Progressive property theory and human flourishing theory, for example, support a more pluralistic property objective than the conventional welfare maximization maxim.[14]

3. **Environmental *res communes* as a new property law sollution?** – In line with the above, it should be noted that recently, several property law mechanisms are being used to promote environmental conservation.[15] One of those (re-) emerging property law devices, transcending the public-private devision and embodying the philosphy of collectiveness, solidarity and cooperation, is known under the concept of "*res communes*".[16] This property law regime of commons essentially is intended to secure equal access for all to common things.[17] The newly adopted Article 3.43 of the Belgian Civil Code (hereinafter: BCC) translates this idea of open access in Belgian property law as follows[18]:

> "Common things [or *res communes*] cannot be appropriated in their entirety. They belong to no one, and are used in the public interest, including the interest of future generations. Their use is common to all and determined by specific rules and regulations."

---

12 S. Gutwirth, "Les communs: avec, malgré ou contre le droit?" (2022) 33 *JT*, (582) 588-589; J. Van de Voorde, "Les droits subjectifs inclusifs en droits belge, français et américain – Analyse à partir du droit aux choses communes (y compris la public trust doctrine), du droit à l'usage des voies publiques et du droit aux bien communaux" (2020) *ERPL*, (1009) 1009-1064 (hereinafter: J. Van de Voorde (2020) *ERPL*).

13 See also V. Sagaert and S. Demeyere, "Le droit des biens et le droit de l'environnement: vers une réconciliation?" (2019) 16 *JT*, (313) 313-323.

14 G. Alexander, *Property and Human Flourishing*, OUP, Oxford, 2019, 14; G. Alexander, E. Peñalver, J. Singer and L. Underkuffler, "A Statement of Progressive Property" (2009) 94 *Cornell Law Review*, (743) 743-744.

15 B. Grimonprez (ed.), *Le droit des biens au service de la transition écologique*, Dalloz, Paris, 2018, 168 p.; V. Sagaert and S. Demeyere, *Contract and Property with an Environmental Perspective*, Intersentia, Antwerp, 2020, 286 p.

16 See on this concept extensively under French law: M.A. Chardeaux, *Les choses communes*, LGDJ, Paris, 2006, 487 p. (hereinafter: M.A. Chardeaux, *Les choses communes*); F. Masson, *La propritété commune*, Panthéon-Sorbonne, Paris, 2016, 457 p. (hereinafter: F. Masson, *La propriété commune*)

17 A. Hucq (2022) 7 *TBBR* (363) 364; J. Van de Voorde (2020) *ERPL* (1009) 1056, No. 67.

18 Draft Bill inserting Book 3 "Goods" in the new Civil Code, *Parl. Doc.* Chamber, 2018-19, No. 54-3348/001 (hereinafter: Draft Bill, No. 54-3348/001).

Contrary to traditional property law anti-common premisses (*supra* no. 2)[19], these common objects or things – as opposed to legal subjects – belong to everyone or to the whole community. *Res communes* are capable of being simultaneously enjoyed and/or used by all. The circle of right-holders to commons is the widest imaginable, since it includes all those subject to rights, both natural and legal persons, without any restriction. No one can be excluded from accessing or using a common thing, whatever their status, capacity or nationality. Common things are therefore seen as "non-exclusive", meaning that no one has the explicit or implicit legal right to exclude another person from accessing or using them.[20] At the same time, commons do not specifically belong to individuals or a state, nor to a specific community.[21] Therefore commons are not the same as public property, in which a state holds property rights, nor as collective property, in which a collectivity holds property rights.[22] Commons are, on the contrary, excluded from any form of property, since they are non-appropriable. As a consequence, no personal nor real rights can be established on these things as a whole. The prepatory works confirm that common things cannot in their entirety belong to a private or public person.[23] Commons are thus excluded from property law in general.

4. **The origin of the commons and their environmental relevance** – The idea of "*res communes*" originates in Greek philosophy and Roman law.[24] Traditionally things like running water, air, landscapes, wildlife fauna and flora, sunlight, etc. were considered to be part of this category.[25] A more "modern" look at the commons category reveals that they contain all kinds of environmentally useful components which could play a quintessential role in protecting and conserving

---

19 On the "tragedy of the anti-commons": J. Buchanan and Y.J. Yoon, "Symmetric Tragedies: Commons and Anticommons" (2000) 43 *J.L. & Econ.* (1) 2; M.A. Heller, "The Tragedy of the Anticommons" (1998) 111 *Harv. Law Rev.*, (621) 624 *et seq.*

20 See about the term "non-exclusive": J.M. Karpoff, "The Tragedy of 'The Tragedy of the Commons': Hardin versus the Property Rights Theorists" (2022) 65 *J.L. & Econ.*, (65) 70, No. 5 (hereinafter: J.M. Karpoff (2022)8 65 *J.L. & Econ.*) .

21 B. Grimonprez, "Les 'biens nature': précis de recomposition juridique" in B. Grimonprez (ed.), *Le droit des biens au service de la transition écologique,* Dalloz, Paris, 2018, (13) 17-18 (hereinafter: B. Grimonprez, "Les biens nature").

22 On public property: J. Page, *Public Property, Law and Society Owning, Belonging, Connecting in the Public Realm,* Routledge, 2020, Abingdon, 178 p.; R. Palmans, J. Toury and T. Leys, *Openbaar domein,* Intersentia, Antwerp, 2019, 274 p.
On collective property: H. Demsetz, "Toward a theory of property rights: the competition between private and collective ownership" (2002) 31 *J.Leg.Stud.*, 653-672.

23 *Parl. Doc.* Chamber, 2019-20, No. 55-0173/001, 108.

24 M.J. Schermaier, "*Res Communes Omnium*: The History of an Idea from Greek Philosophy to Grotian Jurisprudence" (2009) *Grotiana*, (20) 20-21. See also M.A. Chardeaux, *Les choses communes*, 15-18, No. 15-18; A.S. Foures-Diop, "Les choses communes (première partie)" (2011) *RJO*, (59) 60-61.

25 R. Derine and F. Van Neste, *Zakenrecht*, I A, Standaard, Antwerp, 1974, 11-12, No. 6.

ecological balance and biodiversity.[26] In this contribution, we focus on the environmental protection potential of the commons regime.[27] Of course, it must be taken into account that the original *ratio legis* of the French-Belgian legal regime of *res communes*, which dates from the Code Napoléon of 1804, did not have environmental protection as an objective. However, the preparatory works now explicitly link the reinvented notion of *res communes* in the Belgian property law reform with the upcoming sustainable development movement and recent environmental concerns, such as scarcity of resources.[28] As will be set out below (*infra* no. 13), the newly introduced notion of "future generations" is also an example of this sustainability rationale.[29] The question remains however to what extent the reformed *res communes* concept can contribute to a more ecologically inclusive use of resources and how this brings together the traditional model of exclusive ownership and the commons' logic of collectiveness, solidarity and cooperation.

In what follows, four different aspects of the legal regime of Article 3.43 BCC will be discussed. First, we will explore what kind of objects fall under the scope of "common things" (II). Next, we will analyse how the non-appropriability of commons is contested by the common right to use *res communes* (III). Thirdly, we will discuss the restrictions specific to the common right to use (IV). Lastly, the question of wether the common use right is a subjective right is adressed (V). We conclude this contribution with some open remarks.

II. *RES COMMUNES: QUID*? FROM A NATURALISTIC TOWARDS A NORMATIVE UNDERSTANDING

4. ***Res communes* and property law: "things" treated as exiles** – As mentioned in the introduction, according to Article 3.43 BCC, things are considered "common" if they cannot be appropriated in their entirety. The reformed Belgian property law adopts a functional definition of *res communes*. The non-appropriability of a commons as a whole follows from their qualification

26 M.-P. Camproux Duffrène, "Repenser l'article 714 du Code civil français comme une prote d'entrée vers les communs" (2018) 81 *RIEJ*, (297) 297-330 (hereinafter: M.-P. Camroux Duffrene (2018) 81 *RIEJ*); A. Carette, "Een subjectief recht op een volwaardig leefmilieu?" (1998) *TPR*, (821) 821-888 (hereinafter: A. Carette (1998) *TPR*); M.S. De Clippele, "Quel avenir pour les choses communes? in F. Haumont and J. Sambon (eds.), *L'environnement, le droit et le magistrat*, Larcier, Brussels, 2021, (555) 555-584 (hereinafter: M.S. De Clippele, "Quel avenir pour les choses communes?").

27 See in a similar sense: A. Hucq (2022) 7 *TBBR* (363) 363-377.

28 Draft Bill, No. 54-3348/001; Amendment No. 2, *Parl. Doc.* Chamber, 2019-20, No. 55-0173/002, 5; V. Sagaert, *Goederenrecht* in *Beginselen van Belgisch privaatrecht*, Kluwer, Mechelen, 2021, 278 (hereinafter: V. Sagaert, *Goederenrecht*).

29 Amendment No. 2, *Parl. Doc.* Chamber, 2019-20, No. 55-0173/002, 5.

as "things". According to Article 3.38 BCC legal objects or things (Dutch: "*voorwerp*", French: "*chose*") are to be distinguished from legal subjects, like animals and (legal) persons.[30] Next, Article 3.41 BCC stipulates that things that are capable of being appropriated are called "goods" (Dutch: "*goed*", French: "*bien*").[31] Only economically valuable things can be considered as an appropriable good, although the economic value of goods is off course highly variable because of changing markets and subjective understanding of value.[32] Many environmental elements that were deemed worthless, have only recently been perceived as economically valuable and, have consequently, been integrated in the market economy.[33] However, Article 3.43 BCC expressly confirms that *res communes* are non-appropriable in their entirety. *Res communes*, including all kinds of valuable biodiversity elements, are thus excluded from the field of property law, setting them off against private ownership.[34] Common things, because they are mere "things" and no "goods", cannot be the object of property rights (Art. 3.7 BCC).[35] Consequently, these valuable environmental commons are solely governed by public law and traditional public environmental law protection measures.[36]

5. From a naturalistic approach of "commons" ... – The above theoretical analysis about the commons says little about the reasons why the Belgian property law system does not see these *res* as appropriable things (*c.q.* goods). Legal doctrine distinguishes two different explanatory approaches for the non-appropriability of commons in their entirety: an (1) objective or naturalistic approach and (2) a normative approach (for the latter see *infra* no. 7).[37] First,

30 Art. 3.38 BCC states: "*Things, whether natural or artificial, corporeal or incorporeal, are to be distinguished from animals. Things and animals ar to be distinguished from persons.*" See on this distinction: F. Swennen, "Persoon, voorwerp, relatie" (2022) *TPR*, 1253-1274.

31 Art. 3.41 BCC states: "*Goods in the broadest sense are all things that are capable of being appropriated (…).*"

32 Draft Bill No. 54-3348/001, 104 and 108; J. Hansenne, *Les biens: précis*, Faculté de Droit de Liège, Liège, 1996, 11-12 (hereinafter: J. Hansenne, *Les biens*).

33 See R. Chami, *What a Living Whale is Worth – and Why the Economy Should Protect Nature. Ted Talk* (2023) www.youtube.com/watch?v=r wigf0C6zxM, accessed 10.11.2023; B. Grimonprez, "Le droit de propriété à l'ère du changement climatique" in M. Hautereau-Boutonnet and S. Porchy-Simon (eds.), *Le changement climatique: quel rôle pour le droit privé?*, Dalloz, Paris, 2019, (243) 246 (hereinafter: B. Grimonprez, "Le droit de propriété").

34 N. Belaidi and A. Euzen, "De la chose commune au patrimoine commun"(2009) 145 *Mondes*, (55) 63; M.A. Chardeaux, *Les choses communes*, 170 .

35 Art. 3.7 BCC states: "*Property rights can only concern goods as defined in article 3.41, subject to any limitations arising from the nature of the right at hand.*" See N. Carette and R. Jansen, *Handboek goederenrecht*, Intersentia, Antwerp, 2022, 286, No. 507; V. Sagaert, *Goederenrecht*, 161, No. 157.

36 Compare: B. Grimonprez, "Les biens nature", (13) 13.

37 A. Carette (1998) *TPR*, (821) 832, No. 15; A. Hucq (2022) 7 *TBBR* (363) 366; J. Rochfeld, "Penser autrement la propriété: la propriété s'oppose-t-elle aux 'commons'?" (2014) *RIDE*, (351) 357-358 (hereinafter: J. Rochfeld (2014) *RIDE*).

according to the naturalistic approach, *res communes* as a whole are not appropriable because of their own particular nature and scope. The abundance of commons, for example running water, air or sunlight, makes it respectively impossible or undesirable to own them, given the current state of technology.[38] It would therefore be useless and undesirable to appropriate common things as a whole.[39] Article 3.43 BCC, as well as the preparatory works, seem to suggest that the Belgian legislator opted – either intentionally or not – for the traditional naturalistic approach.[40] The Article mentions, without further clarification, the mere physical impossibility or incapability of *res communes* to be appropriated.[41] In this regard, Article 3.43 BCC should be read in conjunction with Article 3.8 BCC, that inscribes the so-called specialty and unity principle in property law, according to which only determinable, delineated goods that can be seen as a unity – corporeal or not – can be the object of property rights.[42] *Res communes,* like for example running water, cannot be materially determined or contained, so that they do not meet these fundamental property law principles, and consequently, cannot be the object of property rights.

6. **Criticism of the naturalistic approach** – However, there are some objections against the objective or naturalistic approach on non-appropriability of common things in their entirety. First, the application of the *res communes* qualification because of sheer abundance of a resource is not necessarily as objective as it seems, since it actually has little to do with the nature of particular *res.* For instance, one can assume that the amount of blue ballpoint pens to be found worldwide is abundant. Why is such stationery not considered a *res communes*? The qualification of things as *res communes* seems, on the contrary, a rather subjective consideration. Another example is air: Since long ago, appropriation of it was considered useless since everyone could have enough of it; today air is indirectly appropriated by emissions trading schemes because of rising levels of air pollution.[43] Although air is still abundant, apparently, (clean) air is no longer taken for granted and becoming scarce, but nonetheless, it still is considered a common good.

---

38 M.A. Chardeaux, *Les choses communes*, 107-131, No. 90-107; J. Ph. Suijling, *Inleiding tot het burgerlijk recht*, Bohn, Haarlem, 1940, 36, No. 33.

39 M.A. Chardeaux, *Les choses communes*, 16-17, No. 17; J. Rochfeld (2014) *RIDE*, (351) 357-358.

40 Contra: J. Van de Voorde (2020) *ERPL* (1009) 1021, No. 12.

41 The exact wording of Art. 3.43 BCC is "*cannot*" be appropriated. Also: Draft Bill No. 54-3348/001, 108: "*il n'est pas possible de se les approprier*".

42 Other criteria for things in order to be appropriable are materiality, susceptibility to human control, autonomy or independency, measurability and economic value. See: V. Tweehuysen, *Het uniciteitsbeginsel in het goederenrecht,* Kluwer, Deventer, 2016, 363 p.; J.C. Van der Steur, *Grenzen van rechtsobjecten*, Kluwer, Deventer, 2003, 124-145.

43 I. Durant, *Droit des biens*, Larcier, Brussels, 2017, 20, No. 3; B. Grimonprez, "Le droit de propriété", (243) 247.

Secondly, as already mentioned, the impossibility of appropriating *res communes*, greatly depends on the ever-changing state of scientific knowledge. Scientific evolution and technical developments can bring certain *res communes* into the realm of appropriable things. An illustrative example is the bottom of the sea, which was considered a commons under Roman law, but – since it is now technically possible to use or capture the entire seabed – it is no longer treated as a natural common according to the original definition, but is considered to be part of the public domain.[44] If the practical use of things depending on the technical possibilities and scientific knowledge were the only criterion for the commons category, this would cause legal uncertainty.

Thirdly, since the naturalistic interpretation of the commons category leads to legal uncertainty, the *res communes* regime does not seem to offer sufficiently firm protection for environmentally valuable elements.[45] Apart from the aforementioned traditional *res communes*, recent scholarship tends to extend the *res communes* concept to environmentally valuable elements like soil, certain species of plants and animals, natural landscapes, biodiversity, ecosystems and the climate in general.[46] In other words, the ecological significance and the need to protect some natural resources are also considered to be criteria for the *res communes* category. This qualification is not at all based on factual or objective criteria regarding the non-appropriable nature of the thing concerned. A certain landscape or an ecosystem could perfectly be entirely appropriated. Nonetheless, these things are considered worthy of *res communes* protection by legal scholarship because of their societal and ecological value. Therefore, in some legal doctrine, these things are considered to be common and thus non-appropriable since the fear exists that private owners shall not protect and safeguard them sufficiently.[47] However these criteria create, again, legal uncertainty, since it is difficult to draw a clear line in the commons qualification criteria. The naturalistic definition of common things, seems to be based on society's subjective changing needs: What is considered useless at a given moment, can become in need of legal protection under the commons regime later on.[48] The interpretation of the category of "*res*

44 M.S. De Clippele, "Quel avenir pour les choses communes?", (555) 559, No. 9; A. Hucq (2022) 7 *TBBR* (363) 366; J. Van de Voorde (2020) *ERPL* (1009) 1019, No. 10.

45 A. Hucq (2022) 7 *TBBR* (363) 366.

46 J. Rochfeld, M. Cornu and J. Martin, *Rapport final de recherche. L'échelle de communalité. Propositions de réforme pour intégrer les biens communs en droit,* 2021, 204 www.gip-recherche-justice.fr/wp-content/uploads/2021/06/Rapport-17-34-final-Juin-2021.pdf, accessed 10.11.2023. Also: M.-P. Camroux Duffrene (2018) 81 *RIEJ*, (297) 319-324; A. Carette (1998) *TPR*, (821) 835; B. Jadot, "L'article 714 du Code civil et la protection de l'environnement" in *L'actualité du droit de l'environnement*, Bruylant, Brussels, 1995, 57, No. 5; J. Van de Voorde, "Het nieuwe goederenrecht en het milieu" (2020) 3 *TMR*, (272) 273, No. 5 (hereinafter: J. Van de Voorde (2020) 3 *TMR*).

47 S. DRAPIER, "Quel régime de responsabilité pour les choses communes endommagées?" (2016) *RJE*, (691) 695.

48 J. Rochfeld (2014) *RIDE*, (351) 357-358.

communes" is thus not purely objective, but it is a rather normative concept, subject to societal values.[49]

7. ... **Towards a normative approach of "commons"** – The three aforementioned objections demonstrate that certain objects are qualified as "common", not because they are factually or objectively non-appropriable as a whole, but because a normative belief exists that it is not desirable that these objects could be freely and individually appropriated and need to be protected. A more fair or realistic approach would be to consider *res communes* protection – at least partially – in a normative way.[50] According to the normative approach, the qualification of things as "common" would no longer depend solely on the nature of these things, but their socio-economic value would also be taken into account as a normative criterion. In order to acknowledge the importance of this normative element with regard to the demarcation of the commons category, a clearer, more substantive and normative definition of *res communes* should be delineated.[51] Under such a new normative definition of *res communes* all kinds of things could principally qualify as commons, as long as it is desirable that the legal protection regime of commons is applicable.[52] Although the new Belgian *res communes*-regime does not include a normative definition, nor a list of common things, we follow the doctrinal argument that the wording of Article 3.43 BCC embraces a normative conception of *res communes*. The references to "*public interest*" and the "*interest of future generations*" exclude the traditional objective approach and give way to the normative interpretation of the commons category.[53] However, two caveats should be made.

First, it should be noted that the factual or objective impossibility to appropriate things because of their technical characteristics or abundance, such as for example air, water or sunlight, remains a valuable criterion for the

49 A. Hucq (2022) 7 *TBBR* (363) 366; J. Van de Voorde (2020) *ERPL* (1009) 1018, No. 10.

50 M.A. Chardeaux, *Les choses communes*, 132, No. 108 and 169, No. 142; B. Jadot, "L'environnement n'appartient à personne et l'usage qui en est fait est commun à tous. Des lois de police règlent la manière d'en jouir" in F. OST and S. GUTWIRTH (eds.), *Quel avenir pour le droit de l'environnement*, FUSL, Brussels, 1996, (74) 78-79, No. 38, 40 and 45 (hereinafter: B. Jadot, "L'environnement n'appartient à personne"); J. Rochfeld (2014) *RIDE*, (351) 358.

51 See in this sense already: W. Dross, "Rapport de synthèse" in *Le changement climatique, quel rôle pour le droit privé?*, Dalloz, Paris, 2019, (275) 278; F. Masson, *La propriété commune*, 11, No. 9; M. Mekki, "L'évolution des limites apportées au droit de propriété: l'exemple des enjeux environnementaux" (2015) *Michel Foucault*, 4, No. 10, https://mustaphamekki.openum.ca/files/sites/37/2015/09/%c3%a9volution-des-limites-foucault.pdf, accessed 10.11.2023; J. Van de Voorde (2020) *ERPL* (1009) 1020, No. 11.

52 A. Hucq (2022) 7 *TBBR* (363) 366.

53 A. Hucq (2022) 7 *TBBR* (363) 366; J. Van de Voorde (2020) *ERPL* (1009) 1021, No. 12. See in the same sense under French law: M.A. Chardeaux, *Les choses communes*, 263, No. 228.

qualification as common things.[54] In fact, the traditional objective interpretation of common things will become part of the normative definition.[55]

Secondly, the current functional definition of common things in Article 3.43 BCC – that describes *res communes* in terms of their legal effect, i.e. non-appropriable as a whole – should be transformed in a more substantial definition. Whether the legislator should include a (non-)exhaustive list of *res communes* or whether an open norm is to be adopted, is open to discussion. For example, in the *Rodota*-proposal on property law, Italian scholars defined commons, so-called "*beni comuni*", as things "*to the enjoyment of fundamental rights and the autonomous development of the individual*", that can be used only "*to the benefit of future generations*".[56] Additionally, the proposal provided an illustrative, non-exhaustive list of things that could be qualified as "*beni comuni*", such as watercourses, lakes, air, forests, high-altitude mountain areas, glaciers, perennial snow, beaches, protected wildlife and flora etc.[57] However, since no definition of *res communes* was inscribed in the Belgian Civil Code, it is still to be seen how the judiciary will interpret the existing provision, especially in the light of changing social conditions and environmental protection goals.

III. WHAT GOES AROUND COMES AROUND: THE REINTEGRATION OF COMMONS INTO PROPERTY LAW THROUGH PARTIAL APPROPRIATION

8. Contrasting the compatible: the phantom of ownership – Traditionally, the non-appropriability of commons in their entirety has been perceived as the distinctive criterion that sets them apart from the traditional ownership model, whether private or public.[58] The *res communes* status is irreconcilable with the powers of an absolute sovereign owner.[59] Moreover, ownership is often seen

---

54 See extensiveley on sunlight: D. Bailleul, *L'énergie solaire. Aspects juridiques*, University of Savoy Mont Blanc-Chambery, Chambery Cedex, 2010, 133.

55 J. Van de Voorde (2020) *ERPL* (1009) 1020, No. 11.

56 The Commission's report is available via www.giustizia.it/giustizia/it/mg_1_12_1.page?contentId=SPS47624, accessed 10.11.2023.

57 F. Cortese, "*What are 'Common Goods' (beni comuni)? Pictures from the Italian Debate*" (2017) 11 *Pólémos*, (121) 125-126; A. Di Robilant, "Property and Democratic Deliberation: The *Numerus Clausus* Principle and Democratic Experimentalism in Property Law" (2014) 62 *AJCL*, (367) 390-394.

58 B. Grimonprez, "Les biens nature", (13) 13; V. Sagaert and S. Demeyere (2019) 16 *JT*, (313) 321, No. 36.

59 M.A. Chardeaux, *Les choses communes*, 67-72, No. 66-67, 91, No. 78 and 170, No. 142; S. Gutwirth, "Les communs: avec, malgré ou contre le droit?" (2022) 33 *JT*, (582) 588, No. 12; V. SAGAERT, "Shaking Hands", (1) 5, No. 8.

as the underlying cause of troubled ecosystems and the climate crisis.[60] In a similar way, *appropriation*-based distribution of natural resources is perceived to be harmful.[61] Consequently, some scholars reject private ownership rights as neo-liberal extractive rights. More inclusive concepts like the *res communes* regime are introduced as more climate-friendly systems. Consequently, the juxtaposition of this "diabolic" and exclusive ownership right against the inclusive *res communes* regime leads to these latter *res* being non-appropriable, non-tradable and excluded from any patrimony.[62] In the end, due to such reasoning, lots of valuable environmental commons are pushed outside the field of property law (and private law in general) towards other legal domains, such as public law. The key question is, however, whether this traditional exclusion of common things from property law is desirable, since various legal factors seem to indicate otherwise.

9. And the walls kept tumbling down: partial appropriation – The latter principle that common things are fully excluded from property law is actually only half true. Whilst excluding full appropriation of *res communes* in their entirety, at the same time, partial appropriation is allowed.[63] This follows from an *a contrario* reading of Article 3.43 BCC. The appropriation of a part of a common thing can follow from the use of the common thing as a whole, such as for example bottling running water or inhaling fresh air.[64] Use equals in that case to partial appropriation. However, partial appropriation is considered to be different from appropriation of the common thing in its entirety. If the partial appropriation compromises the non-appropriability of the whole, it is no longer allowed.[65] The partial appropriation should therefore be in accordance with the conservation obligation that encumbers the common thing in its entirety (*infra* no. 16). Some legal scholars see this partial appropriation as a way of

---

60 B. Akkermans and K. Van Melle, "Regeneratieve eigendom: naar een hernieuwde benadering" in B. Akkermans, B. Hoops, *et al.* (eds.), *Privaatrecht 2050. De weg naar ecologische duurzaamheid*, die Keure, Bruges, 2022, (193) 193-207; B. Grimonprez, "Le droit de propriété", 243-257.

61 J.-P. Chazal, "Le propriétaire souverain: archéologie d'une idole doctrinale" (2020) *RTD civ.*, (1) 1-34; B. Grimonprez, "Le droit de propriété", (243) 245 and 254; U. Mattei and A. Quarta, *The turning point in private law: ecology, technology and the commons*, Edward Elgar Publishing, Cheltenham, 2019, 82-84; M. Serres, "Le droit peut sauver la nature" (2008) 4 *Pouvoirs*, (5) 10..

62 R. Derine and F. Van Neste, *Zakenrecht*, I A, Standaard, Antwerp, 1974, 11-12; A. Hucq (2022) 7 *TBBR* (363) 367; G. Loiseau, "Typologie des choses hors du commerce" (2000) *RTD civ.*, (47) 47-64; J. Van de Voorde (2020) *ERPL* (1009) 1036, No. 31.

63 A. Carette (1998) *TPR*, (821) 834, No. 18; M.A. Chardeaux, *Les choses communes*, 91, No. 80; A. Hucq (2022) 7 *TBBR* (363) 367; V. Sagaert, *Goederenrecht*, 277, No. 293.

64 J. Rochfeld, M. Cornu and J. Martin, *Rapport final de recherche. L'échelle de communalité. Propositions de réforme pour intégrer les biens communs en droit,* 2021, 195, www.gip-recherche-justice.fr/wp-content/uploads/2021/06/Rapport-17-34-final-Juin-2021.pdf, accessed 10.11.2023.

65 A. Hucq (2022) 7 *TBBR* (363) 367.

factual and intentional domination or *occupatio*, and more particularly, as an application of the *res nullius* appropriation regime.[66] Such *res nullii* are goods, not things, without an owner, but which are – opposite to the *res communes* category – factually and legally capable of being appropriated entirely.[67] Like the common law "rule of capture", the first person to take and use resources such as groundwater, oil, gas or wild animals, acquires ownership over these goods.[68] Other examples of *res nullii* are rainwater, fish living in running water, insects, etc.[69] Many of them could be seen as fragments of a larger environmental entirety, like wildlife or ecosystems. *Res nullii* can be seen as the elements or components that together form a larger aggregate, which is in this case a *res communes.*[70] Appropriation of a fraction of a common thing is thus, like the Belgian definition confirms, possible and simply happens by factual possession, just as one could acquire ownership of a *res nullius.* In this regard, some essential parts of natural commons, regardless of their *res communes* protection, could get back into the hands of a private owner through the *res nullius* appropriation regime. Property law thus embraces the commons again via a back door loophole.

10. Bringing the commons back to property law: problems and inconsistencies – The fact that one can partially appropriate commons and, therefore, can regain property rights on these things, poses various issues.

A first theoretical problem that arises, when applying the *res nullius* regime and possession in general on common things, is that it concerns an acquisition that is not "derivative" but "original".[71] This means that the party acquiring the *res* is not bound by earlier rights *in rem* or qualitative obligations that were established before the partial appropriation.[72] As the *res* is "purified" of its earlier encumbrances (in Dutch: "*zuiverende werking*")[73], the acquirer gets a new absolute and exclusive property right. This would imply that the *res*

66 A. Carette (1998) *TPR*, (821) 833-834, No. 18; M.A. Chardeaux, *Les choses communes*, 99-101, No. 85-86; M.S. De Clippele, "Quel avenir pour les choses communes?", (555) 565, No. 19. Contra: F. Masson, *La propriété commune*, 183, No. 419.

67 H. De Page, *Traité élémentaire de droit civil belge*, V/1, Bruylant, Brussels, 1942, 528, No. and 538 (hereinafter: H. DE Page, *Traité*); R. Derine and Van Neste, *Zakenrecht*, I/A, Standaard, Antwerp, 1974, 12, No. 7A; J. Hansenne, *Les biens*, 22, No. 17.

68 See D. Grinlinton, "Evolution, adaption, and invention: Property rights in natural resources in a changing world" in D. Freestone (ed.), *Legal Aspects of Sustainable Development*, Brill, Leiden, 2011, (275) 280 with reference to *Acton v Blundell* [1843] 152 ER 1223; *Ballard v Tomlinson* (1885) 29 Ch D 115, 121; *Ohio Oil Co v Indiana* 177 U.S. 190, 203 (1900).

69 A. Carette (1998) *TPR*, (821) 833, No. 17; H. DE Page, *Traité*, 528, No. 537; J. Hansenne, *Les biens*, 23, No. 17.

70 M.A. Chardeaux, *Les choses communes*, 99-101, No. 86; A. Hucq (2022) 7 *TBBR* (363) 367.

71 M.A. Chardeaux, *Les choses communes*, 92, No. 81.

72 N. Carette and R. Jansen, *Handboek goederenrecht*, Intersentia, Antwerp, 2022, 92, No. 123; V. Sagaert, *Goederenrecht*, 1047, No. 1163.

73 N. Carette and R. Jansen, *Handboek goederenrecht*, Intersentia, Antwerp, 2022, 92, No. 123 and 149, No. 213.

communes protection regime of Article 3.43 BCC does not survive the original acquisition of a part of a common thing.[74] Although it could be argued that the protection regime continues to exist (*infra* no. 16 and 18), the lack of theoretical clarity causes legal uncertainty.

A second question is whether the acquisition of common things through the *res nullius* regime is the only way parts of *res communes* can be appropriated. In fact, commons that supposedly do not belong to anyone individually, are constantly partly appropriated by individuals in various ways, either directly or indirectly.[75] For example, when parties establish an above-ground specific superficies right (NL: "*bijzonder opstalrecht*")[76], this right implies the exclusive privatization of a volume of air above the ground, with the intention to build a structure on or in it.[77] The same goes for a piece of land: which is at the same time considered to be part of the soil as a *res communes*, as well as it is seen as an object of private land ownership. These two examples show that common things, like air and soil, are not partially appropriated merely by possession, but also that the creation of property rights on these things is generally accepted.

A third issue is whether – and if so, to what extent precisely – personal rights can be also established on (parts of) *res communes*? Although allowing the creation of personal rights on commons seems less invasive than property rights, one can imagine very exclusive and extractive personal rights, like long-term (rural) leases that could lead to overexploitation of (agricultural) land.[78] This question has not been addressed yet in legal doctrine. However, if we look into the acquisitive prescription regime of Article 3.18 BCC, some authors state that it is possible to acquire a personal right through possession.[79]

In conclusion, it seems that the term "appropriation" in Article 3.43 BCC is to be understood rather broadly, so that partial appropriation of valuable environmental resources is possible. Consequently, an adequate and effective *res communes* protection regime, preserving those resources, is needed. In the below paragraph, the public domain regime is taken as an example for the use, appropriation and protection of commons.

---

74 See on accession, another way of original acquisition: G. Leray, *L'immeuble et la protection de la nature*, LGDJ, Issy-les-Moulineaux, 2019, 267-268.

75 See also: A. Hucq (2022) 7 *TBBR* (363) 367-368; B. Jadot, "L'environnement n'appartient à personne", (74) 78, No. 33, 35.

76 This concerns a direct and derivative appropriation or acquisition. See V. Sagaert, *Goederenrecht*, 277, No. 293 and 1006-1007, No. 1109.

77 V. Sagaert, "Het opstalrecht in het nieuwe goederenrecht: een eigentijdse volume-eigendom" (2022) *T.Not.*, (531) 535, No. 8 *et seq.*

78 P. Baudinet and G. Cludts, "Relation entre preneur et bailleur au regard de l'évolution technique et écologique de la société" in R. Gotzen (ed.), *Le bail à ferme. Un état des lieux*, die Keure, Bruges, 2015, (491) 498-500; V. Godart and F. Özsarlak, "Het Voorstel van Vlaams Pachtdecreet: eerste verkenning van het nieuwe Vlaamse landbouwlandschap" (2023) *Huur*, (115) 129-130, No. 33, 138-139, No. 64-65 and 142, No. 72.

79 V. Sagaert, "De hervorming van het goederenrecht" (2020) *TPR*, (389) 460, No. 87.

11. Public domain as functional archetype – From the previous paragraph, it follows that commons are not as much beyond the reach of property law. In many different ways, partial appropriation of *res communes* is possible. The property law regime of commons leans towards the regime of public domain goods in this regard. According to Belgian law, a good belongs to the public domain when it is designated by the competent authority, be it explicitly or implicitly, either for the use of all or for a public service.[80] Examples are roads, certain types of waterways, beaches, harbors, cemeteries, etc.[81] The difference between public goods and common things is sometimes unclear. However public goods, contrary to common things, are "goods" and should in that view be appropriable, at least if they become "disaffected" from the public domain.[82] The appropriation of public goods can be justified because these goods are generally considered to be non-excludable, of which the consumption is non-rivalrous.[83] In practice, both categories are still functionally comparable. The use of certain "natural" public domain goods, like beaches and waterways, is also common to all, just like the use of common things.[84] Before the Belgian property law reform, it was discussed which rights of use could be established on public domain goods. The basic premise was that no personal rights, like leases, nor real rights of use were allowed to be established on public domain goods.[85] However over time, numerous statutory and jurisprudential exceptions emerged.[86] The newly adopted Article 3.45 BCC now confirms that both personal and real rights of use are allowed, on the condition that they do not hinder the public purpose of the public domain good.[87] If the use right is incompatible with the public function of the good, the right will cease to exist.[88]

---

80 A. Lemmerling, "Openbaar domein" in V. Sagaert, J. Baeck, *et al.* (eds.), *Het nieuwe goederenrecht*, Intersentia, Antwerp, 2021, (101) 107-109, No. 11-14 and 118, No. 35; J. De Staercke, "De finaliteit en totstandkoming van openbaar domein" in R. Palmans, T. Leys and J. Toury (eds.), *Openbaar domein*, Intersentia, Antwerp, 2019, (1) 13, No. 19 *et seq.*

81 H. de Page, *Traité*, 693-703, No. 794-806; J. Hansenne, *Les biens*, 138-139, No. 121; V. Sagaert, *Goederenrecht*, 239, No. 247.

82 H. de Page, *Traité*, 528, No. 536 and 685-686, No. 787; R. Derine and F. Van Neste, *Zakenrecht*, I A, Standaard, Antwerp, 1974, 171-172 and 184.

83 J.M. Karpoff (2022)8 65 *J.L. & Econ.*, (65) 70.

84 H. de Page, *Traité*, 528, No. 536 and 685-686, No. 787; D. D'Hooghe and M. Van Den Langenbergh, "Naar de opheffing van het leerstuk van het openbaar domein?" in R. Palmans, T. Leys and J. Toury (ed.), *Openbaar domein*, Intersentia, Antwerp, 2019, (243) 245, No. 3.

85 T. Leys and V. Sagaert, "Het gebruik van het openbaar domein door particulieren" in R. Palmans, T. Leys and J. Toury (eds.), *Openbaar domein*, Intersentia, Antwerp, 2019, (79) 79, No. 1; V. Sagaert, *Goederenrecht*, 261, No. 276.

86 A. Lemmerling, "Openbaar domein" in V. Sagaert, J. Baeck, *et al.* (eds.), *Het nieuwe goederenrecht*, Intersentia, Antwerp, 2021, (101) 116-118, No. 30-34; V. Sagaert, *Goederenrecht*, 262-263, No. 277-278.

87 Draft Bill, No. 54-3348/001, 113; L.-S. Pan-Van de Meulebroeke and G. Rolland, "Le nouveau droit des biens: quelques considérations en matière de domanialité publique et de droit administratif" (2022) *Rev.dr.commun.*, (2) 7, No. 25-26.

88 Draft Bill, No. 54-3348/001, 112-113; V. Sagaert, *Goederenrecht*, 264, No. 279.

Although it is not very clear from the wording of Article 3.43 BCC, a functionally similar regime applies to *res communes*. As explained before, common things can be partially appropriated and encumbered with personal or real use rights. For the sake of clarity and legal certainty – but also in order to promote sustainable commercialization and profitability of natural resources – a possible solution could be to align the *res communes* regime with the public domain regime. For example, Article 3.43 BCC can be edited in a way that rights of use are allowed, on the condition that the public interest and the interest of future generations are safeguarded continuously (*infra* no. 16 and 18).

12. **Intermediary conclusion** – From the foregoing follows that, by the broadening of the scope of (partial) appropriation of commons, many environmentally valuable resources are ultimately pulled back into the "absoluteness" of property law. This doesn't necessarily pose a problem for the protection of natural resources as common things, if specific and lasting protection regimes are foreseen. What appears to be quintessential in this regard is the way use rights and appropriation of parts of commons can be managed in order to prevent extractive use of natural resources. This way, the absolute and exclusive nature of ownership and property law in general, can be mitigated and adjusted to environmental protection concerns for commons. The *res communes* property law regime could become more inclusive and sustainable. In the following, we will analyze how such system could be founded in Belgian property law and how overly extractive use can be controlled via public and private law mechanisms for environmentally valuable things.

IV. A USE COMMON TO ALL: RESTRICTED USE IN THE INTEREST OF FUTURE GENERATIONS

13. **Tragedy of the commons: the need for protection** – The risk with *res communes* is that all those entitled to use and appropriate parts of them want to get as much return as possible in the shortest possible time. As explained above, common users can indeed partially appropriate common things, often through the rule of capture (*supra* no. 9). This could, consequently, create a rat race on, for example, natural resources, in which the long-term perspective is lost. Legal-economic literature refers to this problem as the so-called "tragedy of the commons".[89] According to this theory, common things risk being overused and

[89] See a.o. F.A. Friedman, "The Economics of the Common Pool" (1971) *UCLA L. Rev.*, 855-873; H. Gordon, "The economic Theory of a Common-Property Resource: the Fishery" (1954) 62 *J.Pol.Econ.*, 32 *et seq.*; G. Hardin, "The Tragedy of the Commons" (1968) 162 *Science*, (1243) 1244. For an overview: M. Heller, "The tragedy of the Anticommons" (2013) 76 *Mod. L. Rev.*, 1-24 (hereinafter: M. Heller (2013) 76 *Mod. L. Rev.*).

overexploited, if free will and uncontrolled demand prevail in a world of limited carrying capacity of the ecological system.[90] In the words of Garett HARDIN: "*Freedom in a commons brings ruin to all*".[91] In legal-economic literature, two types of standardized solutions can be distinguished for this issue.[92]

A first solution, supported by HARDIN, is to control and regulate the use of common things via public law. This regulatory control can be created through so-called "command-and-control" regulations, that delineate specific practices to achieve environmental goals.[93] Most natural resource and environmental public policies are dominated by command-and-control regulations. For example for fishery, such policies dictate fishing-vessel length, the days of the week or times of the day that a vessel can engage in fishing, net length and mesh size, and other details.[94] From a property law perspective, the use right on common things in this case remains open to all or non-exclusive (*supra* no. 3), meaning that nobody can be excluded from accessing or using a common thing.

A second solution, the alleged "private ownership solution", is to privatize the access to or use of things that are seen as common.[95] This solution emerges from an analysis of the commons problem from a property law viewpoint. Property law theorists, like DEMSETZ, GORDON and SCOTT believe that non-exclusivity of use is the origin of the commons problem.[96] If nobody can be excluded from using a common thing, individual attempts to preserve a resource and limit overexploitation become undermined. In this view, for example, climate change, resulting from carbon emissions, is at its core a problem of non-exclusive use rights to the atmosphere.[97] An individual or entity should therefore be able to have exclusive and exchangeable use rights on common things; this means including the right to exclude others from using it. Following this solution, private property rights and market competition ought to solve the commons issue better than state-controlled regulation.[98] DEMSETZ argues that a clear set of exclusive use rights on commons should be developed, since this would

90 J.M. KARPOFF (2022)8 65 *J.L. & Econ.*, (65) 65-66.

91 G. HARDIN, "The Tragedy of the Commons" (1968) 162 *Science*, (1243) 1244.

92 M. HELLER (2013) 76 *Mod. L. Rev.*, 3 and 7. A third solution strategy to avoid overuse dilemmas are cooperative engagements. See: E. OSTROM, *Governing the Commons: The Evolution of Institutions for Collective Action*, Cambridge UP, Cambridge, 1990, 1-28.

93 J.M. KARPOFF (2022)8 65 *J.L. & Econ.*, (65) 66.

94 J.M. KARPOFF (2022)8 65 *J.L. & Econ.*, (65) 66 with reference to B.C FIELD and M.K. FIELD, *Environmental Economics*, McGraw-Hill, New York, 2017, 471 p.

95 About the "private ownership solution": H. DEMSETZ, "Toward a Theory of Property Rights" (1967) 57 *Am.Econ.Rev.*, (347) 354-359.

96 H. DEMSETZ, "Toward a Theory of Property Rights" (1967) 57 *Am.Econ.Rev.*, (347) 354-359; H.S. GORDON, "The Economic Theory of a Common-Property Resource: The Fishery" (1954) 62 *J.Pol.Econ.*, 124-142; A. SCOTT, "The Fishery: The Objective of Sole Ownership" (1955) 63 *J.Pol.Econ.*, 116–124.

97 J.M. KARPOFF (2022)8 65 *J.L. & Econ.*, (65) 77.

98 M. HELLER (2013) 76 *Mod. L. Rev.*, 4; J.M. KARPOFF (2022)8 65 *J.L. & Econ.*, (65) 70.

minimize the total net costs of developing and enforcing those rights.[99] For example transferable fish quotas and tradable carbon emission rights are considered to be better solutions to respectively overexploited seas and air pollution than classical command and control policies.[100]

14. Solution 1: Non-exclusive use and regulatory protection – At first sight, the Belgian legislator has opted for the first "command-and-control" solution. As previously mentioned, Article 3.43 BCC states that the use of *res communes* is common to all, in accordance with specific laws and, additionally, in the general interest and the interest of future generations (see *infra* no. 16 on the interpretation of the latter). From a property law perspective: the use of these *res* seems to be non-exclusive (*supra* no. 13). In accordance with the first communitarian solution, the common use rights should indeed be limited by public regulations in order to create sustainable management of commons. This is in line with the aforementioned non-exclusive solution: other users cannot exclude a user that breaches the regulations. It is only a governmental body that can sanction a user for breaking the regulations. The Belgian legislator – at least partly – adheres to this regulatory protection by stating in Article 3.43 BCC that the common use is regulated by specific laws.[101] These laws should ensure the integrity and protection of common things and thus include fields as environmental and nature conservation law.[102] Via such state-made laws and regulations, the governmental bodies regain large influence on reglementary access and use of commons. Some authors believe that Article 3.43, like the former Article 714 of the old Civil Code, creates a general legislative competence for the government to enact environmental regulations.[103] In any case, the State has a considerable discretion with regard to regulation of access and use of common things.[104]

15. "Non-exclusive use" as *contradictio in terminis*? – Following the previous paragraph, although appropriation of commons as a whole is principally impossible, partial appropriation and common use is possible, on the condition that this use and, accordingly, partial appropriation is in line with public regulations. How then exactly must such a common use regime be conceived?

99 H. Demsetz, "Towards a theory of property rights" (1967) 57 *Am.Econ.Rev.*, 347-359.

100 J.M. Karpoff (2022)8 65 *J.L. & Econ.*, (65) 70.

101 Van de Voorde states that specific laws contains both *lois particulières* and *lois de police*. See J. Van de Voorde (2020) *ERPL* (1009) 1038, No. 34.

102 C. De Klemm, G.J. Martin, M. Prieur and J. UNntermaier, "Les qualifications des éléments de l'environnement" in A. Kiss and R. Carbenier, *L'Ecologie et la loi: le statut juridique de l'environnement: réflexions sur le droit de l'environnement*, L' Harmattan, Paris, 1989, 56.

103 J. Van de Voorde (2020) *ERPL* (1009) 1038; A. Vandeburie, *Propriété et domanialité publiques en Belgique*, Die Keure, Bruges, 2013, 384, No. 329.

104 A. Hucq (2022) 7 *TBBR* (363) 371; J. Van de Voorde (2020) 3 *TMR*, 277, No. 23.

If we look into general Belgian private law, a user is entitled to use a good for its purpose, to perform all material acts that do not affect the substance or capital value of the good and all legal acts that do not change the property status of the good. Such a broad conception of *res communes* user-powers however may seem contrary to the non-exclusive nature of common things and the wish to protect ecologically valuable objects. Therefore, in our opinion, this is again an indication that Belgian property law also gives leeway to the second ("private ownership") solution strategy. As previously explained, on the basis of the *a contrario* interpretation of Article 3.43 BCC it is indeed possible to appropriate parts of common things, either indirectly, by way of the rule of capture of *res* nullius, either directly, for example by establishing a superficies right on a volume of air (*supra* no. 9-10). In this regard, according to Belgian property law, from a purely technical perspective it seems possible to establish rather exclusive rights on parts of common things. However, for environmental purposes, it is quintessential that the user, either exclusive or non-exclusive, cannot overuse or misuse his or her right of use in order to preserve nature. The key issue is thus not the external exclusivity (i.e. "the right to exclude others") but its internal counterpart (i.e. internal exclusivity or the property powers of the common user).[105] In other words: Exclusive use rights seem to be perfectly compatible with *res communes* on the condition that the exclusive powers or not used in an extractive way, i.e. leading to environmental degradation. In the next paragraph, we elaborate on the Belgian protection regime.

16. Solution 2: Exclusive use and duty of care and conservation – It is clear from the previous paragraph that also the second solution strategy of Demsetz, Gordon and Scott, plays a role regarding the use of Belgian *res communes* (*supra* no. 13). However, the neo-liberal excesses of this exclusive rights-solution have been mitigated by the Belgian legislator by restraining an overly extractive use. The Belgian legislator added by amendment – without giving further explanation on the scope or interpretation of the amendment – to Article 3.43 BCC that *res communes* must be used "*in the general interest, including that of future generations*". This new "common use criterion" implies that common things may only be used if it is in the general interest and in the interest of future generations. Common things may only be used in an interest common to all members of society. How this "general interest" is interpreted, is subject to evolution and primarily determined by the competent governmental bodies.[106] Nature conservation and/or environmental protection are commonly

105 D. Gruyaert, *De exclusiviteit van het eigendomsrecht*, Intersentia, Antwerp, 2016, 890 p.

106 A. Hucq (2022) 7 *TBBR* (363) 369; T. Leys, *De bescherming van het publiek gebruik van privaat vastgoed: tussen particulier en algemeen belang*, KU Leuven, Leuven, 2022, 13. On the difference between individual, common, collective and general interest: M. Kruithof, "Privaatrechtelijke facetten van algemeen belangacties bij de justitiële rechter" (2022) 1-2 *TPR*, (21) 29-36, No. 9-21.

considered to be of general interest.[107] Additionally, common use, in accordance with the general interest, implies that commons should be used in the interest of future generations.[108] This responsibility towards future generations is an attempt to integrate sustainability into property law.[109] The importance and the needs of future generations are also included in the United Nations Brundtland Commission definition of "sustainable development" as: "*development that meets the needs of the present without compromising the ability of future generations to meet their own needs.*"[110] The idea is to conserve natural resources, such as clean water and fertile agricultural land, that are necessary to meet current and future human needs.[111]

The common use criterion – i.e. to use commons in the general interest and in the interest of future generations – creates both a negative and positive duty on the user. On the one hand, it imposes a negative limitation on the access to and use of common things. One can only use a common thing if this use does not cause damage to the thing itself.[112] On the other hand, a positive duty of conservation flows from the common use criterion. All users should take the necessary measures in order to protect the *res communes* from natural degradation or human extractive use.[113]

Although support can be found for the recognition of this kind of positive conservation obligation for the use of commons, several potential drawbacks must be considered. A first, general remark is that, since present and future generations do not necessarily have different interests with regard to the environment, the added value of the "future generations amendment" is unclear.[114] Additionally, it is debated whether the (positive) conservation duty should be enacted in specific laws or an open standard of good behavior should

---

107 A. Hucq (2022) 7 *TBBR* (363) 369.

108 Before the property law reform several scholars already linked common things with the interest of future generations: B. Jadot, "L'environnement n'appartient à personne", (74) 105; J. Rochfeld, "Procès climatiques: une voie pour le commun?" (2020) 18 *RJSP*, (1) 7.
See on intergenerational commons: G. Alexander, *Property and Human Flourishing*, OUP, Oxford, 2019, 106-110 and 119; M. Golding, "Obligations to future generations" in E. Partridge (ed.), *Responsibilities to Future Generations. Environmental Ethics*, Prometheus, Buffalo, 1980, 61 *et seq.*

109 *Parl. Doc.* Chamber, 2019-20, No. 55-0173/002, 5.

110 World Commission on Environment and Development, *Our Common Future*, OUP, Oxford, 1987, 43. Also: E. Gaillard, *Générations futures et droit privé. Vers un droit des générations futures*, LGDJ, Paris, 2011, 673 p.

111 *Parl. Doc.* Chamber, 2019-20, No. 55-0173/001, 108. Also D. Pearce, A. Markandya and E. Barbier, *Blueprint for a Green Economy*, Earthscan, London, 1989, 34.

112 M.-P. Camroux Duffrene (2018) 81 *RIEJ*, (297) 308.

113 This is proposed by Hucq: A. Hucq (2022) 7 *TBBR* (363) 370. See also earlier in French legal doctrine: V. Inserguet-Brisset, *Propriété publique et environnement*, LGDJ, Paris, 1994, 11; F. Ost, "Oser la pensée complexe: l'exemple des communs" in M. Mekki and E. Naim-Gesbert, *Droit public et droit privé de l'environnement: unité dans la divesrité?*, LGDJ, Paris, 2016, 14.

114 See E. Dirix, "Beschermde belangen in het nieuw BW" (2022-23) 35 *RW*, 1362.

be added to Article 3.43 BCC or whether the wording of Article 3.43 already implicitly contains such open standard duty.[115] Based on the contribution of Gruyaert in this book, we tend to say that such open standard of good behavior is already put in place by Article 3.43 BCC, but perhaps a more explicit and concrete delineation of such conservation norm or a list of specified "sub-duties" would be recommendable.[116] Comparable with the French proposal for the reform of Article 714 French Civil Code, the Belgian legislator could have added to Article 3.43 BCC that parts of common things can be appropriated, on the condition that the appropriation does not affect the substance of the common thing, nor the use of others.[117]

However, if such conservation obligation would be generally acknowledged under Belgian law, still the question rises how this obligation can be enforced? We will discuss this enforcement issue briefly in the next section.

V. SANCTIONING HARMFUL ACCESS OR MISUSE OF COMMONS: SUBJECTIVE RIGHT AND COLLECTIVE ACTION

17. Belgian commons: the common use right as a subjective right? – The question of which actors would be able to enforce the *res communes* environmental protection regime, also largely determines which solution (non-exclusive use by all vs. exclusive use rights) will prevail (*supra* no. 14 and 15): If X disturbs the common use right of private person Y, and Y himself can, based on his own subjective right of use, exclude X from accessing or using the common thing in a certain manner (or ask for damages), this would mean that Belgian law is more in line with the exclusive rights solution. As a consequence, judges would have a substantial role in enforcing environmental protection.[118] On the other hand, if only state actors or government bodies were competent to sanction, the non-exclusive solution would prevail. It thus seems that the practical impact of the theoretical discussion between legal scholars on the question whether the common use right constitutes a subjective right or not, is

115 Hucq also raises this question, without giving preference to one of three options. See A. Hucq (2022) 7 *TBBR* (363) 370.

116 See the contribution of D. Gruyaert in this volume, No. 8 and 22.

117 See Art. 714-1 proposition de réforme de l'article 714 du Code civil français in J. Rochfeld, M. Cornu and J. Martin, *Rapport final de recherche. L'échelle de communalité. Propositions de réforme pour intégrer les biens communs en droit,* 2021, 425 www.gip-recherche-justice.fr/wp-content/uploads/2021/06/Rapport-17-34-final-Juin-2021.pdf, accessed 10.11.2023.

118 See F. Auvray, C. Bourucki and P. Gillaerts, "Belgische klimaatzaak: enkel(e) vaststellingen?" (2021) 436 *DJK*, 3-5; M. De Winter, "Belgische klimaatzaak: als het overstroomt in Den Haag, druppelt het in Brussels" (2023) 2 *TBBR*, 99-105; E. Van Gool, "De klimaatzaak als symptoom" (2021-22) 2 *RW*, 42.

not insignificant at all.[119] The recognition of the common use right as being a subjective right of all would entail that legal action is possible. Such legal action could be a quintessential added value for the protection and preservation of the environment and of natural resources.[120] According to Van de Voorde, it is generally accepted in French and Belgian case law and legal doctrine that holders of the common right to use *res communes* also have a procedural right to initiate legal action to protect their subjective right of common use and enjoyment.[121] Although there are strong arguments for accepting the common use right to be a subjective right, there are some counterarguments against or concerns about the acknowledgment of common subjective rights.

First, there are some restrictions: Only the holder of the allegedly infringed right who can proof personal and legitimate interest can bring such action.[122] It is required that the over-access or misuse of the common thing causes a direct personal impact to right holders, because they suffer damage or live near the affected common object.[123] Right holders should proof that they actually use or at least would intend to use the concerned common object themselves.[124] The large group of potential claimants is thus more or less limited.

Secondly, common use subjective rights are different from the classic interpretation of subjective rights. Subjective rights, such as the right of ownership or other limited property rights, are traditionally of a very exclusive nature. On the contrary, the allocation of a subjective right to access and use common things intends to ensure participation of everyone in using and enjoying these things, and is thus to be considered inclusive.[125]

Thirdly, if a common use right would constitute a subjective right, a next question rises whether this would be a contractual or an *in rem* right (of use)?[126] Some authors argue that it concerns a right *in rem* because it gives a holder a direct entitlement to the common object.[127] Other authors argue that it concerns

119 Extensively on this matter: J. Van de Voorde (2020) *ERPL* (1009) 1009-1063.

120 However, too wide an opening for environmental claims also risks the amount of *de facto* unsubstantiated or even abusive claims to rise, *e.g.* when claims without thorough substantive grounds are brought before courts. Such an overly flexible procedural possibility would frustrate the (more legitimate?) interests of *e.g.* more close and/or genuine environmental stakeholders.

121 J. Van de Voorde (2020) 3 *TMR*, (272) 275, vn. 36 with reference to A. Carette (1998) *TPR*, (821) 875-876, No. 75.

122 J. Van de Voorde (2020) *ERPL* (1009) 1054, No. 64.

123 In this regard the notion of neighbour or micro-environment is essential.

124 J. Van de Voorde (2020) *ERPL* (1009) 1055, No. 64.

125 On the notion of inclusivity: S. Dusollier, "Inclusivity in intellectual property" in G. Dinwoodie (ed.), *Intellectual Property and General Legal Principles – Is IP a Lex Specialis?*, Edward Elgar Publishing, Cheltenham, 2015, (101) 101-118. Also: J. Van de Voorde (2020) *ERPL* (1009) 1009-1064.

126 J. Van de Voorde (2020) *ERPL* (1009) 1033, No. 29 *et seq.*

127 J. Van de Voorde (2020) *ERPL* (1009) 1033, No. 29 with reference to M.-P. Camproux-Duffrène, "Entre environnement per se et environnement pour soi: la responsabilité civile pour atteinte à l'environnement" (2012) *Environnement et développement durable*, No. 14, 12.

a mere contractual claim because the central focal point is not the thing or object over which rights can be asserted, but the rights and duties of a legal subject vis-à-vis itself and other legal subjects in relation to environmental common.[128] This mainly theoretical discussion is to a large extent meaningless, because, as SAGAERT and VAN DE VOORDE rightly argue, the distinction between contractual and *in rem* rights is at least partly arbitrary.[129] Moreover, since the specific *res communes* user regime is secured by statute in Article 3.43 BCC the discussion is trivial and the protection appears to be very persistent, i.e. regardless of into whose hands the common would pass.

VI. CONCLUSION: TOWARDS RELIABLE *RES COMMUNES* ENVIRONMENTAL PROTECTION

18. Sustainable private and property law responsibilities – Despite the many remaining uncertainties – *a.o.* regarding the possibility to bring a *res communes* claim to court – we cannot rid ourselves of the intriguing impression that ever more the new regime tends to seek middle ground, moving towards a truly balanced system between the property law approach ("exclusive use" solution) and the public law route ("non-exclusive use by all" solution). A theoretical analysis has shown that although the classical starting point was to push the commons out of property law towards its safe haven, i.e. State and governmental protection, common things are (or could potentially be) almost fully reintegrated into property law by way of partial appropriation. We therefore must endorse and agree with the view of other contributors in this book that the promotion of environmental objectives is no longer solely the responsibility of States and/or public law. Aditionally, private law and more particularly property law has a role to play. The property law responsibilities are abundantly clear with regard to *res communes* after the Belgian property law reform: The preparatory works explicitly mention that the regime is inherently linked with sustainability and the environmental preservation agenda. The revival of the *res communes* regime has thus come with change. The regime has shifted from regulating access to common things, which has been the initial focal point, towards dealing with the scarcity of fundamental natural resources and nature preservation. This shift has made us realize that the notion of what is to be understood as a common thing, other than purely objective, often seems more based on society's rather subjective beliefs and needs. Hence a clear definition of "commons" would probably be favourable.

128 J. VAN DE VOORDE (2020) *ERPL* (1009) 1033, No. 29 with reference to A. CARETTE (1998) *TPR*, (821) 841, No. 28; B. JADOT, "L'article 714 du Code civil et la protection de l'environnement" in *L'actualité du droit de l'environnement*, Bruylant, Brussels, 1995, 61, No. 10.

129 V. SAGAERT, "Het goederenrecht als open systeem van verbintenissen" (2005) *TPR*, 998-1000; J. VAN DE VOORDE (2020) *ERPL* (1009) 1033, No. 29.

Another realization is that because of the new environmental function, the property protection regime of commons is a quintessential centripetal force. In order for this environmental protection regime to play its role effectively, the aforementioned reintegration cannot mean that protection simply ceases to exist. As such, the regime should be made aware of and aligned with the fundamental property law principles (*e.g.* specialty and unity, accession, possession and original acquisition). As these issues are not yet fundamentally addressed in legal doctrine, it may be an interesting subject for further in-depth legal research. The ultimate objective seems to be a protection regime that applies in a thorough functional way, as an overarching duty of conservation. In the words of Grégoire LERAY:

> "Peu importe l'appropriation, dès lors que pèse sur le propriétaire une obligation de conserver la substance de la chose objet de son droit de propriété."[130]

This means that once the legislator – or case law – has determined which objects are worthy of *res communes* protection, they must continuously be protected, whether they are exclusively appropriated or not. In the absence of such a durable protection, the regime is doomed to fail. The specific degree of protection will certainly continue to be the subject of debate. Nevertheless, it appears that the focus of property law has already shifted towards positive obligations and responsibilities.[131] As Henri DE PAGE already mentioned regarding servitudes:

> "Le jour viendra peut-être où l'on admettra qu'une servitude consiste à faire quelque chose, pourvu que ce soit dans un intérêt public. Ce ne serait pas la première fois que les principes individualistes de la législation romaine céderaient devant le droit de demain."[132]

As we realize that the degree of absolute power of owners is strongly dependent on the nature of the object concerned, especially when valuable natural resources are involved, perhaps the same should go for the right of ownership and other property rights encumbering a common thing.

---

130 G. LERAY, *L'immeuble et la protection de la nature*, LGDJ, Issy-les-Moulineaux, 2019, 267-268.

131 See extensively: S. DEMEYERE, *Real obligations at the edge of contract and property*, Intersentia, Antwerp, 2020, 813 p.

132 H. DE PAGE, *Traité élémentaire de droit civil belge*, VI/2, Bruylant, Brussels, 1942, 405, No. 499

THE "RIGHTS OF RELATIONS" BETWEEN HUMAN AND SEEDS

An Ecological and Ontological Approach of the Legal Property Regime Complex of Seeds

Pierre WALCKIERS
Research Fellow, F.R.S.-FNRS,
Affiliated to the Center for Philosophy of Law, UCLouvain[*]

"Recognizing the special relationship and interaction between peasants and other people working in rural areas and the land, water and nature to which they are attached and on which they depend for their livelihood."[**]

LIST OF ABBREVIATIONS

TRIPS	Agreement on Trade-Related Aspects of Intellectual Property Rights[1]
UPOV	International Union for the Protection of New Varieties of Plan[2]
CBD	Convention on Biological Diversity[3]

* I would like to thank Dr Christine Frison for her guidance on my research and for this article. I also thank Vincent Janssen for his helpful comments and suggestions.

** UN Declaration on the Rights of Peasants and Other People Working in Rural Areas, draft version of the 5th OEIWG session (pursuant to para. 1 of Human Rights Council Resolution 36/22), Geneva, 9-13 April 2018.

1 Agreement on Trade-Related Aspects of Intellectual Property Rights, Annex 1C of the Marrakesh Agreement Establishing the World Trade Organization, signed in Marrakesh, Morocco on 15 April 1994.

2 International Convention for the Protection of New Varieties of Plants of 2 December 1961, as Revised at Geneva on 10 November 1972, on 23 October 1978, and on 19 March 1991.

3 Convention on Biological Diversity, Rio de Janeiro, 5 June 1992 [United Nations, Treaty Series, vol. 1760, I-30619]
Agreement on Trade-Related Aspects of Intellectual Property Rights, Annex 1C of the Marrakesh Agreement Establishing the World Trade Organization, signed in Marrakesh, Morocco on 15 April 1994.
International Convention for the Protection of New Varieties of Plants of 2 December 1961, as Revised at Geneva on 10 November 1972, on 23 October 1978, and on 19 March 1991.

NP	Nagoya Protocol on Access to Genetic Resources and the Fair and Equitable Sharing of Benefits Arising from their Utilization[4]
ITPGRFA	International Treaty on Plant Genetic Resources for Food and Agriculture[5]
UNDROP	United Nations Declaration on the Rights of Peasants and Other People Working in Rural Areas[6]
IPR	Intellectual Property Right
ABS	Access and benefit-sharing
MLS	The Multilateral System

I. INTRODUCTION

1. This article aims to critically analyse the international seed "regime complex" from a relational legal prism, imagining and constructing the concept of the "rights of relations" between humans and seeds[7] A regime complex refers to a situation where a subject matter is regulated by several legal rules (on the international, supranational, and national level) with sources, hierarchy, objectives and projects that may be different or even contradictory.[8] In this case, several treaties coexist and coregulate (with some conflict) the seed regime complex. In terms of legally binding rules, this regime complex consists in particular of the International Treaty on Plant Genetic Resources for Food and Agriculture (ITPGRFA), the Convention on Biological Diversity (CBD) and its Nagoya Protocol (NP), the International Union for the Protection of New Varieties of Plants (UPOV), and the Agreement on Trade-Related Aspects of Intellectual Property Rights (TRIPS). Although not legally binding, we should also note the United Nations Declaration on the Rights of Peasants and Other People Working in Rural Areas (UNDROP).[9]

2. Several issues are identified in this regime complex, such as the contradiction between legally binding intellectual property rights (TRIPS, UPOV) that seek to

---

Convention on Biological Diversity, Rio de Janeiro, 5 June 1992 [United Nations, Treaty Series, vol. 1760, I-30619].

4 Nagoya Protocol on Access to Genetic Resources and the Fair and Equitable Sharing of Benefits Arising from their Utilization to the Convention on Biological Diversity, Nagoya, 29 October 2010, UNEP/CBD/COP/DEC/X/1, entered into force on 12 October 2014.

5 International Treaty on Plant Genetic Resources for Food and Agriculture (with annexes), Rome, 3 November 2001 [United Nations, Treaty Series, vol. 2400, I-43345]

6 UN Declaration on the Rights of Peasants and Other People Working in Rural Areas, draft version of the 5th OEIWG session (pursuant to para. 1 of Human Rights Council Resolution 36/22), Geneva, 9-13 April 2018.

7 P. Walckiers, "Vers un 'droit des relations' entre humains et non-humains comme alternative aux droits de la nature" (2022) 1 *Annales de droit de Louvain*, 9-30.

8 K. Raustiala and D.G. Victor, "The Regime Complex for Plant Genetic Resources" (2004) 58 *International Organization*, 277-309.

9 C. Frison, *Redesigning the Global Seed Commons*, Routledge, London, 2018, 71.

privatize access to seeds with an over-intellectual protection of seeds[10] on the one hand and the weak protection of Farmers' Rights or limited Access and Benefit Sharing (ABS) on the other (ITPGRFA, CBD, NP). Other criticisms of the regime complex include unsustainable management and lack of integration of farmers in decision-making.[11]

3. Facing these important criticisms, we propose to reassess this regime complex through the prism of the "rights of relations". Starting from legal philosophy, the "rights of relations" are rights to be imagined (as also the "rights of nature" have been imagined)[12], which do not yet effectively exist, but which could be used in legal arguments. If the rights of nature aim to protect nature for itself, then the "rights of relations" aim to protect all forms of relationships between humans and non-humans. From a legal point of view, we want to inscribe the "rights of relations" in contribution to the theories of the commons.[13] The commons have been an important approach to critiquing the seed regime complex, valuing practices where a group of people autonomously organize around a resource in a sustainable and generative manner.[14] Indeed, some authors argue that managing seeds as commons would facilitate access to the diversity of seeds, and promote their sustainable use and their efficient conservation.[15] These propositions are important in the context of climate change, and especially for developing countries[16], as the protection of genetic diversity is an essential issue for food security.[17] Consequently, our reflection on the "rights of relations" will be in line with the theories of the commons.

4. From an activist point of view, the "rights of relations" seek to break with the rights of nature approach. We believe that the protection of nature for itself,

---

10 S. Safrin, "Hyperownership in a Time of Biotechnological Promise: The International Conflict to Control the Building Blocks of Life" (2004) 98 *American Journal of International Law*, 641-685; C. Frison, *Redesigning the Global Seed Commons*, *o.c.*

11 C. Frison, *Redesigning the Global Seed Commons*, *o.c.*, 52.

12 C.D. Stone, *Should Trees Have Standing?: Law, Morality, and the Environment*, Oxford University Press, Oxford, 2010.

13 E. Ostrom, *Governing the Commons: The Evolution of Institutions for Collective Action*, Cambridge University Press, Cambridge, 1990; F. Capra and U. Mattei, *The Ecology of Law: Toward a Legal System in Tune with Nature and Community*, Berrett-Koehler Publishers, Oakland, 2015.

14 C. Frison, *Redesigning the Global Seed Commons*, *o.c.*, 167; S. Gutwirth and I. Stengers, "Le droit à l'épreuve de la résurgence des commons" (2016) *Revue Juridique de l'Environnement*, 306-343; F. Capra and U. Mattei, *The Ecology of Law*, *o.c.*

15 T. Dedeurwaerdere, "Design principles of successful genetic resource commons for food and agriculture" (2012) 26 *International Journal for Ecological Economics and Statistics*, 31-46; C. Frison, *Redesigning the Global Seed Commons*, *o.c.*, 5.

16 J. Beddington, *et al.*, "Achieving food security in the face of climate change" (2012) *Final report from the Commission on Sustainable Agriculture and Climate Change*, 59 p.

17 M.A. Altieri, "The ecological role of biodiversity in agroecosystems" (1999) 74 *Agriculture, Ecosystems & Environment*, 19-31.

without integrating the populations living there and their relations with this nature, prolongs a neo-colonial logic that is still too present in environmental law. From an anthropological approach, we would like to point out that the separation between nature and culture is far from universal, as it is the result of Western philosophy.[18] Therefore, also other types of relationships with the environment exist. These "ways of seeing the world" or "ontologies" are legitimate and should also be respected in environmental law. This separation between nature and culture (what we refer to as "naturalism" or "dualism"[19]) is also found in the seed regime complex, where plant genetic resources are seen as something appropriable and exploitable.[20] This means that all other forms of relations with the environment and seeds (social, spiritual, etc.) are disregarded in dualistic legal constructs and particularly in the seed regime complex.

5. Our methodology will be interdisciplinary, combining legal technique, legal anthropology and legal philosophy. We will assume a constructive approach to law, where law could evolve and recognize the "rights of relations" between humans and seeds. Our scope will be the seed regime complex (in particular, ITPGRFA), where we do not want to bring an exhaustive study of the regime complex but point out gaps and apply the "rights of relations" rationale. In a first part, the international regime of seed ownership will be presented and questioned. In a second part, we will explore possible ways to mitigate the limitations of the seed ownership regime complex with the concept of the "rights of relations".

II. THE SEEDS LEGAL REGIME COMPLEX: OVERVIEW, PRINCIPLES, AND CRITICISM

6. The seeds legal property regime complex is composed of several rules of international law, addressing different issues.[21] Regarding objectives, a distinction should be made between, on the one hand, rules relating to sustainable conservation of resources and ABS (CBD, ITPGRFA, NP) and on the other hand, rules focusing on intellectual property promoting breeders rights (UPOV, TRIPS).[22] The combination of all these sources of international,

---

18 P. Descola, *Par-delà nature et culture*, Gallimard, Paris, 2005, 623 p.; N. Graham, *Lawscape: Property, Environment, Law*, Routledge-Cavendish, Abingdon, 2010, 225 p.; D. Gardey, "Donna Haraway: poétique et politique du vivant" (2013) 55 *Cahiers du Genre*, 171.

19 F. Ost, *La nature hors la loi. L'écologie à l'épreuve du droit*, La Découverte, Paris, 2003, 346 p.

20 S. Safrin, "Hyperownership in a Time of Biotechnological Promise", *o.c.*, 642.

21 C. Frison, *Redesigning the Global Seed Commons*, *o.c.*, 17.

22 C. Frison, *Redesigning the Global Seed Commons*, *o.c.*, 53.

supranational and national law leads to major overlaps and great complexity in the governance of genetic resources.[23]

7. Several studies have concluded that there are conflicting relationships between UPOV, TRIPS agreements and the ITPGRFA or the CBD given the different objectives.[24] For example, the UPOV treaty on plant variety protection has implications for emerging countries and for Farmers' Rights.[25] This fragmented and divided regime complex favors the rights of breeders and multinationals over the rights of farmers (regarding the access to seeds, the promotion of their traditional knowledge and inclusion in decision-making) and imposes a system of over-appropriation that does not respect the principles of equitable sharing of benefits from the use of genetic resources or their sustainable uses.

A. IPRs CREATE AN UNSUSTAINABLE SYSTEM THAT PROMOTES SEED APPROPRIATION

8. In a transversal way, we criticize the creation of a system that favors the hyper appropriation of seeds (hyper appropriation is to be understood as: "*exclusive ownership and restrictions on the sharing of genetic material*")[26] and the establishment of an "anti-commons" system.[27] In this case, the accumulation of rules on seed management transforms seeds into rival and exclusive goods. Seeds can be appropriated according to state sovereignty over their genetic resources, through intellectual property rights (such as the DUS[28] criteria of UPOV which excludes informal seed exchanges) but also by technical tools (such as genetic use restriction technology: making seeds infertile for

23 J. Tschersich, "Norm conflicts as governance challenges for Seed Commons: Comparing cases from Germany and the Philippines" (2021) 7 *Earth System Governance*, 2.

24 J. Tschersich, "Norm conflicts as governance challenges for Seed Commons", *o.c.*, 2; G.K. Rosendal, "The Convention on Biological Diversity: Tensions with the WTO TRIPS Agreement over Access to Genetic Resources and the Sharing of Benefits" (2006) *Institutional Interaction in Global Environmental Governance: Synergy and Conflict among International and EU Policies*, 79-102.

25 J. Tschersich, "Norm conflicts as governance challenges for Seed Commons", *o.c.*, 3; A. Christinck and M. Tvedt, "The UPOV Convention, Farmers' Rights and Human Rights. An Integrated Assessment of Potentially Conflicting Legal Frameworks" (2015) *Deutsche Gesellschaft für Internationale Zusammenarbeit*, 45.

26 S. Safrin, "Hyperownership in a Time of Biotechnological Promise", *o.c.*, 642.

27 S. Safrin, "Hyperownership in a Time of Biotechnological Promise", *o.c.*, 642.

28 DUS criteria refer to the criteria of distinctness, uniformity and stability required for a plant variety to meet the breeder's right requirement under UPOV (Art. 5). A new variety must be (UPOV, Art. 6): distinct, meaning "clearly distinguishable from any other variety" (UPOV, Art. 7.); uniform: "sufficiently uniform in its relevant characteristics" (UPOV, Art. 8) and stable, as "its relevant characteristics remain unchanged after repeated propagation" (UPOV, Art. 9).

instance).[29] The registration and protection of specific seed varieties imply the standardization of the genetic market and a limitation of access to seeds (and thus also to their use and conservation).[30] This standardization reinforces the nature-culture dichotomy in the appropriation and exploitation of natural resources.

9. Therefore, the hyper appropriation of this regime complex led to the limited and solely economic vision of seeds. Indeed, this regime considers seeds through a commercial (and naturalism) prism where seeds are seen as natural resources which should be controlled and exploited. As a consequence, all other types of relationships and prisms that humans may have with seeds are put aside. However, seeds could be part of various forms of (other) relationships and practices (social, medicinal, spiritual). More specifically, all these relationships are found in local and informal networks of seed management, exchange, sale, and donation.[31] It would therefore be simplistic to view seeds only through a commercial prism.

10. This system of appropriation reveals an unfair legal situation, to the benefit of northern countries and to the detriment of southern countries, which are rich in genetic diversity.[32] This imbalance is also found in access and benefit-sharing processes for genetic resources and plant genetic resources for agriculture. Indeed, several studies show that ABS and the Multilateral System (MLS) have greatly facilitated access, research, and information exchange, with little or no cost or restriction.[33] However, this sharing was more to the advantage of breeders and returns on monetary and non-monetary benefit-sharing were limited.[34] This regime complex favors the countries of the North, which have rich technological resources but no great genetic biodiversity, over the countries of the South, which do have great genetic biodiversity but little technological resources (*ergo* they are providers of genetic resources). There is a race for "green gold" to monopolize the genetic resources of the countries of the South to maximize the gains from their commercialization.[35]

---

29 C. Frison, *Redesigning the Global Seed Commons*, *o.c.*, 54.

30 J. de Mévius, "Impact of the European Union's Seed Legislation and Intellectual Property Rights on Crop Diversity" (2022) 31 *European Energy and Environmental Law Review*, 149.

31 J. Tschersich, "Norm conflicts as governance challenges for Seed Commons", *o.c.*, 4; O.T. Coomes, *et. al.*, "Farmer seed networks make a limited contribution to agriculture? Four common misconceptions" (2015) 56 *Food Policy*, 41-50; M. Pautasso, *et al.*, "Seed exchange networks for agrobiodiversity conservation. A review" (2013) 33 *Agronomy for Sustainable Development*, 151-75.

32 C. Frison, *Redesigning the Global Seed Commons*, *o.c.*, 54, 74.

33 *Ibidem*, 161.

34 *Ibidem*, 106.

35 *Ibidem*, 64; S. Safrin, "Hyperownership in a Time of Biotechnological Promise", *o.c.*, 642.

11. This appropriative and extractive vision of seeds blocks any diversified sustainable alternative as well as common-models. According to Safrin, this "*interactive spiral of increased enclosure, or hyper ownership, results in suboptimal utilization, conservation, and improvement of vital genetic material. It generates tensions between nations and threatens individuals and indigenous communities. The global commons are being subjected to a global tug of war over genetic material at the expense of the global common good.*"[36]

12. Moreover, this hyper appropriation prism is not obvious given the history of agriculture, where seeds were freely accessed, used and sold.[37] This prior open access system ensured sustainable use and conservation of seeds and their diversification, as many genetic varieties were shared and created. In this respect, we need to promote the diversification of genetic resources but also of agricultural practices, rather than their standardization. Considering the climate crisis, access to seed diversity is essential[38] and the erosion of biological diversity is an urgent concern.[39] While the erosion of biodiversity is caused by a multitude of causes, such as climate change, introduction of invasive species, and land change, one should not neglect the political and legal decisions that create a system hostile to any sustainable and responsible use of seeds for instance (think of intensive agriculture, limiting access to seeds through IPRs, etc.).

13. In sum, we find that seeds have changed from being non-rivalrous and non-exclusive goods to rivalrous and exclusive goods.[40] Given the significant constraints, there is an urgent need to revise appropriation paradigms in the seed regime complex to unlock access to seeds.[41]

B. IMBALANCE OF RIGHTS PENALIZING FARMERS

14. Several international Treaties and Declarations recognize rights of farmers, indigenous people and people living in rural areas. Farmers Rights are particularly recognized by the ITPGRFA, by the CBD and the Nagoya Protocol (linked with the protection of traditional knowledge), and also by UNDROP. It is also possible to rely on customary practices, partially recognized in international law.

---

36 C. Frison, *Redesigning the Global Seed Commons*, *o.c.*, 64.

37 *Ibidem.*

38 C. Frison, *Redesigning the Global Seed Commons*, *o.c.*, 25.

39 *Ibidem*; T. Wheeler and J. von Braun, "Climate change impacts on global food security" (2013) 341 *Science*, 508-513.

40 C. Frison, *Redesigning the Global Seed Commons*, *o.c.*, 26.

41 C. Frison, *Redesigning the Global Seed Commons*, *o.c.*, 26; K. Pistor and O.D. Schutter, *Governing Access to Essential Resources*, Columbia University Press, New York, 2015, 378 p.

15. Various studies have shown that protection is not sufficient for Farmers' Rights and is still limited because of IPRs.[42] Despite their valuable contribution to the preservation of agrobiodiversity[43], peasant populations and small farmers suffer from a lack of sufficient international regulation to preserve their rights and relationship with their land or seeds[44] In this context, Farmers' organizations have been lobbying for a long time for the recognition of their rights.[45] Several elements of Farmers' Rights are nonetheless limited: For example, access to seeds (reuse of farm seeds), protection of traditional knowledge, participation in decision-making, etc.

16. While ensuring full sovereignty of the state on these issues, the ITPGRFA declares different rights for farmers: "*protection of traditional knowledge relevant to plant genetic resources for food and agriculture* [...], *the right to equitably participate in sharing benefits arising from the utilization of plant genetic resources for food and agriculture* [and] *the right to participate in making decisions, at the national level, on matters related to the conservation and sustainable use of plant genetic resources for food and agriculture.*"[46] Paragraph 3 of Article 9 highlights the importance for farmers of the rights "*to save, use, exchange and sell farm-saved seed/propagating material.*" In that sense, it indicates that the treaty cannot be interpreted to limit these rights, but their realization is subject to national legislation. (Preamble, paragraph 7 & 8, Art. 9). Therefore, Article 9 of the ITPGRFA is not sufficient to protect the right of farmers to save, use, exchange and sell farm-saved seed, as recognition remains at the discretion of each state.

17. Besides, there is UNDROP which provides a stronger, more protective interpretation of Farmers' Rights, but it is not a binding source of international law.[47] However, it is possible to recognize and highlight the contributions of UNDROP as an additional argument for the legal field. First, international law

42 H.M. Haugen, "The UN Declaration on Peasants' Rights (UNDROP): Is Article 19 on seed rights adequately balancing intellectual property rights and the right to food?" (2020) 23 *The Journal of World Intellectual Property*, 288-309; P. Claeys and M. Edelman, "The United Nations Declaration on the rights of peasants and other people working in rural areas" (2020) 47 *The Journal of Peasant Studies*, 1-68.

43 M. Halewood, I. López Noriega and S. Louafi, *Crop Genetic Resources as a Global Commons*, Routledge, London, 2012, 82; E. Demeulenaere, "A political ontology of seeds: The transformative frictions of a farmers" movement in Europe" (2014) *Focaal*, 8.

44 S. Le Teno, C. Frison, and S. Cogolati, "The right to seeds" in M. Alabrese, A. Bessa, M. Brunori, P. Filippo Giuggioli (eds), *The United Nations' Declaration on Peasants' Rights*, Routledge, London, 2022, 119-133; P. Mcmichael, "Peasants Make Their own History, But Not Just as They Please..." (2008) 8 *Journal of Agrarian Change*, 209.

45 S. Le Teno, C. Frison, and S. Cogolati, "The right to seeds", *o.c.;* E. Demeulenaere, "A political ontology of seeds", *o.c.*, 69.

46 ITPGRFA, Art. 9.2.

47 S. Le Teno, C. Frison, and S. Cogolati, "The right to seeds", *o.c.* 121; C. Frison, *Redesigning the Global Seed Commons*, *o.c.*, 90.

must be interpreted in a coherent manner with the principles and rights of the UNDROP declaration. In this way, UNDROP could be applied to complement and enrich the right to food, which is legally binding.[48] In addition, states may incorporate this declaration into their domestic law, making it legally binding (as is the case for Colombia).[49] Moreover, this declaration can be mobilized in jurisprudence, to integrate other rights in the discussion.[50] Nevertheless, from a strictly legal point of view, the proclaimed right "*to save, use, exchange and sell farm-saved seed/propagating material*" is not legally binding under international law.[51]

18. In contrast, intellectual property rights are legally binding and meticulously enforced at the national level. Indeed, there is a contradiction between Farmers' Rights (ITPGRFA, UNDROP) and Farmers' Privileges (UPOV). Although the UPOV Convention primarily protects the rights of breeders, it optionally allows states to allow farmers to save seeds for the next harvest on their own land. This right to plant the seed is known as the "Farmers' Privilege" (which is not the same as "Farmers' Rights"). This privilege is seen as a tool for balancing plant breeders' rights and farmers' rights, while the UPOV Convention is denounced as only privileging the commercial interests of plant breeders.[52] Under the UPOV Convention, Farmers' Privileges are granted by Contracting Parties on a voluntary basis, but they are strictly limited regarding the type of crops and their use (only for reuse on a small farm, prohibiting exchanges, gifts, and sales within Farmers' networks).[53]

19. This imbalance is also reflected in the lack of recognition of traditional knowledge other than scientific (Western) knowledge. The ITPGRFA and the CBD recognize the need to protect and promote the traditional knowledge of indigenous and local communities, including the equal sharing of benefits in the use of such traditional knowledge and practices.[54] Although the explicit recognition (by a.o. the ITPGRFA, the CBD and its NP) traditional knowledge is not seen as equivalent to scientific knowledge mainly because of

---

48 S. Le Teno, C. Frison, and S. Cogolati, "The right to seeds", *o.c.*, 121; F. Batur and C. Golay, "Briefing 19: Practical Manual on the Right to Seeds in Europe" (2021*) Geneva Academy*, 19.

49 C. Golay, "Le droit à la terre et la déclaration UNDROP" (2021) *Geneva Academy*, 46.

50 F. Batur and C. Golay, "Briefing 19", *o.c.*, 24.

51 ITPGRFA, Art. 9.3.

52 H.B.H. Nguyen and K. Weckström Lindroos, "The Regulation of Farmer's Privilege Under Vietnamese IP Law and the Law of the European Union" (2021) 52 *International Review of Intellectual Property and Competition Law*, 678; J. Sanderson, *Plants, People and Practices: The Nature and History of the UPOV Convention*, Cambridge University Press, Cambridge, 2017, 265 p.

53 H.B.H. Nguyen and K. Weckström Lindroos, "The Regulation of Farmer's Privilege Under Vietnamese IP Law and the Law of the European Union", *o.c.*, 678.

54 CBD, Art. 8 (j); ITPGRFA, Art. 9.2 (a).

our neo-colonial vision on traditional knowledge.[55] Traditional and scientific knowledge are not perceived as equal: One is deemed merely "cultural" and outdated, the other is synonymous with progress and innovation. There is also an important imbalance in that the seed regime complex offers a whole range of legal protection for proprietary (patentable) knowledge and inventions that do not apply to traditional knowledge.[56] Moreover, traditional knowledge would be seen as exotic knowledge that could be appropriated and commercialized without cost; and that it is only in the form of Western scientific knowledge that knowledge would have economic value.[57] Yet, we argue that the protection of traditional knowledge within and beyond the community is essential for sustainable and equitable seed use.[58] It is the traditional knowledge that materializes the link between communities and seeds.

20. This disregard is notably reflected in the notion of "passive beneficiaries" in the context of the MLS in the ITPGRFA.[59] In the seed regime complex, farmers, especially in the Global South, are seen as passive beneficiaries of measures taken in their favour or in favour of biodiversity. Moreover, the benefit-sharing system will consider farmers as passive beneficiaries of Western technology and scientific knowledge (think of pesticides, improved and genetically modified seeds, etc.). This passive beneficiary position contributes to deconstructing the relationship between farmer and seed.

21. Again, the imbalance of the Farmers' Rights is also seen in their lack of inclusion in the decision-making processes. For example, small-scale farmers are often not informed or consulted about key decisions on plant variety rights and cannot participate.[60] There is indeed a lack of participation of seed stakeholders in the international seed governance process even though that the role of communities (on a local as well as a global level) in seed governance is crucial for knowledge production, innovation, and human-seed coevolution.[61]

---

55 M. Sunder, "The Invention of Traditional Knowledge" (2007) 70 *Law and Contemporary Problems*, 97-124; L. Whitt, *Science, Colonialism, and Indigenous People, The Cultural Politics of Law and Knowledge*, Cambridge University Press, Cambridge, 2009, 57; S.N. Ali, "Bio-Colonial Co-Optation of Knowledge: An Eco-Imperialist Investigation of Anita Desai's The Village by the Sea and Uzma Aslam Khan's Thinner than Skin" (2021) 5 *Journal of Contemporary Poetics*, 52.

56 J. Tschersich, "Norm conflicts as governance challenges for Seed Commons", *o.c.*,8.

57 L. Whitt, *Science, Colonialism, and Indigenous People and Knowledge*, *o.c.*, 27

58 J. Tschersich, "Norm conflicts as governance challenges for Seed Commons", *o.c.*, 4; F. Girard and C. Frison (eds), *The Commons, Plant Breeding and Agricultural Research: Challenges for Food Security and Agrobiodiversity*, Routledge, London, 2020, 301 p.

59 C. Frison, *Redesigning the Global Seed Commons*, *o.c.*, 203.

60 A. Christinck and M. Tvedt, "The UPOV Convention, Farmers' Rights and Human Rights. An Integrated Assessment of Potentially Conflicting Legal Frameworks", *o.c.*, 7.

61 C. Frison, *Redesigning the Global Seed Commons*, *o.c.*, 209.

22. The recognition of these rights for farmers and indigenous communities is essential to contribute to the strengthening and the self-determination of these groups, but also to construct a common and polycentric use of seeds. Yet Farmers' Rights are supposed to allow peasants to regain autonomy (notably by being able to resow the products of their harvest, and by valorizing their traditional knowledge, etc.). Not guaranteeing these rights at the international level in the same way as intellectual property rights is to hinder the relationship between peasant and seed. As a marker of this imbalance, the ITPGRFA leaves the recognition of these rights to the Contracting Parties.[62] In addition, Farmers' Rights are proclaimed in the UNDROP, but this is not *stricto sensu* a binding source of international public law. However, UPOV allows Contracting Parties to grant Farmers' Privilege, for small farmers, to reuse certain seeds under specific conditions. As a result, there is a clear imbalance between Farmers' Rights and intellectual rights.[63]

III. THE "RIGHTS OF RELATIONS" BETWEEN HUMAN AND SEEDS

23. Having described the regime complex of seeds, and in particular the resulting problems, we will propose to apply the "rights of relations" to them. Starting from legal philosophy, we argue for constructing a relational approach to law: Protecting the relationships that we have with the environment, or, with seeds (as essential part of the environment). We will first present the "rights of relations" as a legal argument. Then we will apply it to the human-seed relationship. For us, the "rights of relations" will be useful to defend access to seeds, to fight against the hyper appropriation of seeds and to promote traditional knowledge.

A. ORIGIN AND PERSPECTIVES

24. In a few words, these "rights of relations" are a legal concept and argument to protect relationships that we may have with nature (and, conversely, the relationship that nature may have with us). Indeed, the "rights of relations" angle present itself as an alternative legal prism to the "rights of nature". Rather than protecting nature for itself (through the "rights of nature"), this concept of the "rights of relations" focuses on the protection of all forms of relationships

---

62 A. Christinck and M. Tvedt, "The UPOV Convention, Farmers' Rights and Human Rights. An Integrated Assessment of Potentially Conflicting Legal Frameworks", *o.c.*, 5.

63 S. Le Teno, C. Frison, and S. Cogolati, "The right to seeds", *o.c.*, 121; C. Golay, "Research Brief: The right to seeds and Intellectual Property Rights" (2020) *Geneva Academy* 7, 2.

(subjective, social, spiritual, political, etc.) that we may have with it.[64] Thus, this approach seeks to highlight, acknowledge and protect all forms of relations that we may have with nature, without necessarily trying to define them and put them in any legal categories. Taken in an abstract sense, the "rights of relations" may protect many forms of relationship: It may protect the indivisible bonds between the Maori people and Te Awa Tupua of the Whanganui River[65]; the "rights of relations" may highlight the relationship between a ZADs community and the area they defend; or the protection of the relationship between farmers and their seeds.[66] Without imposing an ontological definition of nature[67], the relational perspective thus seeks to protect all the complex forms of relationships between humans and non-humans, and precisely in this case: seeds and humans.

25. Going beyond the "rights of nature" and the object-subject dichotomy[68], we want to explore alternatives to the classical occidental narratives distinguishing nature and politics (which we call "naturalism" or "dualism").[69] Whether for ecological reasons (the advent of the Anthropocene), ontological reasons (with the proliferation of hybrids) or legal reasons (the demands to rethink the law in a *commoning* way)[70], we think it is interesting to explore other paths than the separation between nature and culture, which seems neither sustainable nor just.[71]

26. In addition, the relational perspective is more appropriate for considering the different ontological constructions, and more specifically regarding Indigenous Peoples and Local Communities.[72] It is now clearly stated that the separation between nature and culture is neither universal nor timeless.[73] Indeed, peoples have established different animistic relationships that link the

---

64 P. Walckiers, "Vers un 'droit des relations' entre humains et non-humains comme alternative aux droits de la nature", *o.c.*, 10.

65 E. Hsiao, "Whanganui River Agreement – Indigenous Rights and Rights of Nature" (2012) 42 *Environmental Policy and Law*, 371-375; A. Tanas and S. Gutwirth, "Une approche 'écologique' des communs dans le droit" (2021) *In Situ. Au regard des sciences sociales*, 8.

66 A. Escobar, *Sentir-penser avec la Terre. L'écologie au-delà de l'Occident*, Le Seuil, Paris, 2018, 100.

67 P. Descola, *Par-delà nature et culture, o.c.;* A. Escobar, *Sentir-penser avec la Terre, o.c.*, 100.

68 By the concept of "rights of nature" we understand all attempts to protect the environment "in itself". B. Latour, *Politiques de la nature*, La Découverte, Paris, 2004, 64; Ost, *La nature hors-la-loi, o.c.*, 158.

69 F. Ost, *La nature hors la loi, o.c.*, 158; A. Escobar, *Sentir-penser avec la Terre, o.c.*, 100.

70 Gutwirth and Stengers, "Le droit à l'épreuve de la résurgence des commons", *o.c.*, 317.

71 B. Latour, *Facing Gaia: Eight Lectures on the New Climatic Regime*, Polity Press, Cambridge, 2017, 143; C. Bonneuil and J.-B. Fressoz, *L'événement anthropocène: la Terre, l'histoire et nous*, Points, Paris, 2016, 56.

72 A. Escobar, *Sentir-penser avec la Terre, o.c.*, 16, 61, 100; G. Blanc, *L'invention du colonialisme vert: Pour en finir avec le mythe de l'Éden africain*, Flammarion, Paris, 2020, 356 p.

73 P. Descola, *Par-delà nature et culture, o.c.*, 9; A. Escobar, *Sentir-penser avec la Terre, o.c.*, 21.

social and the natural.[74] If peoples show a relationship of continuity with – what the modern West considers as – "nature", then it seems essential to us to take their ontologies into account and to refrain from imposing this universal hypostatized dualism.[75] In our view, if environmental law and the regime complex of seeds impose an ontological vision of naturalism, then it perpetuates a neo-colonial logic.[76] Therefore, only a particular type of ontological set called "nature" would be protected, at the expense of other sets.[77] This is the case with approaches that protect the environment "in itself": From the creation of large natural parks while excluding the people living in them (often Indigenous people)[78]; to the classification of seed types apart from their ecosystem and their interaction with it, etc.[79]

27. Facing these issues, the "rights of relations" introduce an ontological turn and a paradigm shift to protect all the complex forms of relationship that we may have with our environment. Without pronouncing on its ontological status, the "rights of relations" will defend all the relations between humans and seeds. Pragmatically, the preservation of the diverse and varied relationship of a community ensures an indirect preservation of the human and non-human communities.

28. As an example, the Whanganui River Claims Settlement Act is prominent and promising when talking about the "rights of relations".[80] Indeed, Article 14 of the Te Awa Tupa Act grants legal personality to Te Awa Tupua which is "*an indivisible and living whole from the mountains to the sea, incorporating the Whanganui River and all of its physical and metaphysical elements.*"[81] In addition, the Whanganui River Claims Settlement Act pays great attention to maintaining the indivisible links between Te Awa Tupua and Maori community.[82] Therefore, the protection of the inalienable bonds and

---

74 P. Descola, *Par-delà nature et culture*, 223.

75 C. Larrère and R. Larrère, *Penser et agir avec la nature*, La Découverte, Paris, 2018, 11, 62; A. Escobar, *Sentir-penser avec la Terre*, *o.c.*, 16.

76 M. Blaser, "Ontological Conflicts and the Stories of Peoples in Spite of Europe: Toward a Conversation on Political Ontology" (2013) 54 *Current Anthropology*, 547-568.

77 P. Descola, *Par-delà nature et culture*, *o.c.*, 350; A. Escobar, *Sentir-penser avec la Terre*, *o.c.*, 33-36.

78 G. Blanc, *L'invention du colonialisme vert*, *o.c.*; A. Escobar, *Sentir-penser avec la Terre*, *o.c.*, 100.

79 T. Wattnem, "Seed laws, certification and standardization: outlawing informal seed systems in the Global South" (2016) 43 *The Journal of Peasant Studies*, 850-867; C. Bonneuil and J.-B. Fressoz, *L'événement anthropocène*, *o.c.*, 103; E. Marris, *Rambunctious Garden: Saving Nature in a Post-Wild World*, Bloomsbury, London, 2011, 210 p.

80 A. Tanas and S. Gutwirth, "Une approche 'écologique' des communs dans le droit", *o.c.*, 8.

81 Whanganui River Claims Settlement Act, March 20, 2017 no.7/2017, Art. 13; T. Deleuil, "*Je coule donc je suis*: la reconnaissance des droits du fleuve Whanganui par le droit néo-zélandais?" (2020) 45 *Revue juridique de l'environnement*, 440.

82 Whanganui River Claims Settlement Act, March 20, 2017 no.7/2017, Art. 13 (d).

relationships between Maori and Te Awa Tupua implies preserving all human and non-human parts of this community and respecting and promoting animistic relationships between these indigenous peoples. Therefore, Article 69 of the Te Awa Tupa Act deplores the many infringements of Maori customs and practices that have degraded the relationship with the river.[83]

29. In sum, this new paradigm aims to ensure the legal possibility of inheriting, constructing, and conserving hybrid living communities of relations between subjects and objects, nature and culture, humans and seeds.[84] Assuming this relational prism makes it possible to build a legal framework that protects the bonds of interdependence (still unidentified for the most part) and to devote a fair place to ecological and cultural complexities.

B. THE "RIGHTS OF RELATIONS" AS A LEGAL AND POLITICAL ARGUMENT

30. In terms of legal technique, the "rights of relations" do not (yet) exist in positive law. Rather, it is a legal claim to invent and build these "rights of relations" (in a similar way to the development of the rights of nature). We base ourselves on a constructive approach to law in which positive law reflects social constructs and values.[85] As soon as values change, the law may also be "rebuilt".[86] Therefore, we could imagine the law making an environmental, social and ontological transition in order to reconnect with nature and not dominate it.

31. In order not to limit ourselves to abstract theory, we believe that the "rights of relations" should be articulated in several different specific legal arguments. Building on the development of commoning[87], the "rights of relations" would be an argument that a group of individuals (human and non-human) can mobilize to protect their relationships with a resource on which they all collectively depend.[88] According to this logic, different farmers could

83 Whanganui River Claims Settlement Act, March 20, 2017 no.7/2017, Art. 69; A. Tanas and S. Gutwirth, "Une approche 'écologique' des communs dans le droit", *o.c.*, 12-13.

84 A. Tanas and S. Gutwirth, "Une approche 'écologique' des communs dans le droit", *o.c.*, 14.

85 L. De sutter and S. Gutwirth, "Droit et cosmopolitique. Notes sur la contribution de Bruno Latour à la pensée du droit" (2004) 56-57 *Droit et Société*, 265; MM.P. Camproux-Dufrène, "Les communs naturels comme expression de la solidarité écologique" (2020) 45 *Revue juridique de lenvironnement*, 691.

86 M. Petel, "La nature: d'un objet d'appropriation à un sujet de droit. Réflexions pour un nouveau modèle de société" (2018) 80 *Revue interdisciplinaire d'etudes juridiques*, 207-239.

87 F. Capra and U. Mattei, *The Ecology of Law*, *o.c.*, 216; S. Gutwirth and I. Stengers, "Le droit à l'épreuve de la résurgence des commons", *o.c.*, 320.

88 Gutwirth and Stengers, "Le droit à l'épreuve de la résurgence des commons", *o.c.*, 315.

mobilize their "rights to relations" to protect the connections and co-evolution they have with their seeds or their land. Applied to the seed regime complex, the "rights of relationship" between humans and seeds or between farmers and their land could be included in legal arguments about access to land and seeds for communities that have been excluded from them.[89] As a result, the "rights of relations" would be an adequate way to guarantee a community responsible and sustainable use of resources while cultivating interdependence between humans and seeds within an ecological way of acting.[90]

32. In addition, the "rights of relations" may be based on existing legal constructions or on jurisprudential reasoning. Taking inspiration from the commoning[91], it could be described as "resurgent" because it will reinvest in existing legal structures.[92] Therefore, it is not necessary to change the legal system to try to make use of the "rights of relation". It would be possible to invoke it to interpret existing legal bases (sometimes forgotten)[93], implicit rights and customs[94], modern legal constructions ("rights of nature", "ecocide", etc.), or by crossing it with the most fundamental principles of human rights (*e.g.* right to a healthy environment, right to food).[95] In parallel to science or economics, the law has the ability to create "another world" by legal fictions; it can thus legally create or make these relationships to exist.[96] A legal recognition of the "rights of relations" would create new identities in positive law, such as the complex relations between humans and non-humans, between human and seeds, etc. Moreover, the "rights of relations" could be the object of strategic use of the law (as with Whanganui River).

33. Parallel to the legal level, the affirmation of the "rights of relations" may constitute a new language for understanding the ontological conflict.[97] The "rights of relations" between humans and seeds allows for the reaffirmation of the social and ontological context in which seeds evolve. Seeds are not

---

89 *Ibidem*, 320.

90 *Ibdiem;* D. Bollier, *Think Like a Commoner: A Short Introduction to the Life of the Commons*, New Society Publishers, New York, 2014, 196 p.

91 F. Capra and U. Mattei, *The Ecology of Law*, *o.c.*; S. Gutwirth and I. Stengers, "Le droit à l'épreuve de la résurgence des commons", *o.c.*, 315.

92 S. Gutwirth and I. Stengers, "Le droit à l'épreuve de la résurgence des commons", *o.c.*, 315.

93 S. Vanuxem, "La compensation écologique comme mécanisme de droit analogiste" (2019) 44 *Revue juridique de l'environnement*, 115-144; A. Tanas and S. Gutwirth, "Une approche 'écologique' des communs dans le droit", *o.c.*, 8.

94 A. Christinck and M. Tvedt, "The UPOV Convention, Farmers' Rights and Human Rights. An Integrated Assessment of Potentially Conflicting Legal Frameworks", *o.c.*, 6.

95 A. Christinck and M. Tvedt, "The UPOV Convention, Farmers' Rights and Human Rights. An Integrated Assessment of Potentially Conflicting Legal Frameworks", *o.c.*, 40.

96 M.-A. Hermitte, "Le droit est un autre monde" (1999) *Enquête*, 17-37.

97 M. de la Cadena and M. Blaser, *A World of Many Worlds*, Duke University Press, Durham, 2018, 232 p.

internal objects that could be exploited and modified, but integral parts of the community space and of the ecosystem as a whole.[98]

34. Finally, the "rights of relations" may be mobilized in local claims, assuming their perspectives, responding to different ontologies, but above all reaffirming the importance of the relationship between humans and seeds Therefore, the relational approach may initiate alternative paths to a more ecological and inclusive approach to the seed regime complex.[99] Applied to the human-seed relationship, this approach will highlight the interactive and co-evolutionary links between humans and seeds, whether physical or metaphysical, cultural, spiritual, medicinal, etc. This protection of relations will allow to re-link the regime complex, where not only the economic relation should be considered. In addition, the "rights of relations" may reinforce Farmers' Rights and promote traditional knowledge.

C. THE "RIGHTS OF RELATIONS" AS AN ALTERNATIVE TO THE ECONOMIC PERSPECTIVE

35. As described above, we condemn an underlying naturalist prism in the regime complex. This economic logic is found in intellectual property rights (TRIPS, UPOV) but also with treaties and conventions on the equitable and sustainable management of biological resources (CBD, NP, ITPGRFA). Indeed, the ABS and MLS mechanism endorse the monetization of seeds and biological resources in exchange for a fair distribution of benefits.[100] As a result, the underlying relational logic of this regime complex remains economic and extractivist: Nature, genetic resources and seeds are perceived as a set of inanimate and neutral axiological objects[101], susceptible to appropriation, transformation, and commercialization.[102] In a nutshell, economic relations with seeds are privileged, and all other forms of relations, co-evolution, etc. are put aside.

98 S. Gutwirth, "Le contexte du droit ce sont ses sources formelles et les faits et moyens qui exigent son intervention" (2013) 70 *Revue interdisciplinaire d'études juridiques*, 108-116.

99 F. Capra and U. Mattei, *The Ecology of Law*, *o.c.* 216; K. Anker, P.D. Burdon, G. Garver, and M. Maloney, *From Environmental to Ecological Law*, Routledge, London, 2020, 268 p.; A. Escobar, *Sentir-penser avec la Terre*, *o.c.*, 30.

100 P.M. Yentcharé, "Partager les fruits de l'innovation avec les communautés autochtones ou locales: les 12 travaux d'Hercule?" (2016) 30 *Revue internationale de droit économique*, 107; N. Berta, R. Debref, and F.-D. Vivien, "Economics and the Environment since the 1950s: An Overview" (2021) 79 *Cahiers d'économie politique*, 7-30.

101 P. Descola, *Par-delà nature et culture*, *o.c.*, 57; A. Escobar, *Sentir-penser avec la Terre*, *o.c.*, 74.

102 S. Safrin, "Hyperownership in a Time of Biotechnological Promise", *o.c.*, 642; M. Petel, "La nature: d'un objet d'appropriation à un sujet de droit", *o.c.*, 213; F. Ost, *La nature hors la loi*, *o.c.*, 47.

36. By the "rights of relations", we want to go beyond this imbalance between economic relations and seeds and take a more holistic approach, i.e. to all other relations (social, spiritual, medicinal), which, for the majority, are not yet recognized or identified. Ignoring such relationships would be cultural relativism and would ignore the ontological dimension of seeds.[103] Indeed, and more particularly in animist societies or in developing countries, seeds are linked to a whole other field of dimensions: social, cultural, spiritual, medicinal, etc. Taking the example of a seed exchange network in biodiversity conservation and use, this holistic approach to seed relationships allows a better understanding of the multifunctionality of agriculture and the seed exchange network.[104] It "*recognizes agriculture as a multi-output activity producing not only commodities (food, feed, fibres, agrofuels, medicinal products and ornamentals), but also non-commodity outputs such as environmental services, landscape amenities and cultural heritages.*"[105]

37. In a decolonial way, the "rights of relations" will seek to give legal legitimacy to the different relations that we may have with the environment and seeds. In this sense, the objective of this legal construction is to give equal recognition to the different ontologies and to limit the supremacy of the naturalist ontology. In the example of seeds, a modern position would dismiss the animistic arguments (i.e. or seeds would be spiritual beings, or members of a community).[106] Indeed, these non-naturalistic relationships would be considered as mere beliefs and cultural considerations that would fade away before the so-called "true reality" of science and economics. On the contrary, this dualist and extractivist position considers seeds only as sets of exploitable and appropriable inert objects.

38. Breaking with the single naturalistic prism, the relational approach between humans and seeds that we propose aims to protect all the relationships and dimensions that humans and seeds share. In a way, it is a question of taking seriously a phenomenological approach to the relationships and dimensions that humans and non-humans (as seeds) may have.[107] To conclude, if the regime complex classifies, simplifies and commodifies seeds and biological resources[108],

---

103 A. Escobar, *Sentir-penser avec la Terre*, *o.c.*, 125; T. Ingold, *The Perception of the Environment: Essays on Livelihood, Dwelling and Skill*, Routledge, 2021, London, 12.

104 C. Frison, *Redesigning the Global Seed Commons*, *o.c.*, 63; M. Pautasso, *et. al.*, "Seed exchange networks for agrobiodiversity conservation. A review", *o.c.*, 157.

105 V. Shiva, *The Vandana Shiva Reader*, University Press of Kentucky, Lexington, 2015, 227 p.; C. Frison, *Redesigning the Global Seed Commons*, *o.c.*, 51.

106 A. Escobar, *Sentir-penser avec la Terre*, *o.c.*, 124.

107 A. Escobar, *Sentir-penser avec la Terre*, *o.c.*, 125.

108 S. Safrin, "Hyperownership in a Time of Biotechnological Promise", *o.c.*, 642; C. Bonneuil and J.-B. Fressoz, *L'événement anthropocène*, *o.c.*, 56.

the "rights of relations" will protect all the complex connections, relationships, and interpretations between human and seeds[109]

D. THE CONTRIBUTION OF THE "RIGHTS OF RELATIONS" TO FARMERS' RIGHTS

39. As we have seen above, access to seeds (and, ipso facto, the farmer-seed relationship) is undermined by the seed regime complex favoring the commodification of agriculture and private property.[110] In our opinion, a key aspect of Farmers' Rights is access, control, and management of seeds[111] However, Farmers' customary seed rights and peasant's informal seed system were limited and outlawed.[112] The seed regime complex favors IPRs over Farmers' Rights.[113]

40. In this imbalance context between Farmers' Rights and IPRs, the "rights of relation" may offer additional arguments to preserve a right "*to save, use, exchange and sell farm-saved seed/propagating material.*" The "rights of relations" could be claimed as both individual and collective rights. In this way, community networks and joint seed management could be recognized as legitimate actors.

41. From a technical point of view, the integration of the "rights of relations" may be placed in continuity with the Farmers' Rights. Indeed, these may constitute a starting point for legally invoking these "rights of relations" in legal discourses. "Recognizing the special relationship and interaction between peasants and other people working in rural areas and the land, water and nature to which they are attached and on which they depend for their livelihood", and by proclaiming a right to seeds UNDROP (Art. 19) would be adequate to introduce the "rights of relations".

42. Moreover, UNDROP fits into the political corpus of human rights. Indeed, UNDROP recognizes human rights as the highest sources of law and should therefore take precedence over IPRs.[114] According to some authors, the right to seeds (Art. 19 UNDROP) could be linked with other sources of Human

---

109 D. Magda, I. Doussan, and S. Vanuxem, "La transition agroécologique permet-elle de renouer le lien aux non-humains ? Regards croisés d'écologue et de juriste" (2020) *VertigO – la revue électronique en sciences de l'environnement* https://journals.openedition.org/vertigo/28077, accessed 09.11.2023.

110 C. Frison, *Redesigning the Global Seed Commons*, *o.c.*, 62.

111 S. Le Teno, C. Frison, and S. Cogolati, "The right to seeds", *o.c.*, 121.

112 T. Wattnem, "Seed laws, certification and standardization", *o.c.*, 850.

113 S. Le Teno, C. Frison, and S. Cogolati, "The right to seeds", *o.c.*, 121-122; C. Golay, "Research Brief: The right to seeds and Intellectual Property Rights", *o.c.*, 2.

114 C. Golay, "Research Brief: The right to seeds and Intellectual Property Rights", *o.c.*, 2.

Rights and international law that implicitly recognize it.[115] Finally, Farmers' Rights may be interpreted as legal recognition of practices and customs that farmers have always had and that should be protected.[116] In a political, creative, and activist use of the law, we believe that the Farmers' Rights recognized by UNDROP combined with ITPGRFA and other sources and principles of international law would be an interesting basis to start a legal argument on the "rights of relations".

43. In sum, the "rights of relations" could be inspired by these Farmers' Rights and offer other arguments to overcome their lack of legal effectiveness and their imbalance *vis-à-vis* the IPRs. In that sense, arguing for the "rights of relations" between farmers and their seeds, it would allow putting forward Farmers' Rights, to make them more solid.

E. FROM THE "RIGHTS OF RELATIONS" TO RELATIONAL KNOWLEDGE

44. The seed regime complex, through the CBD and ITPGRFA, protects genetic resources and associated "traditional" knowledge by several means: benefit-sharing funds, global information systems, promotion of sustainable use of resources, protection of Farmers' Rights, etc.

45. However, the protection of traditional knowledge was not sufficient in the regime complex. The regime complex has a naturalistic prism that privileges a Western scientist's approach and disregards traditional knowledge. We perceive a neo-colonial approach in that knowledge from Western science is always privileged over other methods of knowledge.[117] In this case, this deficiency is explained by a Western philosophical structure that devalues traditional knowledge about scientific knowledge.[118]

46. The perspective offered by the "rights of relations" want to criticize this supremacy of the Western scientific discourses and promote traditional knowledge. One of the ways in which we want to link our "rights of relations" is a relational approach to knowledge. Where the modern sciences have posed a

---

115 H.M. Haugen, "The UN Declaration on Peasants' Rights (UNDROP)", *o.c.*, 289.

116 A. Christinck and M. Tvedt, "The UPOV Convention, Farmers' Rights and Human Rights. An Integrated Assessment of Potentially Conflicting Legal Frameworks", *o.c.*, 47.

117 D. Magda, I. Doussan, and S. Vanuxem, "La transition agroécologique permet-elle de renouer le lien aux non-humains ?", *o.c.*, no. 21; M. Sunder, "The Invention of Traditional Knowledge", *o.c.*, 117.

118 This is also found in Western anthropology, where traditional knowledge is seen as a cultural approach to seeing a unique world that only Western science may demonstrate; A. Escobar, *Sentir-penser avec la Terre*, *o.c.*, 127.

distance to their objects of knowledge, we wish to legitimize the links with them. Taking the "situated knowledge" from HARAWAY and "pluriverse" of ESCOBAR as an inspiration, we believe that different knowledge should assume their links and interconnections with the "objects" they study. In this case, in the traditional knowledge, there is a form of valorization of the links between the populations, their knowledge, and their practice.[119]

47. In the end, we believe that the "rights of relations" enable and legitimizes other forms of knowledge. This relational approach would consider traditional and indigenous knowledge in this ontological conflict. In this traditional knowledge, the links with the land are valued and protected. Although further research will be necessary, the "rights of relations" could be inspired by the "pluriverse" and the "situated knowledge" to assume links with our knowledge and therefore, "reason with the heart".[120]

IV. CONCLUSION

48. This article introduced the concept of the "rights of relations" and applied it to the regime complex of seed. The seed regime complex presents a contradiction between the protections of intellectual property rights (TRIPS, UPOV) and their sustainable and fair use (CBD, NP, ITPGRFA).

49. Our criticisms have been gathered in two main points. First, the system of seed ownership in the regime complex creates a system of hyper-ownership of seeds. Seeds are seen as a natural object that could be appropriated and commercialized. In this context, any Access and Benefit Sharing would be a fragile form of compensation for resource providers in this logic of exploitation and appropriation of nature. The second issue is the imbalance between IPRs and Farmers' Rights (especially access to seeds). Several principles resulting from this imbalance prevent all relationships between farmers and their seeds: Seeds are protected only in their economic dimensions, access to land and seeds is limited for farmers, traditional knowledge is not valued, etc.

50. Facing different challenges to the international seed regime complex, we have proposed the "rights of relations". Leaving the object-subject dichotomy, the "rights of relations" are rights to be imagined, which could allow rethinking environmental law (having a dualistic approach). Although the "rights of relations" do not exist in the positive law, we mobilize a constructive approach

---

119 P.M. YENTCHARÉ, "Partager les fruits de l'innovation avec les communautés autochtones ou locales", *o.c.*

120 A. ESCOBAR, *Sentir-penser avec la Terre*, *o.c.*, 29.

of the law to use the "rights of relations" in the legal argumentation: It could be derived from the resurgent legal structure or be articulated in jurisprudential interpretation. From a pragmatic point of view, the "rights of relations" may have multiple implications for individuals, communities and surrounding public and private organizations. It may lead to symbolic recognition or concrete rights (creation of new legal entity, financial means, etc.).

51. Applied to the seed's regime complex, the "rights of relations" could fight against the predominance of the economic perspective of appropriation of seeds. Indeed, the "rights of relations" aim to cover spiritual relations, social relations, etc. Second, the "rights of relations" will provide additional arguments to protect Farmers' Rights. Indeed, Farmers' Rights conflict with the IPR and are not sufficiently recognized in ITPGRFA (left to the discretion of states) and UNDROP (not legally binding). In this case, the "rights of relations" could fill the gaps in the regime complex to try to consolidate Farmers' Rights. Thirdly, the "rights of relations" have been linked with the relational theories of knowledge (situated knowledge and pluriverse) to give legitimacy to traditional knowledge.

52. To conclude, rethinking philosophically and legally from the perspective of the "rights of relations" allows us to restore strength to the relations between humans and non-humans, and to privilege access to seeds, respect for ontologies and forms of relations, and finally, to pose epistemic questions. This is how we propose this project of the "rights of relations" between humans and seeds, which has yet to be constructed and developed with local actors and practitioners.

PART IV

PROPERTY RIGHTS ON WATER AND THE UNDERGROUND

MARINE GENETIC RESOURCES IN AREAS BEYOND NATIONAL JURISDICTION

A New Governance Model for these Ocean Commons?

Maria Carro-Pitarch
Postdoctoral researcher and EU Law Lecturer (ACIF 2021), University of Valencia

I. INTRODUCTION

The foreseen tragedy of the commons in relation to the oceans and their living resources is close to becoming irreparable.[1] In the context of a very fragmented and sectorial regulation of our oceans, the international community has been trying to fill the existing legal gaps in the regulation of marine biological diversity in areas beyond national jurisdiction (hereinafter: "ABNJ").

These areas encompass more than two thirds of the oceans and are considered the largest reservoir of biodiversity on the planet. ABNJ in the oceans are the sum of "the high seas" and "the Area". The high seas are negatively defined by the United Nations Convention on the Law of the Sea (hereinafter: "UNCLOS" or "the Convention") as "*all parts of the sea that are not included in the exclusive economic zone, in the territorial sea or in the internal waters of a State, or in the archipelagic waters of an archipelagic State*" (Art. 86 UNCLOS), while the Area is defined as "*the seabed and ocean floor and subsoil thereof, beyond the limits of national jurisdiction*" (Art. 1 UNCLOS). The first areas are ruled by the principle of "freedom of the seas", while in the second one, the principle of "common heritage of humankind" is applicable.

For more than twenty years, within the United Nations, devoted negotiators from almost all States and international organizations have been striving to find a solution in the form of an international legally binding instrument on the conservation and sustainable use of marine biological diversity of areas beyond national jurisdiction under the auspices of the United Nations Convention on

1 G. Hardin, "The Tragedy of the Commons" (1968) 162 *Science* 1243, 1248.

the Law of the Sea, generally known as the Agreement of Biodiversity Beyond National Jurisdiction or the "BBNJ Agreement".

On 4 March 2023, the president of the negotiations, ambassador Rena Lee, proudly announced to the world that "*the ship ha*[d] *reached the shore*", meaning that the text of the BBNJ Agreement had finally been agreed upon. On 19 June of the same year, the definitive text was adopted by consensus and is open to ratification since 20 September by those States or regional economic integration organizations that would like to become parties and become bound by it.[2]

The BBNJ Agreement addresses mainly four elements that together constitute the so-called "Package Deal", which regulates: (a) marine genetic resources (hereinafter: "MGR"), including the fair and equitable sharing of benefits; (b) measures such as area-based management tools, including marine protected areas; (c) environmental impact assessments; and (d) capacity-building and the transfer of marine technology[3], as well as certain crosscutting issues, such as institutional arrangements, the financial mechanism or settlement of disputes, among others.

While this historic moment for the Law of the Sea sets out the foundations for a more comprehensive regulation, there are certain aspects of the adopted text which have not been peacefully accepted by all negotiators, and that will possibly continue to generate discussions and discrepancies in the years to come. This is particularly the case for the part on the regulation of MGR. The diverging views among the negotiators on the optimal regulation of this Part are founded in the delimitation of the legal status of such resources, which has caused an ideological debate at the core of the discussions between delegations from the Global North and the Global South.

The objective of this chapter is, after this brief introduction (I), to succinctly conceptualize MGR as commons and the possible ways of governing them (II). Afterwards, it identifies the confrontation between the two models that have been proposed during the negotiations of the BBNJ Agreement (III), highlighting the principal debate that has lied at the core of the dispute; as well as the final regime adopted by Agreement (IV), which still needs to enter into force. This contribution ends with some concluding remarks (V).

2 As of January 2024, more than 80 States and regional economic integration organizations have signed the Agreement, but none have ratified it yet. A complete list of signatories is available at https://treaties.un.org/Pages/ViewDetails.aspx?src=TREATY&mtdsg_no=XXI-10&chapter=21&clang=_en. All electronic sources referenced throughout this paper were accessed on 25 June 2023.

3 Letter dated 30 June 2011 from the Co-Chairs of the Ad Hoc Open-ended Informal Working Group to the President of the General Assembly, A/66/119 (30 June 2011).

II. MARINE GENETIC RESOURCES OF AREAS BEYOND NATIONAL JURISDICTION: GLOBAL COMMONS IN NEED OF GOVERNANCE?

There has been a progressive evolution in international law towards a higher consideration of the general interests of the international community. As part of this development, the conviction has been growing that vital resources of the planet ought to be seen as common property that must be protected and exploited in the benefit of humankind as a whole.[4]

The delimitation of the notion of "global commons" was highly debated in legal literature for a long time[5], particularly in the context of international law, "*as* [ABNJ] *have come under increasing economic and environmental pressure.*" Nevertheless, "*multiplicity of semantic inflections, conceptual configurations and legal articulations*" remain when discussing the legal status of these commons.[6]

The traditional notion of commons refers to the high seas, the atmosphere, Antarctica, and outer space.[7] These are all spaces located in the ABNJ that are, *a priori,* accessible to all States, who can therefore (over)use them, creating a risk of overexploitation. The notion of global commons, however, has been expanded to encompass other areas and resources[8], which is where the discussion originates on whether marine genetic resources are global commons and how they should be governed.

The first necessary step to answer this question is to establish what MGR are. Following the notion already used in the Convention on Biological Diversity (Art. 2), the new BBNJ Agreement defines them as "*any material of marine plant, animal, microbial or other origin containing functional units of heredity of actual or potential value*" (Art. 1.8 BBNJ Agreement).

Beyond the delimitation of the scope of the notion of global commons, the governance model established to regulate these commons is relevant. In practice, as Juste Ruiz highlights, different models have come forward, namely: (a) freedom of access and exploitation; (b) common interest or

---

4 J. Juste, "La gobernanza de los *global commons* como patrimonio colectivo en el Derecho Internacional" (2018) 34 *Anuario Español de Derecho Internacional* 133, 149, 133.

5 See: S. Ranganathan, "Global Commons" (2016) 27 (3) *The European Journal of International Law* 693, 717; D. Bodansky, "What's in a Concept? Global Public Goods, International Law, and Legitimacy" (2012) 23 (3) *European Journal of International Law* 651, 668.

6 V. De Lucia, "The Concept of Commons and Marine Genetic Resources in Areas beyond National Jurisdiction" (2018-19) 5 *Maritime Safety and Security Law Journal* 1, 22, 1.

7 United Nations, "UN System Task Team on the Post-2015 UN Development Agenda" (Thematic Think Piece) (2013), 5. www.un.org/en/development/desa/policy/untaskteam_undf/thinkpieces/24_thinkpiece_global_governance.pdf.

8 *Ibid.*, 9.

concern of humankind; and (c) common heritage of humankind (hereinafter: "CHH").[9]

Within the first model, these global commons are considered to be unowned spaces to which all humans have an equal right of access and exploitation. This regime was already enshrined in the Part VII of UNCLOS as applicable to the high seas. In this sense, the high seas are open to all States (Art. 87 UNCLOS), but no State may validly claim to subject any part of the high seas to its sovereignty (Art. 89 UNCLOS). However, the freedoms established in the Convention are not limitless, as they must be exercised in accordance with certain conditions established by the Convention itself and by International Law.[10]

The second governance model, based on the common interest or concern of humankind, has the objective of ensuring the conservation of global commons for the benefit of all States. This model, which applies to commons that are located both in areas within or beyond national jurisdiction[11], was implemented for the first time in the Antarctic Treaty of 1959[12], and later, in the Outer Space Treaty of 1967.[13]

In the 1987 Brundtland Report the United Nations General Assembly acknowledged the concept of "common concern for the planet and interlocked ecological and economical threats"[14], together with the idea that climate change is a common concern of mankind.[15]

The concept of common concern of humankind has not been entirely defined, but is considered to consist of three dimensions: (a) firstly, the spatial dimension, that includes environmental elements that require collective action to protect them; (b) secondly, the temporal dimension, which encompasses the long-term effects of the concern; and (c) thirdly, the social dimension, which stresses the need to engage all sectors of society in an equitable sharing of burdens in the protection of the environment.[16]

---

9 J. Juste, *op. cit.*
The original term in English, already used in UNCLOS (*common heritage of mankind, CHM*), has been adapted in the new BBNJ Agreement with a gender-neutral formulation (*common heritage of humankind*), which is the one used throughout this paper.

10 For a more detailed study of the regime established by UNCLOS, see: T. Scovazzi, *Elementos de Derecho Internacional del Mar* (*Edición española a cargo de Valentín Bou Franch*), Tecnos, Madrid 1995.

11 J. Juste, *op. cit.*, 141.

12 The Antarctic Treaty was signed on 1 December 1959, it entered into force in 1961, and to this date has a total number of 56 Parties to the Treaty. Available at: www.ats.aq/e/antarctictreaty.html.

13 Formally known as the Treaty on Principles Governing the Activities of States in the Exploration and Use of Outer Space, Including the Moon and Other Celestial Bodies (1967). It entered into force on 10 October 1967 and has 113 State-Parties, and 89 Signatory States. Data available at: https://treaties.unoda.org/t/outer_space.

14 United Nations, Our Common Future: Report of the World Commission on Environment (1987) www.un-documents.net/our-common-future.pdf, 7

15 Protection of Global Climate for Present and Future Generations of Mankind, GA Res. 43/53, A/RES/43/53 (6 December 1988).

16 S. Lothian, "Forget Me Not: Revisiting the Common Concern of Humankind Concept in the BBNJ Context" (2021) 38 (3) *Environmental and Planning Law Journal* 1, 20, 12; L. Horn,

This notion was suggested as a solution to prevent an impasse between delegations during the negotiations of the BBNJ Agreement in respect to the principles applicable to the MGR (that is explained in the following section). It was suggested that the common concern of humankind had the possibility to unite more delegations and also to reinforce key principles such as inter- and intra-generational equity, international solidarity or shared decision-making.[17]

The third model, the common heritage of humankind, remains one of the most controversial governance models, as it has been the source of many discussions in the negotiations for the adoption of international treaties or conventions in which it has been proposed[18], and the subject of a prolific literature on its origin and content.[19] The CHH is characterized, generally, by four elements: (a) peaceful use; (b) non-appropriation; (c) exploitation of resources through an international regime or international management; and (d) fair sharing of benefits.[20]

The origin and popularity of this model can be traced back to the 1960s[21], when the Maltese Ambassador, Arvid Pardo, proposed to the UNGA in 1967 that the "*the deep seabed and ocean floor beyond the limits of national jurisdiction should be subject to a new international regime known as the 'common heritage of* [hu]*mankind'*."[22]

It is applicable to the Area and its resources, as established by UNCLOS. The notion of "resources" of the Area, under UNCLOS, is limited to mineral ones[23], which for years has left open the question as to what regime should apply to the non-mineral or living resources encountered in the Area.

"Climate Change and the Future Role of the Concept of the Common Concern" (2015) 2 (1) *Australian Journal of Environmental Law* 24, 27.

17 This proposal was made by the International Union for Conservation of Nature during the work of the Preparatory Committee. S. Lothian, *op. cit.*, 3 and 20.

18 In this line, Duncan French highlights that the CHH "*has failed to find traction beyond the seabed*", to which Lothian adds that it has not been given any effect in relation to Antarctica. *Ibid.*, 8.
For a more complete retelling of the failure of the inclusion of the CHH in the Antarctic Treaty, against the revindications of the developing countries, see: R. Bermejo & V. Bou, "La celebración del Protocolo al Tratado Antártico sobre la protección del medio ambiente: orígenes y negociaciones" (1993) IX *Anuario de Derecho Internacional* 155, 201.

19 For all, see: K. Baslar, *The Concept of the Common Heritage of Mankind in International Law*, Martinus Nijhoff Publishers, Boston 1997.

20 J. Juste, *op. cit.*; J. Murillo, "Common Concern of Humankind and Its Implications in International Environmental Law" (2008) 5 (2) *Macquarie Journal of International and Comparative Environmental Law*, 133, 135. The categorization is extracted from the Resolution of the United Nations General Assembly 2749 (17 December 1970) and reflected in Part XI of UNCLOS.

21 K. Mickelson, "Common Heritage of Mankind as a limit to exploitation of the Global Commons" (2019) 30 (2) *The European Journal of International Law* 635, 663.

22 United Nations General Assembly, Agenda Item 92, *Examination of the Question of the Reservation Exclusively for Peaceful Purposes of the Seabed and the Ocean Floor, and the Subsoil Thereof, Underlying the High Seas beyond the Limits of Present National Jurisdiction, and the Use of Their Resources in the Interests of Mankind (General Debate)*, 22nd Session, First Committee, 1515th Meeting, A/C.1/PV.1515 (1 November 1967).

23 Art. 133 (a) UNCLOS.

However, it is generally known that the original regime of CHH established in Part XI had to be severely modified for the Convention to enter into force. When the efforts to reach consensus were exhausted, UNCLOS was submitted to vote, and it received 130 votes in favour, 4 against and 17 abstentions. The majority of these last two categories was comprised by the so-called developed States, as they understood that the regime would discourage mining activities and create excessive burdens for research and the industry. Thus, the paradox in 1994 was that UNCLOS would enter into force without the participation of those States that actually had the technological means to engage in this sort of activities.[24]

To remedy the situation, a new Agreement Relating to the Implementation of Part XI of the UNCLOS was negotiated, and both the Agreement and the Convention entered into force in 1994 with quasi-universal participation. The content of this Agreement severely changed the concept of CHH in its form and substance[25], significantly "*undermin*[ing] *the hopes of developing states.*"[26]

Later on, it was also declared that the moon and its natural resources are CHH.[27] Many States decided against signing this treaty, particularly because of the common heritage ideal.[28]

III. THE NEGOTIATIONS OF THE BBNJ AGREEMENT: THE CONFRONTATION BETWEEN TWO MODELS OF GOVERNANCE OR TWO GUIDING PRINCIPLES

The potential application of marine generated resources in the industry have made them the object of public and private interest for both their conservation but also their use and exploitation. MGR can be used to advance in scientific research and, as such, can be the key to new technologies that may be patented in

---

24 For a more comprehensive account of the facts, see: T. Scovazzi, "The Concept of Common Heritage of Mankind and the Genetic Resources of the Seabed beyond the Limits of National Jurisdiction" (2007), 25 *Agenda Internacional* 11, 24.

25 *Ibid.*

26 A. Jaeckel, "Benefitting from the Common Heritage of Humankind: From Expectation to Reality" (2020) 35 *The International Journal of Marine and Coastal Law* 660, 681, 661.

27 Art. 11.1 Agreement Governing the Activities of States on the Moon and Other Celestial Bodies. Adopted in 1979 by the Resolution of the General Assembly 34/68, it entered into force in July 1984.

28 C.R. Buxton, "Property in Outer Space: The Common Heritage of Mankind Principle vs. the First in Time, First in Right, Rule of Property" (2004) 69 (4) *Journal of Air Law and Commerce* 689, 707, 699.

the biotechnology industry.[29] This interest has been palpable at all stages of the negotiation process of the BBNJ Agreement.

This process started in 2004 with the recommendation of the United Nations Open-ended Informal Consultative Process on Oceans and Law of the Sea ("UNICPOLOS") and has passed through the creation of an *Ad hoc* Open-ended Informal Working Group to study issues relating to the conservation and sustainable use of marine biological diversity beyond areas of national jurisdiction that met between 2004 and 2016[30], a Preparatory Committee[31] that held meetings in 2016 and 2017, and five periods of sessions of the intergovernmental conference[32] (IGC) that were held between 2018 and 2023.

In the vein of these twenty years-long negotiations, two regimes or models of governance of MGR have been proposed and defended, mainly, by two big groups: the Global South, which has fought vehemently in favour of the inclusion of the CHH[33]; and, the Global North, that has expressed its pronounced interest in the recognition of freedom of access to the resources object of this study.

At the early stages of the process, the final report of the Preparatory Committee showed a first sign of divergence in the negotiations, especially since it mentioned that "*with regard to the common heritage of mankind and the freedom of the high seas, further discussion is needed.*"[34]

The division between Northern and Southern states was quite evident in their statements to the Committee. The G77 and China reaffirmed that the CHH

---

29 Ten states, in 2011, accounted for more than 90% of patents deposited with marine genes, of which three states (USA, Germany and Japan) accounted for 70%. The lack of regulation to date of MGRs found in the ABNJ resulted in access to these resources on a first-come, first-served basis. S. Arnaud-Haond, J.M. Arrieta & C. M. Duarte, "Marine Biodiversity and Gene Patents" (2011) 311 *Science* 1521, 1522.

30 General Assembly Resolution 59/24, *Oceans and the law of the sea*, A/RES/59/24 (17 November 2004), par. 73.

31 General Assembly Resolution 69/292, *Development of an international legally binding instrument under the United Nations Convention on the Law of the Sea on the conservation and sustainable use of marine biological diversity of areas beyond national jurisdiction*, A/RES/69/292 (19 June 2015), 1(a).

32 General Assembly Resolution 72/249, *International legally binding instrument under the United Nations*
Convention on the Law of the Sea on the conservation and sustainable use of marine biological diversity of areas beyond national jurisdiction, A/RES/72/249 (24 December 2017).

33 Observers during the IGCs highlighted that this principle was mentioned 41 times during IGC-1, 56 times during IGC-2, 18 times during IGC-3, 8 times during IGC-4 and, at least, 82 times in IGC-5. R. Tiller, E. Mendenhall, E. De Santo & E. Nyman, "Shake it Off: Negotiations suspended, but hope simmering, after a lack of consensus at the fifth intergovernmental conference on biodiversity beyond national jurisdiction" (2023) 148 *Marine Policy* 1, 9.

34 Report of the Preparatory Committee established by General Assembly resolution 69/292: Development of an international legally binding instrument under the United Nations Convention on the Law of the Sea on the conservation and sustainable use of marine biological diversity of areas beyond national jurisdiction, A/AC.287/2017/PC.4/2 (31 July 2017) https://documents-dds-ny.un.org/doc/UNDOC/GEN/N17/237/36/PDF/N1723736.pdf?OpenElement.

should "*underpin the new regime*" governing MGRs in ABNJ and should be "*at the core of the new instrument*".[35] In contrast, Iceland remarked that the CHH is only applicable to mineral resources under Article 133 of UNCLOS, and, the freedom of the seas (under Art. 87 of UNCLOS) is more appropriate as far as MGRs are concerned.[36] Failing this, it pointed out that a practical and potentially hybrid solution must be found. The European Union (EU) and its Member States, as well as Norway, advocated at the time for a pragmatic solution, without entering into the ideological debate between the two principles.[37]

In the first IGC, which took place from 4 to 17 September 2018, when debating which principles should appear in the text of the future Agreement, the CHH was proposed, together with a "no text" alternative, and the "freedom of the high seas". Delegations' attitudes to the debate between these principles differed widely. On the one hand, the EU stressed that the negotiations of the instrument did not depend on the determination of the legal status of MGRs, thus postponing the debate. On the other hand, the Russian Federation emphasised the necessary application of the freedom of the high seas to MGRs (including those in the Area)[38], while the Republic of South Korea pointed to the imperative of ensuring free access to these resources in accordance with the freedom of the seas enshrined in UNCLOS and, above all, that the instrument need not address the CHH.[39] The United States of America (U.S.), in its final

35 The Group of 77 and China, *Development of an international legally binding instrument under the United Nations Convention on the Law of the Sea on the conservation and sustainable use of marine biological diversity of areas beyond national jurisdiction-Group of 77 and China's Written submission* (5 June 2016) www.un.org/depts/los/biodiversity/prepcom_files/rolling_comp/Group_of_77_and_China.pdf.

36 Iceland, *Iceland's written submission to the Preparatory Committee established by the General Assembly Resolution 69/292: development of an international legally binding instrument under the United Nations Convention on the Law of the Sea on the conservation and sustainable use of marine biological diversity beyond national jurisdiction* (December 2016) www.un.org/depts/los/biodiversity/prepcom_files/rolling_comp/Iceland.pdf.

37 European Union and Member States, *Development of an international legally binding instrument under UNCLOS on the conservation and sustainable use of marine biological diversity of various areas national jurisdiction (BBNJ process)- written submission of the EU and its Member states. Marine genetic resources, including questions on the sharing of benefits* (22 February 2017) www.un.org/depts/los/biodiversity/prepcom_files/rolling_comp/EU_Written_Submission_on_Marine_Genetic_Resources.pdf>; Norway, *Preparatory Committee established by General assembly resolution 69/ 292: development of an international legally binding instruments under the United Nations Convention on the Law of the Sea on the conservation and sustainable use of marine biological diversity of areas beyond national jurisdiction. Comments by Norway* (December 2016). www.un.org/depts/los/biodiversity/prepcom_files/rolling_comp/Norway.pdf.

38 President's aid to negotiations, A/CONF.232/2019/1* (03 December 2018); IISD, Summary of the First Session of the Intergovernmental Conference on an International Legally Binding Instrument under the UN Convention on the Law of the Sea on the Conservation and Sustainable Use of Marine Biodiversity of Areas Beyond National Jurisdiction: 4-17 September 2018 (2018) 25 (179) *Earth Negotiations Bulletin*, 3.

39 Republic of Korea, *General Statement by the Republic of Korea. CIG-1.* www.un.org/bbnj/sites/www.un.org.bbnj/files/rok.pdf.

statement, expressly noted its scepticism about reaching a practical compromise on the benefit-sharing regime because of the numerous references to the CHH during IGC-1 by other delegations.[40]

In the IGC-2, held from 25 March to 5 April 2019, when the tensions were still high about this matter, Colombia pointed out that choosing any other starting point for the Agreement than the CHH would mean maintaining the *status quo* (i.e. continuing to use the resources without any guarantee of their conservation). In contrast, the countries from the Global North, and especially the U.S., pointed out that the objective of the Agreement is in no way to change the international economic order, which is what they understood the CHH would do, and that access to MGRs should remain free and unrestricted.[41]

It must be pointed out that the definition of *status quo* differs greatly among States. As Marciniak highlights the meaning of this notion can be understood as the "*full application of the high seas freedom or imperfect application of CHM principle*"[42], depending on their interpretation of the current regime under UNCLOS.

The debate rapidly became stagnant even with the first draft of the Agreement[43], which did not include any of the contentious principles in an attempt to overcome the blockage. However, the multiple references to this principle during IGC-3[44], which was took place from 19 to 30 August 2019, forced the reappearance of this principle in the following drafts.[45]

---

40 United States of America, *General Statement.* www.un.org/bbnj/sites/www.un.org.bbnj/files/united-states-opening-statement-bbnj-igc-session-1docx.pdf.

41 R. Tiller, E. Mendenhall, E. De Santo & E. Nyman, "A soft treaty, hard to reach: The second inter-governmental conference for biodiversity beyond national jurisdiction" (2019), 108 *Marine Policy,* 1-8, 3.

42 K. J. Marciniak, "Marine Genetic Resources: Do They Form Part of the Common Heritage of Mankind Principle", in L. Martin, C. Salonidis, C.G. Hioureas, I.A. Laird, B. Sabahi & A.M. Whitesell, *Natural Resources and the Law of the Sea: Exploration, Allocation, Exploitation of Natural Resources in Areas under National Jurisdiction and Beyond* (pp. 373-405), Juris Publishing Editors 2017, p. 404.

43 Draft text of an agreement under the United Nations Convention on the Law of the Sea on the conservation and sustainable use of marine biological diversity of areas beyond national jurisdiction, A/CONF.232/2019/6 (17 May 2019).

44 The best illustration of the impasse was Palestine's intervention in the name of the G-77 and China about the general principles of Art. 5 of the Agreement: "*The principle of Common Heritage of Mankind, the polluter pays, the principle of Common Heritage of Mankind, the precautionary principle/ approach, the principle of Common Heritage of Mankind, equity, did I mention the principle of Common Heritage of Mankind? The ecosystem approach, best available scientific information and traditional knowledge of indigenous peoples and local communities, and of course the principle of Common Heritage of Mankind.*"
Declaration by Palestine, on behalf of the G-77 and China, on general principles and approaches (Art. 5) Working Group on Cross-cutting Issues, in: R. Tiller, E. Mendenhall, E. De Santo & E. Nyman, "Stuck in the middle with you (and not much time left): The third intergovernmental conference on biodiversity beyond national jurisdiction" (2020) 117 *Marine Policy* 1, 9, 4.

45 Since 2019, four draft texts have been published and one draft agreement: (1) Draft text (…), *op. cit.*; (2) Revised draft text of an agreement under the United Nations Convention on the

In the IGC-4, held from 7 to 18 March 2022, the President of the conference highlighted that the matter of access and benefit sharing, a key aspect of the new regime of MGR in the Agreement, is "*driven with ideological positions concerning acquisition and status of property, seen especially in the opposition between the concepts of common heritage and free market enterprise.*"[46] Continuing with their previous position, the G77 and China insisted that the CHH principle is "underlying legal and moral principle" for MGRs, while the so-called technologically advanced countries, based their argumentation to impede the inclusion of the CHH in the imperative necessity of not preventing or hindering research.[47]

The last IGC (IGC-5) required two periods of sessions to be concluded: IGC-5, from15 to 26 August 2022; and IGC-5 *bis,* from 20 February to 4 March 2023. It was the pivotal moment where a compromise was reached, even if only at the final hour. Mexico, for the Core Latin American Group, expressed this idea noting that the most progress had been achieved at this conference, even if "*flexibility had not been shared by all, making it difficult to reach agreement, especially with regard to MGRs and benefit-sharing and on the principle of the common heritage of humankind.*"[48]

According to those present in the room, at the beginning, the interventions of the delegations, when debating about the Article on principles and approaches, every single developed country that took the floor stated that they could not accept the inclusion of this principle and recommended the deletion of CHH. On the contrary, all major developing country coalitions expressed strong support for the principle.[49]

At the culmination of the negotiations of IGC-5 *bis,* it was crystal clear that the developing world had re-embraced the concept as critical to an equitable and

Law of the Sea on the conservation and sustainable use of marine biological diversity of areas beyond national jurisdiction, A/CONF.232/2020/3 (18 November 2019); (3) Further revised draft text of an agreement under the United Nations Convention on the Law of the Sea on the conservation and sustainable use of marine biological diversity of areas beyond national jurisdiction: Note by the President, A/CONF.232/2022/5 (1 June 2022); (4) Further refreshed draft text of an agreement under the United Nations Convention on the Law of the Sea on the conservation and sustainable use of marine biological diversity of areas beyond national jurisdiction, A/CONF.232/2023/2 (12 December 2022); and (5) Draft agreement under the United Nations Convention on the Law of the Sea on the conservation and sustainable use of marine biological diversity of areas beyond national jurisdiction, 4 March 2023.

46 R. Tiller, E. Mendenhall, E. De Santo & E. Nyman, "Direction, not detail: Progress towards consensus at the fourth intergovernmental conference on biodiversity beyond national jurisdiction" (2022) 146 *Marine Policy* 1, 10, 3.

47 *Ibid.*

48 IISD, Summary of the Fifth Session of the Intergovernmental Conference on an International Legally Binding Instrument under the UN Convention on the Law of the Sea on the Conservation and Sustainable Use of Marine Biodiversity of Areas Beyond National Jurisdiction: 15-26 August 2022 (2022) 25 (240) *Earth Negotiations Bulletin* 1, 13, 10.

49 R. Tiller, E. Mendenhall, E. De Santo & E. Nyman, *op. cit.*, 4.

effective BBNJ agreement.[50] The consistency of their position throughout the whole negotiation process did not falter and was rewarded with its inclusion in the final text.

IV. THE FINAL TEXT OF THE BBNJ AGREEMENT

More than twenty years ago, Lyle Glowka already pointed out that "[w]*hile it may be worthwhile to create a legal and institutional regime for the genetic resources of the Area, it is difficult to determine conclusively without further study whether it is useful or even necessary to declare the genetic resources of the Area the common heritage of mankind*."[51] In the same vein, and before the start of the IGCs to adopt the instrument under study, David Leary took up this idea and repeated that invoking the CHH is "*neither useful nor necessary*" as it distracts from the truly fundamental issues.[52]

Throughout the negotiations, the stultified debate generated around the principles debate seemed to prove the aforementioned prognosis of Glowka and Leary, and even put into question the finalisation of the agreement, as none of the parties seemed willing to compromise entirely on this issue.

Nevertheless, after thirty-six hours of non-stop negotiations, the President of the IGC announced to the world, on 4 March 2023, that a consensus had been found on the text of the BBNJ Agreement. This compromise also included a solution to the twenty-year long debate on the most appropriate model of governance of MGR and which principle should guide them.

The final text of the Agreement includes, in its Article 7, about "[g]*eneral principles and approaches*", both principles: (1) the principle of the common heritage of humankind which is set out in the Convention and (2) the freedom of marine scientific research, together with other freedoms of the high seas.

The methodology used to finalise this agreement has been called "overcoming by accumulation", which means that the text adopts a series of regulatory binomials, among which is the inclusion of these two principles.[53] This approach, while it has been useful for achieving a compromise, also raises numerous questions as to how the implementation of the new regime will be adopted.

---

50 R. Tiller, E. Mendenhall, E. De Santo & E. Nyman, "The ship has reached the shore: The final session of the 'Biodiversity Beyond National Jurisdiction' negotiations" (2023) 155 *Marine Policy* 1, 10, 3.

51 L. Glowka, "The Deepest of Ironies: Genetic Resources, Marine Scientific Research, and the Area" (1996) 12 (1) *Ocean Yearbook Online* 154, 178, 170.

52 D. Leary, "Agreeing to disagree on what we have or have not agreed on: The current state of play of the BBNJ negotiations on the status of marine genetic resources in areas beyond national jurisdiction" (2019) 99 *Marine Policy* 21, 29, 25.

53 J. Juste Ruiz, "The BBNJ Agreement comes ashore: a preliminary analysis" (2023) *Mepielan e-bulletin* (in press).

Beyond what it is established in the general principles of the Agreement, some of the classic definitory elements of the CHH appear also across the rest of the text. In this sense, activities that are carried out in relation to MGR and digital sequence information (DSI) on MGR of ABNJ shall be carried out exclusively for peaceful purposes (Art. 11.7 BBNJ Agreement).

Moreover, the text stipulates that no State shall claim or exercise sovereignty or sovereign rights over these resources, and no claim or exercise of such shall be recognized (Art. 11.4 BBNJ Agreement).

In this same line, activities related to these resources or DSI on MGR of ABNJ are in the interests of States and for the benefit of all humanity, particularly for the benefit of advancing the scientific knowledge of humanity (Art. 11.6 BBNJ Agreement), as well as promoting the objectives of the Agreement, namely, the conservation and sustainable use of marine biological diversity.

The Agreement also foresees a system for a fair and equitable sharing of benefits. The benefits that are derived from those activities carried out in relation to MGR and DSI of MGR shall be shared. Such benefits include both non-monetary and monetary ones. The full list of options of non-monetary benefits to share will be defined by the future Conference of the Parties (COP) (Art. 14.2.h BBNJ Agreement). Nevertheless, some of the benefits already contemplated in the text include access to samples, to DSI, to data, as well as transfer of marine technology or capacity-building (Art. 14.2 BBNJ Agreement).

The modalities for the sharing of monetary benefits will be decided by the COP, taking into consideration the recommendations made by the Access and Benefit sharing Committee which is established under Article 15 of the Agreement. *A priori* the decision will be made by consensus, unless it is found to be impossible, in which case it will be adopted by a three-fourths majority of the Parties present and voting (Art. 14.7 BBNJ Agreement).

The monetary benefits will be shared through a special fund established under Article 52 of the same Agreement and which will consist of various paying modalities. Firstly, it is envisaged that the developed Parties of the Agreement will make annual contributions until a COP decision is made, at which time there will be various modalities for paying. Contributions are possible in the form of milestone payments, contributions related to the commercialization of products, a tiered fee payable periodically based on a series of indicators to be defined or other modalities decided by the COP (Art. 14.7 BBNJ Agreement).

The written compromise achieved in the BBNJ Agreement in respect to the principles debate and the new regime established, however, does not necessarily solve the question of which model of governance will reign these resources as two challenges lay ahead. On the one hand, the text was formally adopted on 19 June of the same year, but it still needs sixty ratifications to enter into force.[54]

[54] In previous drafts of the Agreement, the number of instruments of ratification, approval or accession which was envisaged, was considerably lower, as it required only thirty (Art. 61 of

On the other hand, there is still a lot of normative and institutional development of this Agreement which will define the way such resources are regulated. The multiple references to the future development of the COP and the committee, among other institutional arrangements, are an indication of this.

V. CONCLUDING REMARKS

Two thirds of our oceans and their resources have lived in a legal limbo over the past decades, regulated through a patchwork of Conventions and sectorial treaties that have tried to create and implement an effective global ocean governance. Despite this, it has been clear for a long time that action was needed in terms of establishing a comprehensive regime for the ABNJ, and particularly for the conservation and sustainable use of marine biological diversity in them.

During the negotiations of this Agreement, one of the key aspects that generated debate, was the establishment of a legal regime for MGR. Since the early stages, the debate was presented as an ideological battle between the Global North and the Global South, favouring a regime that consolidated freedom of access and use, on the one hand, and the common heritage of humankind, on the other hand.

From a *status quo,* in which MGR can be accessed on a first-come, first-served basis, on the condition that the general environmental obligations established in UNCLOS were observed, the BBNJ Agreement has taken a leap forward to a more complete regulation of MGR.

This paper started off with the question what governance model is established through this new Agreement. The final answer must necessarily be a nuanced one. In the BBNJ Agreement two principles, seemingly opposed, will guide the new regime on MGR of ABNJ. Both the freedom of the high seas and the common heritage of humankind are enshrined in the text. This duality, while positive for it has provided consensus to adopt the Agreement, will also likely cause implementation issues.

The new regime for these resources will have to overcome, primarily, two challenges. On the one hand, the Agreement still needs to enter into force. As stated before, sixty ratifications are needed for this to happen, a number considerably larger than what was first foreseen. Moreover, there is always the risk that history repeats itself, and that what happened with Part XI of UNCLOS in 1994 occurs again. On the other hand, even if the Agreement enters into force with a quasi-universal participation, there is still a lot of normative and institutional development needed to effectively implement the Agreement. In this sense, the application of an important part of the regime of MGR has

the further refreshed draft text). Anyhow, the Agreement will enter into force 120 days after the date of deposit of the sixtieth instrument (Art. 68 BBNJ Agreement).

been delegated to the future work of the COP and the Committee on Access and Sharing of Benefits that will be adopted according to the Agreement.

Nevertheless, the adoption of this BBNJ Agreement and the establishment of a new regime for MGR of these areas is positive overall. The Agreement is a necessary foundation for the developments to come. In addition to this, the twenty-year long negotiations have shown a clear call on the part of the Global South for rethinking the way global commons should be reigned. As the President of the IGC announced to the world, "*the ship has reached the shore*"; now, we add, it is necessary to guarantee the rest of its journey.

WATER RIGHTS AND RECODIFICATION

Lessons from Chile

Jill ROBBIE
Professor of Property Law and Natural Environment, University of Glasgow

Pedro CISTERNA GAETE
PhD Researcher, University of Edinburgh

I. INTRODUCTION

Humanity, together with all the other non-human communities on Earth, is facing an ecological emergency. An urgent challenge in this context is how to reform our laws, and in particular our property laws, in order to halt the over-exploitation and destruction of natural resources, and facilitate the protection and restoration of our natural environment. Urgent and substantive processes of reform are necessary to ensure the continued survival of all species in a sustainable and equitable manner. Water law is one of the most difficult and yet most important areas of law to reform, due to the necessity of water for all forms of life, but also the multiple and conflicting demands on water use. This chapter will discuss water rights and recodification, and will examine the case study of Chile.

Chile provides a fascinating case study for water rights reform due to the implementation of a water rights regime in the 1980s which was inspired by neo-liberal ideology. This water rights regime has had significant negative social and environmental consequences, and as a result, is in the process of being reformed. However, the challenges encountered in these reform processes show the difficulties of implementing transformative change in a modern, democratic context. Although the circumstances of Chile appear exceptional, the examination of this country as a case study has broader lessons for other jurisdictions seeking to reform their property laws and policies.

The first part of this chapter will provide an overview of three themes of water law reform in a global context, these being: recognising the limitations of neo-liberal governance models; protecting marginalised people; and finally, tackling the ecological emergency. The second part of this chapter will then go on to consider how these themes have played out in the context of Chile. A concluding section will draw together the lessons which can be drawn from the Chilean example.

II. THEMES OF WATER LAW REFORM IN A GLOBAL CONTEXT

Before this section provides an overview of three important themes of water law reform in a global context, it is necessary to define the term "water right". A water right is a right to, or regarding water, which is enforceable against other individuals and which is recognised by law or custom.[1] Water rights can include the entitlement to consume water, such as the abstraction of water for domestic or agricultural purposes, or use water for non-consumptive purposes such as hydropower or navigation.[2] Water rights have historically been intimately connected with land rights because the owners of land usually have the best opportunity to access and use the water running through their land.[3] However, modern water rights regimes have also allowed water rights to be separated from the land.[4] When water rights can be separated from the land, this gives the possibility to implement a water rights market, where rights are bought, sold and transferred. The theory behind water rights markets is that they are a mechanism to facilitate the transfer of entitlements to use water to productive and effective users, and all users will be incentivised to use water in the most efficient way possible.[5]

Whether a water right is recognised as a property right in the context of water markets is important because the advocates of neo-liberal policies will argue that strong and stable property rights are crucial to the functioning of a market system.[6] However, if a jurisdiction does indeed recognise water rights as property rights this will (depending on the individual country) have important consequences in terms of constitutional protection of the right in question and whether the State can subsequently interfere with, regulate, or cancel the right

1 J. Robbie, "Water Rights" in J.M. Smits, J. Husa, C. Valcke, and M. Narciso (eds.), *Elgar Encyclopaedia of Comparative Law*, Elgar, Cheltenham 2023, p. 587.

2 S. Hodgson, "Modern Water Rights: Theory and Practice" Legislative Study 92, Food and Agriculture Organization of the United Nations, 2006, pp. 5-6.

3 *Ibid.* pp. 9-19.

4 D. Caponera, *Principles of Water Law and Administration: National and International*, Routledge, Abingdon, 3rd edn., revised and updated by M. Nanni, 2018.

5 See an overview in M. Hantke-Domas, "Water Markets" in A. Rieu-Clarke, A. Allan and S. Hendry (eds.), *Routledge Handbook of Water Law and Policy*, Routledge, Abingdon 2017; J.W. Dellapenna, "Fundamental Concepts of Property in Water and the Role of Markets in Water Governance" in J.W. Dellapenna and J. Gupta (eds.), *Water Law: Elgar Encyclopaedia of Environmental Law*, Elgar, Cheltenham, Vol X, 2021; B. H. Thompson, "Water Markets Agonistes" in V. Casado-Pérez and R. Larson (eds.), *A Research Agenda for Water Law*, Elgar, Cheltenham 2023.

6 See, for example, V. Casado-Pérez, "Missing Water Markets: A Cautionary Tale of Government Failure" (2015) *N.Y.U. Envtl. L.J.* 157.

in question.[7] The recognition of a water right in property law and the overall constitutional context of a country, are therefore important factors to consider when reforming a water rights regime.

A. RECOGNISING THE LIMITATIONS OF NEO-LIBERAL APPROACHES

To move onto outlining three important themes of water reform in a global context, in line with public policy debates more generally from the second half of the 20th century onwards, the field of water law contains advocates in favour of neo-liberal approaches to governance. In the context of water, such advocates argue that water is an economic good, should be recognised as such, and markets should be used more widely in the context of water management. In many countries around the world, water is also a scarce resource, and therefore, it is argued, markets are the way to allocate this scarce resource effectively.[8]

However, there has been significant resistance to the recommendation of the widespread implementation of water markets. Water markets have not spread nearly as quickly as their advocates would have hoped, and where they have been implemented, the drawbacks of such systems have become apparent.[9] Market-based approaches struggle to acknowledge or take account broader systemic issues such as inequality or environmental concerns.[10] For example, small-scale farmers can be priced out from water markets which are dominated by powerful commercial organisations with significant resources, and this can have grave

---

7 See discussion in J. Gray and L. Lee, "Water Entitlements as Property: A Work in Progress or Watertight Now?" in C. Holley and D. Sinclair (eds.), *Reforming Water Law and Governance: From Stagnation to Innovation in Australia*, Spinger, Singapore 2018; H. J. Bosch, J. Gupta and H. Verrest, "A Water Property Right Inventory of 60 Countries" (2021) 30 *Review of European, Comparative & International Environmental Law* 263; and in relation to constitutional protection of property rights in general, B. Akkermans, "A Comparative Overview of European, US and South African Constitutional Property Law" (2018) 7(1) *European Property Law Journal* 108.

8 T. R. Lee, *Water Management for the 21st Century: The Allocation Imperative*, Elgar, Cheltenham 1999; J.W. Dellapenna, "The Market Alternative" in J.W. Dellapenna and J. Gupta (eds.), *The Evolution of the Law and Politics of Water*, Springer, 2009; B. H. Thompson, "Water Markets Agonistes" in V. Casado-Pérez and R. Larson (eds.), *A Research Agenda for Water Law*, Elgar, Cheltenham 2023.

9 In relation to Chile, see C.J. Bauer, "Water Conflicts and Entrenched Governance Problems in Chile's Market Model" (2015) 8(2) *Water Alternatives* 147; M. Prieto, M.C. Fragkou and M. Calderón-Seguel, "Water Policy and Management in Chile" in P. Maurice (ed.), *Encyclopaedia of Water: Science, Technology and Society*, Wiley, New Jersey 2020 and discussion below.

10 See discussion, e.g., in C. Howe, "Water resource planning in a federation of states: Equity versus efficiency" (1996) 36 *Natural Resources Journal* 29; S. Gomez and P. Loh, "Communities and Water Markets: A Review of the Model Water Transfer Act" (2008) 14 *Hastings West-Northwest Journal of Environmental Law and Policy* 689.

implications for the viability of rural communities.[11] The contribution of water to ecosystems and the survival of non-human species is also not automatically factored into such approaches.[12] Therefore, there is a recognition that we need to adopt a holistic approach to water management which considers the broad range of interests involved, not just the economic value of water. Indeed, the concept of Integrated Water Resources Management (IWRM) has gained broad acceptance in water governance in recent years.[13] The Global Water Partnership defines IWRM as "*based on the equitable and efficient management and sustainable use of water and recognizes that water is an integral part of the ecosystem, a natural resource, and a social and economic good, whose quantity and quality determine the nature of its utilisation.*"[14]

B. PROTECTING MARGINALISED PEOPLE

The second theme in water law reform in a global context is the acknowledgement of the need to protect historically marginalised people. Modern water rights regimes are often characterised by systems where water rights are granted and regulated by the State through a formal process.[15] However, as VAN KOPPEN states, the "*more powerful and administration proficient benefit most from this. They can most easily obtain these first-class entitlements.*"[16] Modern water rights systems can therefore be dominated by those with the resources to understand the law, negotiate the rights regime and have their rights to use water legally recognised. This can be extremely detrimental in countries where there are plural water rights regimes and where water is governed by customary regimes, which are not appreciated or understood by State institutions.[17]

---

11 J.W. DELLAPENNA, "The Market Alternative" in J.W. DELLAPENNA and J. GUPTA (eds.), *The Evolution of the Law and Politics of Water*, Springer, 2009, pp. 381-382.

12 *Ibid.* pp. 381-383; C. HOLLEY and D. SINCLAIR, "Water Markets and Regulation: Implementation, Success and Limitations" in C. HOLLEY and D. SINCLAIR (eds.), *Reforming Water Law and Governance: From Stagnation to Innovation in Australia*, Springer, Singapore 2018.

13 In the context of the EU, see M. VAN RIJSWICK and A. KEESSEN, "The EU Approach for Integrated Water Resource Management: Transposing the EU Water Framework Directive within a National Context – Key Insights from Experience" in A. RIEU-CLARKE, A. ALLAN and S. HENDRY (eds.), *Routledge Handbook of Water Law and Policy*, Routledge, Abington 2017.

14 Global Water Partnership (GWP), "The Need for an Integrated Approach" (2017) www.gwp.org/en/About/why/the-need-for-an-integrated-approach/ accessed 28.09.2023.

15 S. HODGSON, "Modern Water Rights: Theory and Practice" Legislative Study 92, Food and Agriculture Organization of the United Nations, 2006, pp. 36-48; D. CAPONERA, *Principles of Water Law and Administration: National and International*, Routledge, Abington, 3rd edn., revised and updated by M. NANNI, 2018, pp.176-182.

16 B. VAN KOPPEN, "Customary Water Rights and Legal Pluralism" in A. RIEU-CLARKE, A. ALLAN and S. HENDRY (eds.), *Routledge Handbook of Water Law and Policy*, Routledge, Abington 2017, p. 18.

17 B. VAN KOPPEN, P. VAN DER ZAAG, E. MANZUNGU and B. TAPELA, "Roman Water Law in Rural Africa: the Unfinished Business of Colonial Dispossession" (2014) 39:1 *Water*

As a result, reform processes are considering the needs of those who have been historically disadvantaged through water rights regimes such as indigenous peoples and those without formal water rights. Debate is ongoing as how to best recognise and protect informal water uses and customary uses, which support the survival and livelihoods of a diverse range of small-scale users.[18] This movement runs together with how to implement the human right to water and sanitation, and what this means for water rights regimes.[19] Although the human right to water and sanitation is separate and distinct from water rights as defined above, water rights in all their forms are crucial to the realisation of the human right to water and other fundamental rights.[20] In this context, a human rights-based approach to IWRM has been proposed recently as a beneficial foundation for reformed water governance.[21] It is argued that a human rights-based approach can give a normative framework to IWRM, and can also assist prioritising and balancing the complex aims of IWRM. Further, a human rights-based approach can be supplemented by the systems approach of IWRM.[22]

C. REFORM TO TACKLE THE ECOLOGICAL EMERGENCY

Finally, urgent attention is being given to how water rights regimes need to be reformed to tackle the current ecological emergency including biodiversity loss and climate change.[23] Climate change is affecting the availability, quality

International 49; B. Van Koppen, "Customary Water Rights and Legal Pluralism" in A. Rieu-Clarke, A. Allan and S. Hendry (eds.), *Routledge Handbook of Water Law and Policy*, Routledge, Abington 2017.

18 See generally B. Van Koppen, G. Giordano and J. Butterworth (eds.), *Community-Based Water Law and Resource Management in Developing Countries*, Cabi, Wallingford 2007; B. Cosens, "Indigenous Rights to Water" in J.W. Dellapenna and J. Gupta (eds.), *Water Law: Elgar Encyclopaedia of Environmental Law*, Elgar, Cheltenham, Vol X, 2021.

19 See, e.g., I.T. Winkler, *The Human Right to Water: Significance, Legal Status and Implications for Water Allocation*, Hart Publishing, Oxford 2012; I.T. Winkler, "The Human Right to Water" in A. Rieu-Clarke, A. Allan and S. Hendry (eds.), *Routledge Handbook of Water Law and Policy*, Routledge, Abington 2017; M. Langford and A. F. S. Russell (eds.), *The Human Right to Water: Theory, Practice and Prospects*, Cambridge University Press, Cambridge 2017; E. Morgera et al, "The Right to Water for Food and Agriculture" Legislative Study 113, Food and Agriculture Organization of the United Nations, 2020.

20 L. Cotula, "The Property Rights Challenges of Improving Access to Water for Agriculture: Lessons from the Sahel" (2008) 9:1 *Journal of Human Development* 5; E. Morgera et al, "The Right to Water for Food and Agriculture" Legislative Study 113, Food and Agriculture Organization of the United Nations, 2020.

21 See WaterLex et al, "Human Rights-Based Approach to Integrated Water Resources Management", 2017.

22 See discussion in E Morgera et al, "The Right to Water for Food and Agriculture" Legislative Study 113, Food and Agriculture Organization of the United Nations, 2020, pp. 77-100.

23 J.W. Dellapenna and J. Gupta, "Water Law: its Role, Shortcomings, and Potential" in J.W. Dellapenna and J. Gupta (eds.), *Water Law: Elgar Encyclopaedia of Environmental Law*, Elgar. Cheltenham, Vol X, 2021, pp.493-494.

and quantity of water across the world, as well as increasing the frequency and magnitude of extreme weather events such as heatwaves and storms, which all contribute to uncertainty regarding environmental conditions.[24] This puts pressure on water rights regimes, which may have been based on environmental conditions which no longer exist or which are constantly changing. This can mean that there is a misalignment between "paper water rights" and the "wet water" availability, especially where there has been overallocation of water rights.[25] This is a stark example of what Graham calls de-physicalisation of property rights, where the law does not reflect the underlying physical conditions.[26] The disconnect between legal and physical reality facilitates the overexploitation of water resources and does not provide sufficient protection for ecosystems and non-human communities.[27]

Discussion inevitably leads to suggesting greater State control over allocated water rights in order to reallocate or limit rights in the event of sudden scarcity or other crisis.[28] However, regulators may then be faced with the argument that this interferes with constitutionally protected property rights.[29] Adaptive management, where governance is required to flex and respond to changing needs and conditions involving multiple actors operating at different scales, clashes against the argument that strong and stable property rights held by individuals are needed in order to incentivise efficient water use and investment in water infrastructure.[30]

This brief overview only mentions three of the many themes, and challenges, which exist in relation to reforming water law in a global context.[31] However,

---

24 See overview in United Nations, World Water Development Report 2020: Water and Climate Change, 2020.

25 See in relation to Chile, C.J. Bauer, "Water Conflicts and Entrenched Governance Problems in Chile's Market Model" (2015) 8(2) *Water Alternatives* 147; R. Burgos, "The Current Reform of the Chilean Water Code: An Attempt to Contest the Commoditised Treatment of Water" (2017) TLI Think! Paper 82/217.

26 N. Graham, "Dephysicalised Property and Shadow Lands" in R. Bartel and J. Carter (eds.), *Handbook on Law, Space and Place,* Elgar, Cheltenham 2021. See also N. Graham, *Lawscape: Property, Environment and Law*, Routledge, Abington 2011.

27 M. Davis, L. Godden and N. Graham, "Situating Property within Habitat: Reintegrating Place, People, and the Law" (2021) 6 *Journal of Law, Property and Society* 1.

28 See, e.g., R. Craig, "Adapting Water Law to Public Necessity: Reframing Climate Change Adaptation as Emergency Response and Preparedness" (2010) 11(4) *Vermont Journal of Environmental Law* 709.

29 C.J. Bauer, "Water Conflicts and Entrenched Governance Problems in Chile's Market Model" (2015) 8(2) *Water Alternatives* 147.

30 N. L. Engle et al, "Integrated and Adaptive Management of Water Resources: Tensions, Legacies, and the Next Best Thing" 2011 16(1) *Ecology and Society* 19; K. Akamani, "The Role of Adaptive Water Governance in Enhancing the Transition towards Ecosystem-Based Adaptation" (2023) 15 *Water* 2341. See also T. Dietz, E. Ostrom and P. C. Stern, "The Struggle to Govern the Commons" (2003) 302 *Science* 1907.

31 For others see, J.W. Dellapenna and J. Gupta, "Water Law: its Role, Shortcomings, and Potential" in J.W. Dellapenna and J. Gupta (eds.), *Water Law: Elgar Encyclopaedia of Environmental Law*, Elgar, Cheltenham, Vol X, 2021, pp.493-494.

what is clear is that water rights, and property rights more generally, must be reconsidered in the light of stark and intersecting worldwide problems. Due to the diversity of human communities, ecosystems, climates and geographies around the world, there is no one-size-fits-all solution to these problems. Nevertheless, lessons can be learned from jurisdictions which have undertaken radical transformations in the governance of their natural resources.[32] The next section will provide an overview of the reform processes in Chile in relation to water and conclude with reflections on the broader implications of the Chilean experience.

III. NEO-LIBERAL WATER: THE RADICAL CHILEAN WATER RIGHTS APPROACH

This section analyses the complexity of property law reforms in times of ecological emergency by taking the Chilean water rights system and its radical market approach as a case study. First, the section will provide a little historical context to help the reader understand the circumstances under which Chile developed a radical market approach to water rights. Then, it will give an overview of the two main legal instruments supporting the Chilean neo-liberal system of water rights, namely, the Water Code and the 1980 Chilean Constitution, and their critical consequences for inequality and ecosystem protection. The section will then go onto examine the challenges and difficulties of the reform processes in relation to the Water Code and the Constitution, illustrating the long influence of the imposed neo-liberal regime in Chilean water policies. Finally, in the light of the result of the 2022 Chilean referendum, the section offers some broader considerations for developing property law reforms in the context of global challenges.

A. IMPOSING A NEW REGIME

In 1973, Chile suffered a *coup* led by military forces which overthrew the democratically elected government of President Salvador Allende.[33] The dictator Augusto Pinochet remained in power for years until democratic political

32 South Africa is another jurisdiction which has dramatically reformed its water laws and polices after the end of Apartheid, see overview in M. Kidd, "South Africa: The Development of Water Law" in in J.W. Dellapenna and J. Gupta (eds.), *The Evolution of the Law and Politics of Water*, Springer, 2009.

33 L.Z. Qureshi, *Nixon, Kissinger, and Allende: U.S. Involvement in the 1973 Coup in Chile*, Lexington Books, Maryland 2008.

parties won the 1988 referendum on 5 October.[34] In addition to the atrocities and human rights violations committed during this period[35], the dictatorship implemented several neo-liberal policies in essential sectors of the economy.[36] The neo-liberal thinker Milton Friedman introduced a radical market approach to the Chilean economy through former Chilean students of the University of Chicago (the Chicago Boys).[37] This approach aimed to privatise all sectors of the economy, reducing the State to having merely a subsidiary role.[38]

A key instrument used for institutionalising a radical market approach to several sectors of the Chilean economy was the 1980 Constitution, which still rules the country, and which has a strong emphasis on protecting private property rights.[39] Pensions, healthcare, and natural resources were reformed under the Pinochet Constitution, seeking to privatise most of the services and State assets. Regarding water rights, the 1980 Constitution was complemented by the Water Code of 1981.[40] Under this legal framework, water resources also became privatised.[41] The 1980 Constitution and the 1981 Water Code were the central legal instruments supporting the privatisation of water resources, and are important in different ways.

B. THE 1980 CONSTITUTION AND 1981 WATER CODE

It is crucial to explain how these legal instruments imposed the privatisation of water rights in the Chilean legal system. Although Article 5 of the Water Code recognised water as a public good, it also stated that "*individuals are granted*

---

34 "Chile's 1988 Plebiscite and the End of Pinochet's Dictatorship – Association for Diplomatic Studies & Training" https://adst.org/2014/11/chiles-1988-plebiscite-and-the-end-of-pinochets-dictatorship/ accessed 21.08.2023.

35 M. Klein, "The Human Rights Violations of the Pinochet Regime and Their Legacy" (2003) *Revista Europea de Estudios Latinoamericanos y del Caribe / European Review of Latin American and Caribbean Studies* 107.

36 A.J. Bruey, "Neoliberalism in Chile", in *Oxford Research Encyclopedia of Latin American History*, Oxford University Press, Oxford 2020.

37 S. Edwards, *The Chile Project: The Story of the Chicago Boys and the Downfall of Neoliberalism*, Princeton University Press, Princeton 2023, p. 71.

38 *Ibid.* p. 111.

39 B. Alemparte, "Towards a Theory of Neoliberal Constitutionalism: Addressing Chile's First Constitution-Making Laboratory" (2022) 11 *Global Constitutionalism* 83.

40 C.J. Bauer, "Bringing Water Markets down to Earth: The Political Economy of Water Rights in Chile, 1976–1995" (1997) 25 *World Development* 639, 641.

41 *Ibid.* Bauer has written extensively, in English, on the water regime in Chile. See, e.g., C.J. Bauer, *Against the Current: Privatization, Water Markets and the State in Chile*, Springer, New York 1998; C.J. Bauer, *Siren Song: Chilean Water Law as a Model for International Reform*, Routledge, Abington 2004; C.J. Bauer, "Dams and Markets: Rivers and Electric Power in Chile" 2010 49(3-4) *Natural Resources Journal* 583; C.J. Bauer, "Water Conflicts and Entrenched Governance Problems in Chile's Market Model" (2015) 8(2) Water Alternatives 147. See also G. Donoso (ed.), *Water Policy in Chile*, Springer, 2018.

the right to use [water], *in accordance with the provisions of this Code.*"[42] Furthermore, in Article 6, the same legal instrument established that water rights have similar protection and characteristics to property rights, making them transferable like any other good.[43] The rule specifies that "*the right to use water is the domain of its owner, who may use, enjoy and dispose of it in accordance with the law* [i.e. the Water Code]."[44] Further, the 1980 Constitution, in its Article 19.24[45], establishing private property as a fundamental right, determines that "*the rights of individuals, constituted or recognised in accordance with the law, will grant their holders ownership over them.*"[46] Therefore, according to this rule, the holders of rights to use water have ownership of these rights, and the Constitution protects that dominion. This protection arises from the constitutional protections established in Article 19, paragraph 20 of the 1980 Constitution[47], according to which owners cannot be threatened, disturbed, or deprived of the free exercise of their rights.

Clarifying this strong protection of property rights over water use, the Chilean Constitutional Court in 1997 indicated that "*the Constitution ensures dominion not over the waters themselves, which constitute national assets for public use, but over the right to use them constituted in accordance with the law.*"[48] Considering all the above, the recognition made by Article 5 of the Chilean Water Code regarding water as a public good is negated by several conditions and limitations which aim to reduce the State's role in water management and to empower the private one. Therefore, the notion of water as a public good was more an illusion than a real and practicable concept.

The understanding of establishing ownership over rights, such as in the case of the right to use water, is part of an accepted theory within legal Chilean literature, the "reification of rights".[49] This notion argues that the Chilean private law system[50], conceives of rights as objects of property, turning them into commodities transferable in markets like any other good. This approach is based on an interpretation of Article 576 of the Chilean Civil Code and Article 19.24 of the Chilean Constitution, which defines "*there is property over corporeal and incorporeal goods*", including any right in the latter category.[51]

42 Water Code 1981, Art. 5.

43 *Ibid.* Art. 6.

44 *Ibid.*

45 Constitution of the Republic of Chile, 1980, Art. 19, para. 24. See discussion in V. Ponce de León Solís, "Property Over Incorporeal Goods: The Cornerstone of the Chilean Neoliberal Constitution" in J. Robbie and B. Akkermans (eds.), *Property Law Perspectives VIII*, Eleven, The Hague 2021.

46 Constitution of the Republic of Chile, 1980, Art. 19, para. 24.

47 *Ibid.* Art. 19, para. 20.

48 Chilean Constitutional Court, 260, para. 8, 1997.

49 See, D. Penailillo, Los Bienes, 2022, p.22. In Spanish, "*la cosificación de derechos*".

50 *Ibid.*

51 *Ibid.* p.24.

As a result, water rights are also property objects operating under this category.

Another vital element of water regulation in Chile is the concept of neutrality.[52] The Chilean literature uses this concept to explain that the 1981 Water Code did not define any priority use or condition for consuming or transferring water rights. This neutrality in allocating water rights restricted the States capacity to guarantee minimum water rights to those who are particularly vulnerable and in need, or to define limits on consuming water to protect the ecological functions of the environment.

The elements described above permitted the development of a de-regulated water market that functioned as with any other commodity, ignoring water's ecological and social functions. Supply and demand determined the allocation of water, benefiting those with more resources to acquire and use water rights, to the detriment of historical marginalised people and ecosystems.[53] As no condition of use or priority was established, speculation was also a common practice and in 1997, the General Direction of Water "*estimated that 87% of the granted non-consumptive use rights*" were unused.[54] Indeed, all of these factors represent an undesirable scenario for achieving the standards analysed in the first section of this chapter, and reforms were urgently needed to achieve improved distributive and sustainable outcomes.

C. PROBLEMATIC REFORMS: WATER CODE REFORM AND CONSTITUTIONAL PROCESSES

Since the arrival of democracy in Chile, some reforms to the Water Code have been implemented. However, they have not substantively affected the neo-liberal core of the water rights system in the country. For instance, law 20.017 from 2005[55] established a minimum ecological flow[56], defined as the "*minimum*

52 A. Vergara Blanco, "Bases y dogmas que permiten o impiden mercados de derechos de aguas: mercado en Chile y cuasi mercado en España" (2018) *Revista de Administración Pública* 339, 346.

53 J. Budds, "Power, Nature and Neoliberalism: The Political Ecology of Water in Chile" (2004) 25(3) *Singapore Journal of Tropical Geography* 322; J. Budds, "The 1981 Water Code: The Impacts of Private Tradable Water Rights on Peasant and Indigenous Communities in Northern Chile" in W. Alexander, *Lost in the Long Transition: Struggles for Social Justice in Neoliberal Chile,* Lexington Books, Maryland 2009; D. A. Lovera Parmo, "Indigenous Peoples and the Sale of Water Rights: The Case of Chile" in M. Langford and A. F. S. Russell (eds.), *The Human Right to Water: Theory, Practice and Prospects*, Cambridge University Press, Cambridge 2017.

54 R. Hearne and G. Donoso, "Water Markets in Chile: Are They Meeting Needs?" in K W. Easter and Q. Huang (eds.), *Water Markets for the 21st Century: What Have We Learned?*, Springer, 2014, p. 111.

55 Law 20.017, Reforming Water Code, 2005.

56 *Ibid.* Art. 129 bis.

value of discharge that needs to be maintained in a river to ensure good (or optimum) conditions for the existing ecosystems."[57] In establishing water rights, this minimum ecological flow requires to be defined. This reform intended to make relevant progress in assessing the environmental aspects of watercourses; however, in reality, its effectiveness is questionable. First, although Article 129*bis* of the law 20.017 incorporates the minimum ecological flow; the rule does not apply to those with already constituted water rights, applying only to rights established in 2005 onwards.

Second, the bill of this reform was introduced in 1992 by the government of Patricio Aylwin, and warned that "*the accumulation of water rights in a disproportionate manner without any current or foreseeable future use, but only the possibility of profiting from them* [...] *constitutes the seed of severe difficulties for the future development of the country.*"[58] This declaration reflects the long awareness of Chile's scarcity and accumulation of water resources, notably before the current critical climate situation. In parliamentary sources, there are also statements by reformer senators who ended up approving the reform project but criticising the small progress achieved by the reform.[59] Indeed, adopted after twelve years of legislative procedures due to strong opposition from conservative voices, the project's original aims changed substantively, illustrating the difficulty of reforming the law to limit the water rights of already constituted holders in the context of strongly protected constitutional rights.

Reflecting the inability of the Water Code to deal with the social and ecological challenges of water resources in Chile, in 2011, parliamentarians from progressive political parties presented a bill for reforming the water rights regime comprehensively. The parliamentary proposal identified the overarching reasons for water rights reform initiatives in Chile between 1992 and 2010. The list included the restatement of water as a public good, the recognition of the multiple functions of water to solve the accumulation of water rights, and the protection of the environment in establishing and utilising water rights. After a decade of discussion, a process of reform has made water rights more suitable for responding to ecological and social crises.[60] The 21.435 law of 2022 modified the Water Code, incorporating, amongst other elements, priority uses of water, ecosystem approaches, the recognition of the human right to water, and the temporality in establishing water rights. The latter was the most polemic point of the legislative discussion, where conservative parties insisted that water rights should be set in perpetuity because making them time-limited

---

57 M. Greco, Francesco Arbia and R. Giampietro, "Definition of Ecological Flow Using IHA and IARI as an Operative Procedure for Water Management" (2021) 8 *Environments* 77, 1.

58 See, Law 20.017, History of the Law, available at: www.bcn.cl/leychile/navegar?idNorma=239221 accessed 30.08.2023.

59 See, *Ibid.*

60 *Ibid.*

affects the juridical security of the system and the development of long-term investments.[61]

Specifically, the reformed Article 5 of the Water Code incorporated an interesting approach, asserting that establishing water rights is "*based on the public interest*"[62] and they "*may be limited in their exercise.*"[63] Public interest in this context means safeguarding human consumption and sanitation, ecosystem preservation, water availability, aquifer sustainability, and, in general, is aimed at promoting a balance between social, economic and environmental needs in the use of the water. Furthermore, the same rule recognised the human right to water and ended with the neutrality principle by stating that "*the use for human consumption, domestic subsistence use and sanitation will always prevail.*"[64] However, there are still ongoing challenges in relation to water management because the basic principles of a market-based system remain unchanged, with the maintenance of a strong constitutional protection of property rights at its core.

At the level of constitutional reform, there have been attempts to completely overhaul the market-based water rights system. In parallel to the reforms of the Water Code, the Constitutional Convention established by the 2021 referendum discussed the recognition of water rights in the constitutional draft. The Convention draft defined water in Article 134 as a common good and not subject to property.[65] This rule was under notable scrutiny, mainly because it would have completely transformed the water rights system instituted since 1981. To replace the existing system, the constitutional draft proposed administrative authorisations for water use, assigned by the State as the custodian of water resources. This constitutional draft was rejected in a referendum in 2022[66], where although polls showed necessary support for stating that water is a common good, this could not be said about other aspects of the constitutional reforms.

---

61 This is a classic neo-liberal argument that seeks to protect and strengthen existing property rights. See V. Casado-Pérez, "Missing Water Markets: A Cautionary Tale of Government Failure" (2015) N.Y.U. Envtl. L.J. 157; B. H. Thompson, "Water Markets Agonistes" in V. Casado-Pérez and R. Larson (eds.), *A Research Agenda for Water Law*, Elgar, Cheltenham 2023.

62 Water Code, Art. 5 reformed by Law 21.435.

63 *Ibid.*

64 *Ibid.*

65 Constitutional Convention Draft, 2022, Art. 134; on the difference between common good and public good, see, M. de Jongh, "Public Goods and the Commons: Opposites or Complements?" (2021) 49(5) *Political Theory* 774-800. The interpretation of private, public and common property is highly context dependent in relation to water rights, see discussion in J. Robbie, "Water Rights" in J.M. Smits, J. Husa, C. Valcke and M. Narciso (eds.), *Elgar Encyclopaedia of Comparative Law*, Elgar, Cheltenham 2023, p. 587.

66 See, The Guardian, "Chile Votes Overwhelmingly to Reject New, Progressive Constitution" (4th Sept 2022) available at: www.theguardian.com/world/2022/sep/05/chile-votes-overwhelmingly-to-reject-new-progressive-constitution, accessed 05.10.2022.

On 6 March 2023, Chile started a second constitutional process, where a democratically elected body was responsible for developing another draft. Regarding water rights, the Constitutional Council proposal recognised the right to water and the priority of human use. Still, it continued recognising individual property notions but incorporated the limitations and restrictions defined by the law in accordance with the latest Water Code reform. In addition, in its transitional clauses, the constitutional proposal protected the water use rights recognised by the 1980 Constitution, limiting any chance of redistributing water resources.

In general, the draft took a more conservative approach in different aspects but again there was rejection of the proposal in the Constitutional Referendum held on 17 December 2023. In the end, after decades of legislative discussions, the Water Code reform and two constitutional processes, the same market-based approach developed under the 1980 Constitution and the 1981 Water Code, however nuanced, will remain in place. Despite the progress achieved by the 2022 Water Code reform in improving the distribution of water and ecological functions, there are still negative social and environmental impacts due to the water rights regime in place, and the concentration of water rights remains problematic. According to a recent 2020 study, 1% of the water rights holders have 79.02% of the total volume of water available in the system.[67]

D. PROPERTY RIGHTS AMID POLITICAL DEBATE

The changing approaches in Chile, from radical market notions to proposals eliminating property rights over water, illustrate a deep political debate and notable ideological confrontations. Historically, property is a central topic in political debates, developed under different ideologies and is a crucial factor in defining political relations.[68] As stated by Fox O'Mahony and Roark, private property "*performs an important role in mediating relationships between individuals and the state, as these are played out in the context of economic, social and cultural values in each jurisdiction. By examining how states regulate property relationships (including who has access to property claims), we can better*

67 J. Correa-Parra, J.F. Vergara-Perucich and C. Aguirre-Nuñez, "Water Privatization and Inequality: Gini Coefficient for Water Resources in Chile" (2020) 12 *Water* 3369.

68 See, e.g., A.J. van der Walt, "The South African Law of Ownership: A Historical and Philosophical Perspective" (1992) 25 *De Jure* 446; A.J. van der Walt, "Tradition on Trial: A Critical Analysis of the Civil-Law Tradition in South African Property Law (1995) 11:2 *South African Journal on Human Rights* 169; G. Muller, G. J. Pienaar, R. Brits, B. V. Slade and J. van Wyk (eds.), *Transformative Property Law: Festschrift in Honour of A J van der Walt*, Juta, Cape Town 2018; L. Brace, *The Politics of Property: Labour, Freedom and Belonging*, Edinburgh University Press, Edinburgh 2022; L. Fox O'Mahony and M. L. Roark, *Squatting and the State: Resilient Property in an Age of Crisis*, Cambridge University Press, Cambridge 2022.

understand what it means to be a member of that society."[69] As property is such a sensitive issue, any transformative change involving property rights requires consideration of the multiple factors at play in that particular jurisdiction. As van der Walt noted, "*ownership as a legal institution is shaped by its social function in a particular society, and that it will take on different forms in different societies and at different times.*"[70]

The current situation in Chile is that, despite being highly vulnerable to future climate change impacts[71], suffering severe droughts and experiencing a critical problem of inequality in relation to water rights, the country is still immersed in a system based mainly on market paradigms and the constitutional protection of property rights over water. This is evidence of the lasting influence of the legal structures imposed by the dictatorship and the strong opposition to any meaningful change from conservative political wings which have created obstacles to any substantive reform.

Considering the above, it was perhaps surprising that the Chilean people rejected a constitutional draft which proposed to reform the water rights regime extensively; a draft which emphasised the public interest in water and its ecological and environmental functions. However, it is important to understand that all proposals about property law in this time of ecological crisis require consideration of the feasibility of those changes, both at legislative and constitutional level. Political factors play a significant role in defining the success or failure of any reforming intention, especially when property is at the centre of the debate. Although many of the transformative views appear logical or necessary to scholars and politicians, the way those transformations are presented for public support is also essential. The 2022 Chilean referendum shows that even though many constitutional reforms are needed to make the Chilean legal system equitable and sustainable, especially regarding water, the people decided otherwise. This is the challenge of attempting transformative change in a modern, democratic context. Although the existing regime was imposed during a dictatorship, the overhaul of that regime must be achieved through a deliberative, participatory, and democratic process.

There are many lessons to learn from the Chilean case study regarding the feasibility of democratic transformations at the legislative or constitutional level on topics related to property law. First, it is essential to acknowledge that, despite the existing evidence of the lack of sustainability, the unfairness, and the accumulation which characterises a particular resource distribution system,

---

69 L. Fox O'Mahony and M. L. Roark, *Squatting and the State: Resilient Property in an Age of Crisis*, Cambridge University Press, Cambridge 2022, p. 24.

70 A.J. van der Walt, "The South African Law of Ownership: A Historical and Philosophical Perspective" (1992) 25 *De Jure* 446, 448.

71 Chilean Government, Nationally Determined Contributions, 2020, p.17, available at: https://cambioclimatico.mma.gob.cl/wp-content/uploads/2020/08/NDC_2020_Espanol_PDF_web.pdf accessed 05.10.2023.

reforming such a system by incorporating ecological and distributive justice notions is complex and takes time. In Chile, there is significant consensus that the neo-liberal approach to water rights will not result in a fair distribution of water resources or the protection of ecosystems, especially when factoring in the impacts of climate change. However, the Chilean citizens voted to maintain an unfair and unsustainable water rights regime regardless. How to implement the necessary change to tackle the global challenges of inequality and ecological emergency, while giving due regard to the time, resources and deliberation which are necessary, is an intractable problem facing law reformers.

Second, debates around property, such as water rights in the Chilean constitutional referendum, are the target of fake news.[72] Abstract concepts, such as property rights, are difficult to explain in electoral campaigns, especially binary referendums where the question requires a "yes" or "no" answer.[73] The political campaigns supporting reforms require a deep understanding of the concepts in discussion but also need strategies to communicate these concepts in clear and accessible ways. If the campaigns around property topics are fragmented and intangible in political debates, spreading fake news to block reform proposals is effortless. The 2022 Chilean referendum, specifically the debate around water and housing, highlights the importance of establishing simple language to communicate with citizens and gain their support in reforming property law systems.

Finally, as legal systems confront the effects of the ecological emergency, transitions to new legal approaches will become more frequent. In this context, debates and decisions around adapting property law to changing environmental conditions will be central to the political debate.[74] In this context, how transformative property law approaches incorporate public discussion into their proposals will be crucial to the feasibility of achieving urgent reforms to face ecological challenges.[75] We require to bridge the gap between the theoretical debates about transformation, and the lived reality of the communities and environments most in need, in order to learn how to effect the reform which is necessary.

---

72 See, Reuters, "Chile Battles Flood of 'Half Truths' as Constitution Vote Nears" (8th August 2022) available at: www.reuters.com/world/americas/chile-battles-flood-half-truths-constitution-vote-nears-2022-08-29 accessed 05.10.2023.

73 The Scottish independence referendum and Brexit referendum experience also show the difficulty of voting "yes" or "no" to a question which will have dramatic and complex consequences.

74 See also H. Doremus, "Climate Change and the Evolution of Property Rights" (2011) 1 *U.C. Irvine L. Rev.* 1091.

75 How to achieve deliberation within constitutional reform processes is not easy in itself – see O. Doyle and R. Walsh, "Constitutional Amendment and Public Will Formation: Deliberative Mini-Publics as a Tool for Consensus Democracy" (2022) 20(1) *International Journal of Constitutional Law* 398.

IV. CONCLUSION

In recent years, the field of law and sustainability has been maturing with the result that we now have many concepts, approaches, toolkits and frameworks to draw upon when drafting our water rights, property law and constitutional reform proposals. How these reform proposals make the journey from the realm of academic literature to the statute book, together with the legitimacy to effect change on the ground, is, however, still work in progress. Countries which have experienced or are attempting dramatic transformations, such as Chile, have much to teach us in this context. In these countries, the property debates are in the open air, and the advocates on either side of the debate are unmasked. It is obvious how much is at stake in these discussions, and how the unpredictable nature of political debate will continue to produce obstacles to necessary change.

However, the public awareness of human impacts on the wellbeing and critical functioning of both human communities and ecosystems has arguably never been higher. As part of this raised awareness, momentum is building towards initiatives, proposals and transformations which challenge the destructive patterns and institutional structures of the past. The Chilean constitutional draft from 2022 represents one of these initiatives. Although it did not succeed, it is part of a trajectory towards a changed paradigm where our laws and policies operate equitably within the ecological carrying capacity of the planet. The lessons learned in Chile will now be useful for future initiatives which seek to achieve a transition to sustainability.

OWNERSHIP OF UNDERGROUND RESOURCES IN ICELAND NEW ISSUES AND CHALLENGES

Víðir Smári PETERSEN
Professor, University of Iceland
External PhD Candidate, University of Maastricht

I. INTRODUCTION[1]

The classic *ad coelum* rule[2], where the vertical ownership of land extended up to "heaven" and down to "hell" became impractical in the 20th century. The revolution in transportation, when airplanes could fly in airspace and trains could run underground, raised questions about the content of *ad coelum*. A literal interpretation of the rule would mean that a pilot committed trespass every time she flew over private property without permission. In 1946, the US Supreme Court claimed in *United States v Cosby* that *ad coelum*, at least its classical version, had "*no place in the modern world*" because the airspace had become "*a public highway*".[3]

One alternative to the *ad coelum*, common in many jurisdictions, is a rule where the landowner enjoys the spaces above and below her surface to the extent necessary for the ordinary enjoyment and use of the property.[4] For the sake of clarity, we can call these types of alternatives "ordinary use" rules. Another

---

1 A paper on the same topic has already been published by the author in Icelandic. See V. PETERSEN, "Eignarréttur að auðlindum í jörðu – Ný álitaefni og áskoranir" (2022) 72 *Tímarit lögfræðinga* 383-430. However, this book chapter is not a translation of the Icelandic paper. It has been largely rewritten to better suit an international audience. The Icelandic version also contains more discussion on issues that are nuanced and/or local. The author has largely skipped those discussions in the main body of this book chapter, but some of it is included in the footnotes.

2 The full name of the rule is *Cuius est solum, eius est usque ad coelum et ad inferos*, which translates to English as "*one who owns the soil owns also the sky and to the depths.*" See e.g., T.W. MERRILL and H.E. SMITH, *The Oxford Introductions to U.S. Law: Property*, Oxford University Press, New York 2010, pp 31-32.

3 United States v. Causby, 328 U.S. 256, 261 (1946).

4 See e.g., L.D. LASHBROOK, "Ad Coelum Maxim as Applied to Aviation Law" (1946) 21 *Notre Dame L. Rev.* 143, 144.

alternative are bright-line rules where ownership is defined by an objective measurement. There are myriads of possibilities to designing such rules. An example would be to state that ownership is limited to a certain depth, say 500 meters. Hot water and geothermal power could also be defined by temperature or even the method of drilling. Laws can also prescribe that certain specifically defined resources are subject to ownership, but others, such as oil and gas, are beyond the landowner's rights. Again, for the sake of clarity, we can call these alternatives (in whatever form) objective rules.

The purpose of this paper is to discuss certain issues and questions about ownership of underground resources in Icelandic law. The primary legislation on this issue is Act No 57/1998 on Underground Resources, which covers geothermal heat, groundwater and other matters that can be found underground, including minerals, oil, and gas.[5] Oil has not (yet) been discovered in Iceland, but the most important resources that are subject to the laws are geothermal heat and groundwater. More than 95% of drinking water in Iceland is extracted from groundwater sources.[6] Moreover, more than 90% of domestic heating is driven by geothermal power and geothermal is also responsible for around 30% of our electricity production (the remaining 70% is hydropower).[7] Despite the great importance of underground resources in Iceland, there is still legal uncertainty as to whether ownership is covered by an "ordinary use" rule or an objective one.

In this paper I will address the following four questions: (1) Does the principle of "ordinary use" still apply in Iceland, despite the entry into force of Act No 57/1998 on Underground Resources? (2) How should we determine the landowner's underground ownership? Does the landowner have property rights as deep as his financial means allow (an individualized rule), or should the right only extend to a depth that is ordinary for the general use of the land (a general rule)? (3) Who owns the resources at a depth beyond the landowner's private property rights? Are those resources ownerless, or owned by the State? (4) Can the State pass legislation with an objective rule on the ownership of natural resources (for instance that such rights are limited to a depth of 500 meters), without paying compensation to landowners?

Although the paper has an Icelandic focus, the results can hopefully be applied in other jurisdictions that have similar problems. Indeed, many jurisdictions must be dealing with the question of what amounts to "ordinary use" and how it should be determined.

---

5 The use of surface water is not subject to Act No 57/1998 but falls instead under the Water Act No 15/1923.

6 E.D. Sveinbjörnsdóttir, "Hvaðan fáum við kranavatnið?" [2008] *Vísindavefurinn* www.visindavefur.is/svar.php?id=50312, accessed 27.09.2023.

7 OS-2020-T008-01: *Húshitun á Íslandi eftir orkugjafa 1952-2019* (Excel sheet from the National Energy Regulatory) and OS-2021-T009-01, https://orkustofnun.is/gogn/Talnaefni/OS-2021-T009-01.pdf, accessed 27.09.2023.

II. ORDINARY USE OR "DOWN TO HELL"?

Until 1998, it was widely accepted by Icelandic scholars in the 20th century that an unwritten principle applied to ownership of underground resources. According to this principle, the ownership of underground resources extended to a depth which was considered necessary for the landowner to use their property in an ordinary or reasonable manner.[8] This rule can rightly be called the unwritten principle of "ordinary use".

In 1998, Act No 57/1998 on Underground Resources came into force. According to Article 3 of the Act, the owner of private property has *ownership* of underground resources. There is no reference to ordinary use in the provision or an indication that ownership rights are limited in any way. The obvious question is then, did Article 3 of the 1998 Natural Resources Act override or repeal the unwritten principle of ordinary use? Did the surface owner suddenly become the owner of all underground resources "down to hell"?

The Supreme Court came close to answering this question in two decisions from 2008 but was hesitant to clearly state how the two rules should interact.[9] To simplify, I will focus on the case that concerned the Almannaskarð-tunnel.[10] In 2004, the Icelandic Road Administration started building a tunnel in the Southeast of Iceland through Almannaskarð. To commence the tunnel project, the Road Administration had to expropriate several properties, as is customary in such projects. In one of the cases, the Road Administration refused to pay compensation for certain minerals, mostly gravel and rock, that were incidentally discovered while digging through the property. According to an expert estimate, it was around 150 times more expensive to dig for these minerals than the selling price was on an open market. The minerals were deep in the ground and the market price was low. Therefore, it would have been terribly inefficient for the landowner to dig for the minerals on her own. Because of this inefficiency, the Supreme Court held that the minerals did not belong to the surface owner *neither* according to the unwritten principle (because it was not an ordinary use to dig for simple minerals at a great depth) *nor* Article 3 of the 1998 Natural Resources Act (because the inefficiency meant that the minerals

---

8 See e.g., Ó. Lárusson, *Eignaréttur I*, Hlaðbúð, Reykjavík 1950, p. 46; Þ. Örlygsson, "Um eignarhald á landi og náttúruauðlindum" in K. Jónasdóttir et al. (eds), *Afmælisrit: Gaukur Jörundsson sextugur*, Bókaútgáfa Orators, Reykjavík 1994, p. 559; V.M. Matthíasson, *Fasteignir og fasteignakaup*, Bókaútgáfan Codex, Reykjavík 2008, p. 120; Kristín Haraldsdóttir: "Introduction to the Legal Environment in Iceland for Utilisation of Geothermal" [2010, published online 2015] *Journal of Energy & Natural Resources Law*, 28:1, 18-19, DOI: 10.1080/02646811.2010.11435236, accessed 27.09.2023. See also a further analysis of the academic discussion in V. Petersen, *supra* note 1, 391-394.

9 *Hrd. 21 February 2008 (644 and 645/2006).*

10 That is case *No 644/2006*. The other case, *No 645/2006*, concerned a different tunnel in Fáskrúðsfjörður.

were in fact not a *resource* within the meaning of the Act[11]). The Supreme Court applied both rules simultaneously without explaining why.

At a minimum, it can be inferred by the decision that the Court did not believe that Article 3 of the Natural Resources Act repealed the unwritten principle completely. Otherwise, the Court would not have referred to the principle. But do both rules apply, and which one should prevail in case of conflict? Even though both rules pointed in the same direction in the Almannaskarð-case, there can be tension between them. Let us imagine a geothermal deep drilling project 4 kilometers into the ground. This can be an efficient project if the surface owner can sell access to the resource for more than it costs to drill for it. But it will be difficult to argue that drilling 4 kilometers into the ground amounts to "ordinary use" by the owner. Indeed, it would be very unusual for the average surface owner to be engaged in such a project. What should then happen when there is a conflict between the two rules? Is it sufficient to establish ownership of an underground resource, according to Article 3 of the 1998 Natural Resources Act, to prove that the exploration and processing of it is efficient?

The two rules can be reconciled by interpreting Article 3 in accordance with the unwritten principle. Such reconciliation can justify the Supreme Court's decision and it also seems to be consistent with the will of the legislature. The preparatory works of the Natural Resources Act suggest that the purpose of Article 3 was *not* to change what had previously been considered the applicable law, but rather to clarify that the right amounted to *ownership* of all underground resources but not merely a right to use certain resources.[12] It is specifically stated in the preparatory works that the purpose was to *confirm* (in Icelandic: *staðfest*) that the owner of the surface also owned underground resources, which was held to be consistent with the widely accepted view about the content of surface ownership.[13] Thus, there are convincing arguments for interpreting Article 3 in accordance with the unwritten principles, which means that underground resources are still owned with the implied assumption that the ownership only extends to a depth which is considered a part of the landowner's ordinary use

---

11 This part of the decision has been criticized by Icelandic scholars. They have argued that efficiency is not a condition for a mineral to be considered a resource according to Act No 57/1998. The Supreme Court could, instead, have argued that the minerals amounted to a resource but that the landowner should not be compensated because it was incredibly inefficient to explore and exploit it. Thus, he did not suffer any loss. See Þ. Örlygsson, K. Axelsson and V. Petersen, *Eignaréttur I: Almennur hluti*, Fons Juris, Reykjavík 2020, pp. 41-42 and 47.

12 Alþt. 1997-1998, A-deild, p. 2562. Before 1998 there were specific laws on the rights to use minerals and geothermal heat, but no specific laws or provisions on, for instance, groundwater, oil, or gas. The purpose of Act No 57/1998 was to unequivocally state that *all* resources were subject to the landowner's ownership, and to clarify that the landowner's rights amounted to ownership but not merely rights to use.

13 Alþt. 1997-1998, A-deild, p. 2564.

of her property. Consequently, the rule of ordinary use is still alive and well in Icelandic law.

III. HOW SHOULD THE UNDERGROUND OWNERSHIP BE DETERMINED?

What is the landowner's "ordinary use" of underground resources? Is it at 100 meters, 500 meters or even 10,000 meters? Does the right to geothermal extend further than the right to minerals or groundwater?[14] Should we perhaps define the ownership of geothermal power by reference to heat, for instance that a landowner owns geothermal power up to 200°C but anything above that is beyond her property rights? Or even by the method of drilling, i.e. that drilling close to the surface belongs to the owner, but deep drilling is beyond ownership?

Icelandic case-law does not provide answers to which metric or method should be used to estimate what amounts to ordinary use. The rule is highly subjective and open to interpretation. But, at a minimum, we know that the ownership of natural resources is not a fixed constant. It can change with time. What was considered unusual 50 years ago may be ordinary today due to technological developments. For instance, in an article published in 1956 the author, Ólafur Jóhannesson, believed that a drilling for geothermal power of 80 meters, which had been achieved on two properties in Iceland at the time, was beyond what any ordinary agricultural landowner could handle.[15] Today, this would not be considered abnormal, because technological developments and the increased wealth of the average owner has made it much cheaper and more realistic to drill further into the ground.[16]

But the question still arises whether the ownership of underground resources should be determined by the private financial means of each individual owner (an individualized rule) or whether it should extent to a depth that is ordinary for the average landowner and her ordinary use of the land (a general rule)? To illustrate let us imagine the following example: Jack, a poor person, owns Blackacre and can only dig 10 meters into the ground. Jill, a rich person, buys

14 The use of geothermal energy is usually at a further depth than for instance digging for minerals. See K. Axelsson, H. Hrafnkelsson and D. Kristjánsdóttir, "Um jarðrænar auðlindir og framtíðarnýtingu þeirra" (2007), 4 *Tímarit Lögréttu* 113, 117.

15 Ó. Jóhannesson, "Um eignar– og umráðarétt jarðhita" (1956) 6 *Tímarit lögfræðinga* 134, 154.

16 In Iceland, there are currently drilling projects that go 3-4 kilometers into the ground. Those projects are, however, conducted by large power companies and not individuals. To date, the deepest human-made hole in the world is the Kola Superdeep Borehole in Russia, which went over 12 kilometers into the ground and took 20 years to complete. See e.g., C. Lau, "China is drilling some of the world's deepest holes in hunt for natural resources" [2023] CNN https://edition.cnn.com/2023/07/21/china/china-second-superdeep-borehole-intl-hnk/index.html, accessed 27.09.2023.

Blackacre and can afford to dig 100 meters into the ground. Does the ownership increase from 10 to 100 meters when Jill buys the property? Or if we turn the example around, would the ownership drop from 100 meters to 10 meters if Jack bought Jill's property?

An individualized rule is illogical and goes against the principle of *nemo dat quod non habe*, i.e. that one cannot give what one does not have (*nemo dat* for short).[17] Under a regime that recognizes an individualized rule, the underground ownership of Blackacre *should* increase from 10 to 100 meters when Jack sells to Jill, because Jill can afford to dig ten times deeper than Jack. But the principle of *nemo dat* would prevent that from happening because Jill cannot get more ownership rights than Jack, the previous owner. Ownership of underground resources cannot be like an accordion that expands and shrinks depending on the individualized circumstances of the owner. In the extreme, under an individualized regime, Jack's ownership could extend dramatically by simply winning the lottery.

Accordingly, a general rule that looks at the circumstances of the *average owner* is more logical because it provides stability in the ownership of natural resources and is consistent with the *nemo dat* principle.[18] What should be the average owner and how we should determine that "metric" is of course still an open question that is difficult to answer. The *average owner* metric, however, does not mean that the ownership should be the same for every property. If it is cheaper and more convenient to dig and drill for resources on Whiteacre than Blackacre, for instance due to the natural circumstances of the property, the owner of Whiteacre should own resources at a greater depth than the owner of Blackacre.

It must be reiterated that technological and economic development can extend or diminish the ownership of natural resources. Of course, technological developments should generally *extend* ownership because it becomes cheaper to

---

17 The principle of *nemo dat* is considered one of the general ground rules of property law. See S. Van Erp, "General Issues: Setting the Scene" in S. Van Erp and B. Akkermans (eds.), *Cases, Materials and Text on National, Supranational and International Property Law*, Hart, Oxford and Portland, Oregon 2012, p. 93. On *nemo dat* in Icelandic law reference is made to V. Sólnes, "Sönnunarfærsla í eignarréttarmálum" in K. Benediktsdóttir (ed), *Hæstiréttur og Háskóli Íslands – Rit til heiðurs Hæstarétti 100 ára*, Fons Juris, Reykjavík 2020, pp. 339-342.

18 Icelandic scholars have not been clear about whether they lean towards an individualized or a general rule. It can be inferred by Ólafur Jóhannesson's article from 1956 that he favored a general rule of the average owner. See Ó. Jóhannesson, *supra* note 15, 143. Sigurður Líndal, at first blush, seems to suggest an individualized rule in a speech from 1983, which was later published as an article. See S. Líndal, "Eignarréttur á landi og orkulindum – erindi flutt á aðalfundi SÍR", addressing the general meeting of the Association of Icelandic Electrical Suppliers in 1983, p. 21. I have argued that Líndal's words should be taken with a grain of salt because it is not clear whether he is arguing for an individualized rule. Even if he were arguing for such a rule, he does not seem to have realized the practical problems of it, for instance its relationship with the principle of *nemo dat*. See V. Petersen, *supra* note 1, pp. 403-404.

dig and drill for resources, but economic declines can pull in the other direction. Change in land use can also affect the extent of ownership. For instance, if a landowner changes the use of her property from agricultural use to a residential one, the ownership may decrease, because an agricultural owner should, all things being equal, require more use of underground resources than a residential owner.[19] This is though of course very context dependent.

To summarize, landowners' underground ownership is determined by the following four things: 1) the ordinary use, 2) of the average owner, 3) of that property, 4) in its current use.

IV. WHO OWNS THE RESOURCES BELOW "ORDINARY USE"?

As the previous discussion suggested, the ownership of underground resources is limited to a certain depth. When the use stops being ordinary and starts being extraordinary, ownership ends. For the sake of clarity, we can call this line the "ownership boundary". The previous discussion also suggests that we do not know whether the ownership boundary is at 100, 500 or even 10,000 meters (or if it is determined for some resources by heat, methods of drilling/digging etc.). Another question that becomes interesting is who, if anyone, owns the resources *below* the ownership boundary?

According to Icelandic property law, the State does *not* have superiority or priority when it comes to ownerless property.[20] If no one can prove ownership of a thing it is considered ownerless (*res nullius*). In other words, the State is not the automatic owner of *res nullius*. However, the State can by law and its capacity as the legislature, claim ownership of unowned property, and in 1998, the Icelandic State enacted laws claiming ownership of all unowned *land*. Such areas are now known as public lands (Icelandic: *þjóðlendur*). The Act only prescribes that unowned *land* is owned by the State, but there are no provisions that cover natural resources below private land.[21]

---

19 It may be mentioned that in Book III of the Belgian Civil Code (Art. 3.63) there is a reference to the "view of the use and condition of the land" in determining whether an owner can object against uses by a third party. I want to thank Flore Vavourakis, PhD Researcher at KU Leuven, for drawing my attention to the importance of "use" in determining the scope of underground ownership and providing me with the reference to the Belgian Civil Code.

20 This has been confirmed in Supreme Court decisions such as *Hrd. 1955:108, Hrd. 1981:182* and *Hrd. 1981:1584*. See V. Petersen, "Eru almenningar stöðuvatna þjóðlendur?" [2021] *Vefrit Úlfljóts* https://ulfljotur.com/2021/06/27/eru-almenningar-stoduvatna-thjodlendur/ accessed 27.09.2023. See also V. Sólnes, *supra* note 17, 337.

21 I have argued elsewhere that the State has more rights to underground resources in public land than owners of private land. By enacting Act No 58/1998 on Public Lands and the Determination of the Boundaries of Private Land, Public Land and Upland Ranges, the State claimed ownership of unowned land and effectively converted unowned land to public land

Thus, resources below the ownership boundary in private land are unowned (*res nullius*), which means that they can be acquired by *occupatio*.[22] This does not mean, however, that there will be a Wild West Gold Rush for natural resources below the ownership boundary, because those that want to explore and exploit the resources still need to apply for licenses to the Icelandic National Energy Regulatory.[23] The National Energy Regulatory can decide to advertise (procure) licenses for exploration and exploitation, to give everyone interested a chance to submit bids, instead of simply granting a license to the first applicant.[24]

There have been numerous proposals over the years to include a provision in the Icelandic Constitution on "national ownership" which would stipulate that everything that is not privately owned is owned by the "nation".[25] Essentially, this means that all resources that were previously unowned would become subject to State ownership. The label "national ownership" means that there would be stricter rules on the use and exploitation of such resources, and the government would be under an obligation to charge reasonable fees for the use of resources subject to national ownership.[26] There is political unanimity about including a provision on national ownership in the Constitution, but the political parties have been unable to settle on the appropriate wording.

A provision of national ownership would obviously solve the issue of *res nullius* because no resources would be unowned anymore.[27] Owners and companies wishing to explore and exploit resources below the ownership boundary would need to obtain a license and pay reasonable fees to the government. But this still begs the following question: Where does national ownership *begin* when we do not know where the ownership boundary is? The

owned by the State. Art. 2(1) specifically states that the State owns *all rights and resources* in public lands, which suggests that the State claimed limitless rights in public land. See V. Petersen, *supra* note 1, pp. 405-406. This is why the following discussion about *res nullius* and *occupatio* is limited to ownership of resources in private land.

22 For comparison it can be mentioned that the Norwegian Supreme Court held in a decision from 1998 that groundwater did not belong to landowners and, thus, was an ownerless resource that could be acquired by *occupatio*. See *Rt. 1998:251*. Thus, it is not an unusual finding in Nordic property law that underground resources are ownerless. Following the Supreme Court's decision, the Norwegian water resource laws (n. *vannressursloven*) were amended, and groundwater is now subject to the ownership of landowners irrespective of the depth where it is discovered. For further academic readings on the situation in Norway I refer to E. Stavand and G. Stenseth, *Fast eiendoms tingsrett*, Gyldendal, Oslo 2016, pp. 68-72; K.E. Taraldrud, *Oversikt over rettigheter til fast eiendom*, Cappelen Damm Akademisk, Osló 2016, pp. 41-42; T. Falkanger and A.T. Falkanger, *Tingsrett* (9th ed), Universitetsforlaget, Osló 2022, pp. 102-103; T. Falkanger, "Eierløs fast eiendom i våre dagers Norge?" (2019) 58 *Lov og Rett* 3, 14-15.

23 See Chapters III, IV and VIII of Act No 57/1998 on Underground Resources.

24 See Art. 19 of Act No 57/1998 on Underground Resources.

25 The latest proposal was put forth by Katrín Jakobsdóttir, the Icelandic Prime Minister, in 2021, but the bill only made it through one discussion out of three. Alþt. 2020-2021, A-deild, doc. 787 – case 466.

26 Alþt. 2020-2021, A-deild, doc. 787 – case 466 (p. 30).

27 V. Petersen, *supra* note 20, pp. 10-11.

proposals have not included any suggestions in that respect – national ownership should simply begin where private ownership ends.

The proposals have also been silent on the future interplay between private and national ownership. Let us imagine that the Icelandic Constitution contained a provision of "national ownership" and that when the provision was enacted the ownership boundary of Blackacre was at 500 meters, which was the ordinary use of the land at the time. This means that everything below 500 meters should be subject to national ownership. But ten years later, technological developments have made it much easier and cheaper for landowners to conduct drilling and digging, and now the ordinary use of the average landowner of Blackacre is 800 meters. The proposals do not answer whether the national ownership should shrink by 300 meters in these ten years or whether private ownership should be "frozen" from the date of the constitutional amendment.[28] It is obviously important to clarify this in future proposals.

V. CAN THE STATE ADOPT AN OBJECTIVE RULE WITHOUT PAYING COMPENSATION TO LANDOWNERS?

A final consideration is whether the legislature could decide to switch from a subjective standard of ordinary use to an objective rule, for instance by prescribing that the owner would own resources down to 500 meters in the ground, but resources at a further depth would be owned by the State (or the "nation"). By enacting such a rule, the government might be interfering with ownership. For instance, if the ownership of underground resources at Blackacre is now at 600 meters, an objective rule of 500 meters would diminish the landowner's rights by 100 meters.

Under Icelandic law, the right to ownership is protected by both Article 72(1) of the Icelandic Constitution and Article 1 of Protocol 1 to the European Convention of Human Rights (hereinafter A1P1). An unlawful interference with said provisions usually results in the payment of compensation. The question of whether an objective rule amounts to such an unlawful interference will of course depend on facts and context and would also require a detailed analysis of the constitutional aspects of ownership. However, for the sake of analysis, I wanted to sketch a few preliminary points that deserve special attention, if the legislature were to consider such a provision.

The question of what amounts to ordinary use is not solely a legal one. The legislature will have to conduct geological research when trying to answer where and how to draw the ownership boundary. The Icelandic Supreme Court has

[28] See a further discussion of this in V. Petersen, *supra* note 1, pp. 410-411.

emphasized that the legislature is under a constitutional obligation to thoroughly prepare legislation that may interfere with constitutionally protected rights, such as the right to ownership.[29] Indeed, if legislation is poorly prepared it will undermine the ability of authorities to determine whether the least restrictive alternative is being chosen.[30] Thus, the quality of the democratic process is important when determining the constitutionality of regulations that interfere with property rights.[31]

When the legislature has conducted the necessary technical research, the role of lawyers becomes more important, because they must carefully examine, among other things, whether a proposed legal rule is proportionate and make sure that it does not result in discrimination. The legal analysis includes determining whether there is an appropriate balance between the public interest and the interests of owners (proportionality stricto sensu).[32]

A decision to adopt an objective rule would be in the public interest because it eliminates legal uncertainty, which would enhance the ability to protect and control the use of underground resources. Eliminating *res nullius* would also enable the government to charge reasonable fees for the use of resources below the ownership boundary, which guarantees the public's fair share in the use of resources that are not privately owned. Currently, it is impossible or at least very difficult to ensure that the public enjoys the fair share because we do not know with certainty where the ownership boundary is.[33]

But how would an objective rule affect landowners? This will of course depend on context and implementation, but it is important to mention that it will often be unclear whether the effects are negative. When determining the effects, we must compare the situations pre-rule and post-rule. Negative effects could be nonexistent, for instance if the technological research indicates that no landowners can go below 600 meters and the legislature decides to err on the side of caution and enact an objective rule which establishes ownership down

---

29 See *Hrd. 26 October 2022 (20/2022)* and K.H. Ragnarsson, "Skipta gæði lagasetningar máli við endurskoðun dómstóla á stjórnskipulegu gildi laga?" (2021) 74 *Úlfljótur*, 219, 219-250.

30 See *Hrd. 12 May 2016 (511/2015).*

31 The European Court of Human Rights has also emphasized the importance of proper preparatory work by the legislature. In *Maurice v. France*, no 11810/03, ECHR 2005-IX, the Court awarded a broad margin of appreciation to French authorities because the preparation was of high quality and thorough. Conversely, in *Hirst v. UK (no 2)*, no 74025/01, ECHR 2005-IX, the Court awarded a narrower margin due to the low quality of the preparatory work. See also further K.H. Ragnarsson, *supra* note 29, 232-234, and M. Saul, "The European Court of Human Rights' Margin of Appreciation and the Processes of National Parliaments" (2015) 15 *Human Rights Law Review*, 745, 745-759.

32 On proportionality in Icelandic law and its relationship with the proportionality analysis of the European Court of Human Rights see e.g., K.H. Ragnarsson, "Allt kann sá er hófið kann – Um inntak stjórnskipulegrar meðalhófsreglu" (2017) 13 *Tímarit Lögréttu*, 150.

33 The Icelandic Supreme Court has held that there are rich and obvious public interests in protecting and ensuring the efficient use of resources. Thus, controlling the use of resources (at seabed in that case) was reasonable and justifiable. See *Hrd. 27 September 2007 (182/2007).*

to that depth (or even a little further). This rule would obviously not negatively affect any landowners. On the contrary, all landowners will benefit from the rule, and some may benefit greatly. Such a rule might also be mutually beneficial for owners and the State because it increases clarity (which would presumably be one of the State's objectives) without harming private interests.

But if the State decides to put the ownership boundary closer to the surface, say at 500 meters, some landowners may claim that there is an interference with their ownership rights. However, the laws are already unclear on how deep their ownership extends and currently the rights most likely only include "ordinary use". Thus, a frustrated landowner would have to prove that his "ordinary use" would be at a further depth than the objective rule. Also, an objective rule would not "take away" the landowner's right to underground resources but would at best curtail the use and enjoyment of such rights. The rule would, therefore, not amount to expropriation or deprivation, but would instead be a regulation that determined the use and enjoyment of a certain "stick" of the landowner's "bundle".[34] It is much more likely that such interferences go uncompensated than when property is taken in its entirety.[35]

The legislative trend in Iceland for the past decades has been to curtail the use and enjoyment of land and natural resources in the public interest (for instance to protect the environment, animal welfare or sustainability) without any means of compensation, except in the exceptional case.[36] An objective rule regarding the ownership of underground resources, that is both technically sound and proportional, could be seen as a logical step in the same direction.[37] It is at least not an illogical step or a surprising departure from the current trends.

---

34 The A1P1 case-law is clear in this respect, i.e. that losing one stick in the bundle of rights is not enough to amount to a deprivation of one's property. Instead, the interference will be examined under the control of use rule. See e.g., F. McCarthy, "Protection of Property and the European Convention on Human Rights", (2017) 6 *Brigham-Kanner Property Rights Conference Journal*, 299, 312, and *Alatulkkila and Others v. Finland*, no 33538/96, § 66 (28 July 2005), *Posti and Rahko v. Finland*, no 27824/95, § 95 ECHR 2002-VII, and *Guðjónsson v. Iceland* (dec.), no 40169/05 (2 December 2008). This is less clear from Icelandic case-law and scholarship but can still be inferred by *Hrd. 1964:573*, *Hrd. 27 September 2007 (182/2007)* and *Hrd. 28 October 2011 (340/2011)*.

35 The Icelandic Supreme Court has developed a criterion for determining whether a regulation should go uncompensated or lead to the payment of compensation. The Court looks at the facts holistically but specifically examines the reasons for the regulation, its overall purpose and consequences, its nature and how general and widespread the effects are. See *Hrd. 28 October 2011 (340/2011)* and a detailed discussion of each point in B. THORARENSEN, *Stjórnskipunarréttur – Mannréttindi* (2nd ed), Bókaútgáfan Codex, Reykjavík 2019, pp. 519-529. See also a discussion in K. Axelsson and Á. Ragnarsdóttir, *Eignarnám*, Fons Juris, Reykjavík 2021, pp. 27-31.

36 K. Axelsson, "Um skorður umhverfisréttar við nýtingu lands og náttúruauðlinda" (1996) 46 *Tímarit lögfræðinga*, 81, 87-88, and V. Petersen, *supra* note 1, 420-421.

37 Gaukur Jörundsson has mentioned that general trends and attitudes in the law can matter when determining whether a regulation should result in the payment of compensation. See G. Jörundsson, *Um eignarnám* (PhD thesis), Bókaútgáfa Menningarsjóðs, Reykjavík 1969, p. 403.

Also of importance is the fact that the rule would be general, meaning that it would apply equally to all landowners and not single out a particular subset of them. General rules are, from both the perspective of the Icelandic Constitution[38] and A1P1[39], more likely to go uncompensated than rules that are more concentrated and only affect certain owners or a subset of owners. Of course, the rule might, when applied and implemented, disproportionately affect some owners compared to the larger part of them. Owners that are disproportionately affected could argue that they must bear, in the A1P1 terminology, an "individual and excessive burden" and that it would be unreasonable for them to tolerate it without any means of relief. However, the owners would have to demonstrate that the burden is not only individual but "excessive", which is probably only in cases where an owner can prove that the objective rule is at a *considerably* lower depth than the situation was pre-rule, or that his interests are *substantially* affected in other ways. And even though the State had to pay compensation to some owners that have truly been disproportionately affected, the rule would remain constitutional, given that it is otherwise justifiable and lawful.

Additionally, some landowners may reasonably claim that they already acquired legitimate expectations in the continued exploitation of a resource, for instance because they have a valid license to exploit it for thirty more years. The legislature can take such interests into account and ameliorate negative effects by allowing current licensees to continue their operations, at least for a certain period[40], or by implementing other mitigating measures.[41] It should though be noted that expectations need to reach a degree of certainty and concreteness for them to become "legitimate".[42] A landowner that does not have a license but plans to apply for one soon would be unlikely to enjoy protection on account of the doctrine of legitimate expectations.

---

38 On the Icelandic perspective see K. Axelsson and Á. Ragnarsdóttir, *supra* note 34, pp. 28-29, and B. Thorarensen, *supra* note 34, pp. 519-520.

39 When it comes to the control of use rule, an owner is usually not entitled to compensation unless he has experienced an individual and excessive burden (sometimes also referred to as a disproportionate and excessive burden). See e.g., *Broniowski v. Poland* [GC], no 31443/96, § 150, ECHR 2004-V.

40 It could jeopardize the purpose behind the regulation if all licenses were valid until they expired. Imagine licenses that are held for over 50 more years or indefinite licenses. When the public interest is high the legislature could decide to let all licenses expire within say 5-10 years after the laws are enacted. An Icelandic example is *Hrd. 27 September 2007 (182/2007).* An A1P1 example is *Fredin v. Sweden (no. 1)*, no 12033/86, § 54 (18 February 1991).

41 The Icelandic Supreme Court has looked favorably at measures that mitigate or ameliorate disproportionate and excessive burdens. See *Hrd. 27 September 2007 (182/2007), Hrd. 25 March 2021 (38/2020)* and *Hrd. 15 November 2018 (855/2017).*

42 See *Béláné Nagy v. Hungary*, no 53080/13, § 75 (13 December 2016): "*A legitimate expectation must be of a nature more concrete than a mere hope and be based on a legal provision or a legal act such as a judicial decision.*" The Icelandic Supreme Court has recently held that legitimate expectations enjoy protection under the Icelandic Constitution and that the content of such rights should be interpreted in accordance with A1P1. See *Hrd. 2 November 2022 (15-17/2022).*

To summarize, landowners will not be entitled to compensation by default if an objective rule is enacted, even though they are able to prove that it interfered with their ownership rights, as they were pre-rule. The outcome will be very dependent on facts and context, for instance how elaborately the legislature prepared the process leading up to the rule and whether it respected the principle of proportionality by carefully examining ways to ameliorate excessive and disproportionate burdens.

TO WHOM BELONGS THE WATER?

Someone, No One and Everyone Appropriating Freshwater in the Low Countries

Flore Vavourakis
FWO Fellow
PhD researcher at the Institute for Property Law, KU Leuven

Marie-Laure Degroote
FWO Fellow
PhD researcher at the Institute for Property Law, KU Leuven

As the demand for freshwater soars and climate change alters its availability, the scarce natural resource becomes extremely valuable. The division of rights to freshwater is therefore increasingly contested. In property theory, legal water qualifications determine who has which right to which freshwater. Traditionally freshwater is qualified as res nullius, res privata, res communis or res publica. Which qualification prevails depends on the temporary location of water molecules in the hydrologic cycle. For instance, rainwater is qualified differently than water in public waterways or groundwater. We analyze the legal water qualifications and the matching (private and public) rights to water from a practical point of view. Through this unconventional approach, we question the casualness with which freshwater qualifications are accepted in property theory. Rather than debating water rights from an appropriation point of view, this article argues that legal scholarship should rephrase its question from: Who has a (limited) property right to which freshwater? to Who is, temporarily, responsible for the water? Both public and private actors should take up their responsibilities vis-à-vis the vital natural resource. This is indispensable to achieve sustainable water management in which a shift from draining to retaining freshwater is attained. In shaping the shared responsibility between public and private actors, the symbolic concept of the commons is bodied out: All water should be qualified as a common regardless of its temporary location in the hydrologic cycle. This need not imply abandoning the traditional property law qualifications. On the contrary, their co-existence with the qualification of water as a common could contribute to sustainable water management. The common qualification does, however, imply calibrating granted water rights to adapt their scope to the current context of climate change.

I. TODAY'S WATER AVAILABILITY

1. **Adapting to increasing hydrological extremes** – Every water molecule present on Earth today has been on this planet for billions of years.[1] Water moves around in a continuous cycle above, on and underneath the surface of the Earth.[2] For centuries the amount of freshwater circulating in this hydrologic cycle allowed many civilizations to thrive.[3] Yet, growing populations and expanding industrialization drastically increase the demand for freshwater. Due to these changing circumstances societies are confronted with the scarcity of the natural resource.[4]

Additionally, climate change alters the ancient hydrologic cycle. As the temperature rises, the time dimension of the hydrological cycle is disrupted, resulting in longer periods of drought and peaks of intense rainfall.[5] In Belgium and the Netherlands, the risks associated with these increasing hydrological extremes are negatively influenced by historically grown land

1 On the origin of water: C. Ceccarelli and F. Du, "We Drink Good 4.5-Billion-Year-Old Water" (2022) 3 *Elements* 18, pp. 155-160.

2 NASA, "Precipitation Education: Hydrologic cycle", https://gpm.nasa.gov/education/water-cycle/hydrologic-cycle, accessed 20.11.2023; National Oceanic and Atmospheric Administration (U.S. Departement of Commerce), "The Hydrologic cycle", 2023, www.noaa.gov/jetstream/atmosphere/hydro, accessed 20.11.2023; TU Delft, "Hydrologische kringloop" in L. Stougie (ed.), *Webdictaat Analyse van energiesystemen*, 2023, https://eduweb.eeni.tbm.tudelft.nl/TB142E/?hydrologische-kringloop accessed 20.11.2023.

3 S. Habibbeh Hosseiny, O. Bozorg-haddad and D. Bocchiola, "Water, culture, civilization, and history" in O. Bozorg-Haddad (ed.), *Economical, Political, and Social Issues in Water*, Elsevier, Amsterdam 2021, pp. 189-216; UNESCO, "Water from the Dawn of Civilization" (2009), www.unesco.org/archives/multimedia/document-1557 accessed 15.11.2023.

4 European Environment Agency, "Water scarcity conditions in Europe (Water exploitation index plus)", January 2023, www.eea.europa.eu/en/analysis/indicators/use-of-freshwater-resources-in-europe-1 accessed 16.11.2023; ING Economics Department, "Too little, too much. The diverse sectoral challenges of water", www.ing.com/Newsroom/News/Industrialisation-is-putting-the-worlds-water-resources-under-huge-pressure.htm accessed 16.11.2023; UN Water, "Water Scarcity", www.unwater.org/water-facts/water-scarcity accessed 16.11.2023.

5 Expertenpanel Hoogwaterbeveiliging, *Advies aan de Vlaamse Regering: Weerbaar waterland. Ons voorbereiden op wat al gebeurt*, July 2022, (hereinafter: Expertenpanel hoogwaterbeveiliging 2022), www.vlaamsewaterweg.be/sites/default/files/download/weerbaar_waterland_expertenpanel_hoogwaterbeveiliging_advies.pdf accessed 20.11.2023, pp. 43-45; IPCC, *Sixth Assessment Report: Climate Change 2022: Impacts, Adaptation and Vulnerability, the Working Group II contribution*, February 2022, Chapter 4, pp. 605-611, www.ipcc.ch/report/ar6/wg2/ accessed 20.11.2023.

and water management. The practice of draining lands for agriculture and construction, hardening surfaces, straightening naturally meandering rivers, building in floodable areas and deforestation have all contributed to the risks the Low Countries currently face. When peaks of intense rainfall reach the region, freshwater does not get the opportunity to infiltrate into the soil, nor to gradually fill meandering rivers. Instead, the water causes floods or is drained quickly, leaving the population and nature with too little reserve for times of drought.[6]

Although a zero-risk outcome is unattainable[7], the risks of both water shortages and floods can and should be reduced. To do so, we need not turn to civil engineering alone. Nature-based solutions offer a promising alternative: Restoring the natural absorbent potential of soil and giving water more space to flow more slowly will reduce the risk of water shortages and floods.[8] Soil quality and water protection are thus undeniably interconnected.[9]

Nature-based solutions have two important advantages *vis-à-vis* technical adaptation strategies based on civil-engineering. On the one hand, restoring the sponge function of the soil results in improvements with regard to other (environmental) challenges. Wetlands retain a lot of CO_2[10], better soil and water quality improve biodiversity[11], green areas create a much needed

---

6 Expertenpanel hoogwaterbeveiliging 2022, pp. 37-41.

7 Expertenpanel hoogwaterbeveiliging 2022, pp. 69-70.

8 EEA Report No. 1/2021, *Nature-based solutions in Europe: Policy, knowledge and practice for climate change adaptation and disaster risk reduction*, 2021, www.eea.europa.eu/publications/nature-based-solutions-in-europe accessed on 22.11.2023; Expertenpanel hoogwaterbeveiliging 2022, pp. 73-75; J. Maes and S. Jacobs, "Nature-based solutions for Europe's sustainable development" (2017) 10 *Conservation letters* 121, pp. 121-124; K. Heylen, "Hoe wapenen we ons tegen wateroverlast? 'We moeten rivieren plaats geven en dat betekent ook onteigeningen'", *vrt nws* 17 November, 2023, www.vrt.be/vrtnws/nl/2023/11/17/wateroverlast-wat-kunnen-we-doen-om-ons-hiertegen-te-wapenen accessed on 18.11.2023; N. Seddon, A. Chausson, P. Berry, C.A.J. Girardin, A. Smith and B. Turner, "Understanding the value and limits of nature-based solutions to climate change and other global challenges" (2020) 375 *Phil. Trans. R. Soc. B* 1, pp. 1-12.

9 Rijkswaterstaat, "Water", www.bodemplus.nl/opgaven/water/ accessed on 17.11.2023.

10 A.M. Nahlik and M.S. Fennessy, "Carbon storage in US wetlands" (2016) 7 *Nat Commun* 1, pp. 1-9; C.E. Lovelock, J.W. Fourqurean and J.T. Morris, "Modeled CO2 Emissions from Coastal Wetland Transitions to Other Land Uses: Tidal Marshes, Mangrove Forests, and Seagrass Beds." (2017) 4 *Front. Mar. Sci.* 1, pp. 1-11; D. Abdul Malak, A.I. Marin, M. Trombetti and S. San Roman, *Carbon pools and sequestration potential of wetlands in the European Union*, European Topic Centre on Urban, Land and Soil Systems, Vienna and Malaga 2021, 62 p.; K.W. Krauss, Z. Zhu and C. L. Stagg (eds.), *Wetland Carbon and Environmental Managment*, Wiley, New Jersey 2021, 480 p.

11 K. Cheng, X. Xu, L. Cui, Y. Li, J. Zheng, W. Wu, J. Sun and G. Pan, "The role of soils in regulation of freshwater and coastalwater quality" (2021) 376 *Phil. Trans. R. Soc. B* 1, pp. 1-10; T.A. Groh, "Grounded in Soil: Water Quality Benefits from Healthy Soils", *Penn State Extension*, https://extension.psu.edu/grounded-in-soil-water-quality-benefits-from-healthy-soils accessed 20.11.2023.

cooling effect[12] in our cities and improve the living standard.[13] Technical solutions are less apt to reaching multiple targets at once.[14] On the other hand, compared to nature-based-solutions, technical solutions require heavy investments while being less flexible. Given the uncertain further evolution of climate change[15], the flexibility of nature-based-solutions should be fully utilized.

2. **Paradigm shift from draining to retaining freshwater** – In the past the Netherlands and Belgium mainly repelled water excess. Infamous floods forged the collective memory of water as a burden, and drainage was at the core of water management.[16] As both countries now deal with the additional challenge of drought, a paradigm shift towards retaining water is urged for.[17] The shift from draining to retaining water goes hand in hand with the prioritized choice for nature-based-solutions, only turning to technical solutions where necessary.[18] For this to happen, changes need to be implemented on public and private land.

In Belgium and the Netherlands, property theory tends to ignore this emerging freshwater transition in the discussion of (property) rights on water. Traditional legal water qualifications are repeated without looking at the changed context in which this division of (property) rights to freshwater operates. In this article we analyze and criticize the contemporary role of the water qualifications *res nullius, res privata, res publica* and *res communes*. By doing so, we hope to induce a more practically oriented debate about water in property theory, a discussion that surpasses the axiological dimension of the commons.

12 N. Testelmans, "Cooling effect of European forests mapped for the first time" (2021), *KU Leuven news*, https://nieuws.kuleuven.be/en/content/2021/the-cooling-effect-of-European-forests-mapped-for-the-first-time accessed 19.11.2023; W. Liu, H. Zhao, S. Sun, X. Xu, T. Huang and J. Zhu, "Green Space Cooling Effect and Contribution to Mitigate Heat Island Effect of Surrounding Communities in Beijing Metropolitan Area" (2022) 10 *Front. Public Health* 1, pp. 1-16.

13 T. Fast, *Expertenadvies Vlaams Departement Omgeving: Gezonde Leefomgevingskwaliteit*, 2020, p. 8, https://omgeving.vlaanderen.be/nl/wat-is-een-goede-leefomgevingskwaliteit accessed 18.11.2023.

14 Expertenpanel hoogwaterbeveiliging 2022, pp. 73-75.

15 Expertenpanel hoogwaterbeveiliging 2022, p. 71; Koninklijk Nederlands Meteorologisch Instituut, *KNMI' 23 klimaatscenario's voor Nederland*, 2023, pp. 13-15, www.knmi.nl/kennis-en-datacentrum/achtergrond/knmi-23-klimaatscenario-s accessed 20.11.2023.

16 J. Wynant, "Klimaatverandering houdt geen enkele rekening met onze 'nostalgie' naar uitgeregende zomers" (2021), *Knack*, www.knack.be/nieuws/klimaatverandering-houdt-geen-enkele-rekening-met-onze-nostalgie-naar-uitgeregende-zomers/ accessed 12.08.2023.

17 Expertenpanel hoogwaterbeveiliging 2022, pp. 20-21; R. Didde, "Sponsbodem moet water vasthouden" (2018), *Binnenlands Bestuur*, www.binnenlandsbestuur.nl/ruimte-en-milieu/sponsbodem-moet-water-vasthouden accessed 20.11.2023.

18 Expertenpanel hoogwaterbeveiliging 2022, pp. 73-84.

II. PROPERTY LAW MEETS HYDROLOGY[19]

3. Different water location, different legal qualification – As water molecules move throughout the hydrologic cycle and as humans intervene in this cycle by collecting, using, polluting and discharging water, the property qualification of freshwater changes.[20] Belgian and Dutch property law reflect a similar approach with regard to water: Rainwater is qualified as a *res nullius*[21], certain surface and groundwater is in – private or public – ownership[22], water, e.g. bottled water or effluent water, can be sold on a market, and virtual water – despite its (re)distributive relevance – is not accounted for.[23] An important difference between the two legal systems is that Dutch law provides

---

19 Hydrology is the study of the distribution and movement of water both on and below the Earth's surface, as well as the impact of human activity on water availability and conditions. See: National Geographic Society, "Hydrology" (2023), https://education.nationalgeographic.org/resource/hydrology/ accessed 10.11.2023.

20 F. Vavourakis, "De verschillende dimensies van het watervraagstuk: miskent het Belgische recht het blauwe goed?" (2022-2023) 8 *RW* 282, p. 282.

21 **BE:** Art. 3.43, second para. Belgian Civil Code (hereinafter: CC); Court of Appeal of Liège 17 December 1980, *JL* 1984, (576) pp. 576-577; Trib. Nivelles 13 February 1995, *T.Aann.* 1995, 2, (162) p. 166; A.M. Draye, T. Nulens and B. Vanheusden, *Het juridische statuut van de watermolens*, studie in opdracht van het ministerie van de Vlaamse Gemeenschap, 2005, p. 40, www.molenechos.org/juridische_nota_stuwrechten.pdf accessed 10.07.2023; C. De Smedt and S. Baert, "Oneigenlijke erfdienstbaarheden tot privaat nut" in G. Baert (ed.), *Bestendig handboek privaatrechtelijk bouwrecht*, Larcier-Intersentia, Antwerp 2017, (II.12-1) II.12-19; H. De Page and R. Dekkers, *Traité élémentaire de droit civil belge*, V, Bruylant, Brussels 1975, p. 886, no. 1000; J. Hansenne, *Les biens. Précis*, II, Collection de la Faculté de Droit de Liège, Liège 1996, p. 750, no. 790; J. Kokelenberg and J. Del Corral, "Eigendomsoverdracht- en titel" in R. Derine, H. Cousy, J. Couturier, W. Delva, J. Herbots and R. Vekeman (ed.), *Het onroerend goed in de praktijk*, Kluwer, Antwerp 2022, (I.E-1) I.E.1.-4; S. Snaet and M. Muylle, "Waterregeling" in R. Derine, H. Cousy, J. Couturier, W. Delva, J. Herbots and R. Vekeman (eds.), *Het onroerend goed in de praktijk*, Kluwer, Mechelen, (I.D.11-1) I.D.11-22; V. Sagaert, *Goederenrecht* in *Beginselen van Belgisch Privaatrecht*, Kluwer, Mechelen 2021, p. 279, no. 295; **NL:** Art. 5.4 Dutch Civil Code (hereinafter: DCC); See implicitly: G.E. Van Maanen, "Van de vogelen des hemels en de stranden der zee. Publiek domein en ander overheidseigendom" (1992) 6074 *WPNR* 970, p. 974.

22 See *infra* no. 4; Many civil law jurisdictions distinguish between public and private waters. The traditional distinction is, however, not so clear-cut in practice. See: S. Hodgson, "Exploring the concept of water tenure" (2016) 10 *FAO Land and water discussion paper* 1, pp. 15-16.

23 Virtual water is water required to produce a commodity. See: E. Morgera, E. Webster, G. Hamley, F. Sindico, J. Robbie, S. Switzer, T. Berger, P.P. Silva Sànchez, M. Lennan, R. Martin-Nagle, E. Tsioumani, R. Moynihan and A. Zydek, "The right to water for food and agriculture" (2020) 113 *FAO legislative study* 1, pp. 48-49; J.W. Dellapenna and J. Gupta, "Water law: its role, shortcomings, and potential" in J.W. Dellapenna and J. Gupta (eds.), *Water law* in *Elgar encyclopedia of environmental law*, Volume X, Elgar, Cheltenham 2021, pp. 491-492; M.M. Aldaya, P. Martínez-Santos and M. Ramón Llamas, "Incorporating the Water Footprint and Virtual Water into Policy: Reflections from the Mancha Occidental Region, Spain" (2010) 5 *Water Resources Management* 942, pp. 955-956; R. Larson and A.D. Tarlock, "Inter-jurisdictional water allocation federal systems: lessons for international water law" in S.C. McCaffret, C. Leb and R.T. Denoon (eds.), *Research Handbook on International Water Law*, Elgar, Cheltenham 2019, pp. 59-81.

a clearer general principle excluding non-individualized water from private ownership[24], while Belgium holds on to a more traditional (Roman-French) theory of flowing water as a common good *(res communis)*.[25]

4. ***Res nullius, res privatae, res publicae*** **and** ***res communes*** – Legal scholarship generally considers the abovementioned legal qualifications depending on the temporary location in the hydrological cycle as self-evident.[26] Their impact in practice and the coherence of these legal qualifications vis-à-vis each other is rarely questioned in Belgian and Dutch scholarship. Critically analyzing private water law requires a good understanding of the qualifications' traditional meaning in property law.

First of all, rainwater is qualified as a *res nullius*, which translates to *a good that belongs to no one*. Traditionally, the category of *res nullius* is divided into two subcategories: *Res nullius sensu stricto,* goods that never had an owner before, and *res derelictae,* goods that were previously owned, but which the owner abandoned.[27] Obviously, rainwater belongs to the first subcategory. The

---

24 Art. 5.20, 5.25, 5.26, and 5.27, first para. DCC; A.C. van Schaick, "Kroniek van het zakenrecht (2001-2008), Deel I" (2008) 7 *NTBR* 38, p. 38; S.E. Bartels and A.A. van Velten, *Zakenrecht, Eigendom en beperkte rechten* in *Mr. C. Assers Handleiding tot de beoefening van het Nederlands Burgerlijk Recht (5)*, Kluwer, Deventer 2017, no. 97; C.J.J.M. Stolker, "Commentaar op art. 5:40 BW: Voorbijstromend water" in H.B. Krans, C.J.J.M. Stolker and W.L. Valk (eds.), *T&C BW*, Kluwer, Deventer 2023 (update); H. Havekes, "Wie is juridisch eigenaar van het water?" (2020) 4 *De Landeigenaar* 10, pp. 10-11; W.H.M. Reehuis, A.H.T. Heisterkamp, G.E. Van Maanen and G.T. De Jong, *Pitlo. Het Nederlands burgerlijk recht. Deel 3. Goederenrecht*, Kluwer, Deventer 2019, p. 462, no. 537 (free circulating water is a *res nullius* until someone appropriates it).

25 Roman law also contained a complex mix of private, communal and public rights in water. See: D. Schorr, "Water rights" in M. Graziadei and L. Smith (eds.), *Comparative Property Law: Global Perspectives*, Cheltenham, Elgar 2017, pp. 281-284; See e.g. book II, Title I of the Institutes of Justinian (English version: https://www.gutenberg.org/files/5983/5983-h/5983-h.htm): "[…] *Thus, the following things are by natural law common to all—the air, running water, the sea, and consequently the seashore. No one therefore is forbidden access to the seashore, provided he abstains from injury to houses, monuments, and buildings generally; for these are not, like the sea itself, subject to the law of nations. On the other hand, all rivers and harbours are public, so that all persons have a right to fish therein.* […] *Again, the public use of the banks of a river, as of the river itself, is part of the law of nations; consequently everyone is entitled to bring his vessel to the bank, and fasten cables to the trees growing there, and use it as a resting-place for the cargo, as freely as he may navigate the river itself. But the ownership of the bank is in the owner of the adjoining land, and consequently so too is the ownership of the trees which grow upon it. Again, the public use of the seashore, as of the sea itself, is part of the law of nations; consequently everyone is free to build a cottage upon it for purposes of retreat, as well as to dry his nets and haul them up from the sea. But they cannot be said to belong to any one as private property, but rather are subject to the same law as the sea itself, with the soil or sand which lies beneath it.* […]"

26 F. Masson, "L'eau comme patrimoine commun" in J. Rochfeld, M. Cornu and G.J. Martin (eds.), *Rapport n° 17-34: rapport final de recherche: L'Echelle de communalité: propositions de réforme pour intégrer les biens communs en droit*, 2021, pp. 140-155, www.gip-recherche-justice.fr/wp-content/uploads/2021/06/Rapport-17-34-final-Juin-2021.pdf accessed 20.7.2023.

27 **BE:** H. De Page and R. Deckers, *Traité élémentaire de droit civil belge*, V, Bruylant, Brussels 1952, p. 538, no. 537 and p. 720, no. 824; M. Muylle, *De duur en de beëindiging van zakelijke*

qualification of freshwater as *res derelicta,* in other words, water abandoned by its owner, is not ruled out, but is irrelevant for rainwater that moved away from any previous owners through natural processes like evapotranspiration[28] and condensation[29].[30] The defining characteristic of the (umbrella) category of *res nullius* is its appropriability, meaning that a private individual (or a public authority) can subject it to a private ownership right.[31] In Belgium, rainwater or abandoned water (e.g. effluent water) can simply be appropriated through occupation, i.e. by capturing it (physical element) with the intention of becoming its owner (*animus rem sibi habendi*; intentional element).[32] In Dutch law, mere possession suffices. The intentions of the possessor are irrelevant.[33] In principle the first person to occupy a *res nullius* becomes its rightful owner. Sometimes, however, public law imposes additional requirements (e.g. permit conditions) for a valid appropriation.[34] If there is a valid appropriation, the water becomes

rechten, Intersentia, Antwerp 2012, p. 87, no. 119; N. Carette and R. Jansen, *Handboek goederenrecht*, Intersentia, Antwerp 2022, p. 287, no. 508; P. Lecocq, *Manuel de droit des biens - Tome 1*, Larcier, Brussels 2012, p. 135, no. 33; S. Boufflette, "A l'attention des propriétaires distraits ou négligents: le sort des objets trouvés au regard du droit des biens (annotation under Court of Appeal Bergen 10 October 2005)" (2008) 3 *TBBR* 157, p. 158, no. 4; S. Demeyere, "De onderschatte rol van wilsautonomie in het huidige en in het nieuwe goederenrecht: kwalitatieve verbintenissen als proefstuk" (2019) 3-4 *TPR* 1055, p. 1108, no. 48; V. Sagaert, *Goederenrecht* in *Beginselen van Belgisch Privaatrecht* Kluwer, Mechelen 2021, p. 279, no. 295 and p. 1213, no. 1409; **NL:** A.C. van Schaick, "Kroniek van het zakenrecht (2001-2008), Deel I" (2008) 7 *NTBR* 38, p. 38; H.J. Snijders and E.B. Rank-Berenschot, *Goederenrecht* in *Studiereeks burgerlijk recht 2*, Kluwer, Deventer 2022, p. 174, no. 206; S.E. Bartels and A.A. van Velten, *Zakenrecht, Eigendom en beperkte rechten* in *Mr. C. Assers Handleiding tot de beoefening van het Nederlands Burgerlijk Recht (5)*, Kluwer, Deventer 2017, no. 59.

28 U.S. Geological Survey's Water Science School, *Evapotranspiration and the Water Cycle*, 12 June 2018, www.usgs.gov/special-topics/water-science-school/science/evapotranspiration-and-water-cycle#overview accessed 17.11.2023.

29 U.S. Geological Survey's Water Science School, *Condensation and the Water Cycle*, 8 June 2019, www.usgs.gov/special-topics/water-science-school/science/condensation-and-water-cycle accessed 17.11.2023.

30 **FR:** F. Quillere-Majzoub, "À qui appartiennent les nuages? Essai de définition d'un statut des nuages en droit international public" (2004) 50 *Annuaire français de droit international* 653, p. 665.

31 **BE:** Art. 3.43, second para. CC; **NL:** Art. 5.4 DCC.

32 **BE:** Court of Appeal of Ghent 4 January 2002, *RW* 2004-05 (144) pp. 144-145; S. Boufflette, "A l'attention des propriétaires distraits ou négligents: le sort des objets trouvés au regard du droit des biens (annotation under Court of Appeal Bergen 10 october 2005)", (2008) 3 *TBBR* 157, 158, no. 3; V. Sagaert, *Goederenrecht in Beginselen van Belgisch Privaatrecht*, Kluwer, Mechelen, 2014, 699, no. 901.
The appropriation of goods without an owner is regulated in Art. 3.59 §2 CC. According to the latter Art., appropriation is only possible after fulfilling the obligations of Art. 3.58 CC (obligations of a finder). However, it would be absurd applying these obligations to water, so we intentionally exclude them in this case.

33 Art. 5:4 DCC; A.C. Van Schaick, *Rechtsgevolgen en functies van bezit en houderschap*, Kluwer, Deventer, 2024, 105, no. 84; P.J. Van Der Plank, "Art. 5:4 BW, aant. 6" in F.J. Vonck (ed.), *Groene Serie zakelijke rechten*, Kluwer, Deventer, 2019.

34 Art. 3.2 CC.

a publicly or privately owned good (*res privata*). Nonetheless, because water molecules are constantly moving, the qualification of *res nullius* may disappear before it is captured: If water infiltrates into the soil, it becomes, at least according to some scholars, property of the owner of the soil through accession.[35] Others would argue that infiltrated water is still *res nullius* as long as nobody actively captures it.[36] If rain ends up in a stream or in a pond, it will follow the legal qualification of that larger body of water in which it is integrated.

Unlike the broad acceptance of rainwater as an appropriable *res nullius*[37], the legal qualification of surface water is less clear-cut. It is generally accepted in Belgian and Dutch law that the owner of the land surrounding stagnant water (e.g. a pond) also owns the water itself.[38] For the so-called flowing water (in streams) a distinction is made between the riverbed, i.e. the ground underneath the water, which is in private or public ownership (*res privata*), and the water flowing through it, which is not, as such, appropriated, not in the Netherlands (as it is non-individualized water, qualified as a *res nullius*; see *supra* no. 3) nor in Belgium (as it is qualified as a *res communis* or a *res nullius*).[39] In Belgium, streams are categorized according to their navigability. The riverbed of a navigable stream is part of the public domain (*res publica)*.[40] The riverbed of an unnavigable stream is presumably also part of the public domain but a

---

35 Art. 3.8, § 2 j. 3.55 j. 3.130 CC; J. Goedertier, "Het regiem der ondergrondse waters" (1953-1954) 36 *RW* 1957, p. 1659 and p. 1672; V. Sagaert, *Goederenrecht* in *Beginselen van Belgisch Privaatrecht*, Kluwer, Mechelen 2021, p. 205, no. 210.

36 Court of Appeal of Liège 17 December 1980, *JL* 1984, (576) pp. 576-577; Trib. Nivelles 13 February 1995, *T.Aann.* 1995, 2, (162) p. 166.

37 J. Gupta and H.J. Bosch, "Changing 'ownership' in water law: comparative experiences in the developing world" in J.W. Dellapena and J. Gupta (eds.), *Water law* in *Elgar encyclopedia of environmental law*, Volume X, Elgar, Cheltenham 2021, p. 321.

38 BE: A.M. Draye, T. Nulens and B. Vanheusden, *Het juridische statuut van de watermolens*, studie in opdracht van het ministerie van de Vlaamse Gemeenschap, 2005, p. 40, www.molenechos.org/juridische_nota_stuwrechten.pdf accessed 10.07.2023; F. Van Neste and S. Snaet, "Natrekking" in R. Derine, H. Cousy, J. Couturier, W. Delva, J. Herbots and R. Vekeman (eds.), *Het onroerend goed in de praktijk*, Kluwer, Mechelen (I.G.-1) I.G.4-1; NL: Art. 20, 1d DCC; H. Havekes, "Wie is juridisch eigenaar van het water?" (2020) 4 *De Landeigenaar* 10, pp. 10-11.

39 H. De Page and R. Dekkers, *Traité élémentaire de droit civil belge*, V, Bruylant, Brussels 1975, p. 902, no. 1019; K. De Schepper, "Beweegbare onroerende eigendom: over de juritectuur van drijvende woningen" (2022) 1-2 *TPR* 283, pp. 318-319.

40 Art. 538 old CC; Cass. 7 November 1856, *Pas.* 1857, I, (94) p. 100; Trib. Bruges 12 December 1990, *RW* 1990-91, (994) p. 994; A.M. Draye, T. Nulens and B. Vanheusden, *Het juridische statuut van de watermolens*, studie in opdracht van het ministerie van de Vlaamse Gemeenschap, 2005, p. 55, www.molenechos.org/juridische_nota_stuwrechten.pdf accessed 10.07.2023; D. Déom, P.-Y. Erneux, D. Lagasse and M. Pâques, *Domaine public, domaine privé, biens des pouvoirs publics* in *Rép.not.*, XIV, *Le droit public et administrative*, VII, Larcier, Brussels 2008, no. 47; H. De Page and R. Dekkers, *Traité élémentaire de droit civil belge*, V, Bruylant, Brussels 1975, pp. 704-705, no. 798 and p. 902, no. 1019; J. Dujardin, M. Van Damme, J. Vande Lanotte and A. Mast, *Overzicht van het Belgisch Administratief Recht*, Kluwer, Mechelen 2021, p. 345, no. 342; J. Hansenne, *Les biens. Précis*, I, Collection de la Faculté de Droit de Liège, Liège 1996, pp. 138-139, no. 121.

riparian owner can rebut this presumption.[41] Even though it is often assumed otherwise, the qualification as *res publica* does not equal public ownership: A privately owned riverbed can also be part of the public domain. The defining feature of a *res publica,* such as a riverbed, is not its property status but the fact that it is managed by public authorities to guarantee that it can be used by anyone in accordance with its purpose.[42] For this reason, the ownership of *res publicae* is restricted in some ways (*e.g.* it cannot be acquired through prescription, and the power of disposal of the owner is restricted).[43] In Dutch law the ground underneath public navigable waterways is similarly presumed to be the property of the Dutch state. This presumption is not applicable *vis-à-vis* other authorities that are or were traditionally in charge of the maintenance of the waterway.[44]

All water that can freely circulate to other parcels qualifies as *res nullius* in Dutch law.[45] Water confined to one parcel, like in some ponds, is in private property of the owner of the surrounding land.[46] However, the fact that freely circulating water is (temporarily) situated in the exclusive property sphere of the land owner, does entail that the owner can exclude others from accessing the water from his property.[47] Others can only use the space above and below the land as long as it is at a depth or height to which the owner of the land has no

---

41 Art. 16 Ord.Br. 16 May 2019 houdende het beheer en de bescherming van onbevaarbare waterlopen en vijvers, *BS* 28 June 2019, 66.308; art. D.34 Code Wallon de l'environnement 27 May 2004, *BS* 23 September 2004, 68.724; art. 16 wet 28 December 1967 betreffende de onbevaarbare waterlopen [Vlaams Gewest], *BS* 15 February 1968, 1403; Constitutional Court 14 October 2021, no. 137/2021, *TMR* 2022, 1, p. 133, B.19-B.23.

42 Cass. 15 March 2018, *T.Gem.* 2019, 2, 87, annotation S. De Winter; P. Jongbloet, "In en uit het openbaar domein" in R. Palmans, T. Leys and J. Toury (eds.), *Openbaar domein*, Intersentia, Antwerp 2019, pp. 59-61; V. Sagaert, "De hervorming van het goederenrecht" (2020) 1-2 *TPR* 389, pp. 497-498, no. 143.

43 S. Snaet and M. Muylle, "Waterregeling" in R. Derine, H. Cousy, J. Couturier, W. Delva, J. Herbots and R. Vekeman (eds.), *Het onroerend goed in de praktijk*, Kluwer, Mechelen (I.D.11-1) I.B.20-20; V. Sagaert, *Goederenrecht* in *Beginselen van Belgisch Privaatrecht*, Kluwer, Mechelen 2021, pp. 256-257, no. 270 and pp. 1196-1197, no. 1380.

44 Art. 5.27 DCC; C.J.J.M. Stolker, "Commentaar op art. 5:27 BW: Eigendom openbare vaarwateren" in H.B. Krans, C.J.J.M. Stolker and W.L. Valk (eds.), *T&C BW*, Kluwer, Deventer 2023 (update).

45 Art. 5.20, 5.25, 5.26, and 5.27, first para. DCC; A.C. van Schaick, "Kroniek van het zakenrecht (2001-2008), Deel I" (2008) 7 *NTBR* 38, p. 38; S.E. Bartels and A.A. van Velten, *Zakenrecht, Eigendom en beperkte rechten* in *Mr. C. Assers Handleiding tot de beoefening van het Nederlands Burgerlijk Recht (5)*, Kluwer, Deventer 2017, no. 97; C.J.J.M. Stolker, "Commentaar op art. 5:40 BW: Voorbijstromend water" in H.B. Krans, C.J.J.M. Stolker and W.L. Valk (eds.), *T&C BW*, Kluwer, Deventer 2023 (update); H. Havekes, "Wie is juridisch eigenaar van het water?" (2020) 4 *De Landeigenaar*, p. 10-11; W.H.M. Reehuis, A.H.T. Heisterkamp, G.E. Van Maanen and G.T. De Jong, *Pitlo. Het Nederlands burgerlijk recht. Deel 3. Goederenrecht*, Kluwer, Deventer 2019, p. 462, no. 537 (free circulating water is a *res nullius* until someone appropriates it).

46 Art. 20, 1d DCC.

47 Art. 5.21, first para. DCC; C.J.J.M. Stolker, "Commentaar op art. 5:20 BW: De grond" in H.B. Krans, C.J.J.M. Stolker and W.L. Valk (eds.), *T&C BW*, Kluwer, Deventer 2023 (update); F.J. Vonck, "Art. 5:20 BW, aant. 5 Water buiten open gemeenschap" in F.J. Vonck (ed.), *Groene Serie Zakelijke rechten*, Kluwer, Deventer; W.H.M. Reehuis, A.H.T.

interest of forbidding use.[48] The owner of a parcel adjacent to freely circulating water, can use the water for reasonable purposes (irrigation and drinking water for cattle are explicitly named as examples) as long as he does not cause nuisance to others.[49] For public water there is an additional condition to individual use, namely that it must be reconcilable with the public destination of the water.[50]

In Dutch law, groundwater is a *res nullius*, belonging to no one, until it is brought at the surface by a spring, well or pump.[51] In Belgium the legal qualification of groundwater stirs more debate. It is discussed whether groundwater is a *res nullius*, a *res communis* or part of the private property on land through accession (*res privata*).[52] To understand this discussion, it is important to know that there are no substantive legal criteria in Belgian law for determining which resources qualify as *res communes*. *Res communes* are commonly described as resources that belong to, or that affect the whole of a community.[53] Belgian law does stipulate legal features of *res communes*: They do not belong to anyone, they cannot be appropriated in their entirety and their use is common to everyone.[54] Scholarship almost unanimously qualifies flowing water as *res communes*, but continues to disagree on the question which water "flows".[55] The classification seems artificial since the doctrinal distinction between flowing and non-flowing water is not sufficiently based on scientific grounds (groundwater is not stagnant, instead it flows through

---

Heisterkamp, G.E. Van Maanen and G.T. De Jong, *Pitlo. Het Nederlands burgerlijk recht. Deel 3. Goederenrecht*, Kluwer, Deventer 2019, pp. 461-462, no. 536.

48 Art. 5.21, second para. DCC; C.J.J.M. Stolker, "Commentaar op art. 5:40 BW: Voorbijstromend water" in H.B. Krans, C.J.J.M. Stolker and W.L. Valk (eds.), *T&C BW*, Kluwer, Deventer 2023 (update).

49 Art. 5.40, first para. DCC.

50 Art. 5.40, second para. DCC; C.J.J.M. Stolker, "Commentaar op art. 5:40 BW: Voorbijstromend water" in H.B. Krans, C.J.J.M. Stolker and W.L. Valk (eds.), *T&C BW*, Kluwer, Deventer 2023 (update).

51 Art. 5.20, 1c DCC; C.J.J.M. Stolker, "Commentaar op art. 5:20 BW: De grond" in H.B. Krans, C.J.J.M. Stolker and W.L. Valk (eds.), *T&C BW*, Kluwer, Deventer 2023 (update).

52 Art. 3.130, 3.55 and 3.63 DCC; J. Goedertier, "Het regiem der ondergrondse waters" (1953-1954) 36 *RW* 1657, p. 1659; V. Sagaert, *Goederenrecht* in *Beginselen van Belgisch Privaatrecht*, Kluwer, Mechelen 2021, nos. 209-210.

53 **BE:** J. Van de Voorde, "Het nieuwe goederenrecht en het milieu" (2020) 3, *TMR* 272, p. 273, no. 5; M.S. De Clippele, "Quel avenir pour les choses communes?" in F. Haumont and J. Sambon (eds.), *L'environnement, le droit et le magistrat*, Larcier, Brussels 2021, (555) p. 560, no. 10; **FR:** F. Terré and P. Simler, *Droit civil: les biens in Précis Dalloz*, Dalloz, Paris 2018, 10, no. 7; M.-A. Chardeaux, *Les choses communes, LGDJ*, Paris 2006, p. 3, no. 1; M.-P. Camproux Duffrène, "Repenser l'article 714 du Code civil français comme une prote d'entrée vers les communs" (2018) 81 *RIEJ* 297, p. 300; P. Berlioz, *La notion de bien*, LGDJ, Paris 2007, p. 39, no. 122.

54 Art. 3.43, first para. CC.

55 A. Carette, "Een subjectief recht op een volwaardig leefmilieu" (1998) *TPR* 821, p. 831, no. 14; F. Van Neste, *Goederen, bezit en eigendom* in *Beginselen van Belgisch Privaatrecht*, V, Story-Scientia, Ghent 1990, p. 13, no. 6; J. Goedertier, "Het regiem der ondergrondse waters" (1953-1954) 36 *RW* 1657, p. 1659; J. Van de Voorde, "Het complexe goederenrechtelijke statuut van energie" (2019) 2 *MER* 117, p. 128.

different property spheres[56]; natural bodies of surface water are connected to groundwater and surface water within distinct property spheres[57] etc.)

Dutch property law does not recognize *res communes* as a distinct category.[58] Instead of discussing water's flowing nature, it makes a more logical distinction between individualized water and water that is still connected to other water ("freely flowing").[59] While the first category is susceptible to ownership, the latter cannot be owned as such. This, however, does not prevent people from individualizing water and subsequently appropriating it. Belgian private law could use some of the Dutch down-to-earth formulation. Still, the Belgian qualification of (some) water as a common holds an important advantage over Dutch law: It clearly states – within private law – that water should only be used in the general interest, *including that of future generations*.[60] In other words, the inappropriability of "flowing" water as a *res communis* does not prevent people from exclusively using (small) amounts of water, but delineates the way in which everyone may use water. This distinguishes the contemporary Belgian qualification from traditional *res communes*. The inappropriability of *res communes* used to be descriptive rather than prescriptive. *Res communes* were considered to fall outside the scope of property law because it was deemed technically impossible to gain control over these objects.[61] Today the common qualification is increasingly crystallizing the idea that, for socio-ecological reasons, certain scarce resources should not be monopolized.[62]

5. Inappropriable *res communes* vs. appropriable *res nullius* – At first glance, *res nullius* and *res communes* are two opposite legal qualifications.

---

56 C.R. Fitts, *Groundwater science*, Elsevier, Boston 2013, pp. 13-16.

57 C.R. Fitts, *Groundwater science*, Elsevier, Boston 2013, p. 125; VMM, *Moeten we ons zorgen maken over lage grondwaterstanden?*, www.youtube.com/watch?v=baIVCV-0vLo accessed 08.08.2023.

58 See for instance: A.C. Van Schaick, *Rechtsgevolgen en functies van bezit en houderschap* in *Monografieën nieuw BW*, A-serie 14, Kluwer, Deventer 2024, pp. 106–107, no. 85; H. Hennekens, *Openbare zaken naar publiek- en privaatrecht*, Tjeenk Willink, Deventer 2001, p.18 and p. 51.

59 Art. 5:20, first para. d) DCC; S.E. Bartels and A.A. van Velten, *Zakenrecht, Eigendom en beperkte rechten* in *Mr. C. Assers Handleiding tot de beoefening van het Nederlands Burgerlijk Recht (5)*, Kluwer, Deventer 2017, nos. 96-97.

60 Art. 3.43, first para. CC.

61 F. Ost, *la nature hors la loi. L'écologie à l'épreuve du droit*, la Découverte, Paris 1995, p. 60; J. Van De Voorde, "Het nieuwe goederenrecht en het milieu" (2020) 3 *TMR* 272, pp. 273-274.

62 Explanatory memorandum no. 2, *Parl.St.* Kamer (BE) 2019-20, no. 173/2, p. 5; A.C. van Schaick, "Kroniek van het zakenrecht (2001-2008), Deel I" (2008) 7 *NTBR* 38, p. 38; B. Coriat, "Le retour des communs" (2013), *Revue de la regulation*, no. 18 et seq; J.L. Vivero-Pol, "Food as Commons or Commodity? Exploring the Links between Normative Valuations and Agency in Food Transition" (2017) 9 *Sustainability* 442, pp. 442-451; M. de la Fuente, "A personal view. The water war in Cochabamba, Bolivia: Privatization triggers an uprising" (2003) 23 *Mountain Research and Development* 98, pp. 98-100; W. Dross, *Droit Civil. Les Choses*, LGDJ, Paris 2012, p. 580, no. 320-1.

The first category being characterized by its appropriability, the latter by its inappropriability.[63] Consequently one may wonder if a qualification as *res nullius* at some stage in the hydrologic cycle and a qualification as *res communes* in another stage is coherent. Yet, *res nullius* and *res communes* are connected qualifications since partial appropriation of *res communes* remains possible.[64] In that sense, a small part of a greater common can be identified as a *res nullius sensu stricto*.[65] For instance, water from a river can be bottled and sold as a commodity.[66] Some authors see this (partial) appropriation as a mere (common) use of the good.[67] Regardless, from a property law point of view, there is no watertight distinction between legal qualifications on the basis of the (in) appropriability of freshwater.[68]

6. **Duality** – Above all, these different legal qualifications of freshwater reveal a factual tension between the protection and the appropriation of water inherent in human interaction with the natural resource. Water is generally viewed from a protection perspective when qualified as a common or part of the public domain, whereas it is viewed through the lens of its useful appropriation as a commodity when it is qualified as a *res nullius* or when private (property) rights are awarded upon it (*res privata*). This tension between water as worthy of protection and water as an appropriable good is inevitable. Water law has the challenging task

63 Art. 3.43, first and second para. CC; A.C. van Schaick, "Kroniek van het zakenrecht (2001-2008), Deel I" (2008) 7 *NTBR* 38, p. 38; H. De Page and R. Dekkers, *Traité élémentaire de droit civil belge*, V, Bruylant, Brussels 1975, p. 540, no. 542 and p. 888, no. 1004; V. Sagaert, *Goederenrecht* in *Beginselen van Belgisch Privaatrecht*, Kluwer, Mechelen 2021, p. 277, no. 293; V. Sagaert and S. Demeyere, "Le droit des biens et le droit de l'environnement: vers une réconciliation" (2019) 16 *JT* 313, p. 321, no. 36.

64 Court of Appeal of Ghent 11 September 2007, *TGR* 2008, nr. 2, (155) p. 155; A. Lebrun, "L'environnement, son défenseur et le juge civil" (1990) 1 *Amén.* 47, pp. 47-51; H. Schoukens, "Het toekennen van rechten aan de natuur: had Darwin dan toch gelijk?" (2020) 2 *TMR* 124, p. 138, no. 31 and p. 150, no. 62; S. Snaet and W. Neven, "Eigendom" in G. Baert (ed.), *Bestendig handboek privaatrechtelijk bouwrecht*, 2017, (II.4-1) II.4-12 – II.4-13.

65 **BE:** A. Hucq, "Code civil et enjeux écologiques: le cas des choses communes" (2022) 7 *TBBR* 363, p. 367; B. Jadot, "L'article 714 du Code Civil et la protection de l'environnement" in *L'actualité du droit de l'environnement*, Bruylant, Brussels 1995, p. 55, no. 3; M.-L. Degroote, "Deel III. Basiscomponenten van het recht. Hoofdstuk III. Rechtsobject" in R. De Corte, B. De Groote and D. Bruloot (eds.), *Privaatrecht in hoofdlijnen. Volume 1 – Inleiding tot het recht*, LeA Uitgevers, Leuven 2022, pp. 222–223, nos. 302A and B; **FR:** M. Rémond-Gouilloud, "Ressources naturelles et choses sans maître" (1985), *D.* 27, pp. 27–34.

66 M.-A. Chardeaux, *Les choses communes*, LGDJ, Paris 2006, p. 93, no. 82.

67 **BE:** A. Carette, "Een subjectief recht op een volwaardig leefmilieu" (1998) *TPR* 821, pp. 832-833, no. 16; B. Vanheusden, "Soil and land stewardship: hefboom voor meer bodemzorg en hoe past dit binnen ons eigendomsrecht?" (2019) 2 *TOO* 143, p. 145; V. Sagaert, *Goederenrecht* in *Beginselen van Belgisch Privaatrecht*, Kluwer, Mechelen 2021, p. 293, no. 307; **FR:** C. Larroumet and B. Mallet-Bricout, *Les biens, droits réels principaux, Tome II*, Economica, Paris 2019, p. 649, no. 967.

68 S. Leprince, "De l'usage de l'eau, ou comment le droit wallon évolue pour appréhender la raréfaction de la ressource" in J. Sambon (ed.), *L'environnement, le droit et le magistrat*, 1e édition, Larcier, Brussels 2021, pp. 608-611.

of regulating the delicate balance between the protection of the water system and interference with it. The concepts of *res communes*, *res publicae*, *res privata* and *res nullius* each represent a way of dealing with the duality in the human interaction with water on an individual and a societal level. The qualifications can be interpreted coherently: *Res publicae* and *res communes* emphasize that private property rights on water are not absolute but subject to limitations in the general interest.[69]

In that regard the distinction between *res publicae* and *res communes* is less sharp than it might seem. Whereas the commons are often presented as the third path, an alternative to the private-public dichotomy[70], protection of the general interest is key to both the *res publicae* and the *res communes* categories. Traditionally navigable rivers were qualified as *res publicae* because navigation was important for trade.[71] Today, the general interest also encompasses sustainable water management from a socio-ecological point of view[72], more often associated with *res communes* (see *supra* nos. 4-5). As a result, the distinction between *res publicae* and *res communes* is blurring.[73] Meanwhile, we increasingly observe that (groups of) private individuals act in favor of an objective that exceeds their economic self-interest and contest the approach to the general interest chosen by public actors for a lack of socio-ecological awareness.[74] Collective private water management and public water management are not so much different from an appropriation point of view, but

---

69 A. Hucq, G. Rolland and C. Romainville, "L'eau, la terre, l'environnement: trois biens communs en quête de reconnaissance concrete en droit belge" (2022) 33 *JT* 607, p. 607; U. Mattei, A. Quarta, and F. Valguarnera, "Meeting the Challenge of the Commons: An Emerging Field of Common Core Research" in U. Mattei, A. Quarta, F. Valguarnera and R.J. Fisher (eds.), *Property Meeting the Challenge of the Commons*, Springer, Cham 2023, pp. 24-25.

70 D. Misonne, M. de Clippele and F. Ost, "L'actualité des communs à la croisée des enjeux de l'environnement et de la culture" (2018) 2 *RIEJ* 59, p. 79; E. Schlager and E. Ostrom, "Property-Rights regimes and natural resources: a conceptual analysis" (1992) 69 *Land Economics* 249, pp. 259-260; U. Mattei, A. Quarta, and F. Valguarnera, "Meeting the Challenge of the Commons: An Emerging Field of Common Core Research" in U. Mattei, A. Quarta, F. Valguarnera and R.J. Fisher (eds.), *Property Meeting the Challenge of the Commons*, Springer, Cham 2023, p. 10.

71 D. Lagasse, *Droit de la voirie. Droit de la domanialité publique* in *Répertoire pratique du droit belge*, Brussels, Larcier 2019, pp. 80-81, no 91.

72 See Art. 1.3, fourth para. CC.

73 Some authors see a different role for the government depending on whether water belongs to the category of the *res publicae* or the *res communes*. In the first case, the government acts as the owner of the water. In the second case, the government acts as a mere administrator or trustee, without appropriating the water. Regulations of the use of *res communes* would consequently be interpreted more strictly than regulations of the use of *res publicae*. See: D. Déom, P.-Y. Erneux, D. Lagasse and M. Pâques, *Domaine public, domaine privé, biens des pouvoirs publics* in *Rép.not.*, XIV, *Le droit public et administratif*, VII, Brussels, Larcier 2008, nos. 41-42.

74 See e.g. M. Kruithof, "Privaatrechtlijke facetten van algemeenbelangacties bij de justitiële rechter" (2022) 1-2 *TPR* 21, pp. 44-47, nos. 32-41.

represent two different responses to the question: *Who do we trust to manage water sustainably?* The powers of the entrusted water actors are, however, built upon different grounds of legitimation: The input of public authorities, citizens, local farmers, industry and environmental organizations in water management is accepted for different reasons.[75]

III. ACCESS AND CONTROL

7. **Beyond appropriation** – Despite being presented as the main feature of *res communes*, inappropriability is not what protects water.[76] Water cannot be protected by simply forbidding any sort of appropriation. Water is inevitably "appropriated", in the sense that people acquire access to water and control over it, (temporarily) excluding others (rivalry).[77] For example, when farmer X uses water to irrigate his land, farmers Y and Z cannot simultaneously use the same water for the irrigation of their crops. When a factory uses large amounts of cooling-water in its industrial processes, the water is temporarily unavailable for other water actors. If the factory decides to share the effluent water with industrial players close-by, the former has the factual power to include some and exclude others from the water's use. These examples show that theoretical discussions about the (in)appropriability of water as a common and water as the object of (private) rights, in practice amount to the division of access and control over water. Different private and public actors want to obtain and retain legal access to water. However, faced with water's scarcity as compared to societal

---

75 See: A. van Buuren, E.-H. Klijn and J. Edelenbos, "Democratic legitimacy of new forms of water management in the Netherlands" (2011) 28 *International Journal of Water Resources Development* 1, pp. 1-17; M. Alexander, N. Doorn and S. Priest, "Bridging the legitimacy gap – Translating theory into practical signposts for legitimate flood risk governance" (2018) 18 *Regional Environmental Change* 397, pp. 397-408; S. Almazán-Casali, B. Peregrina Puga and M.C. Lemos, "Who Governs at What Price? Technocratic Dominance, Ways of Knowing, and Long-Term Resilience of Brazil's Water System" (2021) 3 *Front. Water* 1, pp. 1-13; S. Trowsdale, K. Boyle and T. Baker, "Politics, water management and infrastructure" (2020) 378 *Phil.Trans.R.Soc.A* 1, pp. 1-13.

76 Not individual appropriation of all water but systemic infringements on water quality and quantity threaten the entire water stock. See: D. Misonne, "Les communs environnementaux" (2022) 33 *JT* 595, p. 599.

77 In this article we refer to the legal concepts of *res communes* and *res publicae*. In economics, goods are categorised in private goods, public goods, common resources, and club goods based on two (factual) characteristics: whether people can be prevented from consuming them (excludability) and whether individuals can consume them without affecting their availability to other individuals (rivalrousness). Freshwater in its natural state (as compared to, for instance, bottled water) is an economic common good given that it is non-excludable but rival. This means that virtually anyone can use this water, but that the consumption by one individual reduces water's availability for other individuals. See: C. White, "Understanding water markets: Public vs. private goods" (2015), Global Water Forum, www.globalwaterforum.org/2015/04/27/understanding-water-markets-public-vs-private-goods/ accessed 20.11.2023.

and ecological needs, they want to have broader control over who is included and who is excluded from accessing water. VAN ERP places the management of access at the core of ownership. Although his analysis was concentrated on the ownership of data, his writings resonate in the water context:

> "[...] whether the apex of data rights is called 'ownership', 'management' or any other term, the debate on data rights should be on content and it should be realistic, pragmatic and taking into account differing interests and stakeholders."[78]

In property theory, the idea of including and excluding people from the use of an object is the battlefield of private property (obtained through title, e.g. buying water, or through occupation of a *res nullius*), public domain and the commons. How legal systems worldwide are dealing with those societal conflicts over water can – according to DELLAPENNA – be classified in three archetypes: (i) common property, (ii) private property and (iii) public ownership.[79] Most legal systems, however, combine elements of the archetypes. Such hybrid systems are widely prevalent.[80] Their prevalence shows that, regardless of the theoretical emphasis on private, public, or common water law, every legal system continues to struggle with third-party access (inclusiveness) and the wider need for sustainable water use.

8. Common property – In DELLAPENNA's classification common property refers to the Hardinian notion of a common[81]: a system of open access, with more or less unregulated water use by a group of potential users. By default, these systems involve landlocked people who largely decide for themselves when, where, how and how much water they use.[82] The riparian rights derived from

---

78 S. VAN ERP, *All good things come to an end, but access remains*, Wolf Legal Publishers, Oisterwijk 2021, pp. 53-56.

79 J.W. DELLAPENNA, "Fundamental concepts of property in water and the role of markets in water governance" in J.W. DELLAPENNA and J. GUPTA (eds.), *Water law* in *Elgar encyclopedia of environmental law*, Volume X, Elgar, Cheltenham 2021, pp. 86-103.

80 D. SCHORR, "Water rights" in M. GRAZIADEI and L. SMITH (eds.), *Comparative Property Law: Global Perspectives*, Cheltenham, Elgar 2017, pp. 283-284; J. GUPTA and H. J. BOSCH, "Changing 'ownership' in water law: comparative experiences in the developing world" in J.W. DELLAPENNA and J. GUPTA (eds.), *Water law* in *Elgar encyclopedia of environmental law*, Volume X, Elgar, Cheltenham 2021, pp. 322-323.

81 G. HARDIN, "The Tragedy of the Commons" (1968) 162 *Science* 1243, pp. 1243-1248; See: D. MISONNE, M. DE CLIPPELE and F. OST, "L'actualité des communs à la croisée des enjeux de l'environnement et de la culture" (2018) 2 *RIEJ* 59, p. 68; S. COGOLATI, *International law to save the commons. The international legal protection of the commons in development*, unpublished. Doctoral Thesis in Law KU Leuven, 2020, p. 13; T. DE MOOR, "From Common Pastures to Global Commons: a Historical perspective on Interdisciplinary Approaches to Commons" (2011) 19 *Natures Sciences Sociétés* 422, p. 425.

82 J.W. DELLAPENNA, "Fundamental concepts of property in water and the role of markets in water governance" in J.W. DELLAPENNA and J. GUPTA (eds.), *Water law* in *Elgar encyclopedia of environmental law*, Volume X, Elgar, Cheltenham 2021, pp. 89-92.

Roman law represent this type of water division.[83] This system does not work in case of (imminent) water shortages, does not avoid a tragedy of the commons and is too vague to resolve disputes. Generally phrased, limitations to use water "reasonably" are just not clear enough when water is not plentiful.[84] The moderate riparian rights systems in Belgium[85] and the Netherlands[86] today can be explained by the historical struggle of the Low Countries with floods rather than water shortages (see *supra* no. 1).

9. **Private property** – The second archetype entails the attribution of exclusive rights on water. By inserting a priority order, such systems hope to avoid a tragedy of the commons. The problems associated with free access to water are thought to be solved by granting certain users (or uses) priority over others. Usually, however, the allocation of water rights happens on a first come, first served basis, the same logic which underlies the *res nullius* concept. The regulatory framework in most Western States of the United States infamously illustrates the unwanted outcomes of such private property in water law.[87] The first come, first served system has the major disadvantage that the lowest priority users lose all their rights before the highest priority users have to diminish their water use at all. Since there is no maximization of marginal productivity, nor adequate risk pooling, this system violates two basic economic principles.[88] Put simply, in times of (imminent) water shortages the users granted the highest priority are not incentivized to show solidarity because the (economic) risks lie with lower priority users alone.

10. **Public property** – The last category distinguished by DELLAPENNA is public ownership within a permit system. This system is not sacrosanct in protecting water quality and quantity either because competent authorities tend to give long-term certainties to companies, thereby not granting permits with a

83 J.W. DELLAPENNA, "Fundamental concepts of property in water and the role of markets in water governance" in J.W. DELLAPENNA and J. GUPTA (eds.), *Water law* in *Elgar encyclopedia of environmental law*, Volume X, Elgar, Cheltenham 2021, pp. 91-92.

84 E. RYAN, "A short History of the Public Trust Doctrine and its intersection with private water law" (2020) 38 *VA. ENVTL. L.J.* 135, pp. 183-185.

85 Art. 3.130 CC.

86 Art. 5.39 and 5.40 DCC.

87 C. SMIT, "The Reasonable Use Doctrine, the Public Trust Doctrine, and Surface Water Rights in California: Exploring the Frontiers of Water Rights Reform in an Era of Scarcity and Instability" (2021) 45 *ENVIRONS Environmental law and Policy Journal* 71, pp. 76-77; E. GARNER, R. MCGLOTHLIN, L. SZEPTYCKI, C. BABBITT and V. KINCAID, "The sustainable groundwater management act and the common law of groundwater rights. Finding a consistent path forward for groundwater allocation" (2020) 38 *UCLA Journal of Environmental Law and policy* 163, p. 163 and pp. 170-186.

88 J.W. DELLAPENNA, "Fundamental concepts of property in water and the role of markets in water governance" in J.W. DELLAPENNA and J. GUPTA (eds.), *Water law* in *Elgar encyclopedia of environmental law*, Volume X, Elgar, Cheltenham 2021, pp. 92-94.

(clear) time limit. Even if permits are limited in time, they are often renewable and rarely not renewed.[89]

In introducing a system of permits, the intention has generally been to replace one kind of property right based on a land tenure, i.e. a traditional formal[90] water right, with another, i.e. a modern formal water right.[91] As permits are designed to provide an equivalent degree of security as traditional formal water rights[92] in order to prevent claims of expropriation, they create a form of quasi-property right. Although modern formal water rights confer a right of use and not an ownership right, they nevertheless create a form of quasi-property right given that modern formal water rights are, just like traditional formal water rights, capable of being asserted against third parties and the state.[93] The introduction of permits can, however, amount to regulatory licensing[94] instead

89 S. Hodgson, "Exploring the concept of water tenure" (2016), 10 *FAO Land and water discussion paper* 1, pp. 18-19.

90 Formal water rights are defined by formal law. Besides traditional formal water rights, based on land tenure, and modern formal water rights, based on permits, the literature describes e.g. regulatory licensing, agency control, water supply contracts, investment contracts, *de minimis* uses and minimal flow requirements as forms of formal water rights. The term "formal" emphasizes that there also exist water relationships that are not defined by formal law e.g. customary or local water tenure, water tenure under religious law, informal tenure, assumed and impossible tenure and unrecognized tenure. Water tenure, rather than water right, is used to refer to the relationships, whether legally or customarily defined between people, as individuals or groups, with respect to water resources. Thinking in terms of water tenure instead of water rights should further the understanding of relationships with water resources as they actually are, rather than show how laws and regulations suggest that they should be.
See: S. Hodgson, "Exploring the concept of water tenure" (2016) 10 *FAO Land and water discussion paper* 1, p. xiii-xiv and p. 4.

91 Almost all traditional formal water rights derive as a matter of law from existing land tenure rights. They are increasingly unable to effectively regulate access to water resources because they are outdated in terms of hydrological knowledge and technological abilities. In addition, they are often difficult to quantify and to enforce. Many countries thus move away from traditional formal water rights to modern formal water rights that are distinct from land tenure rights. Modern formal water rights are permit-based long-term rights that depend on monitoring. See: S. Hodgson, "Exploring the concept of water tenure" (2016) 10 *FAO Land and water discussion paper* 1, pp. 15-16.

92 Generally speaking, from the perspective of the right holder, the longer duration of a right equals more security. However, the duration of a right is not always conclusive. An indefinite right that is incapable of effective delineation or that cannot exclude others from the resource will not provide much security. See: S. Hodgson, "Exploring the concept of water tenure" (2016) 10, *FAO Land and water discussion paper* 1, p. 43.

93 A common element of the idea of property is the right to exclude others either from a physical space or from the right to use the substance of the property right. If permit holders can exclude others form using the water, their modern formal water right is similar to a property right. However, not all modern formal rights entail the right to sell or dispose, which is why the term quasi-property is coined. See: S. Hodgson, "Exploring the concept of water tenure" (2016) 10 *FAO Land and water discussion paper* 1, pp. 16-19.

94 Sometimes called command and control regulation. See: B. Lankford and N. Hepworth, "The cathedral and the bazaar: Monocentric and polycentric river basin management" (2010) 3 *Water Alternatives* 82, pp. 82-101.

of modern formal water rights. When permits are of short duration (e.g. one year), they do not result in a quasi-property right over water. Even if they may be renewable, their short duration and personal nature makes them less capable of being enforced against third parties and the state than modern formal water rights.[95] The Rodotà commission in Italy emphasized the temporariness of permits.[96] However, the temporal dimension of water rights is still too often ignored by lawmakers.

Besides determining the end date of water permits, authorities should also consider permit conditions imposing actual water use within a given period of time to avoid water speculation and hoarding.[97] Apart from the risk of being caught and punished, short-term regulatory licenses give too little incentive for compliance and are criticized for lacking the security businesses need for investing in expensive long-term water projects.[98] However, hydrological changes and increasing water demands beg the question how much legal certainty law can provide when it is not respecting the physical limits of the water system.[99] The concept of the commons is put forward as a way of staying within the planetary boundaries.[100]

11. Hybrid systems and compensation – Gupta and Bosch emphasize that most legal systems have hybrid water law in which traditional private water rights are combined with more recent public water permits. The fear that a public authority would have to pay compensation when simply abolishing and replacing the system of individual water rights, is used to explain this widespread

---

95 S. Hodgson, "Exploring the concept of water tenure" (2016) 10 *FAO Land and water discussion paper* 1, pp. 18-19.

96 D. Misonne, M. de Clippele and F. Ost, "L'actualité des communs à la croisée des enjeux de l'environnement et de la culture" (2018) 2 *RIEJ* 59, p. 73; U. Mattei, "Institutionalizing the Commons: An Italian Primer" (2007), *Commons Blog*, https://commonsblog.files.wordpress.com/2007/10/mattei-italian-commons-chapter-short.pdf accessed 16.11.2023.
If water rights are indefinite or excessively long, it may make it more difficult to allocate additional water for the environment. See: S. Hodgson, "Exploring the concept of water tenure" (2016) 10 *FAO Land and water discussion paper* 1, p. 48.

97 S. Hodgson, "Exploring the concept of water tenure" (2016) 10 *FAO Land and water discussion paper* 1, p. 18.

98 How much security a water right offers largely depends on two elements. On the one hand, it depends on whether the right holder can count on being able to use sufficient amounts of water of sufficient quality over a sufficiently long period. The sufficiency of the quality and quality of the available water and of the period of availability is to be judged for each type of water use. On the other hand, the right holder's security depends on his means of preventing other people from interfering in his use of water resources. See: S. Hodgson, "Exploring the concept of water tenure" (2016) 10 *FAO Land and water discussion paper* 1, p. 43.

99 Dephysicalised property law has abstracted legal constructs from the physical realities of the place in which the law operates. See: N. Graham, "Dephysicalised property and shadow lands" (2019) *Legal studies research paper series the university of Sydney law school* no. 19/83, p. 3.

100 See e.g. W. Steffen, J. Rockström, K. Richardson and S.E. Cornell, "Planetary boundaries: Guiding human development on a changing planet" (2015) 347 *Science*, p. 7.

phenomenon in water law[101], but is elsewhere more generally described as an obstacle for effective climate adaptive legislation.[102] The high degree of regulatory inertia which marks climate adaptive legislation may partially be explained by obstacles in our current constitutional conception of property as a human right. Governments are reluctant to interfere with property rights because (environmental) regulations could possibly trigger a duty to compensate.[103] With regard to water the fear is activated on two fronts: Private water rights themselves, and the ownership of land, factories, agricultural corporations etc. for the exploitation of which water is used or otherwise impacted.

Both Belgian and Dutch water law is hybrid (see *supra* no. 4). Another famous example of a persistent hybrid system is Spain.[104] The Spanish government made an unsuccessful attempt to phase out private water rights to groundwater. Although at first glance the 1985 Spanish Water Law clearly states that groundwater is public property, the majority of Spanish groundwater nevertheless remains privately owned. Only wells drilled since 1986 automatically belong to the public domain. The majority of wells were drilled before 1986 and are most frequently still the object of private ownership. In fact, after the 1985 change in the law, all private owners of wells had a period of three years (no later than December 31, 1988) to join the "registry" (*Registro de Aguas*). The only legal alternative was the inclusion of their well on the "catalogue" (*Catálogo de cuenca*). Existing wells listed in the registry have the legal status of temporary private wells (*aprovechamiento temporal de aguas privadas*).[105] In practice, this means that private ownership is maintained and respected

---

101 J. Gupta and H. J. Bosch, "Changing 'ownership' in water law: comparative experiences in the developing world", in J.W. Dellapenna and J. Gupta (eds.), *Water law* in *Elgar encyclopedia of environmental law*, Volume X, Elgar, Cheltenham 2021, pp. 322-323.

102 V. Petersen, "Constitutional Property Law" in B. Akkermans (ed.), *A Research Agenda for Property Law*, Elgar, Northampton 2024, pp. 39-56.

103 V. Petersen and B. Akkermans, "Eminent domain, regulatory takings and the right to property" in C. Bevan (ed.), *Handbook of Property, Law and Theory*, Cheltenham, Elgar, 2024, pp. 326-344.

104 J. Gupta and H. J. Bosch, "Changing 'ownership' in water law: comparative experiences in the developing world" in J.W. Dellapenna and J. Gupta (eds.), *Water law* in *Elgar encyclopedia of environmental law*, Volume X, Elgar Cheltenham 2021, pp. 322-323.

105 **ES:** Art. 2 Disposiciones Transitorias, Ley 29/1985, de 2 de agosto, de Aguas, *BOE* n° 189, de 8 de agosto de 1985, 25123-25135: "*1. En el plazo de tres años, a partir de la entrada en vigor de la presente Ley, los titulares de algún derecho conforme a la legislación que se deroga, sobre aguas privadas procedentes de manantiales que vinieran utilizándose en todo o en parte, podrán acreditar el mismo, así como el régimen de utilización del recurso, ante el Organismo de cuenca, para su inclusión en el Registro de Aguas como aprovechamiento temporal de aguas privadas. Dicho régimen será respetado por un plazo máximo de cincuenta años. Quienes, al término de dicho plazo, se encontrarán utilizando los caudales, en virtud del título legítimo, tendrán derecho preferente para la obtención de la correspondiente concesión administrativa, de conformidad con lo previsto en la presente Ley.*
El carácter opcional de la alternativa que se regula en este apartado excluye cualquier obligación compensatoria para la Administración hacia quien la ejercite, como consecuencia de la transformación del derecho.

for 50 years. After that period, ownership is automatically transferred to the state without compensation, although an administrative concession would be granted to enable the former owner to continue to use the well. The alternative option of the catalogue offered no such promises to private well owners. Thus, the government hoped that within three years most Spaniards would opt for the temporary security of the registry and that all groundwater would thus automatically become public domain half a century later.[106] However, the desired effect was not achieved. Only 10-20% of well owners joined the registry in time. Those owners will lose their private rights on groundwater between 2036 and 2038. In contrast, those who did not join the registry (an overwhelming 80-90%) will retain their private property on a groundwater well indefinitely.[107]

The reasoning of the Spanish government is strange from an expropriation perspective. Groundwater itself is not contained within the borders of private property on land. When someone abstracts groundwater from a well on his privately owned land, he will inevitably abstract water from underneath other people's privately owned land as well, influencing water's availability and quality for all.[108] The idea of privately owned wells is therefore factually erroneous. One could argue that the argument goes differently; that the government risks

---

2. Transcurrido el plazo de tres años previsto en el apartado 1, sin que los interesados hubieren acreditado sus derechos, aquéllos mantendrán su titularidad en la misma forma que hasta ahora, pero no podrán gozar de la protección administrativa que se deriva de la inscripción en el Registro de Aguas.

3. En cualquiera de los supuestos anteriores, el incremento de los caudales totales utilizados. así como la modificación de las condiciones o régimen del aprovechamiento, requerirán la oportuna concesión que ampare la totalidad de la explotación según lo establecido en la presente Ley.

4. En todo caso, a los aprovechamientos de aguas a que se refiere esta disposición transitoria les serán aplicables las normas que regulan la sobreexplotación de acuíferos, los usos del agua en caso de sequía grave o de urgente necesidad, y en general, las relativas a limitaciones del uso del dominio público hidráulico."

106 J.M. Fornés, A. de la Hera, R. Llamas and P. Martínez-Santos, "Legal Aspects of Groundwater Ownership in Spain" (2007) 32 *Water International* 676, p. 677; See: Art. 4 Disposiciones Transitorias, Ley 29/1985, de 2 de agosto, de Aguas, *BOE* n° 189, de 8 de agosto de 1985, 25123-25135: "1. *Los aprovechamientos de aguas calificadas como privadas por la legislación anterior a esta Ley se podrán inscribir en el Registro de Aguas a petición de sus titulares legítimos, y a los efectos previstos en las disposiciones transitorias segunda y tercera.*

2. Todos los aprovechamientos de aguas calificadas como privadas por la legislación anterior a esta Ley, se declararán por sus titulares legítimos ante el Organismo de cuenca, en los plazos que se determine reglamentariamente.

El Organismo de cuenca, previo conocimiento de sus características y aforo, los incluirá en el Catálogo de aprovechamientos de aguas privadas de la cuenca.

3. Los titulares de aprovechamientos de aguas continentales de cualquier clase, que no los hubieren inscrito en el Registro de Aguas o incluido en el Catálogo de cuenca, podrán ser objeto de multas coercitivas en la forma y cuantía que resulten de la aplicación de los criterios determinados en el artículo 109 de la presente Ley."

107 J.M. Fornés, A. de la Hera, R. Llamas and P. Martínez-Santos, "Legal Aspects of Groundwater Ownership in Spain" (2007) 32 *Water International* 676, p. 678.

108 S. Snaet and M. Muylle, "Waterregeling" in R. Derine, H. Cousy, J. Couturier, W. Delva, J. Herbots and R. Vekeman (eds.), *Het onroerend goed in de praktijk*, Kluwer,

to interfere with the private property of land or business in a disproportionate manner, by removing the "water-stick" from the bundle of rights.[109] This reasoning is difficult to uphold *if* what the public authority aims to do is regulating water to protect its availability for all and *if* decisions about water permits are based on scientifically sound information. Provided that those two conditions – both grounded in the modern commons – are met, the public authority is not interfering in a disproportionate manner with the use of "private wells". The ownership status of the water is thus less relevant than the (limits of the) decision power over the water. This leads back to an old discussion about the public domain: Is the competent public authority an *administrator* or the *owner* (of the water) and what are the limits of its power to award individual rights on the public domain (varying in degree of exclusivity)?[110]

This does not mean that the expropriation framework is irrelevant in the shift towards more sustainable water management. For instance, the government could expropriate private property when it is ill located in a floodable area to restore the natural wet land. The relevant question here is not whether this constitutes an expropriation – it does – but how the compensation should be calculated.[111]

One cannot help to think that the issue of compensation is sometimes used by politicians in view of appeasing social turmoil when the *status quo* is changed. The legislator should dare to change an existing situation if it is no longer in line with the general interest, instead of prioritizing the protection of long-lasting situations at the expense of sustainable water management for current and future generations. For instance, groundwater tables in Flanders would highly benefit if all garden owners were obliged to remove a certain percentage of tiles, cement etc. sealing the soil. If garden owners restore a green area where the water can infiltrate into the ground, less water would run off hardened

---

Mechelen (I.D.11-1) I.D.11-44. See: C.R. Fitts, *Groundwater science*, Elsevier, Boston 2013, pp. 13-16.

109 See: D.R. Johnson, "Reflections on the bundle of rights" (2007) 32 *Vermont Law Review* 247, pp. 247-272.

110 G. Viljoen, "Construing the transformed property paradigm of South Africa's water law: new opportunities presented by legal pluralism" (2021) 54 *The journal of legal pluralism and unofficial law* 193, pp. 203-204. In the U.S.A. the public trust doctrine has gradually transformed from an affirmation of sovereign authority over water resources to a recognition of sovereign responsibility to protect them from present and future generations. See: E. Ryan, "A short History of the Public Trust Doctrine and its intersection with private water law" (2020) 38 *VA. ENVTL. L.J.* 135, p. 138; O.R. Young, "Land use, environmental change and sustainable development: the role of institutional diagnostics" (2011) 5 *International Journal of the Commons* 66, p. 73.

111 See: K. Heylen, "Hoe wapenen we ons tegen wateroverlast? 'We moeten rivieren plaats geven en dat betekent ook onteigeningen'", *vrt nws* 17 November, 2023, www.vrt.be/vrtnws/nl/2023/11/17/wateroverlast-wat-kunnen-we-doen-om-ons-hiertegen-te-wapenen accessed 18.11.2023.

surfaces and be "lost" to the sewerage.[112] To the extent that this infiltration has a limited financial impact on property owners, it should be considered to be part of the social obligation of private owners[113] to contribute to sustainable water management on their private property. The need for compensation does not arise. Instead, public funds could be directed to helping citizens de-harden their gardens and advising them in the search for indigenous plants. The legislative intervention would help to better protect private property against both floods and drought.[114] Private property is thus protected through a relatively small regulatory interference.

IV. SHARED RESPONSIBILITY

12. Public-private symbiosis – We demonstrated that legal water qualifications and typologies of water law, do not suffice to get through to the core of today's challenges of sustainable water management. Alternatively, we suggest looking at the powers attributed by water rights, rather than fixating on formal denominations. We do not dive into the specific contours of those powers here, but consider the basic assumption that water management should be the joint responsibility of both public and private actors inevitably using water and otherwise impacting the water system.

13. The need for private water rights – As water flows across the boundaries of (private) property on land and individual interventions in the water system have a cumulative impact on the natural resource, an external, often public, authorization is deemed necessary to protect water's quality and quantity for all.[115] Despite most legal systems today having at least some form of water permits (see *supra* no. 7), private water rights will always remain relevant because it is impossible nor desirable that public actors manage every human interaction with water. The Netherlands, for example know a relatively high acceptance of the power of central authorities to manage water. This tends, however, to lead

---

112 Vlaams departement omgeving, "Ontharden: impact op wateroverlast", https://omgeving.vlaanderen.be/nl/ontharden-impact-op-wateroverlast accessed 20.11.2023.

113 See on the social function of property and the human flourishing theory: G.S. Alexander and E.M. Peñalver, *An Introduction to Property Theory*, Cambridge University Press, Cambridge 2012, pp. 91-97; S.R. Foster and D. Bonilla, "The Social Function of Property: A Comparative Law Perspective" (2011) 80 *Fordham law review* 101, pp. 101-113; V. Petersen, "Climate Change and the Social Function of Property – a Human Flourishing Reading of Article 1 of Protocol No. 1 to the European Convention on Human Rights" in B. Hoops (ed.), *Takings for Climate Justice – Rethinking Expropriation Law*, IV, Eleven, Den Haag, 2024, pp. 213-245.

114 Expertenpanel hoogwaterbeveiliging 2022, pp. 62-65.

115 G.S. Alexander, "Property as a fundamental constitutional right? The German Example" (2003) 88 *Cornell L. Rev.* 733, pp. 764-765.

to an underestimation of private responsibility towards sustainable water management.[116]

As private actors inevitably impact the water system, be it through water or through land use, they share a responsibility to value water in that interaction. Farmers, industrial players, and citizens should have the room to actively take up that responsibility and cooperate with each other (and with public actors) to manage water more sustainably. Two examples can help to understand the need for private water rights.

First, industrial players are striving towards circular water use. Water sharing can help to achieve that goal. Take for instance company A whose effluent water is of insufficient quality for further use in its own production process. Instead of directly purifying the water – which comes with high energy costs – the effluent water is transferred to company B nearby. Company B can use the effluent water a second time before purification.[117] The companies want to contractually agree on the terms and conditions of their water sharing, for which they need a framework of private water rights.

Second, imagine a drinking water company that wants to establish a local rainwater network in a new residential area. It wants to contract with the owners of the houses in that area to capture and collect rainwater, a *res nullius*, from their roofs, purify it on site and subsequently redistribute it as tap water of drinking quality between them. The drinking water company does not consider itself to be the owner of the water, but wants to organize a form of *commoning*. The local rainwater network will need to transcend the current owners and continue to operate after houses are sold in the future. Servitudes can be used to establish such network.[118]

Innovation and cooperation can improve water management, but require that private actors can construe their water projects on the basis of private water rights. Their engagement *vis-à-vis* the general interest should be recognized in private law. Permits and environmental legislation should coordinate the shared

116 Ons water, *Waterpeil 2020*, 8, https://klimaatadaptatienederland.nl/@212601/waterpeil/ accessed 12.08.2023: "*De valkuil is echter dat Nederlanders een positief beeld hebben van waterbeheer in Nederland, waardoor er een bepaalde vanzelfsprekendheid uitgaat van zowel zoetwater beschikbaarheid, waterveiligheid en waterkwaliteit.*"
One could make the broader argument that centralized public water supplies, threaten to decrease European citizens' knowledge about where 'their' water comes from and which challenges of scarcity and energy costs are associated with it.

117 See www.vmm.be/water/projecten/proeftuinen-droogte accessed 13.10.2023 for similar sustainable water projects subsidized by the Flemish Blue Deal Program.

118 See on conventional water servitudes: H. De Page and R. Dekkers, *Traité élémentaire de droit civil belge*, V, Bruylant, Brussels 1975, pp. 879-880, no. 994; L. Lindemans, *Erfdienstbaarheden*, Larcier, Brussels 1958, nos. 308-316; M. Muylle, "Creatief met privaatrechtelijke erfdienstbaarheden. Perspectieven uit de notariële praktijk" in K. Swinnen and M. Muylle (eds.), *Erfdienstbaarheden* in *Studies privaatrecht*, die Keure, Bruges 2016, pp. 44-47.

effort to sustainable water management, whereas public actors can also be involved more actively in water projects jointly carried out with private actors.

14. Shaping a shared responsibility framework – If we accept the idea of a shared partnership between public and private actors, the next step is to create a framework in which such partnership can thrive. The philosophy of the Belgian "*res communes*" category seems a good starting point. Nonetheless, the legal provision does not provide much information about the practical impact of the commons in Belgian property law beyond mere symbolism (see *supra* no. 5). To give a practical interpretation of freshwater's qualification as a *res communis*, we thus turn to the three scholarly pillars of "the commons" (in a positive, non-Hardinian, sense).[119]

First, commons literature deals with the distribution of scarce, vulnerable, or otherwise valuable objects.[120] With regard to water, contemporary commons have evolved from a descriptive indication of technical inappropriability to a normative question of its equitable distribution (see *supra* no. 4). The second pillar is based on finding an administrator who we trust to manage the equitable distribution of the object (see *supra* no. 6). Each society should consider the co-existence of public and private water management and clearly delineate what the limits of the respective powers of public and private actors are.[121] The last pillar is protection, or rather sustainability.[122] The cumulative impact of various uses on the water system is large. Water use needs to be coordinated to balance planet, people, and profit, the three components of sustainability.[123] Intergenerational responsibility is an inherent part of this last pillar.[124] This means that we should consider the effect of our decisions and actions on future generations. According to us, it should also mean that the *status quo* inherited from past generations can be altered in light of changing circumstances and advancing science.

---

119 D. Misonne, M. de Clippele and F. Ost, "L'actualité des communs à la croisée des enjeux de l'environnement et de la culture" (2018) 2 *RIEJ* 59, p. 61; Y. Emerich, "Les communs en droit privé: à la confluence de l'inappropriable, de la propriété collective et de la technique fiduciaire" (2021) 53 *Ottawa Law Review* 205, p. 218.

120 Y. Emerich, "Les communs en droit privé: à la confluence de l'inappropriable, de la propriété collective et de la technique fiduciaire" (2021) 53 *Ottawa Law Review* 205, p. 218.

121 B. Jadot, "L'environnement n'appartient à personne et l'usage qui en est fait est commun à tous. Des lois de police règlent la manière d'en jouir" in F. Ost and S. Gutwirth (eds.), *Quel avenir pour le droit de l'environnement?*, VUB Press, Brussels 1996, p. 94; D. Misonne, M. de Clippele and F. Ost, "L'actualité des communs à la croisée des enjeux de l'environnement et de la culture" (2018) 2 *RIEJ* 59, p. 61; N. Bernard, "Les communs (déjà) à l'œuvre dans le domaine de l'habitat: l'exemple du community land trust" (2022) 33 *JT* 613, p. 617; S. Gutwirth, "Les communs: avec, malgré ou contre le droit?" (2022) 33 *JT* 582, no. 16.

122 D. Misonne, "Les communs environnementaux" (2022) 33 *JT* 595, pp. 595-601.

123 Report of the World Commission on Environment and Development: "Our common future" (Brundtland-report), annexed to UNGA, UN Doc. A/42/427, 4 August 1987, pp. 42-43.

124 See art. 3.43, first para. CC; B. Hudson, "Time and Tragedy. The problem with temporal commons" in S. Foster and C. Swiney, *The Cambridge Handbook of Commons Research Innovations*, Cambridge University Press, Cambridge 2021, pp. 62-64.

15. Consequences for *res nullius*, *res privatae*, *res publicae* and *res communes* – If we interpret the common qualification of water as a matter of equitable distribution and sustainable management, all water should be qualified as a common, regardless of its temporary location in the hydrologic cycle.[125] This does not necessarily mean that the traditional property law qualifications should be abandoned. We argue that qualifying all water as a common can be reconciled with other private law qualifications since the *common* qualification does not impose a single type of (public or private) water management, nor a specific type of water rights. It only adds the idea of sustainable management and equitable distribution, which every system must respect as its limit. The specific content of this limit evolves as science progresses and the sociological and hydrological context changes.

The common idea should not fade away depending on the temporary location of water in the hydrological cycle. It would make much more sense to qualify each water molecule as a common. The fact that the water owner or user changes, or that a water rights regime is altered should not have an impact on the obligation of striking a balance between people, planet and profit across generations. In other words, the common-qualification depends on the object and can transcend (temporary) property claims. In this way, the common character of water should lead us in our interpretation of other property law qualifications. The traditional feature of a Roman/Belgian *res communis* – inappropriability in its entirety despite the possibility of partial appropriation – is not very relevant as far as we are concerned (see *supra* no. 4).

Whereas the temporary location of water in the hydrologic cycle is irrelevant for water's qualification as a common, it is relevant for the attribution of specific water rights within the limits of the commons-idea. The current scientific state-of-the-art suggests a larger role for private management with regard to rainwater (*res nullius*), compared to surface water and groundwater (*res privata* or *res publica*). The latter two water types require more public control and coordination. The reason for this is the paradigm of water retention (see *supra* no. 2).

The risks associated with floods and drought can simultaneously be reduced by retaining, reusing, infiltrating and separating rainwater from wastewater as much as possible, before the rainwater is stored or gradually disposed of. This concretization of the retention paradigm is visualized by Lansink's ladder. This management tool is mainly known from the context of sustainable waste management. Applied to water management, the main objective is to avoid accelerated discharge of rainwater (visualised in the green top of the ladder).

---

[125] See: F. Masson, "L'eau comme patrimoine commun" in J. Rochfeld, M. Cornu and G.J. Martin (eds.), *Rapport n° 17-34: rapport final de recherche: L'Echelle de communalité: propositions de réforme pour intégrer les biens communs en droit*, 2021, pp. 140-155, www.gip-recherche-justice.fr/wp-content/uploads/2021/06/Rapport-17-34-final-Juin-2021.pd accessed 20.07.2023.

Rainwater should be partly stored for use. The amount of rainwater that needs to be stored is determined by societal water needs. Rainwater should not be stored excessively as it must infiltrate into the soil as much as possible. Through infiltration, significant volumes of rainwater can be kept out of the sewerage (visualised in the red bottom of the ladder) and out of the waterways in times of intense rainfall. In addition, infiltration will feed the groundwater supply. Both effects of increased infiltration are necessary as climate change alters the hydrologic cycle.[126]

Ladder of Lansink

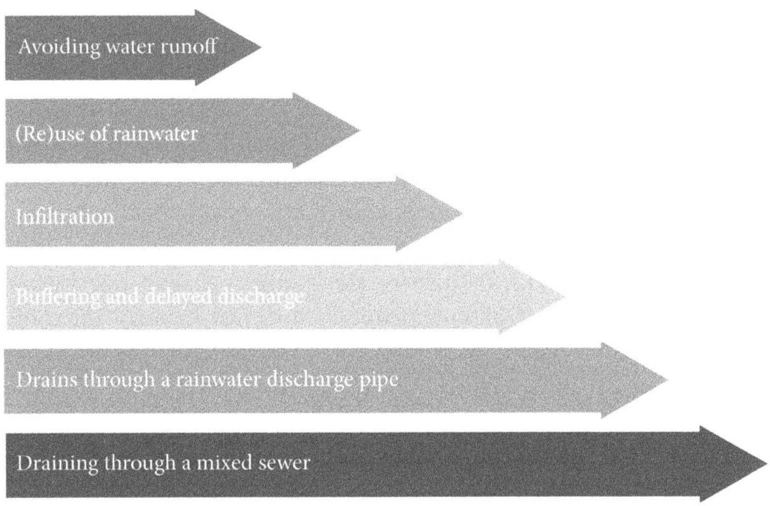

Source: KPMG, *Freshwater is an essential but limited resource*, https://kpmg.com/be/en/home/insights/2022/03/sus-fresh-water-is-an-essential-but-limited-resource.html accessed 18.11.2023.

The mere fact that rainwater is initially a *res nullius* does not mean that its use is limitless after it becomes a *res privata*. In the Flemish Region and in the Netherlands, legislation has therefore translated Lansink's ladder into concrete obligations of water collection and infiltration.[127] In other words, private rights

126 CIW, "Bijlage 3: Principes Ladder van Lansink" in *Rapport opmaak hemelwater- en droogteplan – blauwdruk*, June 2022, pp. 23-25, www.integraalwaterbeleid.be/nl/beleidsinstrumenten/hemelwater-en-droogteplannen/blauwdruk_hwdp.pdf accessed 18.11.2023.

127 **BE:** Art. 1.2.2, first para., 6° Waterwetboek; Decision of the Flemish Government "houdende vaststelling van een gewestelijke stedenbouwkundige verordening inzake hemelwaterputten, infiltratievoorzieningen, buffervoorzieningen en gescheiden lozing van afvalwater en hemelwater", 5 July 2013, see: www.vmm.be/wetgeving/hemelwaterverordening accessed 18.11.2023; **NL:** Art. 2.1 Waterbesluit j. art. 2.9 Waterwet (replaced by the omgevingswet as from 1 January 2024, see: https://unievanwaterschappen.nl/themas/waterwet/ accessed 20.11.2023 and www.helpdeskwater.nl/onderwerpen/wetgeving-beleid/handboek-water/

on water are never absolute given the co-existing commons-qualification. Still the *res nullius* qualification can play a role in water law. It can legally translate the societal conviction that those who invest in rainwater collection should be able to benefit from those investments, to a great extent exclusively so.[128]

V. DARE TO COMMON

16. Inherent limitations of water rights – Sustainable water management is grounded in the idea that all water is valuable. In that sense all water is a common, an object that should be handled carefully in the general interest, including that of future generations. The paradigm of retaining instead of draining water is the basis of sustainable water management in Belgium and the Netherlands according to the scientific state-of-the-art.[129] This water management is the responsibility of private and public actors who must, beyond symbolism, dare to acknowledge the limits of the water system relative to the cumulative human needs. Whether we say that water belongs to someone, to no one, or to everyone, does not change the reality that water is a scarce, rivalrous, but non-excludable good. Instead of losing ourselves in theoretical debates about water's legal qualification as a *res nullius*, a *res privata*, a *res publica* or a *res communis*, we should thus focus on the practical impact of these qualifications within today's context of climate change: *How* should everyone deal with water?

Commons-inspired literature often emphasizes that there can only be a right to use water[130], but this ignores the fact that individuals *de facto* control access to clean and sufficient water for others. Think of a business that wants to share its effluent water with another factory, choosing more or less freely

activiteiten/beheer-watersysteem/droogtemaatregelen/ accessed 20.11.2023); H.K. Gilissen, J.J.H. van Kempen, F.A.G. Groothuijse and H.F.M.W. van Rijswick, "Droogte in de delta – het nieuwe normaal? Naar meer eigen verantwoordelijkheid voor de landbouw" (2019) 11 *Tijdschrift voor Agrarisch Recht (NL)* 697, pp. 702-704; J.M. Havekes and P.J. de Putter, "Wegwijzer Waterwet", Kluwer, Deventer 2014, pp. 56-59.

128 See e.g. VMM, "Uitwerking van een reactief afwegingskader voor prioritair watergebruik tijdens waterschaarste, samenvatting en conclusies", VMM/S004X/201119/2.0, April 2021, www.vmm.be/water/projecten/afwegingskader-prioritair-watergebruik-tijdens-droogte/afwegingskader-2021/vrag-samenvatting_tw.pdf accessed 10.09.2023, p. 13 and pp. 19-20.

129 Expertenpanel hoogwaterbeveiliging 2022, pp. 20-21.

130 The term "water use" covers different consumptive and non-consumptive human interactions with water that jointly impact the water system: Water can be abstracted and removed from the immediate system, e.g. taking groundwater and using it for irrigation, thus causing it to return to the atmosphere by evapotranspiration, or the withdrawal of water from a river to use it as cooling water within an industrial circuit. However, water can be used and subsequently returned to the local system. This water use often impacts the features of the water e.g. temperature, chemical composition. Water use also encompasses use without abstraction e.g. navigation, local generation of hydropower or fishing. See: M. Muller, "Polycentric governance: water management in South Africa" (2012) 165 *Management, Procurement and Law* 193, p. 194.

who that water goes to, but also think of the sale of (bottled) water. Upstream water users enjoy a *de facto* advantage over downstream users in that they can divert and use the water before it flows downstream.[131] Climate adaptation in water law is not so much a matter of private against public or common water management, but rather a discussion about the limits of the cumulative human impact on the water system. How should we determine these limits and who do we trust to respect those limits? Those in power to exclude others from sufficient and qualitative water are both private and public actors. Governments should stipulate clear limits to human access and control over water, but simultaneously leave sufficient leeway for individual and collective cooperation and innovation. Compensation for expropriation is seldom at stake when governments regulate water use in the general interest.

Today's commons-literature risks to ignore that between private, public or common water management no option is inherently better than the other. The success of sustainable water management builds on the principles respected by those managing the water. As the scientific state-of-the-art about water management evolves, it is important to highlight that we are a future generation too. The legal *status quo* is not carved in stone. As the current generation and the generations to come grow to understand that water should be managed differently, they should not be held back by the heritage of past water law stemming from a different societal and hydrologic context. Legal security to water does not exist independent from the reality of today: Retaining instead of draining freshwater should become the new paradigm in Belgium and the Netherlands.

131 S. Hodgson, "Exploring the concept of water tenure" (2016) 10 *FAO Land and water discussion paper* 1, p. 31.

Property Law Series

The *Property Law Series* is dedicated to publishing in-depth books on property law which provide detailed analysis and insight on the conceptualisation and legal practice of property law.

The *Property Law Series* has an 'open' character, allowing authors to submit their work to the Board of Editors. All works in the series are subjected to a peer review, which assesses the quality, depth and academic relevance of the books in the series. The series therefore includes an array of works, from comprehensive monographs, to innovative theses and leading handbooks.

Previously published in the Property Law Series:

1. Julie del Corral, *De leveringsplicht bij de overdracht van roerende lichamelijke goederen*, Antwerp, Intersentia, 2013.
2. Koen Swinnen, *Accessoriteit in het vermogensrecht*, Antwerp, Intersentia, 2014.
3. Sofie Bouly, *Onroerende natrekking en horizontale eigendomssplitsingen*, Antwerp, Intersentia, 2015.
4. Dorothy Gruyaert, *De exclusiviteit van het eigendomsrecht*, Antwerp, Intersentia, 2016.
5. Ann Apers, *Wilsautonomie bij de kwalificatie van goederen*, Antwerp, Intersentia, 2017.
6. Vincent Sagaert (ed.), *De betekenis van erfdienstbaarheden bij vastgoed-transacties*, Antwerp, Intersentia, 2017.
7. Elien Dewitte, *Feitelijke algemeenheden in het privaatrecht*, Antwerp, Intersentia, 2017.
8. Vincent Sagaert, *De zakenrechtelijke structuur van vastgoedprojecten*, Antwerp, Intersentia, 2019.
9. Siel Demeyere, *Real Obligations at the Edge of Contract and Property*, Antwerp, Intersentia, 2020
10. Siel Demeyere, Vincent Sagaert, *Contract and Property with an Environmental Perspective*, Antwerp, Intersentia, 2020
11. Vincent Sagaert, Joke Baeck, Nicolas Carette, Pascale Lecocq, Mathieu Muylle en Annelies Wylleman (eds.), *Het nieuwe goederenrecht*, Antwerp, Intersentia, 2021.

12. Frederic HELSEN (ed.), *The Law and Economics of Secured Lending*, Antwerp, Intersentia, 2021.
13. Vincent SAGAERT, Alexander APPELMANS & Benjamin VERHEYE (eds.) *Digitalisering en vastgoedtransacties*, Antwerp, Intersentia, 2022.
14. Sander BAEYENS, *Vermogensrechten en faillissement*, Antwerp, Intersentia, 2023.

www.ingramcontent.com/pod-product-compliance
Ingram Content Group UK Ltd.
Pitfield, Milton Keynes, MK11 3LW, UK
UKHW051913100926
8556IPUK00006B/865

9 781839 704512